OLD SILVER OF EUROPE & AMERICA

PLATE I

OLD SILVER OF EUROPE & AMERICA

by
E ALFRED JONES

This edition digitally re-mastered and
published by JM Classic Editions © 2008
Original text © E Alfred Jones 1928

ISBN 978-1-905217-97-7

All rights reserved. No part of this book subject
to copyright may be reproduced in any form or
by any means without prior permission in writing
from the publisher.

Addenda et Corrigenda

Add to Preface: "To the Trustees of the Wallace Collection my thanks are due for the loan of the photograph for Plate LXXXI"

Page 162. The date of the ewer by A. S. Durand (Plate XLV) should be c. 1760.

Page 234. 4th line. Hendrik de Keyser was a sculptor and architect, and was the designer only of the figure.

Page 240. 3rd line. *For* "Goltzhius" *read* "Goltzius."

Page 244. 17th line. *For* "brandewijkom" *read* "brandewijnkom."

CONTENTS

LIST OF CHAPTERS

	PAGE		PAGE
AMERICA	1	HUNGARY	247
AUSTRIA	48	IRELAND	255
BALTIC STATES	52	ITALY	265
BELGIUM	57	NORWAY	271
CANADA	65	POLAND	279
CHANNEL ISLANDS	69	PORTUGAL	285
CZECHOSLOVAKIA	71	RUSSIA	292
DENMARK	75	SCOTLAND	302
ENGLAND	84	SPAIN	313
FRANCE	162	SWEDEN	323
GERMANY	180	SWITZERLAND	330
HOLLAND	227	SPURIOUS PLATE	338

LIST OF PLATES

Plate Number	Facing Page	Plate Number	Facing Page
I	Frontispiece	XVII	52
II	4	XVIII	53
III	5	XIX	60
IV	6	XX	61
V	7	XXI	64
VI	10	XXII	65
VII	11	XXIII	74
VIII	12	XXIV	75
IX	13	XXV	80
X	22	XXVI	81
XI	23	XXVII	96
XII	26	XXVIII	97
XIII	27	XXIX	112
XIV	32	XXX	113
XV	33	XXXI	116
XVI	48	XXXII	117

LIST OF PLATES—*Continued*

Plate Number	Facing Page	Plate Number	Facing Page
XXXIII	124	LXV	237
XXXIV	125	LXVI	238
XXXV	128	LXVII	239
XXXVI	129	LXVIII	246
XXXVII	144	LXIX	247
XXXVIII	145	LXX	250
XXXIX	160	LXXI	251
XL	161	LXXII	256
XLI	164	LXXIII	257
XLII	165	LXXIV	264
XLIII	166	LXXV	265
XLIV	167	LXXVI	270
XLV	170	LXXVII	271
XLVI	171	LXXVIII	276
XLVII	172	LXXIX	277
XLVIII	173	LXXX	284
XLIX	180	LXXXI	285
L	181	LXXXII	290
LI	188	LXXXIII	291
LII	189	LXXXIV	296
LIII	192	LXXXV	297
LIV	193	LXXXVI	304
LV	196	LXXXVII	305
LVI	197	LXXXVIII	312
LVII	204	LXXXIX	313
LVIII	205	XC	320
LIX	208	XCI	321
LX	226	XCII	328
LXI	227	XCIII	329
LXII	228	XCIV	332
LXIII	229	XCV	333
LXIV	236	XCVI	336

PREFACE

THEIR Majesties the King and Queen have most graciously granted me permission to examine the Royal collection at Windsor Castle.

In America I am indebted for many courtesies and gifts of photographs to Judge A. T. Clearwater and Mr. Francis P. Garvan, owners of important collections of old American silver; and to Mrs. Charles Prince, Mrs. Robert Soutter and Mrs. Alexander F. Wadsworth for photographs. Miss C. Louise Avery and Mr. Henry W. Kent, both of the Metropolitan Museum, New York, have been unsparing in answering questions and requests for photographs, with the courteous sanction of the Museum authorities. I desire also to express my thanks for help from Mrs. Florence Paull Berger; Mr. Francis H. Bigelow; Mr. Henry W. Belknap, of the Essex Institute, Salem; Mr. Benjamin H. Stone, of the Worcester Art Museum, Massachusetts; Mr. Fiske Kimball, Director of the Pennsylvania Museum; Dr. S. W. Woodhouse, junr.; Mr. William C. Lane, of the Harvard College Library; Mr. A. J. Wall, of the New York Historical Society; and Miss Lisa Jennison, of the Museum of Fine Arts, Boston, the authorities of which have courteously granted the use of illustrations. Mrs. Lucas Brodhead, of Versailles, Kentucky, has generously sent me some photographs and notes of Kentucky silversmiths.

For the chapter on the silver of the Baltic States I have had cordial help from Mr. H. Montgomery Grove, H.B.M. Consul-General at Reval; Mr. Alexander Hartmann, of Reval; Dr. K. K. Meinander, of the National Museum, Helsingfors; and Mr. J. E. P. Leslie.

To M. M. Laurent, of the Museum of Decorative Art in Brussels, I am under obligation for information and photographs; and to Mr. A. B. Denton Thompson, British Vice-Consul at Brussels, for answers to questions.

The Archbishop of Quebec and Father Elias Roy, of the College of Levis, have been most helpful.

From Mr. S. Carey Curtis, author of two brochures on the

PREFACE

Church plate of the Channel Islands, I have had several photographs and information.

My investigations into the history of silver in Czechoslovakia have been made easy by Dr. F. X. Jirix, Director of the Museum of Industrial Art, Mr. Lennox Petrie and Mr. J. W. Taylor, Vice-Consuls, all of Prague.

All requests for photographs of, and questions concerning, Danish plate have been courteously met by the authorities of the National Museum at Copenhagen.

M. Puiforcat, of Paris, has not only given me facilities for examining his highly important collection of French plate, but has generously presented me with many photographs. My thanks are also due to Mme. Martin Le Roy; M. J. J. Marquet de Vasselot for many services; and to Mr. Junius S. Morgan for his gift of photographs. Acknowledgment has been made in the text to M. Henry Nocq's invaluable book on Paris marks.

For the chapter on German plate I am indebted to the Baroness James de Rothschild for permission to use photographs from my catalogue of her notable collection; and to Dr. Marc Rosenberg personally, as well as to his indispensable work, *Der Goldschmiede Merkzeichen* (3rd edition). My other helpers include Herr W. Mundt, of Emden; Dr. Victor Schultze, of the University of Greifswald; and the Director of the Kunstgewerbe Museum in Berlin.

In Holland I have had several enthusiastic contributors, namely, Miss C. J. Hudig, of the Rijks Museum, Amsterdam; Mr. Carel J. A. Begeer; Mr. M. W. Wieweg and Mr. N. Ottema, both of Leeuwarden; Mr. A. O. van Kerkwijk, of The Hague; Mr. A. van E. Dorens, Gemeente Museum, Arnhem; and Dr. H. P. Coster, of Groningen Museum.

M. Jules de Végh, Director of the Museum of Applied Art at Budapest, has been most indefatigable in contributing valuable information upon ecclesiastical and secular plate in Hungary, much of which cannot be included here for lack of space. He has also sent many photographs.

In my search for Irish silver, Mr. Dudley Westropp, Director

PREFACE

of the National Museum of Ireland, has shown forbearance, while Mr. George W. Thornley, of the Assay Office in Dublin, has contributed notes of interest.

A contributor to the chapter on Norwegian silver is Mr. Thor Kielland, whose important books on the subject are mentioned in the text. Mr. Einar Lexow, of the Bergen Museum, has also helped.

In Poland my helpers were Dr. Leonard Lepszy, of Cracow, an acknowledged authority; Dr. Mary Fredo-Boniecka, also of Cracow; Mr. Frank Savery, H.B.M. Consul at Warsaw; M. F. B. Czarnomski, of the Polish Legation in London; and Professor B. Gembarzewski, Director of the National Museum at Warsaw.

To Mr. Ernest A. Sandeman I offer cordial thanks for much help in regard to Portuguese silver. Likewise to Senhor Luciano Martius Freire, Director of the National Museum of Art in Lisbon, for several communications.

For notes on Russian and Swedish silver I am indebted respectively to Dr. Ellis H. Minns, of Cambridge, and Dr. Gustaf Upmark, of Stockholm.

His Majesty the King of Spain most graciously allowed me to examine the Royal plate at Madrid and to illustrate a piece. From Señor Pedro M. de Artinano, of Madrid, I have received photographs of, and interesting information on, Spanish silver.

His Excellency M. Paravicini, Swiss Minister in London, has taken the warmest interest in all questions relating to old Swiss silver.

My gratitude is due for photographs and help to Earl Spencer; Viscount Lee of Fareham, P.C., G.B.E., K.C.B.; Lord Dalmeny; Baron and Baroness Bruno Schröder; Mrs. Leopold de Rothschild; Messrs. Alinari, of Florence; Mr. A. O. Anderson, M.A., of St. Andrews; Messrs. B. T. Batsford, Ltd.; Messrs. Ernest Benn, Ltd.; Mr. Frederick Bradbury; Messrs. Brook and Son, of Edinburgh; Messrs. Cartier Bros., of Paris and London; Messrs. Crichton Bros.; Messrs. Christie, Manson and Woods; Mr. F. P. Croshaw; Mr. Llewellyn Davies, of Cardiff; Mr. Hugh Gurney, of H.M. Diplomatic Service; Mr. H. C. Norman; Mr. E. E. M. Nielsen;

PREFACE

Messrs. Sotheby and Co.; Mr. J. D. C. Wilton, British Vice-Consul at Vienna; the Society of Antiquaries of London; the authorities of the British Museum and the Victoria and Albert Museum; and Mr. Laurence Haward, Director of the Manchester Art Gallery.

Finally, I desire to thank most warmly those owners of old silver mentioned in the text for permission to record and illustrate their treasures in this little book.

E. ALFRED JONES.

INTRODUCTORY NOTE

WITHIN these pages an attempt has been made to compile, for the first time in any language, a brief historical account of the old domestic silver of Europe and America.

The charming silver wrought in the American Colonies begins with that of Robert Sanderson (1608–93), a London silversmith settled in Boston. Further north on the American continent there were the Canadian silversmiths, while south of the United States some excellent work was executed in Mexico after the Spanish conquest.

In Europe the next chapters are concerned with the silver of Austria, the Baltic States and Finland, followed by a note on the talented Flemish goldsmiths and their work. Nor is the silver of the Channel Islands and of Czechoslovakia forgotten in the survey. A summary will be found of the history of domestic silver in the three Scandinavian countries of Denmark, Norway and Sweden and the salient features of the more popular objects described.

The historical sequence of English plate is traced so far as is possible from extant specimens, as is that of France. Domestic silver of the eighteenth century, the " golden age " of furniture and of metal work in general in France, is exceedingly rare, as is emphasised in the text.

German silver, from the rise of Augsburg and Nuremberg as the most prosperous cities in the sixteenth century, was wrought not only in those, the two most important centres of the goldsmith's craft, but also in many other places. For adequate treatment of the subject, and of the immense number of cups and other vessels produced for rich patricians, princes and guilds, much more space would be needed than can be spared here.

The development of Dutch silver and its several interesting and characteristic household vessels, especially those contemporaneous with the great school of painting in the seventeenth century, has been traced and the names of the more prominent silversmiths mentioned.

In Ireland and Scotland there were skilful goldsmiths, many of

INTRODUCTORY NOTE

whose surviving works are described, including the two typical objects of each country, the dish-ring and the quaich, respectively.

Illustrations are included of the three old national vessels of Russia, the bratina, kovsh and charka, which were not infrequently made of gold, enamelled and enriched with precious stones. Many specimens are historic.

Included are short notices of the art of the goldsmith in Hungary and Italy, Poland and Portugal, Spain and Switzerland, concluding with a short chapter on spurious old silver.

A correction must be made of a statement on page 31 that no American punch ladles have survived. One or two examples have been brought to the notice of the author too late for inclusion.

It has been found impossible in the limited space to include even a short outline of the development of spoons in Europe and America, an important branch of the subject of old silver which must be reserved for another volume.

Changes of ownership of two important objects have occurred since the printing of the text. The impressive English wine-bottle, described on page 118 as in the possession of Captain C. D. Rotch, has found a permanent home in the Victoria and Albert Museum, while the unique German salt from the Holford sale at Christie's, mentioned on page 314, has passed into the collection of Baron and Baroness Bruno Schröder.

A mazer bowl of the fifteenth century, a relic of the Chief of the Clan MacGregor, was sold in November 1927 at Hurcomb's for £10,000 to Messrs. Crichton Bros.

OLD SILVER OF EUROPE AND AMERICA

AMERICA

PLATE I.

No. 1 Plain beaker, by Edward Winslow, of Boston (1669–1753). H. 5¾ in.
Collection of Francis P. Garvan, Esq.
No. 2 Engraved beaker, by Jacob Boelen, of New York (1654–1729). In the same collection.
No. 3 Engraved beaker, by Henricus Boelen, of New York. Dated 1731. H. 6¼ in.
Reformed Church, Bergen, New Jersey.
No. 4 Engraved beaker, by Benjamin Wynkoop, of New York, 1711. H. 7¼ in.
Collection of Judge A. T. Clearwater.

PLATE II.

No. 1 Tankard, c. 1730, by Thomas Millner, or Miller, of Boston.
First Congregational Society, Chelmsford, Massachusetts.
No. 2 Large tankard, by Robert Sanderson, of Boston (1608–93).
Owner, Mrs. Alexander F. Wadsworth.
No. 3 Tankard, by Paul Revere (1735–1818).
No. 4 Tankard, by Henry Hurst, of Boston (c. 1665–1717), the property of Dudley L. Pickman, Esq.
No. 5 Tankard, by Jeremiah Dummer, of Boston (1645–1718).
South Parish, Portsmouth, New Hampshire.

PLATE III.

Six tankards by New York silversmiths :—

No. 1 By Henricus Boelen (1697–1755).
No. 2 By Peter Quintard (1699–1762).
No. 3 By Jacob Boelen (1654–1729). Collection of Judge A. T. Clearwater.
No. 4 By Jacobus van der Spiegle (working 1685–1705).
No. 5 By Peter van Dyck (1684–1750).
No. 6 By Nicholas Roosevelt (freeman 1735).
(Nos. 1, 2, 4, 5 and 6 are in the collection of Francis P. Garvan, Esq.)

PLATE IV.

No. 1 Tankard, attributed to John de Nise, of Philadelphia. Early 18th century.
Pennsylvania Museum.
No. 2 Tankard, c. 1725, by William Vilant, of Philadelphia. In the same Museum.
No. 3 Snuff box, by Jacob Hurd (1702–58), of Boston. Collection of Francis P. Garvan, Esq.
No. 4 Tankard, by Joseph Richardson (1711–70), of Philadelphia.
Collection of Francis P. Garvan, Esq.
No. 5 Tankard, c. 1725, by Francis Richardson, of Philadelphia. Owner, Dr. Isaac Starr, Jun.

PLATE V.

No. 1 Mug, by Jacob Hurd, of Boston (1702–58). Owner, Mrs. Lydia B. Taft.
No. 2 Tankard, by Samuel Vernon (1683–1737), of Newport, Rhode Island.
Worcester Art Museum, Massachusetts.
No. 3 Mug, by Paul Revere. In the same Museum.
No. 4 Mug, by William Cowell, of Boston (1682–1736).
First Church of Christ, Hartford, Connecticut.
No. 5 Mug, c. 1725, by Simeon Soumaine, of New York.
Collection of Francis P. Garvan, Esq.

PLATE VI.

No. 1 Sweetmeat box, by John Coney, of Boston (1655–1722).
Museum of Fine Arts, Boston.
No. 2 Caudle cup. H. 3 in., 1665, by Robert Sanderson and John Hull, of Boston.
Second Church, Dorchester, Massachusetts.
No. 3 Caudle cup. H. 3¼ in., by Robert Sanderson, of Boston (1608–93).
Museum of Fine Arts, Boston.
No. 4 Caudle cup. H. 3¼ in., by Jeremiah Dummer, of Boston (1645–1718).
First Congregational Church, Chelmsford, Massachusetts.
No. 5 Caudle cup. H. 4¾ in., by William Cowell, of Boston (1682–1736).
Church of Unity, Neponset, Massachusetts.

PLATE VII. SEVEN PORRINGERS.

No. 1 Attributed to Joseph Newkirke, of New York. Early 18th century.
Judge A. T. Clearwater's collection.
No. 2 By John Coney (1655–1722), of Boston. Collection of Francis P. Garvan, Esq.
No. 3 By Jeremiah Dummer (1645–1718), of Boston.
Worcester Art Museum, Massachusetts.
No. 4 By William Homes (1717–83), of Boston. Collection of Francis P. Garvan, Esq.
No. 5 By Andrew Tyler (1692–1741), of Boston. Worcester Art Museum, Massachusetts.
No. 6 By Bartholomew Schaats (1670–1758), of New York.
Collection of Francis P. Garvan, Esq.
No. 7 By Richard Humphreys, of Philadelphia, c. 1770. Pennsylvania Museum.

PLATE VIII.

No. 1 Spout cup, by John Edwards, of Boston, 1706. H. 5¼ in.
Worcester Art Museum, Massachusetts.
No. 2 Spout cup, by John Edwards (1670–1746), of Boston.
Metropolitan Museum, New York.
No. 3 Small bowl, by Benjamin Wynkoop, of New York. Early 18th century.
New York Historical Society.
No. 4 Spout cup, by Benjamin Hiller (1687–1739), of Boston.
Owner, Captain C. D. Rotch.

AMERICA

PLATE IX.

No. 1 Trencher salt, by John Coney, of Boston (1655-1722). Museum of Fine Arts, Boston.
No. 2 Trencher salt, by same maker as No. 1. Judge A. T. Clearwater's collection.
No. 3 Salt, by Joseph Richardson, of Philadelphia (1711-70).
Collection of Francis P. Garvan, Esq.
No. 4 Salt, c. 1700, by John Edwards and John Allen, of Boston. H. 6 in.
Owner, Nathan Hayward, Esq.
No. 5 Cup and cover, 1749. H. 12¼ in., by William Swan, of Worcester, Massachusetts.
Essex Institute, Salem, Massachusetts.

PLATE X.

No. 1 Punch bowl. D. 11¼ in., H. 9 in., by John Coney, of Boston (1655-1722).
Owner, Mrs. Henry Parish.
No. 2 Punch bowl. D. 11 in., H. 5¼ in., by Paul Revere (1735-1818).
Owner, Mrs. Marian Lincoln Perry.

PLATE XI.

No. 1 Inkstand, by John Coney, of Boston (1655-1722). Metropolitan Museum, New York.
No. 2 Large cup and cover. H. 11 in. By Edward Winslow, of Boston (1669-1753).
Owner, Mrs. Lois B. Rantoul.
No. 3 Inkstand, by Philip Syng, the younger (1703-89), of Philadelphia.
Independence Hall, Philadelphia.
No. 4 Kettle, by Cornelius Kierstead (1674-1753), of New York.
Owner, Miss Anne S. van Cortlandt.

PLATE XII.

No. 1 Teapot, by John Coney, of Boston (1655-1722). Judge A. T. Clearwater's collection.
No. 2 Teapot, by Adrian Bancker, of New York (1703-61). In the same collection.
No. 3 Teapot, by Jacob Hurd, of Boston (1702-58). Museum of Fine Arts, Boston.
No. 4 Teapot, by Joseph Richardson, of Philadelphia (1711-84).
Metropolitan Museum, New York.
No. 5 Teapot, ascribed to Josiah Austin, of Charlestown, Massachusetts (1719-80).
In the same Museum.
No. 6 Teapot, by Benjamin Burt, of Boston (1729-1809).
Collection of Francis P. Garvan, Esq.
No. 7 Teapot, by Paul Revere. Owner, Mrs. Charles Prince.
No. 8 Teapot, by Paul Revere, c. 1797. Worcester Art Museum, Massachusetts.
No. 9 Tea service, by Paul Revere, 1799. Boston Museum of Fine Arts.

PLATE XIII.

No. 1 Chocolate pot, by Edward Winslow (1669-1753), of Boston. H. 9¼ in.
Judge A. T. Clearwater's collection.
No. 2 Coffee-pot, by Paul Revere (1735-1818). H. 13¼ in.
Owner, Mrs. Thomas Bailey Aldrich.
No. 3 Coffee-pot, probably by Christopher Robert, of New York, c. 1751. H. 10¼ in.
Owner, Mrs. Bayard Bowie, jun.
No. 4 Coffee-pot, by John Coney (1655-1722), of Boston. H. 9¼ in.
Owner, Mrs. Robert Soutter.
No. 5 Coffee-pot, by Paul Revere (1735-1818). Worcester Art Museum, Massachusetts.

PLATE XIV.

Five plain casters:—
No. 1 By Edward Winslow (1669–1753), of Boston.   Collection of Francis P. Garvan, Esq.
No. 2 By John Edwards (1670–1746), of Boston.   Worcester Art Museum, Massachusetts.
No. 3 By Benjamin Hiller (1687–1739) of Boston.   Collection of Francis P. Garvan, Esq.
No. 4 By John Coburn (1725–1803), of Boston.   Worcester Art Museum.
No. 5 By John Burt (1691–1745), of Boston.   Owner, Mrs. Lydia B. Taft.

PLATE XV.

No. 1 Plain salver, c. 1765, by Daniel Christian Fueter, of New York.
Metropolitan Museum, New York.
No. 2 Tumbler cup. H. 2 in. By Philip Goelet, of New York, c. 1740.
Collection of Judge A. T. Clearwater.
No. 3 Bowl and cover, by John Brevoort, of New York, c. 1750.
Metropolitan Museum, New York.
No. 4 Pair of sauce boats, by Joseph Richardson (1711–70), of Philadelphia.
Metropolitan Museum, New York.
No. 5 Sauce boat, by Paul Revere (1735–1818).   Worcester Art Museum, Massachusetts.
No. 6 Lemon strainer, by Philip Syng, the younger (1703–89), of Philadelphia.
Collection of Francis P. Garvan, Esq.
No. 7 Brazier (one of a pair), by Jacob Hurd (1702–58), of Boston.
Collection of Francis P. Garvan, Esq.
No. 8 Brazier, by Philip Syng, the younger (1703–89), of Philadelphia.
Pennsylvania Museum.
No. 9 Plain tazza, by Jacob Hurd (1702–58), of Boston.   Museum of Fine Arts, Boston.

THE history of the silversmith in America probably begins with one Thomas Howard, of Jamestown, whose name is recorded in the register of the Virginia Company in 1620. That he was a practical worker in the precious metals is doubtful. He was probably like the silversmiths of 1608, mentioned by the redoubtable Captain John Smith as employed for the purpose of finding gold in Virginia, or a mere member of the Goldsmiths' Company in London, like Sir Hugh Myddelton, Sir Robert Vyner and other so-called goldsmiths in the seventeenth century.

More tangible is the history of Robert Sanderson (1608–93), of Boston, the first silversmith in America whose works live after him, though the English goldsmith, John Mansfield, had emigrated to Boston six years earlier, in 1634. Sanderson had learned his craft in London and would seem to have carried with him to his new adventure in Massachusetts the actual stamp used by him on silver wrought in London (illustrated in Sir C. J. Jackson's *English*

PLATE II

PLATE III

AMERICA

Goldsmiths and Their Marks for 1635–6). This mark was on a silver salver of that year, which, by an interesting coincidence, was found in America. The early records of Goldsmiths' Hall having been destroyed, the number of identifiable marks anterior to 1697 is but few, and, therefore, the attribution of the mark on this salver cannot be made with certainty.

Several examples of the work of Robert Sanderson have survived in American Churches and in private ownership, together with other specimens, bearing his marks and those of his partner, John Hull (1624–83).

About 150 names of silversmiths have been recorded at Boston before the year 1800, and include such early masters of the craft as John Allen; John Burt and his three sons, Benjamin, Samuel and William; John Coburn; John Coney; William Cowell; John Dixwell; Jeremiah Dummer, apprentice of John Hull; John Edwards and his three sons, Joseph, Samuel and Thomas; William Homes; the Hurd family; Knight Leverett; John Noyes; the Reveres; William Simpkins; Andrew Tyler and Edward Winslow. Of these the most prolific was Jacob Hurd (1702–58), and the most conspicuous by reason of his part in the American Revolution and not of his superior workmanship is Paul Revere, many of whose choicest works are in the collection of Mrs. Nathaniel B. Thayer, the owner of Mrs. Paul Revere's miniature portrait by Copley, in a gold frame by Revere himself. Silver was also wrought at nine other places in Massachusetts.*

Until 1906 American-wrought silver was as unknown as was the music of Bach in the early nineteenth century, for most educated Americans regarded all their old family silver, and, indeed, their furniture, as of English workmanship if in New England, or as Dutch if in New York. The exhibition of American silver in that year in the Boston Museum of Fine Arts was, however, to many visitors, a revelation of the unsuspected riches in the art of the American silversmith. To the present writer, although made aware of the existence

---

* The price of silver in America in 1706–1714 was 8s. 6d. an ounce. In 1733 it had risen to £1 1s., and in 1743 to £1 10s. In 1747 it reached the high figure of £3 an ounce, and in 1750 it fell to £2 10s. (*Collections of Colonial Soc. of Mass.*, vii, 279).

of American-made silver by his study of the book of the late Mr. J. H. Buck, the pioneer in research on the subject, this exhibition was a complete surprise, both in the quantity and the beauty of the old silver wrought in Boston in the seventeenth and eighteenth centuries.

It may be said with Longfellow that it is

> " Old and yet ever new,
> Simple and beautiful always."

Subsequent exhibitions in Boston, New York, Philadelphia and other places have added to the knowledge of the subject.

American Colonial silver in general is dependent for its undoubted charm on the simplicity of its lines and graceful forms, and the absence of the prodigality of ornament which mars the beauty of much contemporary European work. Just as Colonial furniture in New England is in the main inspired by English fashions, so is the silver of the mother country ever the source of inspiration of the early silversmiths of Boston, the most important town in the American colonies in the seventeenth and early eighteenth centuries. Well might Daniel Neal remark in 1720 that the colonists " affect to be as English as possible."

That the sight of a convivial New England party, with its tankards and porringers on highly polished tables and other veritable mirrors of social life, was a painful sight to the puritan John Adams, may be judged from his letter to his wife, Abigail, dated from Passy, June 3, 1778, in which he says that ". . . luxury, wherever she goes effaces, from human nature the image of the Divinity. If I had power I would forever banish and exclude from America all gold, silver, precious stones, alabaster, marble, silk, velvet and lace." To such manifestations of puritan spirit are due the incredible destruction of countless treasures in all the arts at the English Reformation. Fortunately, the sentiments of John Adams were not sufficiently strong in Boston in Colonial days to stop the flourishing craft of the silversmith.

The dazzling display of silver plate in New York between 1763 and 1775 was particularly observed by British officers (stationed in that province and city) as guests at elegant entertainments and

PLATE IV

PLATE V

dinners, "equal if not superior to any nobleman's," while the sideboard of William Walton, a wealthy merchant in that city before the Revolution, is said to have "groaned with the weight of brilliant massive silver." Not all this silver was, however, wrought by American silversmiths; old inventories indicate England as the source of many objects.

Over eighty silversmiths are recorded in New York itself before the Revolution. Men of Dutch birth or descent predominate in the early history of the art. A few received their training in England. Others were Huguenot refugees or their descendants—Le Roux, Hastier, Goelet, Pelletreau, Moulinar and Huertin—who have left no "French" influence in their work or designs, as did their compatriots in England after the revocation of the Edict of Nantes in 1685.

To the celebrated William Penn's account book we are indebted for the names of the earliest silversmiths in Philadelphia. First comes, in 1698, the name of one Johan Nys, or John de Nise, supposed to have been a Huguenot refugee, first in Holland and afterwards in America, and probably the maker of the tankard on Plate IV (No. 1). Five pieces are attributed by Mr. H. F. Jayne and Dr. S. W. Woodhouse, jun., in their article in *Art in America* for October, 1921, to the hands of this craftsman.

The second, Francis Richardson, is of double interest from the fact that he was the first American-born silversmith to ply his craft in Philadelphia. Born in New York in 1681, he removed to the Quaker city nine years later; but no records have come to light of the name of his teacher in the craft. He left a competent silversmith in his son, Joseph, of whom more hereafter.

The name of Cesar Ghiselin is entered in 1702 in the account book of the Quaker Proprietor. He is supposed to have been a Huguenot, who first sought refuge in England and thence about 1690 at Annapolis, the old capital of Maryland, removing later to Philadelphia, where he died in 1733 or 1734. Three pieces, fortunately, have survived as memorials of his skill, and two of these are of historic importance: a beaker and a plate given by a devout spinster, Margaret Tresse, to the historic Christ Church, Philadelphia. Both display a robust simplicity in contrast with the Louis XIV decoration, introduced into England by the Huguenot refugees. These vessels are illustrated on Plate 113 in *The Old Silver of the American Churches*.

Joseph Richardson (1711-70) was perhaps the most conspicuous of the Philadelphia silversmiths in the eighteenth century, and wrought pleasant bits of silver in accordance with the changing fashions of his time. Three of his day-books for the years 1733-40 are in the possession of the Pennsylvania Historical Society. One item is for eight square milkpots, which suggest the plain octagonal pieces of silver so popular in England early in the eighteenth century, and occasionally made in America. A prized piece from his hands is a silver coffee pot, which has been handed down to his great-granddaughter.

Joseph Richardson had two sons, Joseph and Nathaniel, both of whom followed their father in the ancient and honourable craft of the goldsmith. The former rose to be assayer to the United States Mint in 1808.

Another family also gave three generations of silversmiths to Philadelphia—the Syng family. Philip Syng was born in 1676 in Ireland, and appears to have learned his craft in Dublin, though his name is not recorded as a member of that guild. He emigrated in 1712, accompanied by his son, Philip, then aged nine. The only specimens of his craft still extant are a flagon and a baptismal basin—two historic relics, given in 1712 to Christ Church, Philadelphia, by Colonel Robert Quary, Surveyor-General of the Customs in America, and illustrated with the Ghiselin silver just mentioned. Like all the early work executed by the first silversmiths of Philadelphia, the basin is plain and simple, yet withal dignified, while the flagon is a copy of an English one given by Queen Anne to the same church, of which Syng was a vestryman. Philip Syng, the elder, removed in or shortly after 1723 to Annapolis and died there in 1739, leaving his atelier to his son and pupil, Philip, soon to achieve prominence not only as a capable silversmith but also as a public man during his long life of eighty-six years. His best known work is the famous silver inkstand on Plate XI (No. 3), made for the Provincial Assembly of Pennsylvania and used at the signing of the ever-memorable Declaration of Independence. Two more works of the second Philip Syng are the rare brazier and lemon strainer on Plate XV (Nos. 8 and 6).

To these names must be added William Vilant, maker of the tankard on Plate IV (No. 2); and Richard Humphreys, one of the most prolific and skilful of craftsmen and maker of pieces described later; also Abraham Carlisle, son of the Philadelphia loyalist of this name who was executed for his loyalty in 1778. After serving his apprenticeship Carlisle worked as a journeyman silversmith and supported his widowed mother. He was the maker of an interesting silver tea-caddy illustrated in the article by Mr. Jayne and Dr. Woodhouse already mentioned.

Philip Syng, the third, died a premature death at the age of 27 and left but few works after him.

With the rapid rise of Philadelphia as the largest city in 1760 came an increasing output of silverware, as fine as the furniture of Savery and other cabinet makers. Indeed, the high position of Philadelphia in 1765 as a centre of craftsmanship, in furniture and silver, is confirmed in a letter of Samuel Morris, the well-known Philadelphia merchant, in which he says that household goods may be bought there "as cheap and as well made from English patterns." "In the humour people are in here (he adds) a man is in danger of becoming invidiously distinguished, who buys anything in England which our tradesmen can furnish." He appears, however, to have despised silver without hall-marks, for in the same letter he mentions his sale of four old battered porringers and other silver, weighing 44 ounces, for 8s. an ounce, to Joseph Richardson, as "they were country made & not having ye Hall mark would not exceed that price, indeed I had try'd others before him and they would not give more" (*Penn. Mag. of Hist. and Biog.*, xix, 531–2).

As at New York so at Philadelphia, certain characteristic features are common in the silver. Such things as urn-shaped vessels for the table surmounted by pierced galleries* are typical of the work of such prominent men as Joseph Lownes, Christian Wiltberger, John McMullin, Abraham Dubois and John Le Telier towards the end of

---

* These were probably copied from the silver galleries of Old Sheffield Plate teapots.

the eighteenth and the beginning of the nineteenth centuries. A tea service by the last-named silversmith shows a peculiarity in the repetition of the gallery to the feet of the vessels. A circular teapot was another popular product of the Philadelphia silversmiths. Many of the tea and coffee services of the early nineteenth century, wrought at Philadelphia and New York, are more conspicuous for their ungainly appearance than for grace of form.

One common practice of Philadelphia craftsmen was the engraving of the owners' arms or initials in a shield or medallion, suspended from a flowing knot, below which are two laurel branches or ears of wheat, adapted, however (without the wheat), from American and English engraved bookplates of the end of the eighteenth century. An example of such engraving is illustrated on a tankard by John Myers, about 1796, in the Pennsylvania Museum catalogue, 1917, p. 44. The question of engraving arms and devices on silver, by an engraver as distinct from the actual silversmith, is discussed on a later page in this chapter.

The late Mr. George M. Curtis has told the story of the silversmith's craft in Connecticut in an excellent little book published in 1913, and illustrates specimens of Connecticut work and the earliest piece of Sacramental silver in that State—a plain beaker of 1668 by William Rouse of Boston, whence came most of the silver into Connecticut before about 1708.

Job Prince (1680–1703), of Milford, was probably the pioneer silversmith, but none of the work executed in his short life has so far been identified. Examples by the next silversmith, René Grignon, a Huguenot (who settled at Norwich from other parts of New England about 1708 and died in 1715) have, however, survived, including a small plain mug, illustrated by Mr. Curtis, and a porringer, described by Mr. Bigelow.* Next was Cornelius Kierstead,† Dutch by descent, who had exercised his craft in New York before settling about 1722 in New Haven, and wrought several important things, on some of which he combined with New England designs traces of New York

---

* The work mentioned throughout this chapter is Mr. Francis H. Bigelow's *Historic Silver of the American Colonies*, 1917.

† A silver kettle by him is illustrated on Plate XI.

PLATE VI

PLATE VII

ornament, such as the modified leaf-like ornament on a two-handled cup. Pierre or Peter Quintard, another silversmith of Huguenot extraction, worked in New York from 1731 to 1737, the date of his migration to Connecticut, where he died in 1762, leaving a caudle cup in the Congregational Church at Stamford and two beakers in the Metropolitan Museum in New York as memorials of his skill. One Timothy Bontecou (1693–1784), also of Huguenot descent, was born in New York and settled in New Haven, and although he had learned his craft in France there is no French influence in the pair of late candlesticks attributed to him and illustrated by Mr. Curtis.

Two of Connecticut's most prosperous and skilful craftsmen were Pygan Adams (1712–76), maker of a plain coffee pot illustrated in Miss C. Louise Avery's catalogue of Judge A. T. Clearwater's important collection of American silver on loan at the Metropolitan Museum, New York; and John Gardiner (1734–76), craftsman of the cup of Dr. Yeldall in the Berkeley Divinity School at Middletown and illustrated in the present author's book on the Old Silver in American Churches.

Among many other silversmiths in Connecticut in the eighteenth century, noted by Mr. Curtis, are John Potwine, from Boston, and the versatile Amos Doolittle, engraver of book-plates and maps, printer on calico and publisher of mezzotints.

Virginia* and South Carolina were in more intimate touch with the mother country than with New England, which was virtually a foreign country to the southern colonists, who imported all their silver and porcelain and personal jewellery from England before the Revolution. Here and there the names of silversmiths of the end of the eighteenth and the beginning of the nineteenth centuries have come down, but they were probably repairers of silver ware or makers of trifles, such as spoons and sugar tongs, which any skilled blacksmith was capable of hammering. One interesting piece of silver in Judge Clearwater's collection deserves notice: the map case presented to General Lafayette in 1825 by Richard J. Manning, Governor of

* For silver made for General George Washington at Alexandria, see *Antiques*, Feb. 1927.

South Carolina, which has the mark of L. Boudo, of Charleston, whither one James Nichols, a silver caster, aged 24, had emigrated from London in 1774.

Savannah in Georgia had a silversmith in Ebenezer Whiting, who, in his advertisement in the *Georgia Gazette* for May 1, 1788, declares his intention to sell tankards, teapots, coffee pots and other silver, made (presumably under his supervision) by "one of the first workmen from New York," who could execute the work "in as elegant taste as the English imported." Unfortunately, the name of the New York craftsman is not disclosed. It is to be hoped that silver bearing the distinctive mark of Ebenezer Whiting, or preferably that of his anonymous journeyman, may yet be found in Georgia.

Annapolis, the old capital of Maryland, was in constant communication with the mother country and probably imported all the silver needed by the high provincial officials and prosperous lawyers, merchants and planters, as there is no record of any silver made by a resident craftsman, though the names of James Chalmers and James Hamilton, silversmiths, are mentioned in 1758 and 1766. The Philadelphia silversmith, Philip Syng, may have worked in Annapolis before his death there in 1739.

Of English workmanship was the silver plate used at weddings and at the elegant suppers, with the cheerful glass and convivial songs, provided by the Maryland women, as related by an English admirer of their beauty and social accomplishments, William Eddis, Surveyor of the Customs, in one of his published letters from America (1769–1777).

The author has failed to trace the precise reasons for the emigration of eight goldsmiths and silversmiths as "indented servants" from England to Maryland in 1774, named in documents in the Public Record Office in London (T. 47/9 and 47/10). They may have intended to work as journeymen silversmiths. The names are Edward Bailey, aged 21; Charles Gray, aged 25; Henry Hughes, aged 18; Robert Moore, age 37; Joseph Nuttall, aged 36; Robert Shropshire, aged 26; and John Strong, aged 25—all from London. James Jackson, aged 19, followed them in 1775.

The names of a few silversmiths, beginning with Gabriel Lewin,

PLATE VIII

PLATE IX

are recorded at Baltimore, the new capital of the State, in the fourth quarter of the eighteenth century. Nothing by Lewin has been definitely identified, but there is a little ladle by Standish Barry, another Baltimore silversmith, in Judge Clearwater's collection.

A covered basin by Louis Buichle, of Baltimore, in the collection of Mrs. Miles White, jun., was shown in the recent exhibition of old American silver at Washington (see an article by Miss C. Louise Avery, in the *Connoisseur*, May, 1926).

Andrew E. Warner was, perhaps, the most successful of the Baltimore silversmiths of the early nineteenth century. He made several important objects, such as the epergne decorated in Louis XVI style in the Hopkinson collection in Philadelphia, and the large tray in Judge Clearwater's collection (illustrated in the catalogue, p. 195), both presented by the citizens of Baltimore to Commodore Stephen Decatur in 1811 for his great naval services. A contemporary, and doubtless a kinsman, was Joseph Warner, the maker of a plain teapot in Judge Clearwater's collection.

New Hampshire had an accomplished silversmith in William Whittemore, of Portsmouth, maker of the historic Pepperell cups in the First Congregational Church at Kittery, Maine.

Newport, and later, Providence in Rhode Island, were centres of silversmithing. Samuel Vernon was, perhaps, the most employed of the Newport silversmiths. One of his tankards is described in this chapter. Others were Samuel Casey, James Clarke, John Coddington, Arnold Collins, Jonathan Otis, Daniel Rogers and John Tanner.

In Kentucky the pioneer silversmith was probably Samuel Ayres, who had a shop in Lexington and advertised in the old Gazettes of that State in 1790–1817. But the man whose name has come down as the most prominent silversmith in Lexington is Asa Blanchard, the maker of a large quantity of silver from about 1810 for the early settlers from Virginia, who formed a refined society in that capital.

Beakers were among the earliest objects in silver made in New England. The Churches of New England and New York display an endless procession of secular beakers, accounted for by the fact that, as in the Nonconformist bodies in England, the intervention of a priest in the administration of the Sacrament was deemed unnecessary, and as congregations grew in numbers, new cups were needed, and several cups were handed round simultaneously.

Six classes of beakers are found in American Churches. The first is plain, with a cylindrical body on a moulded base of the same shape as the decorated beakers made in Holland and England in the sixteenth and seventeenth centuries, and is represented by Colonel Francis Wainwright's gift to the First Congregational Church, Ipswich, Massachusetts,* made by Edward Winslow (Plate I, No. 1). The good English-built ship, *Adventure*, and her adventures with pirates, are recalled by the pair of plain beakers, made by John Allen and John Edwards, of Boston, in the First Congregational Church at New London, Connecticut. They were the gift of the owners, who were residents in that port.

Fig. 1.—Beaker by Robert Sanderson (1608-93) and John Hull (1624-83), of Boston.

The second class has a straight body, with a flat bottom, and is encircled with a broad granulated band, leaving the lip and base plain. Five specimens are recorded, including one with the date 1659, and all made in Boston. The granulated band was evidently copied from that on a tall English cup of 1639-40 in the First Church in Boston. The third class is of the same form as the second, but is quite plain, like one by Robert Sanderson and John Hull, in the Old South Church, Boston, as illustrated here. The fourth class has a plain, inverted bell-shaped body, the earliest dated example being 1710.

These two Boston silversmiths had before their eyes an English beaker of the sixteenth century when making the fine beaker for the First Congregational Church at Marblehead.

Another class of beaker, with a fluted body derived from English plate of the fourth quarter of the seventeenth century, is entirely confined to New England Churches. The same fluting may be

---

* The plain old beakers of the same shape from this Church, by John Coney, Jeremiah Dummer, John Allen, John Edwards, and Cornelius Kierstead, illustrated on Plate 78 of the present author's book on *The Old Silver of the American Churches*, have passed into the collection of Mr. Francis P. Garvan.

seen on tall cups and caudle cups by Boston silversmiths, and was especially favoured by Jeremiah Dummer.

Most of the New York beakers are Dutch in character, as might be expected from the Dutch ancestry of the early silversmiths of that city. One of the oldest was copied in 1678 by Ahasuerus Hendricks, the earliest New York silversmith, from a beaker made at Haarlem in Holland in 1660, both of which are in the First Reformed Church at Albany. An important beaker by Jacob Boelen (1654–1729) is in the collection of Mr. Francis P. Garvan (Plate I, No. 2). Another " Dutch " beaker was made in 1731 by Henricus Boelen and belongs to the Reformed Church at Bergen, New Jersey (Plate I, No. 3), while another, of a more religious character in the engraved decoration, has been acquired by Judge Clearwater from the First Church, Kingston, the maker being Benjamin Wynkoop, of New York, 1711 (Plate I, No. 4).

Historic specimens of all the above beakers are illustrated in *The Old Silver of the American Churches*.

Contrary to accepted opinion, the American silver tankard was not exclusively the man's drinking vessel, for his wife's initial shares with his a place of honour on the handle of many examples of this intimate and cherished family possession.

New England tankards of the early period, it need scarcely be said, followed in shape the old English tankards of the time of Charles II, though there are certain embellishments peculiar to Colonial silversmiths. One of the earliest, and certainly one of the noblest, of extant Boston tankards is in the possession of Mrs. Alexander F. Wadsworth, and deserves notice from the fact that its maker was the first of the Boston silversmiths, Robert Sanderson. It is exceptionally large and is plain, except for some engraved flowers on the cover (Plate II, No. 2). Another rare Boston tankard by one of its most important craftsmen, Jeremiah Dummer, was a gift to the South Parish in Portsmouth, New Hampshire, for the personal use of the pastors, by the widow of the pastor, the Rev. William Shurtleff (Plate II, No. 5). Its rarity lies not in the shape or in the fluted or gadrooned shoulder of the cover, comparatively rare as is this second feature, but in the application of a cut tulip on the cover and on the body, at the junction of the handle, in the manner of the "cut-card" ornament of English silversmiths, especially between 1660 and 1690, and carried on until the early part of the eighteenth century. In shape and size and in the application of the "cut-card" tulip it resembles the tankard by the same gifted craftsman, in the possession of Hon. William F. Wharton, exhibited a few years ago at the Worcester Art Museum, Massachusetts. By Jeremiah Dummer is one of the most capacious silver tankards extant—the gift in 1759 of the Rev. Ebenezer Turell to the First Parish, Medford, Massachusetts. Two more tankards of the variety with fluted or gadrooned borders on the covers are worthy of remembrance, not only as important specimens of the handiwork of John Coney of Boston in 1705, but also because past Presidents and *alumni* of Harvard College have received the Sacrament in them in the First Parish, Cambridge. These three tankards are illustrated on Plates 39 and 42 in *The Old Silver of the American Churches*.

Rarer than the Dummer tankards is one by Timothy Dwight (1654-91), embossed along the base with acanthus and palm leaves in the English style of 1670-95, and fitted with a lion thumbpiece. Mr. Bigelow illustrates it (No. 63).

The early flat-topped tankards of the New England silversmiths would seem to date mainly from 1700 to 1730, when they were superseded by tankards of the same shape, but with more tapering bodies, frequently encircled by a narrow moulding, and with domed covers and moulded finials. It must, however, be remembered that the domed-cover tankards without finials had made their appearance about 1715. A tankard by Paul Revere illustrates a late development of this form, with a moulding on the body, a higher domed cover, and a moulded finial resembling those of Colonial furniture, such as are peculiar to New England tankards and are rarely seen on English tankards (Plate II, No. 3). Several tankards have handles terminating in cherubs' faces, cast and chased, and masks, both of which are peculiar to Colonial silversmiths, the former of which may have been inspired by some such faces as those on the flagons of about 1660 in Marlborough House Chapel in London. One of the most uncommon thumbpieces is formed of two dolphins and a mask, as on the tankard attributed to Thomas Millner (or Miller), of Boston, about 1730, in the First Congregational Society, Chelmsford, Massachusetts (Plate II, No. 1), and on the exceedingly rare tankard by Henry Hurst (c. 1665–1717), which has descended to Mr. Dudley L. Pickman (Plate II, No. 4). The embossed fruit and leaf on the Hurst handle is most unusual in a Boston tankard.

A deservedly prized piece is the Boston tankard by Jacob Hurd (1702-58), engraved with the snow *John and Ann*, and showing the domed cover mentioned above; it was a gift to the Second Presbyterian Church in Philadelphia by John Sproat, mariner. A similar tankard by the same maker is known to the author, and is of historic associations in that its original owners were Colonel Elisha Jones, of Weston, Massachusetts, a conscientious loyalist, and his wife, Mary; engraved upon it are the Jones arms.

It is curious that although they have made many mugs of the "bellied" shape, the American silversmiths seldom copied the English tankards of this form, with domed covers, so popular in England in the middle of the eighteenth century. One American tankard of this shape, by Peter David, of Philadelphia, is in Mr. Francis P. Garvan's collection.

There is reason to assume that the old silver tankards in New England Churches (of which more than 130 are described by the author in his book on American Church silver) were frequently used in the eighteenth century for purposes other than the administration of the Sacrament, just as flagons of silver and pewter were requisitioned in English parishes for the ancient "Church Ales" and for serving hot spiced drinks at funerals, as well as at vestry meetings and local festivities. In New England similar hospitable customs prevailed. For example, at the funeral in 1685 of the Rev. Thomas Cobbet, minister at Ipswich, Massachusetts, one barrel of wine and two barrels of cider were consumed by the mourners, and "as it was cold, there was some spice and ginger for the cider." At the funeral of Mary Norton, widow of a pastor of the First Church at Boston, over 51 gallons of wine were served, doubtless in some of the precious and historic old silver cups in the possession of this Church.

Even the peremptory edict of the General Court of Massachusetts in 1742, forbidding the drinking of wine and rum at funerals, did not have the immediate effect of stopping this ancient and hospitable custom.

Some 119 tankards were exhibited at the Boston Museum in 1911 and are included in the catalogue.

The tankard, barrel shaped and cylindrical, hooped like a barrel, was made in large numbers in England towards the end of the eighteenth and the beginning of the nineteenth centuries, but was not popular in America. A specimen with a cylindrical body, made in 1801 by Samuel Williamson of Philadelphia, is in the First Congregational Church at Deerfield, Massachusetts, and is illustrated in the author's book on *The Old Silver of the American Churches*.

The " peg " tankards of Scandinavia and England of the seventeenth century were never made in America, despite Longfellow's allusion to the ancient custom of drinking down to the peg, in his Golden Legend :

" Come, old fellow, drink down to your peg !
But do not drink any farther, I beg ! "

The shape of the tankards by New York silversmiths is not, as might be supposed, Dutch, but purely English, having been modelled on English tankards of 1660 to 1710. But, English as is their shape, there are certain decorative features in these New York tankards which are essentially American. These features may be summarised as follows : Inserted in the flat topped covers of some specimens are coins of gold and silver, and occasionally Dutch and other medals of the seventeenth century. In this feature they depart from English tankards and follow those of Germany and Scandinavia in the seventeenth and eighteenth centuries. An illustration of the custom is provided in the fine tankard, attributed to Abraham Pontran of New York, and bequeathed to the First Presbyterian Church in that city by a New York schoolmaster, one Jeremiah Owen, which is appropriately set with a medallion by Sebastian Dadler, struck in 1634 in commemoration of the death of Gustavus Adolphus of Sweden, the hero of the Protestant peoples; this is illustrated in the present author's book on the old silver in American Churches. Double and other monograms are also a feature on the covers. Another conspicuous decorative motive of these New York tankards is the narrow band of cut acanthus leaves, frequently accompanied by a zigzag wire, applied above the moulded bases. This band of leaves may be seen in Jeremiah Owen's tankard and in the illustrations of several variations in Miss C. Louise Avery's catalogue of Judge Clearwater's collection, p. 24. The handles of many New York tankards are decorated with a cherub's head, swags of fruit, lions, and other ornaments in relief, and on the end with another cherub's head, all of which are typical features. The thumbpiece of several differs from those of New England in that it is formed of an elongated spiral or "corkscrew." Here and there this orthodox "corkscrew" is abandoned for a scrolled thumbpiece of English fashion.

Cornelius Kierstead, of New York, an accomplished silversmith, made several tankards, including one in Trinity Church, New Haven; and one in possession of the New York Historical Society, which is illustrated in the Society's Bulletin for April 1921. A third is on loan from Mr. Lionel A. Crichton in the Victoria and Albert Museum.

The flat-topped New York tankard remained in favour later than the same type in New England and is, in general, larger and of thicker metal. The holding capacity varies from $1\frac{1}{4}$ to $1\frac{3}{4}$ quarts; a few hold more and others less.

Illustrations of six New York tankards are given on Plate III, from the collections of Judge A. T. Clearwater and Mr. Francis P. Garvan, the first of whom is the fortunate owner of a tankard by Gerret Onclebagh, engraved with the Shelley arms and associated by tradition with Giles Shelley, a noted merchant and master mariner of New York.

Samuel Vernon (1683-1737), of Newport, Rhode Island, one of the earliest silversmiths in that town, made tankards with a mixture of New York and Boston tankards in certain features, such as the cut acanthus leaves of the former and the dolphin thumbpieces of the latter. His tankard in the Worcester Art Museum exhibits these features (Plate V, No. 2).

By the courtesy of the Pennsylvania Museum three Philadelphia tankards are shown on Plate IV, beginning with the early example (No. 1) attributed to John de Nise, showing the influence of New York tankards in the modified flat cover, in the small cut leaves applied above the base, in the "corkscrew" thumbpiece, and in the mask on the handle-end. William Vilant is represented (No. 2) by an important specimen of his skill as a maker of tankards, which differs slightly from his equally important tankard in Judge Clearwater's collection (Fig. 86 in the catalogue). The third (No. 5), belonging to Dr. Isaac Starr, jun., of Philadelphia, is by Francis Richardson, and differs from the others in having a moulding on the body and a plain shield on the handle-end, while copying Vilant's notched rat-tail on the handle.

In Mr. Francis P. Garvan's collection are some good examples of Philadelphia tankards by the second Philip Syng and Joseph Richardson, and the later "bellied" type by Peter David, the second of which is illustrated on Plate IV (No. 4).

That the composer of the following delightful epitaph for himself, supposed to be Dr. Myles Cooper, the President of King's College (Columbia University), New York, should have quaffed wine, beer or cider from one of these old silver tankards before his banishment from America at the Revolution, is hardly disputable :

" . . . . liked what'er was good
good company, good wine, good name."

Another popular form of English drinking vessel at the end of the seventeenth and throughout the eighteenth centuries, the mug, also crossed over to America and was there usually called a can, or cann. Three shapes were made. The first is modelled on the English mug of late seventeenth-century date and has a plain, tapering, cylindrical body, like that of the tankard, and may be with or without a moulding around it. Benjamin Hiller, of Boston, made a mug of this kind about 1714 as a gift to the First Baptist Church in Boston from his father and mother-in-law. Several specimens of these mugs are illustrated in the author's book on the old silver of the American Churches. One shown here, in the First Church of Christ, Hartford, Connecticut, is by William Cowell (1682-1736), of Boston (Plate V, No. 4).

A plain mug of the same form was also made by New York craftsmen, and, like the New York tankards, it has characteristics of its own, not seen in New England mugs. A prominent feature is the wide handle with a notched " rat-tail " running down its back, like that on Mr. Francis P. Garvan's tankard by Peter van Dyck (Plate III, No. 5.). Specimens of these, made about 1729 and 1739 by John Hastier and by Peter van Dyck—one of the most accomplished of the New York silversmiths—are in the First Presbyterian Church, Southampton, Long Island. Here is an illustration of a rare mug, with an acanthus leaf applied to the shoulder of the handle, and cut acanthus leaves along the base, like those of the New York tankards. The maker was Simeon Soumaine, of New York, about 1725 (Plate V, No. 5). It is in the collection of Mr. Francis P. Garvan. Mr. Bigelow illustrates several of this type of mug. John McMullin (1765-1843), of Philadelphia, also made mugs of this shape.

The second type of American mug is a copy of an English mug of the early eighteenth century, seen in large numbers in the colleges of Oxford and Cambridge. It has a plain tapering body, rounded at the bottom, and a short moulded foot. Mugs of this form are in American Churches, including one of about 1717, by William Pollard, of Boston, in the First Church in Boston.

The third and most popular class of mug, introduced by English silversmiths in the second decade of the eighteenth century, has a " bellied " body and came into fashion in America about 1730. More than sixty of this type are recorded in American Churches, more than half of which are in three Churches in Salem, Massachusetts. Three of the earliest were made in or soon after 1737 by Jacob Hurd, of Boston, and another came from the workshop of the celebrated Paul Revere. The American mugs exhibit some differences in the handles. Some have plain scrolled handles, as that by Samuel Minott (1732-1803), the Boston silversmith, in the collection of Mr. Francis P. Garvan. Other mugs have a leaf on the handle, turned up at the end to make the holding easier, as in one by Jacob Hurd, in the possession of Mrs. Lydia B. Taft (Plate V, No. 1). In the Worcester Art Museum is an uncommon example with a gadrooned foot, finely engraved with the arms of Orne, by Paul Revere (Plate V, No. 3).

Of this form is the English mug, 1767-8, once the property of the parents of Governor William Paca, a signatory to the Declaration of Independence, which is illustrated on Plate XXXVI (No. 9).

Another form of English drinking vessel, the caudle cup, seems to have been copied by Boston silversmiths as early as 1676, which is the date engraved on the plain gourd-shaped cup given by Margaret Bridges, of Finglas in Ireland, for Sacramental purposes to the First Parish at Concord, Massachusetts, and wrought when its maker, John Coney, was 21 years old.* He was also the maker of five other caudle cups for the same Church a few years later. No fewer than 57 of these plain caudle cups were recorded by the writer in American Churches, chiefly made by the most conspicuous of the Boston silversmiths, and many of them of great historic interest from their association with their pious donors and deserving of preservation as monuments in little. One by Jeremiah Dummer, of Boston, in Mr. Francis P. Garvan's collection, is illustrated in an article by Miss C. Louise Avery in the *Connoisseur*, May, 1926.

Scarcer than the plain variety is the imitation of the common English caudle cup of the reign of Charles II, decorated with flat flowers, which have some resemblance to those on chests and other furniture of New England of the fourth quarter of the seventeenth century. Two specimens by Robert Sanderson have escaped the melting-pot and are illustrated in the present author's book on the old silver of the American Churches. One came from Hollis Street Church in Boston and is now in the Boston Museum of Fine Arts (Plate VI, No. 3). The second belongs to the First Congregational Society in Quincy, Massachusetts, the Church of John Adams. An earlier example than either is in the Second

---

*The caudle cup of President Holyoke, of Harvard College, by John Coney, is illustrated in Mr. W. Coolidge Lane's article in *Trans. of Colonial Soc. of Mass.*, xxiv, 165-176.

PLATE X

PLATE XI

AMERICA

Church, Dorchester, Massachusetts, and bears the marks of Sanderson and his partner, John Hull, with the date 1665, which is within about ten years of the introduction of this type of caudle cup in England (Plate VI, No. 2).

A third variety of caudle cup has a straighter body fluted along the lower part in the manner much favoured by the maker, Jeremiah Dummer (1645-1718), of Boston, like one in the First Congregational Church, Chelmsford, Massachusetts (Plate VI, No. 4). For the prototype of the next caudle cup, the seeker after origins must once again turn to England in the fourth quarter of the seventeenth century. This has an embossed cable band encircling the body below the lip, while the lower part is fluted like the previous cup. The specimen here illustrated was wrought by William Cowell (1682-1736), of Boston, and is in the Church of Unity, Neponset, Massachusetts (Plate VI, No. 5).

Mr. Bigelow illustrates (No. 48) a plain caudle cup with "English" handles of the time of Charles II, but with the unusual addition of a cover, also copied from an English cup; the maker was John Coney, of Boston (1655-1722).

A characteristic American vessel, called a porringer (in no way resembling the English cup of this name), was introduced at the end of the seventeenth century and was made in great numbers, both in silver and pewter, throughout the following century. Although it became so markedly common for all sorts of household purposes, until at last no well-managed home in New England was regarded as decently furnished without at least one, yet the form of the vessel is English in origin and was derived from what is called a "bleeding bowl," on what evidence the author is unable to determine. Such a vessel with a single pierced handle appears to have been made for the first time in London in the second quarter of the seventeenth century and continued to be made in isolated examples for about a hundred years, with slight variations in size and in the pattern of the handle. It was also made of Lambeth Delft ware. The author is inclined to suggest that the "bleeding bowl" may have been intended originally for a wine taster, especially as no evidence of its use is recorded by the Barber

Surgeons Company of London, and especially as that Company have not a single specimen in their important collection of old silver. It is not denied that this little vessel may have been seized in a sudden emergency by the barber surgeon, as the nearest receptacle to his hand, nor is it denied that one is extant, made at Norwich in 1689 and engraved with the initials of the Master of the Barber Surgeons of that city in 1693, in the collection of Mr. John H. Walter.

The American porringer tended to be larger in size than its English prototype, and the single pierced handle was made in a great variety of patterns. Mr. Bigelow illustrates several types of handles in his book, as does Miss Avery in her catalogue of Judge Clearwater's collection, which contains 35 porringers.

No porringer has so far been discovered by the earliest Boston silversmiths, Robert Sanderson and John Hull, but the next generation of Boston craftsmen is well represented by several specimens. Porringers with covers, in the manner of the French écuelle, are great rarities. One is illustrated in Mr. Bigelow's book (No. 213), which is an interesting problem in attribution and *provenance*, while a later one by a Connecticut silversmith, Thomas Harland, is shown in Mr. G. M. Curtis's book. A highly important silver porringer with two handles—a most unusual feature—and a cover, originally belonging to Benjamin Duffield, partner of William Penn (now in the collection of Judge Clearwater on loan in the Metropolitan Museum, New York), is said to have been made probably by Joseph Newkirke, of New York, early in the eighteenth century. It is illustrated here as an object of unusual interest, whoever the maker may have been (Plate VII, No. 1).

Popular as was the porringer in New England in the eighteenth century it never reached the same degree of popularity in the workshops of the New York and Philadelphia silversmiths, and apparently did not penetrate into use in the southern colonies, where culture and education were more akin to the mother country than to the northern colonies before the Revolution.

The so-called "key-hole" pattern in the handle, so named from the elongated oval, seems to have ousted the other patterns from about 1725, though it had been made before that date, notably in the example by John Dixwell, of Boston (who died in that year), in the collection of Mr. Francis H. Bigelow. Forty-two specimens of porringers were exhibited at the Boston Art Museum in 1911.

Evidence of the popularity of the porringer is found in old inventories and wills. Timothy Lindall, a prosperous merchant of Salem, Massachusetts, was the possessor of six. General Timothy Ruggles left two, and Joshua Winslow, of Boston, numbered four among his silver in 1769.

Six typical specimens are illustrated on Plate VII: one by John Coney, of Boston, in the collection of Mr. Francis P. Garvan, the fortunate owner of a rare New York porringer, by Bartholomew Schaats, early in the eighteenth century, and of one by William Homes (1717–83), of Boston. The Boston silversmith, Jeremiah Dummer, made several, including two showing different handles, in the Worcester Art Museum, where there is one with the later type of handle, by Andrew Tyler (1692–1741), of Boston.

The rarity of porringers by Philadelphia silversmiths has already been mentioned. Here is one (in the Pennsylvania Museum) by one of the most skilful of its craftsmen, Richard Humphreys (Plate VII, No. 7). A small early porringer, by John Lent, of New York and Philadelphia, is unusual for the great size of its handle, as may be observed from the illustration in the Bulletin of the Wadsworth Athenæum, Hartford, for April 1924.

An amusing illustration of the use of the porringer in 1771 is mentioned in a letter of Charles Pelham to Henry Pelham, engraver, of Boston, in which a "Porrenger of Water Gruel" was provided for his refractory and eccentric kinswoman, Betty Pelham, who was hinted at as being in the case of Mary Magdalene (*Pelham-Copley Letters*, p. 108). Dr. Benjamin Franklin, in his biography, speaks of his frugality in eating out of a "twopenny earthen porringer" with a pewter spoon. In proof of the use of this vessel for drinking as well as for eating, a silver porringer holding a pint is mentioned in 1742. Thomas Vernon, of Newport, in his journal, kept during his exile as a loyalist in 1776, notes that he had had "a porringer of pudding and milk" at a supper, and that he "drank a porringer and turned in at ten, very sober" (*Rhode Island Tracts*, No. 13, 1881).

The spout cup, or feeding cup, with and without a cover, was another domestic vessel which attained greater popularity in New England than in the country of its origin, England, where the earliest of the few known specimens is in the form of a miniature tankard. This was made in 1642-3 by Timothy Skottowe, of Norwich, and is in the Victoria and Albert Museum. An English glass vessel with a spout, a cover and two handles, of the fourth quarter of the seventeenth century, is called a "syllabub" cup, and was used for the drink of that name made of milk or cream, curdled by the admixture of wine, cider, or other acid, and often sweetened and flavoured. One with two handles, of Bristol Delft ware, dated 1741, in the British Museum, is called a posset cup, doubtless because it was used for a similar drink, made of hot milk curdled with wine, ale, and other beverages and flavoured with spices, which was consumed from the spout in the same manner as the woman partaking of the wine from a spouted cup in the picture of the "Communion" by Matthias Scheits (1640-1700), of Hamburg.

A glance at the covered spout cup of the early eighteenth century by John Allen and John Edwards is sufficient evidence of the source of the shape—an English silver mug, such as that of 1688-9 in St. Michael's Parish, Maryland, illustrated on page 169 of Mr. Bigelow's book, which, in its turn, had been derived from an English silver tankard or a stoneware jug of the sixteenth century. Mr. Bigelow in the chapter on spout cups in his book illustrates another of the same shape without a cover by Samual Haugh (1675-1717), of Boston. The spout cup in the Metropolitan Museum, New York, by John Edwards, of Boston, is of this shape (Plate VIII, No. 2). One of a different form with a wooden handle, the cover decorated with "cut-card" work, by the same John Edwards, is a rare variety and is dated 1706; it is in the Worcester Art Museum, Massachusetts (Plate VIII, No. 1). A taller variety with a domed cover, by the Boston silversmith, Nathaniel Morse (1685-1748), was evidently inspired by some such teapot as that of John Coney, illustrated here (Plate XII, No. 1), or by a coffee pot by the same

PLATE XII

PLATE XIII

AMERICA

maker, No. 248 in the catalogue of the Boston Museum of Art, 1911. One example is merely a cylindrical beaker, with a spout and handle added.

One of these American silver spout cups had been taken to England by a conspicuous mariner and loyalist from Massachusetts, Francis Rotch, and is engraved with his parents' initials. Made by Benjamin Hiller (1687–1739), of Boston, it is slightly different in shape from any illustrated by Mr. Bigelow, and is still in the possession of the English branch of the family represented by Captain C. D. Rotch (Plate VIII, No. 4).

Old wills in Massachusetts indicate that silver spout cups were more common than would seem from the few surviving examples. Joshua Winslow, of Boston, left two in 1769, and that fine old Massachusetts soldier, General Timothy Ruggles, one.

Judging from the extant specimens, the spout cup ceased to be made about the middle of the eighteenth century and was rarely if ever made in New York or Philadelphia.

Another household vessel which was expanded in use, so to speak, by the American silversmith was the brazier, or chafing dish, which was made in England in the reign of Queen Anne, but is rare in silver. It was made in the Low Countries and England of copper or brass, as illustrated in Dutch pictures of the seventeenth century and in Hogarth's picture in the Soane Museum, where a brazier is supporting a pewter plate. A silver tea-kettle on a brazier-like stand with a spirit lamp, by the well-known Huguenot refugee in London, David Willaume, in 1706–7, was sold at Christie's on May 12, 1926, and is illustrated in the sale catalogue.

The earliest American shape would seem to be a deep circular bowl for the hot charcoal, pierced with foliage and other patterns, and resting on a frame of three supports, formed of scrolls and claw and ball and other shapes of feet. A pair, belonging to the estate of the late Miss Sally Pickman Dwight, were made by John Coney, of Boston, before his death in 1722. Later specimens are fitted with handles of wood, as in the specimen by John Potwine (1698–1792), of Boston, in the possession of Mrs. George F. Richardson, and in the important pair by Jacob Hurd, of Boston, in the collection of

Mr. Francis P. Garvan, of New York (Plate XV, No. 7). Differences may be observed in the pattern of the pierced work of these objects.

Eight braziers are included in the catalogue of the exhibition at the Boston Museum in 1911. No specimen by early New York silversmiths has been recorded. Examples by Philadelphia craftsmen are exceedingly rare. In marked contrast with the braziers of Boston is the important example by the second Philip Syng, of that city, in the Pennsylvania Museum (Plate XV, No. 8).

Capable as were the Boston silversmiths of doing pierced work, such as is seen in these braziers or chafing dishes, it is odd that their skill in this direction was never exercised in making bread or cake baskets and sugar basins, as in England.

Metal chafing dishes are in the inventories of Governor Hutchinson, of Massachusetts, and the Boston loyalist, Stephen Deblois.

Almost exotic in comparison with other Colonial silver is the sweetmeat box by John Coney, of Boston, of the end of the seventeenth century, copied from an English box of about 1676, such as that illustrated in Sir C. J. Jackson's *History of English Plate*, No. 1076. It now reposes in the Boston Museum of Fine Arts (Plate VI, No. 1). In one feature only, in the serpent handle on the cover, does it resemble the sweetmeat box by Edward Winslow illustrated in the same book. So different is the Winslow box from any other piece of old American silver, in style and workmanship, that it has given rise to the suggestion that the maker may have been apprenticed in London, where this box was found. Winslow's place of apprenticeship and the name of his master have not, however, been traced.

No American salts have been found earlier than the highly important specimen by Edward Winslow (in the collection of Mr. Philip L. Spalding), and the one, 6 in. high, by John Edwards and John Allen, of Boston, in the possession of Mr. Nathan Hayward, dating from about 1700 (Plate IX, No. 4). Both are of the same octagonal shape, fitted with four scrolls on the top to hold the napkin, and differ only in the absence of a gadrooning from the top of the stem in the Winslow salt. The prototype is an English salt like the pair of 1686–7 of the Saddlers Company (Plate XXX, No. 10).

It is perhaps curious that while one of the English spool-shaped salts of the seventeenth century has been preserved at Harvard since the earliest years of the College, not one salt of this fashion appears to have been made by Boston silversmiths, or, perhaps more accurately, has not survived. An English example is illustrated on Plate XXX (No. 12).

The small English trencher salts of about 1690–1740 were, however, copied in America, as is shown by the oval pair by John Coney, of Boston, in Judge Clearwater's collection (Plate IX, No. 2), and by the similar pair by John Burt (1691–1745), of Boston (Nos. 172–3 in the Boston Museum catalogue for 1911). Coney was also the maker of another shape of trencher salt with a gadrooned edge, in the Museum of Fine Arts, Boston (Plate IX, No. 1), copied from an English salt, as that illustrated later. From about 1735 to 1770 salts on three feet—like those of cream jugs and sauce boats—were made in England and were copied by American silversmiths. One specimen by the Philadelphia silversmith, Joseph Richardson, in the collection of Mr. Francis P. Garvan, is illustrated on Plate IX (No. 3). Another salt of the same form, by Richard Humphreys, is in the Pennsylvania Museum. With these may be included the pair, possibly by Thomas Shields, of Philadelphia, about 1765, in the Metropolitan Museum, New York.

Of the exceedingly few American silver punch bowls, four are of great interest on personal grounds as well as in the history of the silversmith's art in America. The maker of the first, John Coney, of Boston, had evidently seen one of the English "Monteith" bowls of the late seventeenth and early eighteenth centuries (described in the chapter on English plate) before making this unique bowl. It belonged to the distinguished New York lawyer of Scottish birth and member of Gray's Inn, James Alexander, whose American coffee pot is also illustrated here. The arms engraved upon it are those of the powerful New York family of Livingston. The present owner is Mrs. Henry Parish (Plate X, No. 1). Second in date is the bowl, in the Museum of Fine Arts in Boston, of the plain type first seen in England in the first quarter of the eighteenth century, with and without handles and in common use in pottery and porcelain both in England and America in the eighteenth and nineteenth centuries, and a conspicuous feature in convivial gatherings, social and political, in both countries. This bowl was wrought by William Homes (1717–83), the "honest goldsmith," of Boston, and was a gift in 1763 from the officers of the Boston Regiment to Thomas Dawes, Adjutant.

Similar in form is the more famous and historic bowl made by the celebrated Paul Revere (1735–1818) for the fifteen "Sons of Liberty," whose names are inscribed upon it, with symbols of the supporters of John Wilkes, the celebrated English Whig. This precious relic of American history was the object of veneration at many a symposium at the famous Boston tavern, the "Bunch of Grapes," kept by John Marston, one of the fifteen Sons of Liberty. It has descended from the above John Marston to his great-great-granddaughter, Mrs. Marian Lincoln Perry (Plate X, No. 2).

A different variety of punch bowl is the proud possession of Dartmouth College and was the gift to the Rev. Eleazer Wheelock, President of the College, and to his successors for ever, by John Wentworth (the loyalist Governor of New Hampshire) and friends at the first Commencement in 1771. The scrolled rim in the "Monteith" manner is a late survival of some twenty years after the same type had passed out of fashion in England, where it was made with and without cherubs' faces on the fixed or detachable rim. It is illustrated by Mr. Bigelow (No. 310).

Confirmation of the author's suggestion on another page that arms and other devices on English and American silver were frequently added by engravers as distinct from the silversmiths is forthcoming in this bowl, which has the mark of Daniel Henchman (1730–75), silversmith, of Boston, and the initials of his brother-in-law, Nathaniel Hurd,* engraver of the inscription, silversmith and engraver of book-plates.

Of considerable interest to American sportsmen is the old English

---

* Nathaniel Hurd wrought but little silver, only seven pieces by him having been exhibited at, and recorded in the catalogues of, the Boston Museum of Fine Arts in 1906 and 1911. The inference may therefore be drawn that he devoted himself more to the engraving of silver and book-plates.

silver bowl of the same shape as the Homes and Revere bowls, just described, which was won at a horse race at Newmarket—thus named after its more famous English namesake—in South Carolina by a horse named Tryall. This is illustrated in the *Connoisseur* (Vol. LV), and mentioned in the chapter on English plate.

Thousands of silver punch ladles, with whalebone handles, were made in England for use with the Chinese porcelain bowls, imported into the country in the eighteenth century, but none of American make can be identified.

Other accessories of the convivial gatherings of the past are the lemon strainers, with various shapes of handles, such as that by Philip Syng, of Philadelphia, in Mr. Francis P. Garvan's collection (Plate XV, No. 6), and tumbler cups, like the historic example by Philip Goelet, of New York, about 1740, in Judge Clearwater's collection (Plate XV, No. 2). To these may be added the little dram cups or tasters, of which a few are illustrated by Mr. Bigelow with other lemon strainers; and small nutmeg graters for use with hot drinks.

The American silver inkstand (originally called a standish in England) is as great a rarity as an American silver kettle. Unique must surely be the triangular inkstand on three lion feet, by John Coney (died 1722), of Boston, in the Metropolitan Museum, New York (Plate XI, No. 1). Of greater historical but not of intrinsic interest is the inkstand, by Philip Syng, the younger, of Philadelphia, used by the signatories to the famous Declaration of Independence (Plate XI, No. 3). In the shaped border and its rocaille work and the four scrolled feet, the maker was influenced by an English salver, while the receptacles for ink and sand and pens follow English patterns.

The high cost of tea in the early eighteenth century is reflected in the great scarcity of American silver teapots before 1750, the development of which may be traced from the illustrations. First in date ranks the great rarity (once the property of General Jean Paul Mascarene), by John Coney, of Boston (1655–1722), one of the gems in Judge Clearwater's collection (Plate XII, No. 1). The pear-shape of this teapot is derived from English teapots of the first decade of the eighteenth century. In New York was made a charming teapot of similar form, but with certain well-defined characteristics, such as a narrower and longer neck, with the bird's head spout of English kettles and teapots, and the addition of mouldings, at once apparent by a comparison of the illustration of one by Adrian Bancker, of New York (1703–1761), in the same collection (Plate XII, No. 2). Such teapots were made by other New York silversmiths, John Brevoort, Charles and John Le Roux, J. Ten Eyck, Peter van Dyck and Simeon Soumaine. Different in outline and with a domed cover, not unlike those of American tankards, is a teapot ascribed to Josiah Austin (1719–80), of Charlestown, Massachusetts, in the possession of Mrs. Robert N. Toppan and illustrated by Mr. Bigelow (No. 238).

In the second quarter of the century a small globular teapot with and without a slight flat-chased decoration around the edge of the lip and mouth was evolved in England and copied in America, like that by Jacob Hurd (1702–58), of Boston, in the Boston Museum of Fine Arts (Plate XII, No. 3). A charming teapot of this shape, somewhat more extensively chased around the lip, ascribed to Josiah Austin, is in the Metropolitan Museum, New York (Plate XII, No. 5). The lower half of the spout in both is facetted. If the style of the engraved mantling may be regarded as a safe guide, the date may be assigned to about 1750. Of the same shape, with a different form of handle and a simpler foot, is the equally charming teapot by Joseph Richardson (1711–84), of Philadelphia, in the same Museum (Plate XII, No. 4).

The third development in the shape of the teapot shows an inverted pear-shaped body, copied from English teapots of 1750–60, as in the excellent example by Benjamin Burt (1729–1804), in Mr. Francis P. Garvan's collection (Plate XII, No. 6). One of the same shape, by Paul Revere, is in the possession of Mrs. Charles Prince (Plate XII, No. 7). An early specimen chased in rococo on the shoulder, by Samuel Edwards, of Boston, dated 1757, is illustrated in the Boston Museum catalogue, 1911. Slight variations in the height of the bodies, covers and feet, may be observed from the illustrations in Mr. Bigelow's book. A teapot of this shape, chased

PLATE XIV

PLATE XV

with flowers in relief, by John Moulinar, of New York, is illustrated in the catalogue of Judge Clearwater's collection (Fig. 51), and is important as a somewhat rare piece of American decoration.

From about 1775 vast numbers of teapots were made in England both in thin sheet silver and Sheffield Plate, of an oval and octagonal shape, with flat bottoms and straight spouts, not infrequently accompanied by little trays to stand on. For the most part the ornament consisted of bright cut engraving (popular after 1780*) of various patterns, and shields and medallions with floral festoons or ribands in the prevailing fashion in book-plates and in the decoration of Hepplewhite furniture. Others are plain or only slightly decorated. As with most other English fashions in the smaller objects in silver, this form of teapot was soon copied by American silversmiths in considerable numbers and continued into the early nineteenth century.

Interesting for its own sake as well as for its historic association is the teapot with its tray, sugar basin and cream jug, by Paul Revere, 1799, which was a gift to Edmund Hartt, constructor of the frigate *Boston*; this set is in the Boston Museum (Plate XII, No. 9). Paul Revere's charge for a teapot in 1789 was £5 12s. for the silver, and £5 8s. for making and engraving. For the accompanying stand he charged £2 2s. for the silver and £1 10s. for making and engraving, presumably in the currency of Massachusetts. A teapot by Revere, in the Worcester Art Museum, is illustrated on Plate XII (No. 8). A full tea service in the Wadsworth Athenæum, Hartford, was made by John Vernon of New York, about 1795. Lack of space precludes the inclusion here of a plain, simple teapot as an example of the excellent work of Asa Blanchard of Lexington, Kentucky, early in the nineteenth century, which belonged to Governor Isaac Shelby. Mrs. William Powell is the present owner.

Ungainly as are most of the American tea services of the first half of the nineteenth century, a few deserve preservation as examples of fashions, for future historians.

---

* The bright cut engraving was introduced on Old Sheffield Plate about 1789.

From teapots it is a natural step to a discussion of the other accompaniments of the tea-table of the eighteenth century, and here again the American silversmiths follow English fashions. Several stages in the changes of fashion of the cream jug may be traced from the few extant examples, beginning with the earliest English type of the reigns of George I and II through its successor, with a bulbous body and scalloped edge on three feet, as was made in great numbers in England from about 1740 to 1765 and later (Figs. 2 and 4). Mr. Francis P. Garvan is the owner of one of the popular helmet-shaped cream jugs of the late eighteenth century by the famous Paul Revere. A specimen or two of the large cream jugs made in Philadelphia in the early nineteenth century are illustrated with their sugar basins and teapots in the Pennsylvania Museum catalogue for 1921. Illustrations of other shapes are shown by Mr. Bigelow.

The American porringer was doubtless used for sugar as for other household purposes. Bowls, expressly for sugar, are somewhat scarce before the end of the eighteenth century. The charming little bowls with covers, like one shown, by John Brevoort, of New York, about 1750, in the Metropolitan Museum, New York (Plate XV, No. 3), probably served the double purpose of a sugar basin and feeding bowl for a child, the cover of some acting as a saucer. In outline, the Brevoort bowl resembles the contemporary teapots mentioned above. Earlier than this are the plain circular covered bowls, 4 to $4\frac{3}{4}$ in. high, copied from the English bowls of about 1720–35. A charming specimen by John Burt, of Boston, is shown on Plate 6 of the Boston catalogue, 1911, with a similar one by Jacob Hurd, the maker of the rare octagonal bowl and cover on Plate 21 of the same catalogue

A covered sugar bowl, by Paul Revere, repoussé in the English rococo manner of about 1750, is an illustration of the few pieces of American silver thus decorated (Plate 30 in the above catalogue).

The little sugar basin and cream jug by Cary Dunn, of New York, about 1785, in Mr. Francis P. Garvan's collection, show the formal riband and medallions for initials just mentioned.

The most important specimen of an American silver chocolate pot (illustrated on Plate XIII, No. 1) is undoubtedly in Judge Clearwater's collection and is by one of the most famous of American silversmiths, Edward Winslow (1669–1753), of Boston. As will be observed, the decoration of the cover and the body consists mainly of fluting, copied from England. On the top of the cover is some "cut-card" work, also derived from English plate. The acorn finial is removable, for the insertion of a swizzle-stick to stir the contents. The Hutchinson arms engraved upon this unique American chocolate pot are embellished with mantling of Charles II period in England, where it had been virtually discarded before these arms were engraved. Winslow practised the same fluting on one of his most imposing pieces, a large two-handled cup and cover, the property of Mrs. Lois B. Rantoul (Plate XI, No. 2). In this chocolate pot the handle is at right angles to the bird-head spout, as are the handles of many of the earliest English chocolate and coffee pots.

Different in character is Mrs. Robert Soutter's plain chocolate pot by John Coney, fitted with the familiar bird's head spout, above which is some "cut-card" ornament on the body (Plate XIII, No. 4). For solemn dignity it may be compared with the Mascarene teapot by the same skilful craftsman in Judge Clearwater's collection (Plate XII, No. 1). Important, and historic also, is the tall plain coffee pot, with a wooden handle at right angles to the spout, part of the silver plate of James Alexander, the New York lawyer, with the punch bowl on page 29. From him it descended to Lord Stirling of Revolutionary fame and is now the property of his great-great-granddaughter, Mrs. Bayard Bowie, jun. Christopher Robert, of New York, is claimed as the maker about 1751 (Plate XIII, No. 3).

The slightly later type of coffee or chocolate pot, with plain tapering cylindrical body, is represented by one by George Hanners, of Boston (c. 1696–1740), as illustrated on Plate 16 of the Boston catalogue, 1911, and by a similar one by Jacob Hurd, shown by Mr. Bigelow (No. 267). The chocolate pot by Zachariah Brigden (1734–87), engraved with the Storer arms in characteristic "Chippendale" style, illustrated by Mr. Bigelow (No. 266), has a higher domed cover, which indicates a later date than the lower covers of the Hanners and Hurd pots just mentioned.

Another form, fashioned with a long elongated (or pear-shaped) body with an ornamental spout, in imitation of English coffee pots of about 1740–60, was made by Paul Revere and others. One by Revere is a typical example of the form in question (Plate XIII, No. 2); its owner is Mrs. Thomas Bailey Aldrich. A similar one, with a slightly different gadrooned foot, by the same maker, is in the Boston Museum of Fine Arts.

A departure from this form is noticeable in the American coffee pots of some ten or fifteen years later, where the body is longer and ends at the bottom in a sub-base (like the pear-shaped teapots, already mentioned) above the gadrooned or plain foot, which also tends to be higher than in the preceding type. The ornamental spout and the high domed cover are retained. Features of these later coffee pots are the circular and oval medallions and shields, for arms or initials, engraved or cut, with festoons, ribands, wreaths, and branches, in the style of contemporary book-plates. Three specimens may be singled out for mention: one by Paul Revere, about 1797, in the Worcester Art Museum (Plate XIII, No. 5); another by the Boston silversmith, Benjamin Burt (1729–1804), in Mr. Francis P. Garvan's collection; and the third, by Ephraim Brasher, of New York, about 1785, in Judge Clearwater's collection—a collection which contains a bowl, by the same maker, formerly belonging to Commodore Isaac Hull, commander of the *Constitution* in the war of 1812.

In the latter collection is a plain pear-shaped coffee pot, different from any of the above, by John Vernon, of New York, at the end of the eighteenth century.

The precise use is uncertain of an American silver bowl, somewhat smaller than a punch bowl, though probably intended as a slop bowl for the tea-table. Two such plain bowls by Jacob Hurd, of Boston, were exhibited at Boston in 1911 and are described in the catalogue. One, made about 1755 by Daniel Christian Fueter, an emigrant to New York, is in Mr. Lionel A. Crichton's collection of American silver on loan in the Victoria and Albert Museum.

AMERICA

Nothing is rarer in American silver than the kettle, for only two have so far been traced. One is the curious piece by Cornelius Kierstead (1674-1753), of New York, in the possession of Miss Anne S. van Cortlandt, now on loan in the Metropolitan Museum, New York* (Plate XI, No. 4). Nothing like it is known in English silver; the little wire added to the lip, in the manner of New York tankards, stamps it as by a silversmith of that city, apart from the evidence of the maker's mark. It might not be too rash an assumption to picture this kettle standing on a brazier of silver, or even of brass, in its original home. The bird spout has suffered alteration at a later date.

The second kettle is plain, except for the flat chasing on the lip, and conforms in shape to its English prototype; it is, in fact, merely an enlarged copy of American and English teapots, in a slightly more globular form, with a facetted spout ending in a bird's head. The stand and spirit lamp are of the same shape as those of English kettles, such as the interesting piece illustrated later. Jacob Hurd, of Boston, was the maker. Engraved upon it are the arms of Lowell, one of the last owners being none other than James Russell Lowell, from whom it has descended to his granddaughter, Mrs. Stanley Cunningham. An illustration is on Plate 21 of the Boston Museum catalogue, 1911.

Later in the century the kettle was succeeded by a tall tea-urn, fitted with a tap in the manner of the ornate English silver wine fountains of the early eighteenth century. Paul Revere was the maker of two of different patterns. One illustrated by Mr. Bigelow (Fig. 253) was a gift from an admirer to Captain Gamaliel Bradford in perpetuation of his gallant defence in his ship *Industry* against an attack by four French privateers in the Straits of Gibraltar in 1800. The body of the other is divided into hollow sections, like the companion teapot and sugar bowl; it is illustrated on Plate 30 in the catalogue of the Boston Museum, 1911. An urn of a different shape by an unknown American silversmith is in the Boston Museum.

Some little bowls of engaging quality, varying from 5½ to 9¼ in.

---

* The kettle was probably wrought by this silversmith before his migration from New York to New Haven about 1722.

in diameter, were made in New York, and apparently not elsewhere in America, early in the eighteenth century. Three have come down to the present day. Earliest in date is a plain one, 5½ in. in diameter, with two plain solid scrolled handles, by Jacob Boelen, the welcome gift of Miss Margaret S. Remsen to the Metropolitan Museum, New York. In all three bowls the most conspicuous features are the six panels formed by hollow lines, in a similar manner to those of English " Monteith " bowls of the end of the seventeenth century. The main difference between this and the second and larger bowl (9¼ in. in diameter) is in the handles, which were copied by the maker, Simeon Soumaine, from those of English caudle cups of Charles II. The same handles are on the particularly interesting and slightly smaller bowl by Benjamin Wynkoop, in the possession of the New York Historical Society (Plate VIII, No. 3). In the Wynkoop bowl, however, the panels contain flowers, repoussé and chased. The Soumaine and Boelen bowls are illustrated in the catalogue of the exhibition of silver at the Metropolitan Museum, New York, 1911.

Silver salvers are by no means common in America. One of the earliest known, belonging to the estate of Miss Sally Pickman Dwight, was made in Boston by Timothy Dwight (1654-91) and may be described as rare, not from the shape but from the engraving on the wide rim of tulips and other flowers interspersed with an elephant, a lion, a camel and unicorn, evidently inspired by the embossed decoration of these motives on English plate of the time of Charles II. The salver has a truncated foot, in the manner of the seventeenth-century English tazza.

The tazza is not distinguishable from the silver patens of the English Church of the late seventeenth century, such as the historic specimen of 1691-2, with a gadrooned edge, presented by that able but unpopular Colonial Governor, Sir Edmund Andros, to the old Jamestown Church, Virginia; it is illustrated in the present author's book on the old silver of the American Churches, wherein may also be seen an illustration on Plate 36 of a tazza-shaped paten, by Edward Winslow, of Boston (1669-1753). Some such tazza as the Andros piece had served as a model for one engraved with the

AMERICA

Coffin arms, by John Allen and John Edwards, of Boston, early in the eighteenth century, which was exhibited at the Boston Museum in 1911 and is illustrated in the catalogue. John Coney, of Boston, made a similar tazza-salver, also illustrated in the same catalogue, and a paten of the same shape, illustrated on Plate 36 in the above book on American Church silver.

Of the plain silver salvers or tazze on truncated feet without the gadrooned edges of the above specimens, there is one by Jacob Hurd (1702–58), the prolific Boston silversmith, in the Museum of Fine Arts, Boston (Plate XV, No. 9), which has been copied from an English tazza like one of 1725–6 presented to Corpus Christi College, Cambridge, by James de Lancey, afterwards Governor of New York, a member of that college.

Silver tazze for serving glasses of wine were discarded in England early in the eighteenth century and were succeeded by small square or octagonal salvers on four short feet. Perhaps unique in American silver is the dainty little salver (one of a pair) of this kind, by Jacob Hurd, illustrated by Mr. Bigelow (No. 151) as the property of Mr. Hollis French, which exhibits an attempt to decorate the border in the style of the Anglo-French silversmiths in London about 1725. The slightly larger type of salver on four feet was made by American silversmiths in small numbers. A rare and charming specimen by Jacob Hurd was exhibited by Mr. William S. Townshend at Boston in 1911 and is illustrated in the catalogue (No. 648). The common English salver with a plain centre and a rim of scroll and scallop-shell pattern was copied about 1750 by Thomas Hamersly, of New York, as is observed in the catalogue of Judge Clearwater's collection (Fig. 100). The plain salver, with a shaped gadrooned edge, here illustrated (Plate XV, No. 1) was made by Daniel Christian Fueter, a London silversmith who settled in New York in or shortly before 1754. A small pair not unlike the last, by Myers, of New York, about 1770, are in the loan collection of Mr. Lionel A. Crichton in the Victoria and Albert Museum. Paul Revere* made a

---

* In a recent gift of silver by Revere to the Boston Museum by Mr. Henry Davis Sleeper is an excellent example of his work in Lucretia Chandler's salver, thoroughly English in pattern.

large plain salver with multifoil border, decorated with shells, which is illustrated in the above Boston catalogue (No. 894), while an illustration of one with the conventional English border of shells and gadroon by a Philadelphia craftsman is in the catalogue of the Pennsylvania Museum, 1921.

Common as were the later English salvers of the eighteenth century, it must not be assumed from the above observations that they were relatively as common in America.

New York silversmiths appear not to have made the silver tazza.

The custom of serving wine on tazze, both of silver and pottery, in France, is observable from the engraving of the Sixth Apartment at Versailles, 1698, by Antoine Trouvain.

Equally scarce, if not scarcer, are American silver candlesticks before the Revolution. Earliest in date is the well-known example, modelled on the lines of English candlesticks of the reign of Charles II, by Jeremiah Dummer (1645-1718), of Boston, and now owned by Mr. William A. Jeffries, a descendant of the original owner (Fig. 3). A curious composite candlestick, attributed to John Coney, has a baluster stem, similar, though shorter and thicker, to those of English wine cups of the time of James I and Charles I, while the high curved foot, with its gadrooned edges, is not unlike an English salt.

By John Coney are also a pair of baluster candlesticks of true English type of the end of the seventeenth and the beginning of the eighteenth centuries. Both these and the previous candlestick belong to the estate of the late Miss Sally Pickman Dwight and are illustrated by Mr. Bigelow (Nos. 188 and 189).

John Burt (1691-1745), of Boston, followed a familiar English fashion in making the charming pair of candlesticks in 1724,* and in the exceedingly rare snuffer tray and snuffers, shown in Mr. Bigelow's book, which also contains an illustration of a pair of silver candle-brackets of great rarity, by Knight Leverett (1703-53), of Boston.

Casters as distinct from combined salts and casters were first made

---

* These have been presented to Harvard University.

AMERICA

in England in the reign of Charles II and were cylindrical in shape, A rare American caster of this form (illustrated by Mr. Bigelow. No. 220) was made by Gerret Onclebagh, of New York, early in the eighteenth century, after an English model but with a touch of the characteristic New York work in the cut acanthus leaves applied above the foot, in the same manner as the tankards.

Next is a little cylindrical caster with a single handle, copied from English casters of about 1720-45, as in the two examples by John Edwards (1670–1746), in the Worcester Art Museum (Plate XIV, No. 2), and by William Pollard (1690-c.1746), both of Boston, in the Metropolitan Museum, New York. Contemporary with these are taller and exceedingly scarce pear-shaped casters, like those by two early Boston silversmiths, Edward Winslow and Benjamin Hiller—the latter octagonal in shape—both in the collection of Mr. Francis P. Garvan (Plate XIV, Nos. 1 and 3).

Three octagonal casters of the English fashion of about 1715-25, by different Boston silversmiths, showing differences in the pierced covers and in the finials, or absence of a finial, may now be mentioned. The first, by William Simpkins (1704–80), is in the possession of Miss Maud A. Cummings ; the second, by John Burt (1691–1745), was a gift from Thomas Hancock to his niece, Lydia Bowman, and now belongs to Mrs. Lydia B. Taft ; and the third by Paul Revere, the elder (1702–54), is in the Worcester Art Museum. The second of these is illustrated on Plate XIV (No. 5).

A specimen of the taller plain vase-shaped casters, as made in England in great numbers, is shown on the same Plate (No. 4). The maker was John Coburn (1725–1803), of Boston. It is in the Worcester Art Museum.

Mustard pots are by no means common in America. One by the New York silversmith, John Moulinar, is in the collection of Mr. Francis P. Garvan.

English sauce boats with single scrolled handles and three feet, like the feet of salts and cream jugs, succeeded those with solid moulded bases with single or double handles, and were extensively made in the middle of the eighteenth century. None of the earlier fashion would seem to have crossed the Atlantic, but several of the later type are recorded, by John and Samuel Burt, of Boston, and are illustrated in the Boston Museum catalogue for 1911. A boat by Paul Revere, engraved with the Orne arms, is in the Worcester Art Museum (Plate XV, No. 5), and a charming pair by Joseph Richardson, of Philadelphia, are in the Metropolitan Museum, New York (Plate XV, No. 4). An unusual form is shown on Plate 3 of the catalogue just mentioned, where a later shape, by Benjamin Burt, about 1770, is also illustrated.

Little snuff and patch boxes were reserved for the few. Of the highest importance in the history of the arts in America is Judge A. T. Clearwater's box, wrought by a silversmith who preferred to remain anonymous, while his brother craftsman, William Burgis, engraved the " Prospect of the Colledges at Cambridge in New England 1739 " [Harvard College].* This veritable treasure is fully described in the Bulletin of the Metropolitan Museum, New York, February 1924.

Mr. Garvan has a little box by Jacob Hurd, of Boston (Plate IV), the maker of a great rarity in solid gold, engraved with the Dummer arms, which is in the possession of the Misses Loring and is illustrated by Mr. Bigelow. A little box, chased with a Tudor rose, attributed to Francis Richardson, of Philadelphia, is in the Pennsylvania Museum. An early example by the Boston silversmith, John Coney, engraved with the contemporary Jeffries arms, has descended to Mr. William A. Jeffries with the unique Dummer candlestick mentioned on page 40 and is illustrated by Mr. Bigelow.

The two-handled plain cup and cover, $12\frac{3}{8}$ in. high (Plate IX, No. 5), now in the Essex Institute at Salem, was presented in 1749 by the Province of Massachusetts to Colonel Benjamin Pickman (whose arms are engraved), a man of consequence in that old Massachusetts town, for his great services in promoting the famous expedition to Louisburg, also commemorated by some English silver caddies given to Sir William Pepperell, illustrated later. It was made by William Swan (1715-74), of Worcester, Massachusetts, after some such English cup as that by George Wickes, of

---

* The " Prospect " engraved on a copper plate by Burgis was published in 1726.

London, of about 1730, once the property of the celebrated John Hancock and illustrated in Mr. Bigelow's book (No. 117). Another English cup of the same form is also in America, namely, that of 1736–7 (with a later cover of 1745–6), formerly belonging to the Corporation of the mother town of Boston in Lincolnshire, which was examined by the author with much interest, not unmingled with feelings of regret, some years ago at the hospitable board of the St. Botolph Club in Boston; this is illustrated in Buck's *Old Plate*, page 103. Yet another historic English cup of this shape, wrought in London by John Swift in 1756-7, was a race prize in America; it is illustrated later.

An American cup of the same shape, by Jacob Hurd (1702-58), was exhibited at the Boston Museum in 1911 and is illustrated on Plate 21 in the catalogue. The Rowe arms (Plate 33 in the same catalogue) may have been engraved upon it by the maker's son, Nathaniel Hurd. Exhibited at the same time (No. 643) was a similar cup by the same maker, the gift from the merchants of Boston to Edward Tyng, commander of the snow *Prince of Orange*, for taking a French privateer on the American coast in 1744.

Jacob Hurd is remembered for deigning to stamp his mark on a French silver spoon and fork, once the property of Esther Wheelwright, the little American girl who was captured at the age of seven by Indians in Maine and was placed by the French Governor of Quebec, the Marquis de Vaudreuil, in the Ursuline Convent at Quebec, where these precious relics were examined by the author in 1912.

With the cup in the Essex Institute is a tall ewer, $10\frac{1}{8}$ inches high, which was presented by the New England Guards in 1819 to Benjamin Toppan Pickman, grandson of Colonel Benjamin Pickman. It is stamped with the maker's name, *Ward*, presumably Richard Ward, of Boston.

In studying American fashions in silver, a surprising absentee is the characteristic English silver and Sheffield-plate coaster or bottle-stand of the eighteenth and early nineteenth centuries, without which no comfortable house was regarded as decently furnished. It is true that port was not a popular wine in America as it was in

England, but Madeira was drunk in every family with any pretensions to luxury and therefore it is odd that not a single American silver bottle-stand has been found. That the use of such accessories of the hospitable table was not unknown in America just before the Revolution is proved by the inventories of two loyalists, one in Massachusetts and the other in South Carolina, though these were doubtless of English workmanship. Mahogany bottle-stands were apparently made in or imported into America, for 22 are included in the inventory of Gilbert Deblois, loyalist, of Boston.

Nor are any silver wine-labels of the early nineteenth century known to have been made.

Chasing in the rococo manner of the middle of the eighteenth century was not greatly practised in America, and indeed is almost an intrusion in the plain dignified silver. Of the few specimens are a bowl by Richard van Dyke, of New York (illustrated No. 321 in the Boston Museum catalogue, 1906); a cream jug by Jacob Hurd (No. 161 in the same catalogue); and the teapot and basin mentioned earlier.

The Classical revival of about 1770 spread to America and is discernible not only in American-made furniture but also in silver. The influence of the style known as the "First Empire" may be observed in the silver vase at Washington, made in 1812 by Fletcher and Gardiner, of Philadelphia, for presentation to Commodore Isaac Hull for sinking the British frigate *Guerriere* with the frigate *Constitution* in 1812 (see page 36).

Little or nothing has been said in books on old plate on the part played by apprentices and journeymen in making the wares stamped with the marks of their masters. That journeymen were not negligible factors is proved by the will of Paul Lamerie, the Anglo-French goldsmith, who directed that two journeymen should finish all the plate left unfinished at his death. One of these men, Frederick Knopfell, afterwards became a master goldsmith himself.

In America the same custom prevailed, as is revealed in the advertisement of a Savannah silversmith on page 12.

The anonymous engravers of arms on New England silver followed, as would be expected, the changing fashions in the mantling and decorative features of English heraldry, as did American engravers of book-plates. Only one Boston silversmith is definitely known to have engraved arms on the silver made by him, namely, Nathaniel Hurd,* engraver of book-plates for Harvard College and of the Hancock arms on the silver cups made by him for the First Congregational Society at Lexington. He also engraved the inscription on a punch bowl (p. 30). This somewhat categorical statement may be qualified by adding that John Coney, engraver of the first paper money for the American Colonies and one of the most prolific of Boston silversmiths, may have engraved his own silver, as may Paul Revere, engraver as well as silversmith. Likewise, Nathaniel Morse, the Boston silversmith (c. 1685-1748) and engraver of the rare portrait of Matthew Henry, probably engraved the work of some of his contemporary silversmiths in Boston.

The collaboration of engraver and silversmith has not received that attention in America or England which the subject deserves. Notwithstanding the few examples quoted above, where the silversmith was engraver too, the author ventures to suggest that much of the heraldry on plate wrought in both countries was executed by different craftsmen, probably engravers of book-plates. Practical support for the suggestion is afforded by two pieces of plate of 1685 and 1689, at St. John's College, Oxford, where one L. King, engraved and signed the arms. Both pieces are illustrated in Mr. H. C. Moffatt's book on the Oxford plate.

In America the advertisements of engravers of the eighteenth century support the suggestion. Dunlap's *History of the Arts of Design in the United States* (1918) mentions, among others, William Rollinson, an Englishman settled in New York, as an engraver of silver. John Murray was an engraver of silver plate in New York in 1775, and Thackara and Vallance were engaged in the same work at Philadelphia in 1794. Others, both earlier and later, might be cited, including Francis Dewing, who arrived in Boston in 1716 and advertised himself as an engraver of coats of arms and cyphers on silver plate. According to his advertisement in the *Pennsylvania Gazette*,

---

* He was the engraver in 1762 of the rare caricature portrait of the notorious Dr. Seth Hudson.

1748-51, Lawrence Herbert was an engraver on gold, silver, copper and pewter.

Much precious old silver has been lost for ever because its owners and custodians have been persuaded in the past by goldsmiths and others, with the best of intentions, to have their " old-fashioned " plate transformed into new fashions, just as old furniture was thrust aside for the new designs of Chippendale, which in their turn were dubbed within a few years by Sheraton as " now wholly antiquated but possessing great merit at the time they were published."

Several historic objects have perished, including the gold boxes made by New York silversmiths for presentation with the freedom of the city to such Governors as Lord Lovelace, the Earl of Dunmore General Tryon, and others.

For a full appreciation of the old American Colonial silver it should be studied in conjunction with old American furniture, as illustrated in Mr. Luke V. Lockwood's admirable book on furniture ; and with Mr. Fiske Kimball's excellent work, *Domestic Architecture of the American Colonies and of the Early Republic*, 1922.

For those who wish to study the fascinating subject of old American silver in greater detail, ample material is available in the late Mr. Buck's book, already mentioned ; in the illustrated catalogues of the exhibitions in the Museum of Fine Arts at Boston in 1906 and 1911, with their interesting introductions by Mr. R. T. H. Halsey and Miss Florence Paull (now Mrs. Florence Paull Berger) ; the catalogue of a similar exhibition at the Metropolitan Museum in New York, also with an introduction by Mr. Halsey, and the Bulletins of that Museum ; the late Mr. George M. Curtis's work on the old Connecticut silversmiths; Mr. Hollis French's List of American silversmiths (printed for the Walpole Society) 1917 ; the catalogue of an exhibition at the Pennsylvania Museum in 1917 ; Mr. Maurice Brix's book on Philadelphia silversmiths ; the illustrated catalogue of the exhibition of silver at the Worcester Art Museum ; *Historic Silver of the American Colonies*, 1917, by Mr. Francis H. Bigelow, an acknowledged authority on the subject ; Miss C. Louise Avery's admirable catalogue of Judge A. T. Clearwater's collection, 1920 ; and the catalogue (1921) of the silver exhibited in the Pennsylvania Museum, by Dr. S. W. Woodhouse, jun. To this list may be added the present author's book on the Old Silver of the American Churches, containing some hundreds of illustrations of domestic as well as ecclesiastical silver, printed in 1913 for the National Society of Colonial Dames of America.

Fig. 2.
Cream jug, c. 1750.

Fig. 3.
Candlestick, by Jeremiah Dummer, of Boston (1645-1718). H. 10¾ in. Owner, William A. Jeffries, Esq.

Fig. 4.
Cream jug, c. 1735.

AUSTRIA.

PLATE XVI.

No. 1 Nautilus cup, c. 1580, H. 11 in., by Marx Kornblum, of Vienna.
                                                                             Imperial Museum, Vienna.
No. 2 Carved ivory tankard, with silver-gilt mounts, by Ignaz Krautauer, of Vienna, 1816. H. 7¼ in.   Windsor Castle.
No. 3 Carved ivory tankard, with silver-gilt mounts, Vienna, c. 1816. H. 6¼ in.
                                                                              Windsor Castle.
No. 4 Tall cup of silver-gilt and enamel, probably by Wolfgang Zulinger, of Wiener-Neustadt, c. 1462. H. 32 in.   Rathaus, Wiener-Neustadt.
No. 5 Silver-gilt stag, late 16th century, Vienna. H. 10¾ in.
                                                  Waddesdon collection, British Museum.

SEVERAL old towns in Austria had their goldsmiths. Vienna, which flourished under Rudolph IV as the capital and the permanent residence of the German Emperors, had its Court goldsmiths. Many important objects, though suspected as Viennese in origin, cannot be definitely assigned to Vienna goldsmiths because of the absence of marks, the Court goldsmiths having been exempt it is supposed, from guild regulations. Furthermore, the purely household silver of the Austrian Court and much of the silver of the Austrian nobility was melted in the Turkish and Napoleonic wars.

Wenzel Jamnitzer was born in Vienna in 1508 and in 1534 settled in Nuremberg, where he achieved fame as a goldsmith.

A most important cup of the second half of the fifteenth century was wrought at Wiener Neustadt (where it is preserved with other relics in the Rathaus) probably by Wolfgang Zulinger. As will be observed from the illustration on Plate XVI, this great cup is covered with the polished lobes or bosses which are such characteristic features of German plate from this period until the seventeenth century. In form and decoration it is similar to the " St. Christopher " cup of 1486, probably by Hermann Kolmann, of Lüneburg, which is in the important collection of plate of the old city of Lüneburg, now in the Kunstgewerbe Museum, Berlin, and is surely worthy of the most powerful ruler in central Europe

PLATE XVI

AUSTRIA

at the period, Matthias Corvinus (1440-90), King of Hungary. Displayed on the finial are the monogram of this king together with that of the Emperor Frederick III, his rival for the Hungarian Crown, whom he defeated in 1462, the date on the cup, which marks the reconciliation between the two sovereigns. It stands 32 inches high and is illustrated in colour, showing the enamelled decoration, in Becker and Hefner-Alteneck's *Kunstwerke und Geräthschaften* . . . 1852.

One of the earliest and most conspicuous of the Viennese goldsmiths was Erhard Efferdinger, identified from his imposing Gothic monstrance, signed and dated 1524, and bearing the Vienna mark, in the Pfarrkirche at Schattau in Moravia. No specimen of his secular work has, however, been recorded. Of the Renaissance one of the most prominent craftsman was Marx Kornblum (died in 1591), whose fame rests on a few extant specimens of his work which have survived the ravages of war and the changes of fashion and family misfortunes, including an enamelled silver-gilt nautilus cup, in the Imperial collection at Vienna (Plate XVI, No. 1); a dish chased with gods and goddesses, in the Wallace Collection in London; and a tankard of potstone, mounted in silver-gilt, in the British Museum. The names of some of his contemporaries and immediate followers cannot be identified from their marks. One goldsmith, however, Christoph Hedeneck, working between 1574 and 1595, is known from a silver-gilt dish, illustrated in *Chefs-d'œuvre d'orfèvrerie à l'exposition de Budapest*, 1884, by Pulszky, Radisicz and Molinier, an important work on old silver.

The Vienna maker of the late sixteenth-century stag in the British Museum has not been identified (Plate XVI, No. 5).

In the year 1699 was wrought the costly monstrance, set with a great number of diamonds, in the Church of St. Loretto, in Prague, the combined work of Johann Baptist Känischbauer von Hohenreid (1668-1739) and Mathias Stegner, both of Vienna.

Vienna rapidly developed as the social centre of the monarchy during the brilliant reigns of Charles VI (1712-40) and Maria Theresa (1740-80). It was markedly under the influence of the

Louis XIV style in art, and traces of its influence, as well as that of Louis XV and Louis XVI, may be observed not only in silver, but also in ironwork. Anton Mathias Domanek (1713–79) was the maker of the gold toilet service of 53 pieces, chased in the French manner, for the Empress Maria Theresa about 1750, illustrated on Plate 34 in Ilg's *Album Kunstindustrieller Gegenstände des Kaiserhauses*, 1895. Another Viennese silversmith, patronised by the Court and the Austrian nobility, was Ignaz Joseph Würth, who flourished in the last quarter of the eighteenth century, the maker of a silver dinner service which was in the possession of Prince Esterhazy when seen by the author some years ago. By another member of this family of goldsmiths are several tureens with stands, stamped with the mark of J. S. Würth about the same date, and decorated in the Louis XVI style, which are also in the same princely collection.

Some tureens on stands, dated 1779–80 and 1781, in Louis XVI style, and candlesticks of 1781, by Ignaz Joseph Würth, are illustrated in an interesting article on Vienna silver of the eighteenth century by Count Vincenz Latour in *Kunst und Kunsthandwerk*, 1899, pp. 417–429. In the same article are illustrations of a candlestick, ewer, cocoapot, teapot and tray, with touches of rococo ornament, by Anton Mathias Domanek, the maker of the gold toilet service, already mentioned; and of a plain chocolate pot by Johann Georg Stromayr, 1763.

The style of Louis XVI penetrated even to ecclesiastical vessels by Viennese goldsmiths, who, within a few years, were equally under the influence of the "First Empire" in decoration.

There would seem to have been a taste for English plate in Austria, as in Portugal, in the eighteenth century, a taste perhaps stimulated by the advertisements of the London goldsmith, Thomas Daniell, in the *Journal des Luxus und der Moden*, for such things as epergnes, coffeepots and candlesticks. This goldsmith registered his mark with that of his partner, John Wall, at Goldsmiths' Hall, in 1781.

Dr. Marc Rosenberg has noted an enamelled chalice made in 1660, a year before his death, by Michel Dietrich, who, previous

AUSTRIA

to removing to Vienna in that year, had been Court goldsmith at Prague. This is the only piece, ecclesiastical or secular, mentioned as his work by Dr. Rosenberg.

Doubtless some of the agate and other vessels of crystal and stone were mounted in gold and silver by anonymous goldsmiths of the seventeenth century in Vienna, just as were the two large redstone vases from Paraguay, brought to Spain in the time of Philip IV. These vases (in the old Imperial Museum) were mounted in silver in Vienna in 1747.

Three carved ivory tankards at Windsor Castle have silver-gilt Viennese mounts of the early nineteenth century. The ivory carvings were also executed in all probability in Vienna. One, carved with the "Death of Agag," was acquired by Lord Stewart, Ambassador at Vienna between 1814 and 1823 and one of the plenipotentiaries to the famous Congress with his brother, Viscount Castlereagh. Stamped upon the mounts are the Vienna date-letter for 1816 and the mark of the goldsmith Ignaz Krautauer, a goldsmith who became master in 1771 and made plate in the French style of Louis XVI and the "First Empire." The second tankard is carved with a Bacchanalian subject and also bears the Vienna mark, while the carving on the third represents a battle scene. Two are illustrated on Plate XVI (Nos. 2 and 3).

One result of the Congress of Vienna was the patronage accorded to the goldsmiths by the diplomatic corps and others attracted to the city.

Some pieces of plate by Vienna goldsmiths were exhibited at Budapest this year (1927) and are described in the catalogue. One of the examples illustrated is a large *surtout de table* in the rococo style of the year 1755–6, and three ewers of the early nineteenth century.

BALTIC STATES

PLATE XVII.

No. 1 Tankard, probably by Johann Behrend, of Riga, 1691. H. 8¼ in.
"Kompagnie der Schwarzen Häupter," Riga.
No. 2 Oil and vinegar frame, by A. C. Levon, of Abo, Finland, 1790.
National Museum, Helsingfors.
No. 3 Islamic glass, probably of the 14th century, mounted in silver gilt in 1551 perhaps by a Reval goldsmith. H. 11½ in. Hermitage Museum, Petrograd.

PLATE XVIII.

No. 1 Tall cup. H. 28 in. By Hermann Winkelmann, of Riga, 1654.
Schwarzen Häupter, Riga.
No. 2 Tall cup. H. 22 in. Dated 1786, probably made at Reval.
Schwarzhäupterhaus, Reval.
No. 3 Beaker. H. 24 in. By a Riga goldsmith, 1616. Schwarzen Häupter, Riga.

PLATE is known to have been wrought for several centuries at Reval and Riga, the capitals of Estonia and Latvia, respectively.

One Hans Ryssenberch, the elder, was a prominent goldsmith at Reval and was the maker of an important silver-gilt monstrance in 1474, now in the Hermitage Museum at Petrograd. In the same museum is an object of excessive rarity: a horn-shaped cup of Islamic glass, perhaps of the fourteenth century, decorated with an inscription in golden letters on a blue ground, conveying a greeting to an unknown Sultan, and wishing him luck. The glass is also enamelled with four figures, two in red and two in white, and is supported on two silver-gilt feet, formed as claws holding balls. Richly chased on the silver-gilt mount on the lip are hunting scenes in relief, and enamelled on the band in the centre are the arms of the family of Von Drolshagen. At the end are figures of the twelve Apostles, arranged in two rows, separated by mythological and historical figures, including Cleopatra, Lucretia, Hercules and Mucius Scævola, and surmounted by a figure of Christ, all in silver-gilt. On the lower band is an inscription: OLDE . BRUN .

PLATE XVII

PLATE XVIII

DROLSCHAGEN . HER . ICK . THO . ANE . FRAGEN . UND . HED . GEVEN . SINEM . SON . IURGEN . DROLSCHAGEN . IM . IAR . 1551. Chased in relief on the band below the inscription are figures of a young nobleman and a maiden, in contemporary costumes, believed to represent Jürgen Drolshagen and his bride, to whom the horn was probably a gift from the bridegroom's father, Bruno Drolshagen, on their marriage (Plate XVII, No. 3).

The silver-gilt mounts are supposed to have been executed by a goldsmith of Reval at the date inscribed, 1551. It is $11\frac{1}{2}$ in. high. A full illustrated account was published by Baron A. de Foelkersam in *Jahrbuch für Genealogie, Heraldik u. Sphragistik*, 1900, pp. 81–3.

A tall cup and cover, belonging to the Schwarzhäupterhaus in Reval, has English associations, having been the gift of eleven English merchants in 1786. It is embellished around the lip with the arms and names of the donors: Thomas Reningt (probably Remington), William Beaumont, Robert Maisters, Thomas Donn, Robert Mallabar, John Cary, Gabriel Donker, Benjamin Benson, Richard Sykes, William Sill, and Richard Cooke. Below the arms are three panels depicting the siege of a town and its surrender. On the cover are a crown with the inscription, SALUS ET VICTORIA; a horn of plenty, with HERCULES MUNKS; and a laurel wreath with NISI QUI LEGITIME CERTAVERIT. The finial is a cupid blowing a trumpet, and the stem is a warrior holding a shield bearing the head of a Moor, in black enamel, the badge of the Schwarzhäupter. No marks have been found on the cup, but it was probably made at Reval (Plate XVIII, No. 2).

Riga had its own distinctive mark for silver from the sixteenth century, as is illustrated by Dr. Marc Rosenberg,* who mentions three goldsmiths of that time, namely, Hans Unna, the maker of the cup in 1553 for the Glassworkers' guild of Riga; Thomas Smollde; and the unidentified maker of a tankard of 1590 in the Hermitage Museum at Petrograd.

A tall tankard is a peculiar product of the goldsmiths of the

---

* In *Der Goldschmiede Merkzeichen*, which is the work mentioned throughout this book under his name.

Baltic towns and Northern Germany of the end of the sixteenth and the early seventeenth centuries. One by a Lübeck goldsmith, in the Waddesdon collection in the British Museum, is a typical specimen. Two by Riga silversmiths are known.

The " Kompagnie der Schwarzen Häupter " of Riga—a similar body to that at Reval—is in possession of a goodly collection of old plate, intrinsically and historically interesting, wrought in that old member of the Hanseatic League. Ranking first in date is the tall, gilt, beaker-shaped cup and cover, called the " Rigasche Willkommen " (Cup of Welcome), of 1616, surmounted by a finial of a figure in Roman dress holding a lance and standing on three lion feet. Engraved inside the cover is an inscription of welcome.

Encircling the body are two bands, the upper being composed of four shields of arms supported by lions and several human figures, while the lower consists of winged masks. The maker's marks of a Riga goldsmith have not been identified (Plate XVIII, No. 3.)

The second cup, called the " Amicitia pokal," is tall and is divided into six sections. In the upper part of the body are young Bacchus, sea-horses, Ceres and Venus in bold relief. Heads of cherubs, dolphins and satyrs form the decoration of the other parts, while the appropriate stem is a figure of Bacchus on a tun, and the finial is a figure of Mercury. According to the inscription, the cup was a gift of the Riga goldsmiths as a loving cup in 1654. Hermann Winkelmann, head of the Goldsmiths' guild of Riga from 1642 to 1651, was the maker, though the mark of his son, Gert Winkelmann, is stamped on the cup (Plate XVIII, No. 1).

Five massive silver-gilt tankards are contained in the collection. The first is set with 30 thalers, dating from 1574 to 1660, and including a Riga thaler of 1574, five others of 1660, and two Danzig thalers of 1640 and 1649. On the cover, in high relief, are coats of arms of the six donors, in a circle, with their names and the date 1676. It stands 10¼ in. high and rests on three lions holding in their paws shields of Moors' heads, the arms of the Kompagnie. Jürgen Linden, master of the Riga guild of goldsmiths in 1674, was the maker.

The second tankard, 8¼ in. high, is adorned on the cover with four coats of arms and the Kompagnie's badge, all in high relief, and the bearers' names, with the date 1691. It was made at Riga, probably by Johann Behrend (Plate XVII, No. 1).

The third is of the same size as the second, and stands on three large decorated ball feet, of the same variety as the thumb-piece. Decorating the border of the cover are arabesques, flowers and fruit, in relief, and five shields of arms of the donors, with their names. In the centre of the cover is a large medallion depicting Charles XII of Sweden on horseback, at the head of his troops, charging over fallen warriors, all worked in high relief. Visible in the background is the castle of Narva and the camp of the Russians. The following inscription is engraved upon it:

DER SIEGREICHE ENTSATZ DER STADT NARVA ANNO 1700

It is signed *J. G. Eben Fecit* and is stamped with the initials G.D., representing Georg Dehkant, who was master of the Riga guild in 1698. Johann Georg Eben, whose name is signed, became master only in 1703 and died in 1712, and is supposed to have been an apprentice of Dehkant. The vessel commemorates the great victory of Charles XII over the Russians at Narva on November 30, 1700.

The fourth tankard stands on three ball feet decorated with the Kompagnie's badge. The border of the cover is richly decorated with the arms of the five donors and their names in relief, and in the centre is a large medallion of similar workmanship to the last, representing a battle, with the town of Riga in the background, called "Die Schlacht auf der Spilwe bei Riga, 1701." On the cover is also a bust of Charles XII of Sweden in an oval medallion, supported by two cherubs.

The above Johann Georg Eben was the maker of this tankard in 1704, and of the fifth, a year later, set in the cover with a medallion, in the same style, of a spirited representation of a battle, inscribed:

Gemaurthoff d. 17 Juli 1705.

The arms of the six donors are on the cover in relief.

These three last tankards are of the same shape as the second, and resemble many Swedish tankards, as, for example, the specimen illustrated in the chapter on the silver of Sweden.

In possession of the Kompagnie are four large dishes decorated with Biblical scenes, wrought in 1671 and 1672 by the above Jürgen Linden, a successful Riga goldsmith, maker of the first tankard and of a large beaker and cover in the Victoria and Albert Museum. Two other dishes in the same collection were made by the Riga goldsmiths, Heinrich von Köln in 1676 and Andreas Becker in 1684, both decorated with Biblical subjects.

Several other goldsmiths were working in Riga in the seventeenth and eighteenth centuries, including the unknown maker of a " Monteith " bowl, bearing two inscriptions : " From the English factory in Riga " ; and " The English factory at Riga, to Captain Robert Chadwick, of the Royal Navy, Anno 1718," which was sold at Christie's on June 7, 1916.

The subject may be studied in greater detail in two published works : Neumann's *Kunstgewerbe in Livland, Estland u. Kurland* ; and Buchholtz's *Goldschmiedearbeiten in Livland, Estland u. Kurland.*

Finland had its goldsmiths from medieval times, though no secular plate of that period has survived. In the National Museum at Helsingfors are a few pieces of plate, including a charming oil and vinegar frame, in Louis XVI style, by A. C. Levon, of Abo, 1797 (Plate XVII), and a caster of 1770 by another goldsmith of that place.

BELGIUM

PLATE XIX.

No. 1 Dish, 16¼ in. long, and No. 3, companion ewer, 9⅞ in. high, Mons, 1724.
Museum of Decorative Art, Brussels.
No. 2 "Falcon cup." Antwerp, c. 1555. H. 11¼ in.   Clare College, Cambridge.
No. 4 Silver-gilt column, Antwerp, 1559, by the same maker as No. 2. H. 21⅜ in.
Museum, Frankfurt-am-Main.

PLATE XX.

Ewer (H. 18 in) and dish (D. 25 in.), Antwerp, 1558-9.   The Louvre Museum, Paris.

PLATE XXI.

No. 1 Dish, attributed to Jaques van der Spee, of Bruges, c. 1600. D. 21⅜ in.
Museum of Decorative Art, Brussels.
No. 2 Dish, Antwerp, c. 1560. D. 16¼ in.   Corporation of Guildford.

ANTWERP, at the height of its commercial prosperity in the sixteenth century, attracted not only painters but also goldsmiths and other craftsmen. Philip II in 1555 found it the centre of the carrying trade of the world. Merchants, who had forsaken their places of business at Bruges and other towns, were drawn thither as by a magnet. Thirty years later the maritime supremacy of Antwerp had departed.

Would that an illustration could be provided here of the objects from the atelier of Hans of Antwerp, goldsmith and friend of Hans Holbein the younger, some of whose designs for gold and silver plate are said to have been wrought by this silversmith. No opinion can be offered as to whether the golden cup from Holbein's original design (in the Ashmolean Museum, Oxford), intended for Queen Jane Seymour, was ever actually made, and if so, whether the maker was Hans of Antwerp. One definite statement may, however, be made : no such cup is now extant.

The engraver, Balthasar Geertssen (1518–80), during his artistic career at Antwerp, designed a great number of silver vessels and ornaments for goldsmiths, but none of the actual works have survived. Hans Collaert, of the same place, was a designer of jewels and details for goldsmiths and armourers, and one of his designs for a gold cross was executed by Jeronimus Jacobs, of Antwerp, whose works in domestic plate remain unknown, as do those of Master Reynere van Jaesvelt. Nor is any plate known by Nicaise van der Beken, goldsmith of Brussels, who was ordered in 1597 to chase four gold medals for Philip II.

Among the surviving examples of Antwerp plate of the sixteenth century the following may be mentioned: the "Falcon" cup, with its box for spices acting as a pedestal for the bird, 11¼ inches high, at Clare College, Cambridge (Plate XIX, No. 2). The mound is worked in imitation of ground, while the high rectangular box is delicately engraved in front with a laureated bust of a male figure within a laurel wreath, surrounded by foliated scrolls. Two ring handles, attached to monster heads, are affixed at the ends, which are engraved with foliated grotesques. It is stamped with the mark of Antwerp for about 1555; the date-letter C; and pan-pipes in a shield—the mark of an unknown silversmith who made an enamelled silver mirror frame in the royal collections of Denmark at Rosenborg Castle; and a silver-gilt Corinthian column in the Museum at Frankfurt-am-Main. How the distinguished donor and alumnus of the College, Dr. William Butler, acquired this curious conceit of a Flemish goldsmith, is not recorded. A second piece of Antwerp plate in England is the little known rose-water dish, 16½ inches in diameter, decorated with six medallions of Roman busts on the rim and with four cartouches of masks and clusters of fruit in the German manner on the raised centre, which was a gift, with an English silver ewer of 1567-8, by John Parkhurst, Bishop of Norwich from 1560 to 1575, to the Corporation of Guildford, the place of his birth. The arms of the see of Norwich, impaling those of the Bishop, are enamelled in the centre (Plate XXI, No. 2). A Swiss silver beaker, given by the same Puritan Bishop to friends at Zurich, is illustrated later.

The silver Corinthian column just mentioned is of considerable interest in the history of the Reformation, for, according to the Latin inscription, it was a gift in 1559 by the English Church to the Municipal Council of Frankfurt as a perpetual memorial of the hospitality shown to the English refugees, "driven from their country for Christ's sake." The actual donors were probably the exiles who had returned to England shortly after the death of Queen Mary, their persecutor, and who are mentioned in the letter of congratulation to Queen Elizabeth upon her accession to the throne, from the Protestant divine, Alexander Ales, on September 1, 1559* (Plate XIX, No. 4).

Some surprise may be expressed by the gift of a piece of Flemish, rather than of English, plate on this occasion. Such occurrences are, however, not unusual, for Queen Elizabeth presented a German cup to the divine, Heinrich Bullinger, while the three exiled English Bishops sent money for the purchase of the three Swiss silver beakers, described in a later chapter, as gifts to their hosts during their exile. Other instances may be found in the chapters on the silver of the Baltic States and Germany.

Another Antwerp piece is a tazza, covered inside with embossed work in imitation of the waves of the sea, illustrated on Plate 73 in the present author's catalogue of the late Mr. J. Pierpont Morgan's collection. To this list may be added three objects in the Waddesdon collection in the British Museum: a nautilus cup, dated 1581; a rose-water ewer and a very large circular rose-water dish, decorated on the border with the "Plagues of Egypt" and engraved at a later date with the arms of Aspremont de Lynden and Reckheim.

More important than either of these are the silver gilt ewer and dish, of imposing size, of about 1558-9, in the Louvre, two of the finest examples of goldsmiths' work of the Renaissance (Plate XX). The whole of the dish (25 inches in diameter) is chased with five scenes from the victorious expedition of Charles V against Tunis in 1535: the landing of troops, the encampment, the bombardment of Goulette, the capture of Goulette, and the

---

* Public Record Office: S. P. Dom. (Calendar), Elizabeth—Foreign.

battle and the liberation of the Christians, followed by the return to Goulette. Inscription:

EXPEDITIO ET VICTORIA AFRICANA. CAROLI V. ROM. IMP. P. F. AUGUSTO
1535

The ewer is over 18 inches high and is partially enamelled and is richly decorated by a master hand, unfortunately anonymous, with military trophies, masks of divers kinds, garlands of fruit and flowers and other details. A female bust, probably intended for Minerva, forms the spout and serpents are intertwined into the handle, while a satyr, seated below the handle, gives a piquant touch to the ewer. The wide frieze, depicting the embarkation of the triumphant army at the close of the campaign, is the *chef d'œuvre* of the decoration on the ewer. It is supposed that the subject has been inspired by the famous set of tapestries celebrating the same event, designed by Jean Vermay or Vermeyen, in the Royal Palace at Madrid, where the actual armour worn by Charles V on this occasion is preserved in the Royal Armoury. M. Joseph Destrée has written a full account of these historic vessels in *Annales de la Société d'Archéologie de Bruxelles*, 1900, pp. 3-59.

One more piece of Antwerp silver, of the second half of the sixteenth century, deserves recognition, not only because of its own intrinsic merit but as the old cup in which the first Sacrament was celebrated at the formation of the English Reformed Church in a cellar at Flushing in 1571. Two centuries later, in 1772, the cup was used in the English Church at Flushing, as is recorded in the inscription. This is the tazza-like cup in the Rijks Museum at Amsterdam. Inside the bowl is a medallion of Philip II., which alone, apart from other evidence, indicates the secular origin of the vessel.

A tall cup and cover in the style of the German Renaissance, by an unknown goldsmith of Antwerp, is in the Friesch Museum at Leeuwarden, and is illustrated in the catalogue (No. 107).

Dr. Marc Rosenberg enumerates several other pieces with Antwerp marks from the sixteenth to the eighteenth centuries.

The artistic activity of Bruges and other places in Flanders under

PLATE XIX

PLATE XX

BELGIUM

the Dukes of Burgundy, especially under Philip the Good, and the stately banquets and revels of the Court, are reflected in the art of illumination, which reached its zenith under Charles the Bold. Flemish illuminated manuscripts are an interesting study for the life and times of high personages, for glimpses of domestic life and for the drinking vessels in daily use. Attracted by the glamour of the Burgundian Court, goldsmiths and other artists flocked into Flanders, but except for pictures and illuminated manuscripts—things of no intrinsic value for bartering—nothing remains of the splendid secular plate for which the Flemish goldsmiths were famous in the fifteenth century. One splendid piece of ecclesiastical plate should not, however, escape notice—the reliquary of solid gold and enamel, executed in 1466–7 by Gerard Loyet, in the form of a group, showing Charles the Bold and St. George and engraved with the ciphers of Charles and his third wife, Margaret of York, which is now in Liège Cathedral.

The old copper plates of the marks of the goldsmiths' guild of Bruges between 1487 and 1500 are preserved in the Museum there.

A domestic cup (slightly restored) of the sixteenth century, stamped with the mark of Bruges, in Aldbury Church, near Tring, is in outline similar to a design in the book of Hans Brosamer (worked at Fulda, 1536–50, and died at Erfurt, 1552). An English cup of the same shape and with similar fluting is the well-known "Queen Anne Boleyn's Cup," stamped with the London date-letter for 1535–6, in Cirencester Church, which is illustrated in Sir C. J. Jackson's *History of English Plate* (Fig. 185).

The marks stamped on the interesting dish, repoussé and chased in the centre with a bird's-eye view of Bruges, surrounded by a battle scene and with trophies of arms on the rim, are attributed by M. Joseph Destrée to Jacques van der Spee, of Bruges, about 1600, though Dr. Marc Rosenberg gives the maker's mark to Loys van Nievkercke, master in 1607. It is in the Museum of Decorative Art at Brussels (Plate XXI, No. 1).

Ghent had its goldsmiths' guild as early as the fifteenth century, as is proved by the original copper plates of makers' marks from 1484 to 1707, still preserved in the Museum there.

The name of one Corneille de Bont, master in 1471-2, is recorded by Dr. Marc Rosenberg as the maker of four silver-gilt shields in the Museum at Ghent. In the Victoria and Albert Museum is a Flemish dish of the same eight-pointed shape as the rare Dutch dish illustrated on Plate LXVI; it is engraved with floriated arabesques and is stamped with the Ghent mark for 1622.

The *provenance* is unknown of the rare Merode cup—a covered beaker with a band of enamel and Gothic windows—in the Victoria and Albert Museum.

Five reliefs in chased silver—in the Rijks Museum at Amsterdam—depicting events in the life of General Spinola, were executed about 1630 by a Flemish master, signing himself, *Mathias Melin, Belga*.

The picture "Taste," of the Flemish school, by Gonzales Coques (1618-84), in the National Gallery in London, is interesting for the little plain silver caster of cylindrical form (Fig. 5), showing that this shape of caster, but without the handle, was known in Flanders some years earlier than in England.

Fig. 5.

Early Flemish pictures, as well as illuminated manuscripts, afford a glimpse of the sumptuous vessels of gold and silver in daily use. Beakers, to name only one drinking vessel, may be observed in pictures by Hans Memlinc, Gerard David, Roger van der Weyden and Quentin Matsys. In the portrait of Ægidius (Pieter Gillis), painted about 1513 by the last of these artists (in the collection of the Earl of Radnor) is a golden cup, perhaps a favourite drinking cup of the learned Ægidius himself, as was probably the cup in the portrait of Lady Jane Grey, attributed to Lucas de Heere, in the collection of Earl Spencer. It is interesting for the similarity in outline to English cups of the time, notably the rare cup of 1520-1 at Christ's College, Cambridge, illustrated later. Introduced into the great picture of the Adoration of the Kings, by Jan de Mabuse, in the National Gallery in London, are ornate and minutely finished golden vessels, illustrating the transition from the Gothic to the Renaissance. In the very different representation of the same subject, in the same Gallery, by Pieter Brueghel,

1564, are two cups and a most unusual vessel, namely, a ship or nef of golden colour with a body of green stone.

Many painters, as is well known, had received their early training as goldsmiths, therefore the conjecture may be made that some vessels in pictures were inventions of the artists, while in other cases the drawings were doubtless made direct from actual objects.

A good deal of well-wrought plate was executed in the French style at Mons in the eighteenth century, and an example is provided in a fine helmet-shaped ewer, decorated with straps and other ornament in the manner of Louis XIV. "Roman" medallions are set in the ewer and its companion dish, which are engraved with the arms of the Chevalier François Cornet d'Elzius, in 1724. Both vessels are in the collection Drion in the Museum of Decorative Art at Brussels (Plate XIX, Nos. 1 and 3). The plate of Mons is represented in the Victoria and Albert Museum by a pair of frames, repoussé and chased, of the second half of the seventeenth century.

Liège was another place of some importance in the history of the goldsmith's art in the eighteenth century, and the author has seen a ciborium from a church in Canada, stamped with the marks of this place. The above Brussels Museum contains some chocolate pots and candlesticks by unknown silversmiths of Liège.

Yet another important centre was Tournai—celebrated for its architects, sculptors and artists from early times—as may be observed from the work *Orfèvreries Tournaisiennes du XVIIᵉ et du XVIIIᵉ siècle à l'Exposition de Tournai*, with an account of the marks, by E. J. Soil de Moriamé, 1911. In this work are illustrated an octagonal candlestick and other pieces of the first half of the eighteenth century, both ecclesiastical and secular, by Marc Le Febvre, a conspicuous silversmith of Tournai and artist of the altar of marble and silver in the Church of Notre Dame at Courtrai. Other craftsmen are represented by various coffee-pots of the eighteenth century, illustrated in this work

Another account of Belgian silver may be studied in that made at Malines in the eighteenth century, in an illustrated article by Dr. G. van Doorslaer in *Annales de l'Académie Royale d'Archéologie de Belgique*, LXIV (1912).

The work *L'Orfèvrerie Religieuse en Belgique*, by the Abbés L. and F. Crooij, 1911, is useful not only for the illustrations but also for the account of eighteen places where silver was wrought in Belgium ; Antwerp, Audenarde, Bruges, Brussels, Courtrai, Ghent, Grammont, Liège, Louvain, Malines, Mons, Namur, Nivelles, Termonde, Tongres, Tournai, Virton and Ypres.

An interesting problem in *provenance* arises in the magnificent ewer and basin in the possession of Lord Mostyn. According to an old tradition they were the gift of Henry VII, when Earl of Richmond, to a member of the Mostyn family after his escape, about 1483, from Mostyn Hall. The style of the decoration, however, precludes the possibility of so early a date. Moreover, the three marks are not English. The ewer closely resembles in form Archbishop Parker's ewer of 1545-6 at Corpus Christi College, Cambridge, illustrated later, which is the earliest English example extant. With some diffidence the author suggests that these noble vessels may have been wrought, if not in Flanders itself, by a Flemish goldsmith in London. They may be studied from the illustration in the *Burlington Magazine* for May, 1907.

The same difficulties occur in the *provenance* of the Founder's cup at Emmanuel College, Cambridge. Here again the maker was probably a Flemish goldsmith (see *The Old Plate of the Cambridge Colleges*, by E. Alfred Jones).

PLATE XXI

PLATE XXII

CANADA.

PLATE XXII.

No. 1 Monstrance, by Laurent Amyot, of Quebec, c. 1800. H. 16 in.
No. 2 Large Sanctuary lamp, 18th century.
No. 3 Ewer, by François Ranvoyze, of Quebec, c. 1770. H. 9¾ in.
No. 4 Small teapot, probably by Robert Cruickshank, of Montreal, c. 1800.
General Hospital, Quebec.

No. 5 Monstrance, by a silversmith of Montreal, c. 1790. H. 20¼ in.

THE little masterpieces of the old Canadian silversmiths have suffered the same neglect as had the charming work of the Colonial silversmiths of America until a few years ago. Thanks to the intimate knowledge of the subject of the late Father Lionel St. G. Lindsay, of Quebec, and his guidance during the present author's visit to that historic town in 1912, the writer is enabled to write a brief sketch of the old silver preserved in the Churches and convents there, though in doing so he has to record with regret the destruction of many precious objects in the many fires which have since occurred.

As a colony of France, the early missionaries, and such benefactors as Governor Frontenac and the celebrated Champlain, bestowed sacred vessels upon Churches and religious houses, and for many years all the ornaments and vessels necessary for the services of the Church were obtained from the mother country, France. François de Montmorency Laval, first Bishop of Quebec, is believed to have brought many precious objects in 1659. Relics enclosed in costly shrines, wrought by France's most skilful goldsmiths, have been bestowed upon Churches from time to time, only to perish in fires and by the hand of the despoiler. So little regarded was old silver that a part of the collection of the Ursuline Convent in Quebec was sacrificed and melted for the centennial anniversary of this celebrated convent and the metal fashioned into a sanctuary lamp.

Interesting as the old French silver must have been, the author was more concerned in tracing the development of the silversmith's craft in Quebec itself. As early as the first decade of the eighteenth century a silversmith is recorded as working there, namely, one Michel Levasseur, who had prospered so far as to take unto himself two apprentices, Pierre Gauvreau and Jacques Pagé *dit* Carcy, the second of whom established himself on Mountain Hill in Quebec. None of their works have, however, been identified or have survived. Nor can any extant silver be attributed to either of the following silversmiths, named in the census for 1744 in Quebec:

Jean Baptiste Deschevery *dit* Maisonbasse, in Sous-le-Fort Street; Michel Cotton, in Buade Street; Paul Lambert, Joseph Mailloux, François Landron and Francis Lefebvre.

The most conspicuous craftsman in the eighteenth century was François Renvoize, or Ranvoyzé, born in Quebec itself in 1739, son of Etienne Ranvoyzé and grandson of Pierre Ranvoyzé and his wife, Marie Goupel, both emigrants from Caen in Normandy. Whether he learned his craft from one of the above silversmiths in Quebec, or was sent to Paris, cannot be determined. That this French-Canadian silversmith enjoyed considerable patronage from the ecclesiastics and Churches of Quebec is proved by the many examples of his work examined by the author, notwithstanding the serious losses by fire and theft.

An important collection of silver examined was that of the Archbishop of Quebec, containing as it does no fewer than four of the characteristic French écuelles, two of which are engraved with the initials of Joseph Signay, Archbishop of Quebec, and of Joseph Octave Plessis, Bishop of Quebec; and two French ewers of the eighteenth century. But, more interesting of all, are the works, ecclesiastical and secular, of François Ranvoyzé, namely, two large oval dishes, a Holy Water bowl, a pair of candlesticks and a soup ladle, dated 1785. Specimens of his work were found also in the Basilica and in Lorette, where his son became the parish priest. In the Ursuline Convent* there is a skilful copy by him of a French chalice, bearing not only his mark, F R, but also his name,

---

* See page 43 for a notice of the French silver spoon and fork, stamped with the mark of the American silversmith, Jacob Hurd.

CANADA

Ranuouze, engraved upon it. The ewer illustrated is an important example of his work (Plate XXII, No. 3).

François Ranvoyzé would seem to have been an envious man, for he refused to be tempted with a premium to accept an apprentice in the boy, Laurent Amyot, soon to become Quebec's most competent silversmith, lest he should prove to be a formidable competitor. The boy was consequently sent by his father to Paris, to learn the craft, and there he worked hard for two years, from 1784, in the atelier of a goldsmith, whose name, unfortunately, has not been traced. Fully equipped for his craft, young Amyot returned to his home in Quebec and during the remaining 33 years of Ranvoyzé's life was a successful competitor as a maker of silver vessels for Churches and of secular plate. Much of his success may be attributed to the severance of ecclesiastical connection between French-Canada and old France from the French Revolution and the consequent dissolution of the religious houses in France.

A silver sanctuary lamp is an interesting specimen of the work of an accomplished and anonymous Quebec silversmith of the eighteenth century; its weight is $88\frac{1}{2}$ ozs. (Plate XXII, No. 2).

From Amyot's atelier on Mountain Hill came Archbishop Signay's finely wrought ewer; another historic ewer presented to a priest for succouring the English brig, *Rosalind*, of London (Captain Boyle), in 1832; and Bishop Plessis's candlestick, all in the Archbishop's Palace. A curious cocoanut cup, mounted in silver, and a plain beaker, both in the General Hospital in Quebec, founded in 1693, were wrought by him, as were the monstrance (Plate XXII, No. 1); and the large ladle, presented by the author to the Victoria and Albert Museum in memory of Canadian soldiers who fell in the Great War.

A little later came François Sasseville, who began working at the corner of Palace Hill and Charlevoix Street in Quebec.

The author, during his visit to Quebec, was privileged to converse with an old silversmith named Ambroise Lafrance, who was then in possession of the working tools of Laurent Amyot, which had descended to him from the above François Sasseville, then to Pierre L'Esperance, who worked at the same address from 1863 to

1882, and finally to the said Ambroise Lafrance at the same address from 1882 to 1905, when he retired and removed to 26 rue St. Nicholas. Lafrance's youthful son had also been intended for the silversmith's craft and before his premature death had wrought a silver cup and a cross for the author.

A little school of silversmiths had been established in Montreal in the eighteenth century. One name only has been traced, namely, that of Robert Cruickshank, a loyalist refugee from the American Colonies at the Revolution, and perhaps the maker of a charming little teapot (Plate XXII, No. 4) and a spoon of about 1800, stamped with a maker's mark, R C, and *Montreal*, both in the General Hospital in Quebec. The monstrance, illustrated on the same Plate, is marked MONTREAL, and was wrought there at the end of the eighteenth century (Plate XXII, No. 5).

Old silver in Canada may be studied further in the present author's pamphlet, printed from the *Transactions of the Royal Society of Canada*, 1918.

CHANNEL ISLANDS

SILVER plate was made here from the middle of the seventeenth century and probably earlier, and throughout the eighteenth century, when sacred vessels for churches were wrought in goodly numbers. A plain and simple flagon of the eighteenth century, perhaps secular in intention, is one of the most characteristic church vessels. Another is a plain bowl of the seventeenth century in use in Jersey for the Communion.

The most common and popular of the domestic vessels is a christening cup, which was made in large numbers in the eighteenth century, the Jersey types differing but slightly from those of Guernsey.

The researches of Mr. S. Carey Curtis, author of the histories of the old Church plate in these Islands, have brought to light the names of two silversmiths, Pierre Mainguy, probably the maker of a flagon of 1756 in Forest Church, Guernsey, and of the christening cup, mentioned below, and John or James Perchard.

The frequency of makers' marks resembling a fleur-de-lis, accompanied by initials, points to France as the original home of the silversmiths of the Channel Islands, who were exempt from the regulations as to hall-marking of the Goldsmiths' Company in London. Among these men were possibly religious refugees from France, as in London, especially after the revocation of the Edict of Nantes in 1685.

Of the three types of christening cups the most common is the two-handled cup, like the fine Guernsey specimen of about 1760 (Fig. 6), which is a late survival of an old English caudle cup. Next is the goblet; and third is a single-handled mug similar in form to the Guernsey mug, which is inscribed: *M G don de Son Parein & Mareine* 1757, and stamped with the mark of Pierre Mainguy (Fig. 7). Both the specimens illustrated are English in shape and have descended, from the time of the gifts as heirlooms, to

Colonel T. W. M. de Guerin of Guernsey. One of these two-handled cups, bearing the maker's mark of G. H., crowned, as on Guernsey plate of about 1760, is in the collection of Sir John H. B. Noble, Bart.

Fig. 6.
Cup, Guernsey, c. 1760.

Fig. 7.
Mug, by Pierre Mainguy, 1757.

CZECHOSLOVAKIA

PLATE XXIII.
No. 1 Ostrich-egg cup, Prague, c. 1600. H. 15¼ in. Waddesdon collection, British Museum.
No. 2 Carved crystal ewer, gold mounted, Prague, 1655. H. 20 in.
Imperial Museum, Vienna.

THE interesting old city of Prague and capital of Bohemia was renowned in the past for the gold and silver plate and personal ornaments executed there. Coins of the twelfth and thirteenth centuries of no mean merit are among the earliest works of Bohemia in the precious metals. Meanwhile, the art of the goldsmith proper was fostered under Premysl Otakar II, the " Golden King," in the thirteenth century. The growing importance of the goldsmith's craft in Prague is apparent from the establishment of a guild in 1324 and from the increasing number of goldsmiths working in the Goldschmiedegasse (now Karlova) in the reign of Charles IV (1316–78), founder of the University of Prague in 1348. Churches and monasteries were now enriched with many objects in the precious metals. Protection and encouragement were accorded to the art of the goldsmith under this monarch's successor, and a noteworthy example of the time is the reliquary of Brevnov, executed in 1406. Among the medieval objects of Bohemia worthy of mention are the cross of Zavis von Falkenstein in the convent of Hohenfurth; the royal insignia of King Rudolph in Prague Cathedral; the mitre of St. Eligius; and the famous crown of St. Wenzel, all happily preserved to-day.

Many important chalices and ciboria, vessels and ornaments, were consecrated to the service of the Church in Bohemia in the fifteenth and sixteenth centuries, including the great monstrances of Bohdanec, Sedlec, Hostomice, Cheb, Malešice and Ústí nad Labem (Aussig).

Patronage was liberally bestowed on the goldsmiths for ecclesiastical and domestic plate and for personal ornaments by the

Emperor Rudolph II (1552–1612), King of Hungary and Bohemia, whose court at Prague—his favourite residence—was the chief centre of art within the empire. Here was executed for the Emperor in 1608 the superb ewer of jasper and gold by the celebrated Dutch goldsmith, Paulus van Vianen (who had settled there in 1604), illustrated in the chapter on the plate of Holland; and also the large crystal ewer of hexagonal form, executed by an anonymous artist for Ferdinand III in 1655. The crystal body is carved with hunting scenes and mythological figures, and the handle of the same pure quartz is fashioned like a terminal human figure, while the gold mountings are enamelled with festoons of flowers and insects and set with rubies. Carved in relief on the cover is a Phœnix; it is in the Imperial Museum at Vienna (Plate XXIII, No. 2).

Prague is known to have been a flourishing centre for the mounting and carving of domestic vessels of great beauty, fashioned from crystal, jasper, lapis lazuli and other semi-precious stones. The exquisitely enamelled gold and silver mounts, in the style of the Renaissance, are often attributed to Italian and German artists. Unfortunately, the names of these skilled goldsmiths and enamellers cannot be applied specifically to any of the precious objects in these natural materials in the great collection at Vienna. The old Bohemian capital was no less celebrated for the enamelled jewellery executed there under the encouragement of the Archduke Ferdinand of Tirol (1520–95), brother of Maximilian II.

One Michel Dietrich was Court goldsmith at Prague before 1660, when he removed to Vienna and there wrought an enamelled chalice, the only piece of plate by him recorded by Dr. Marc Rosenberg in *Der Goldschmiede Merkzeichen*. His career as a goldsmith in Vienna was short, for he died in the following year.

Two flourishing crafts in Prague in the seventeenth and eighteenth centuries were those of the makers of cases for watches, and the designers and workers of personal ornaments in the precious metals. The eighteenth century witnessed the decline of the goldsmith's craft proper—the makers of domestic plate—in Bohemia.

CZECHOSLOVAKIA

The student of old silver will seek in vain for a representative collection of domestic plate by the goldsmiths of Prague and other places in the country, in the Museum of Industrial Art in the capital. Among the noteworthy pieces are a small silver cup, inscribed: "Matej Kolowratek Mezrichy—Letha 1642," by an unknown goldsmith bearing the initials I Z; and a cocoanut cup mounted in the sixteenth century, with a later cover of the eighteenth century. The collection of old rings and personal ornaments in the Museum must also be mentioned.

What is perhaps the only important piece of plate in England by a goldsmith of Prague is the finely executed ostrich-egg cup, $15\frac{1}{4}$ inches high, by an unknown craftsman of the end of the sixteenth or the beginning of the seventeenth century, which is in the Waddesdon collection in the British Museum (Plate XXIII, No. 1). Except for the characteristically German stem, in the form of a twisted trunk of a tree, the decoration in certain features is a little unusual, in the cartouches enclosing faceted metal in imitation of precious stones and in the cherubs' heads at the bottoms of the four straps supporting the egg, which have little drops like pearls. Inside the cover is a medal of Ieronimus Loter, aged 46 in 1544.

The French style of the First Empire penetrated into the goldsmiths' ateliers of Prague as it did into those of Vienna and other European capitals.

Olomouc (Olmütz) is among the other places in Czechoslovakia where silver was wrought. The names of four men are recorded there in the fifteenth century. Dr. Marc Rosenberg mentions a tankard of about 1575 and a chalice of 1593 by goldsmiths of this place. Opava (Troppau), which had a mint in 1250, registered its own distinctive goldsmiths' mark at the end of the sixteenth century, as is illustrated in Dr. Rosenberg's book. Although other goldsmiths are recorded in the sixteenth century, such as Master Foltyn (Valentin), Hans Wolgemuth, the more conspicuous Liborius Eckert and Georg Gertzner, the earliest goldsmith's mark recorded in this book is that of Jakob Mannlich (Manlig, Manling), who removed thither from Augsburg before 1628 and died there in 1650. Four objects by him are named, including a characteristic tankard covered with granulated work ; this is illustrated in Dr. E. W. Braun's catalogue of the exhibition of old Austrian silverwork at Troppau in 1904, a useful little brochure in which the names of certain goldsmiths of that place are mentioned. Eger, now called Cheb, had a goldsmith at the end of the sixteenth century in Martin Burckhardt, the maker of an ostrich-egg cup, in the Royal Museum at Cassel.

Goldsmiths were working at the following towns, formerly in Hungary : Kassa (now Kosice), Löcse (now Levoca), Komárom (now Komárno), Pozsony (now Bratislava), and Zólyom (now Zilina). At the second of these places Johann Szillassi specialised in ecclesiastical vessels of silver and enamel about 1750–1770, and doubtless executed secular plate.

PLATE XXIII

PLATE XXIV

DENMARK

PLATE XXIV.
No. 1   Silver-mounted horn, c. 1400.   National Museum, Copenhagen.
No. 2   Large two-handled cup, probably by Ægidius Loidt, of Copenhagen, 1577. H. 14¾ in.   National Museum, Copenhagen.

PLATE XXV.
No. 1   Tall tankard, c. 1610.   National Museum, Copenhagen.
No. 2   Plain tankard, by Borchart Rollufsen, of Copenhagen, c. 1649.   National Museum, Copenhagen.
No. 3   Tankard, by Mogens Thommesen Löwenhertz, of Horsens, c. 1695.

PLATE XXVI.
No. 1   Beaker, by Hans Nielsen, of Copenhagen, c. 1703.
No. 2   Cup, c. 1600.
No. 3   Beaker, 1709.
No. 4   Two-handled bowl, for hot liquor, 1608. D. 4⅞ in.
No. 5   One of a pair of octagonal candlesticks, by Philip L. Weghorst, of Copenhagen, 1724. H. 6⅞ in.
No. 6   Small bowl, for hot liquor, 1643.
No. 7   Beaker and cover, with a granulated surface, by a goldsmith at Odense, c. 1650.
No. 8   Beaker, c. 1590.

(All except No. 5 are in the National Museum, Copenhagen.)

NO Scandinavian domestic silver as early as the thirteenth century chalice from Iceland, in the Victoria and Albert Museum, or the chalice of similar form, dating from about 1201, in the church at Sorö, in Denmark, have survived wars and family losses.

The earliest drinking vessel in Scandinavia is the horn, and in the fourteenth and fifteenth centuries it would seem to have been in more common use for this purpose than in any other country in Europe. Of the 40 horns described by Mr. Jörgen Olrik in the illustrated catalogue of the National Museum at Copenhagen in 1909 no fewer than 24 date from that period. Six only of these are mounted in silver, the others having mounts of gilt copper. One of the finest and earliest is the horn of about 1400, finely engraved with the arms of the King of Norway and of several

Norwegian nobles; it was brought from Iceland by Admiral Rabe in 1720. Another interesting example, with Gothic niches enshrining figures on the silver mount, is inscribed with the name of Ivar Vigfusson Holm, a Norwegian Governor of Iceland, who was killed in 1433. A third horn, believed to be of Danish origin, is plainer. Some of the inscriptions on the copper-gilt mounts of the other horns are of a religious character, recalling in this particular the medieval mazer bowls of England. One of the most common inscriptions, occurring as it does six times, is that of the three Kings, Caspar, Melchior and Balthazar, an inscription which is found on the highly important standing mazer cup of about 1490 at Corpus Christi College, Cambridge, and on a mazer bowl of the same date in Holy Trinity Church, Colchester. Another inscription on a Danish horn is *Amor vincit omnia*, which occurs on an Icelandic horn and is common on Danish jewellery. A Scandinavian horn with metal-gilt mounts of the fifteenth century is in the British Museum.

The Danish horn illustrated on Plate XXIV (No. 1), is probably that of the bison and is mounted in silver-gilt and set with a shield, originally enamelled with the figure of an abbot, about 1400. It is assumed from the arms of the Tornekrans family, engraved on the rim early in the sixteenth century, that the horn had belonged to Henrik Christiernson Tornekrans, Abbot of Sorö Abbey, who died in 1538. Some silver mountings are missing from the horn.

According to an old Danish saga the honour of carrying the drinking horn into the hall for the assembled guests was always accorded to a maiden, who stepped into the hall with "the gold-banded horn in her lily-white hands."

> Bold Luselil thus addresses his serving maiden:
> "Go fetch me a horn of wine—fetch me a horn I say."

In medieval times the liquor consumed from these horns was mead and wine, rarely ale from such costly vessels.

Several of the horns came from Iceland, where some were probably mounted in metal by Danish craftsmen (or under their instruction) after the introduction of Danish rule in 1380.

DENMARK

One of the earliest pieces of silver in the National Museum is a bell-shaped cup with a cover (date about 1550), revealing the transition from Gothic to Renaissance in the decoration, probably by a Copenhagen silversmith. The work of a highly-skilled Copenhagen artificer is represented in the National Museum by a two-handled drinking cup of imposing size, holding nearly eight quarts. Two wide bands encircle the body, depicting hunting scenes on one of them, and animals in cartouches, fruit in scutcheons and clusters of fruit on the other, all worked in relief. Along the lip is an inscription in Danish bidding the guests to quaff an ample draught and testifying to the power of wine in driving away sorrow. This cup, which is assigned to the hands of Ægidius Loidt in 1577, was a christening present from a Danish nobleman and his wife to the Crown Prince of Denmark, afterwards King Christian IV. It stands on lion and pomegranate feet, fixed alternately (Plate XXIV, No. 2). Inside the cup are pegs, like those of some Danish tankards, indicating how much each member of a convivial party was pledged to drink when the vessel was circulated, in the same manner as the English silver peg tankards of the seventeenth century (derived, be it remembered) from the Danish tankards. The custom of "drinking down to the peg" is described in the chapter on English plate. No other piece of plate bearing the marks of the same talented Danish goldsmith has been recorded in this Museum or elsewhere in or out of Denmark. Olaf Kolsrad, however, suggests that the silver mounts of a horn may be by Ægidius Loidt (*Beretning Kristiania Kunstindustrimuseums Virksomhed i Aaret*, 1911).

During the Thirty Years War a vast quantity of plate, jewels and other precious things in Denmark were buried in the earth. Many important pieces of silver have been recovered and are now in the National Museum, including beakers of the sixteenth and seventeenth centuries, engraved with conventional straps and arabesques in a manner essentially Danish (Plate XXVI, No. 8). The corded band, set with cherubs' heads, on one beaker, is found on English and German tankards of the late sixteenth century. Not the least interesting cups in the Museum were found in the earth at Viborg and are engraved in the Danish style with fruit and arabesques, hunting scenes and other subjects, like one of about 1600 illustrated (Plate XXVI, No. 2). Their shape has been derived from the green wine glasses, imported into Denmark from Germany and the Netherlands, and a popular feature of Dutch "Still Life" pictures of the seventeenth century. The studs on the lower part of these silver cups are imitated from those on the glass cups. Two other Danish cups of the same shape, dating from about 1625, are illustrated in the Museum catalogue with many varieties of the beaker, other than that shown here.

A shallow two-handled silver bowl was made in Denmark, Norway and Sweden, as well as Holland, in the seventeenth century, and was used for serving hot brandy and liquor. An early Danish example, dated 1608, is illustrated on Plate XXVI (No. 4). Engraved on the plain trefoil-shaped handles are the original owners' initials, probably husband and wife, which are repeated on the bowl, with two shields of arms. The engraved decoration of scrolls and festoons is typically Danish. Such bowls were common in Denmark. Another variety of bowl for the same purpose, somewhat later in date, has a body formed of eight large plain hollow sections, and a single flat handle, engraved with the arms and initials, or initials only, of the owners, and with the date (Plate XXVI, No. 6). Two specimens in the National Museum at Copenhagen are dated 1642 and 1648 and were made at Odense.

Examples of Norwegian and Swedish bowls are illustrated later.

Several characteristic Danish beakers from the sixteenth to the eighteenth centuries are illustrated in the catalogue of the National Museum, mentioned above, and may be compared with those of Norway and Sweden.

The earlier Danish tankards of the sixteenth and early part of the seventeenth centuries, like those of Norway and Sweden, have tall cylindrical bodies. A specimen in the National Museum is engraved in Danish fashion at the top of the body with panels of figures and conventional scrolls and arabesques, while the cover and base are repoussé with masks, small figures and scrolls. This was made in the early seventeenth century (Plate XXV, No. 1). In the catalogue of that Museum are illustrations, on pages 65, 73 and

123, of three tankards of this form, differently decorated. The Norwegian tankard of about 1620, by Johan Slytter, of Bergen, illustrated on Plate LXXVIII is of this same shape.

Later tankards of the seventeenth century made both of silver and wood, in Norway and Sweden as well as Denmark, are shorter and wider, as in the plain example (in the same Museum), standing on three gilt pomegranate feet, attached to leaves applied to the body; the thumbpiece is formed of two acorns. This is engraved with an inscription in Latin to the effect that it was a gift to Johann Schelderup from his distinguished father-in-law, Professor Ole Worm, upon his elevation to the dignity of Bishop of Bergen in 1649. It had evidently been a family possession, for engraved on the cover, within a wreath of flowers, are the arms of Ole Worm with those of his third wife, Magdalene Motzfeldt (Plate XXV, No. 2). The maker was Borchart Rollufsen, of Copenhagen, to whom is attributed two silver spoons of 1633 and 1623 in the National Museum, numbers 41 and 48, respectively, in the catalogue. Of particular interest is the fact that some such Danish tankard as this had served as a model for the English "peg" tankards, made at York in the seventeenth century, as mentioned in the chapter on English plate.

A particularly good specimen of the tankards of late seventeenth century date is illustrated here. In this the body is repoussé and chased with large sprays of flowers above the three lion and ball feet, which are also seen on Norwegian tankards. On the cover are birds and foliage, also repoussé and chased, and a lion and ball thumbpiece. The mask on the end of the handle is also a common motive in Norwegian tankards. Horsens, in Jutland, is claimed as the place of origin, and one Mogens Thommesen Löwenhertz as the maker, about 1695 (Plate XXV, No. 3). Illustrated in Mr. Jörgen Olrik's book *Danske Solvarbejder* (Fig. 54) is another tankard, but with a plain body standing on similar lion and ball feet; the handle is likewise plain, while the cover is embossed with large tulips and other flowers and is set with a medallion of David and Goliath. The maker was Erik Andersen Winther, goldsmith, of Aarhus, about 1691.

The covered beaker with a plain globular finial, on Plate XXVI (No. 7), is worked over with a granulated surface, as in English cups from Charles I to Charles II and in German tankards and other vessels of the seventeenth century. It was made about the middle of the seventeenth century by an unknown silversmith at Odense, in Fünen. Illustrated on the same Plate (XXVI, No. 1) is a beaker of a later variety of about the year 1703. It has a heavily embossed body, with a plain lip, and stands on three large plain ball feet, in the manner of German beakers of this form introduced in the second half of the seventeenth century. The decoration consists of female busts amid large sprays of foliage on a matted ground. Hans Nielsen, of Copenhagen, was the maker. A second specimen is similarly embossed with flowers and foliage, without the busts.

Another type of beaker without feet and embossed with wide bands of flowers and foliage, leaving the lip and bottom plain, is represented in the National Museum catalogue by three specimens, all about the same date, 1700. One illustrated on Plate XXVI (No. 3), is dated 1709.

The Dutch fashion of a windmill cup travelled to Denmark, though it never reached the same degree of popularity. One rare example of these cups (in the National Museum at Copenhagen) is repoussé and chased with formal acanthus foliage and is dated 1709 and stamped with the mark of the maker, Godfred Bolch, master goldsmith at Copenhagen in 1702, and that of the assay-master, Conrad Ludolf. It is illustrated in the catalogue.

Among the Danish silver which should be mentioned are the "Queen's throne," made in 1725 by Nicolai Junge, a prominent goldsmith of Copenhagen; and the three large lions, displayed on ceremonial occasions, wrought in 1668–70 by Ferdinand Küblich, also of Copenhagen, all of which are at Rosenborg Castle. An important specimen of Danish work is the wine-fountain, executed at Copenhagen in 1703 and acquired in 1725 by the Russian ambassador to the Danish Court; this is illustrated on Plate 15 in Baron A. de Foelkersam's catalogue of the old plate in the Winter Palace at Petrograd.

Mention should also be made of the silver statuette of

PLATE XXV

PLATE XXVI

DENMARK

Frederik III of Denmark, by the Copenhagen silversmith, Jorgen Stilcke, who was master in 1651 and died in 1683. It will be found illustrated in Mr. Jörgen Olrik's *Danske Solvarbejder*, 1915, Fig. 33. In this same work is an illustration (Fig. 78) of a plain octagonal candlestick by Nicolaus Fuchs, of Copenhagen, 1721, modelled from an English pattern only a few years earlier in date.

The influence of the French rococo ornament and of the Louis XVI and the First Empire styles on Danish domestic silver is apparent from the book just mentioned.

That Danish plate should be found in Norway is not surprising in view of the historic connection between the two countries in the past. A good specimen of a tankard by a Danish provincial goldsmith in 1688 is illustrated in the excellent catalogue by MM. Kielland and Gjessing of the exhibition of old silver at Stavanger in Norway in 1916. The body is plain and the three feet and the thumbpiece are formed of the conventional pomegranate. Two shields of arms are worked in high relief—not engraved in the more usual manner—on the cover. Described fully in the same catalogue are a pair of interesting candlesticks of octagonal form, plain and cast, by Philip L. Weghorst, of Copenhagen, in 1724, evidently copied from English candlesticks within a few years of the original model (Plate XXVI, No. 5). English influence is also noticeable in the charming pistol-handled silver knife (with a three-pronged fork to match), by a Copenhagen silversmith, whose mark is illegible, while the assay-master was C. Ludolf. The knife and fork are illustrated on Plate 21 in the Stavanger catalogue, which contains on Plate 54 a pair of silver salts with glass linings, also probably inspired by an English pattern, though not equal in workmanship. Michael Gren, of Copenhagen, was the maker of these salts early in the nineteenth century. Characteristically English is the oval teapot, by Peder Krags, of Copenhagen, which is decorated with festoons of flowers and shields in the bright cut work, first seen between 1780 and 1790 in England, and often copied in Danish and Norwegian plate; this is illustrated on Plate 52 of the above Stavanger catalogue.

The names of a few French goldsmiths working at Copenhagen

have been preserved in Mr. Bernhard Olsen's book, *De Kjobenhavnske Guldsmedes Mærker*, including Isaac Dubois, master goldsmith from Paris, who was admitted to the Goldsmiths' Guild of Copenhagen by royal decree in 1688. A cup made by him in 1689 is mentioned in the above work. André le Coq, a Frenchman by birth, was a member of the same guild from 1696 to 1717, and a chalice from his atelier is in the German Reformed Church in the Danish capital. Another goldsmith was Jean Marie Lenoir, who is known to have flourished in Copenhagen between 1722 and 1742; and a fourth was Jerome Paul Lenoir, by whom two chalices, 1754 and 1762, are recorded.

The earliest of these craftsmen may have been Huguenot refugees from France, like Pierre Harache, David Willaume and many more in London, and Bartholomew le Roux and others in New York.

Some notice should be accorded to one Magnus Berg, a carver of ivories, since his ivories have been mounted by silversmiths as cups and tankards. Two of his fine carvings (one mounted in silver by John Bridge of London in 1824-5) are at Windsor Castle. The bowl of the first is finely carved with a boar hunt and is supported by a figure of Hercules as a stem. On the cover are three recumbent female figures, the finial being a figure of Diana. Carved on the body of the second cup is the " Rape of the Sabine Women," and the stem is composed of ivory figures of the " Three Graces." The finial is a figure of Romulus, surrounded by ivory figures of amorini and figures of Romulus and Remus sucking the wolf. Both cups are illustrated on Plate 27 of the present writer's book on the plate at Windsor. The career of this highly skilled and prolific carver in ivory may briefly be told. He was born in Norway in 1666 and left that country at the age of 24 for Copenhagen, where he remained for six years, departing in 1694 for a tour in Germany, Italy and France and returning later to the Danish capital, where he spent most of the remaining years of his life. One of the most important of his ivory plaques is the Apotheosis of Frederik IV," carved about 1730, which is in the historic collections of the Kings of Denmark at Rosenborg Castle.

DENMARK

It was not until late in his career that Berg directed his skill to the carving of cups. His greatest work is the large ivory and silver cup of the "Water Element" in the same royal Danish collections, upon which he was engaged for several years, probably from 1713 until a short time before his death in 1739, except for his enforced absence at a German watering place for the benefit of his health. (L. Dietrichson, *Magnus Berg*, 1912.)

Although there were goldsmiths in Copenhagen in the seventeenth century capable of making plate worthy of a King, Christian IV appears to have thought otherwise, for his considerable gifts of German plate to the Court of Russia were largely by silversmiths of Hamburg. Mr. F. R. Martin has illustrated and described them—they included an English dish and a flagon of the Elizabethan period—in his book on the gifts.

For the old marks of Copenhagen silversmiths, the book by Mr. Bernhard Olsen, *De Kjobenhavnske Guldsmedes Mærker*, 1892, should be consulted. Silver was made at Aarhus, Horsens in Jutland, Hjorring, Odense in Fünen, Randers, Ribe, Ringkobing, Viborg, Vejle, and elsewhere in Denmark.

Nyrop's *Meddelelser om Dansk Guldsmedekunst* (1885) will be found useful.

ENGLAND

PLATE XXVII.

No. 1 Standing mazer cup, c. 1490. H. 5¼ in.
No. 2 Mazer, c. 1390. H. 2¾ in.
No. 3 Beaker, c. 1350. H. 4¼ in.   Trinity Hall, Cambridge.
No. 4 "Rochester" mazer, 1532–3. D. 7¼ in. H. 2¾ in.   British Museum.
No. 5 "Studley" bowl, late 14th century. Total height, 5⅛ in. H. of bowl, 3½ in. D. 5⅛ in.   Victoria and Albert Museum.
No. 6 Horn, first half of the 14th century. L. 24½ in. H. 10⅜ in.

         (Nos. 1, 2 and 6 are at Corpus Christi College, Cambridge.)

PLATE XXVIII.

No. 1 Cup, c. 1450. H. 7 in.   From Lord Methuen's collection.
No. 2 Cup, second half of the 15th century. H. 13¼ in.   Lacock Church, Wilts.
No. 3 Cup and cover, 1520–1. H. 9½ in.   Christ's College, Cambridge.
No. 4 Small cup, c. 1465. H. 5⅞ in.   Marston Church, Oxon.
No. 5 "Rodney" cup, c. 1490. H. 6¼ in.   Lord Swaythling.
No. 6 Small bowl, 1526–7. H. 2¼ in.   Collection of the late J. Pierpont Morgan, Esq.
No. 7 Enamelled cup, 1350–75. H. 15 in.   Corporation of King's Lynn.

PLATE XXIX.

No. 1 Ostrich-egg cup, 1623–4. H. 18¼ in.
No. 2 "Pelican in her piety," 1579–80. H. 15½ in.   H. N. Gladstone, Esq.
No. 3 Cup and cover, 1619–20. H. 16¾ in.
No. 4 "Steeple" cup, 1605–6. H. 25 in.   Lord Dalmeny.
No. 5 Cocoanut cup, c. 1470. H. 8 in.   Gonville and Caius College, Cambridge.
No. 6 Cup and cover, 1611–12. H. 20¼ in.   Christ's College, Cambridge.

         (Nos. 1 and 3 are from the late Lord Swaythling's collection.)

PLATE XXX.

No. 1 Plain oval trencher salt, 1729–30.
No. 2 Pierced oval salt, Sheffield, 1777–8.
No. 3 Circular trencher salt, by Pierre Harache, 1694–5.
No. 4 "Steeple" salt, 1626–7. H. 9¾ in.   Collection of the late Lord Swaythling.
No. 5 "Bell" salt, 1599–1600. H. 8¾ in.   Collection of the late Lord Swaythling.
No. 6 Plain trencher salt, 1727–8.   Sidney Sussex College, Cambridge.
No. 7 Plain trencher salt, 1720–1.   Pembroke College, Cambridge.
No. 8 "Queen Elizabeth's" salt, 1572–3. H. 13¾ in.   Tower of London.
No. 9 Large standing salt, 1592–3. H. 16 in.   Victoria and Albert Museum.
No. 10 Plain octagonal salt, 1686–7. H. 7¾ in.   Saddlers' Company.

ENGLAND

PLATE XXX (continued)

No. 11 "Hour-glass" salt, 1508–9. H. 12¼ in. — Messrs. Crichton Bros.
No. 12 Circular salt, 1661–2. H. 6½ in. — Saddlers' Company.
Nos. 13 & 14 Pair of plain salts, 1741–2. — New York Historical Society.
No. 15 Octagonal trencher salt, 1725–6.
No. 16 Circular trencher salt, 1707–8.
No. 17 Pierced oval salt, 1777–8.
No. 18 Circular fluted trencher salt, 1693–4.

(Nos. 1, 2, 15–18, are in the Manchester Art Gallery.)

PLATE XXXI.

Nos. 1 & 3. Rosewater dish (D. 19¾ in.) and ewer (H. 14¼ in.), 1586–7. — Rijks Museum, Amsterdam.
No. 2 Ewer (H. 9 in.) and dish (15¼ in. long), by Philip Rolles, 1718–9. — Messrs. Crichton Bros.
No. 4 Bishop Parkhurst's ewer, 1567–8. H. 8½ in. — Corporation of Guildford.
Nos. 5 & 6 Ewer (H. 8¼ in.) and dish (D. 18 in.), 1545–6. — Corpus Christi College, Cambridge.

PLATE XXXII.

No. 1 Tall flagon, 1613–4. H. 15¾ in. — The Kremlin, Moscow.
Nos. 2 & 3 Pair of flagons, 1604–5. H. 13 in. — Lord Dalmeny.
No. 4 Tankard of marble, mounted in silver-gilt, c. 1575. H. 9¼ in.
No. 5 Stoneware flagon, mounted in silver-gilt, 16th century. H. 5½ in. — Worcester Art Museum, Massachusetts.
No. 6 Flagon of Rhodian ware, mounted in silver-gilt, 1586–7. H. 10¼ in.
No. 7 German stoneware flagon, mounted by C. Eston, of Exeter, c. 1590. H. 10½ in.
No. 8 Globular tankard, 1556–7. H. 6 in.

(Nos. 4, 6, 7 and 8 are from Lord Swaythling's collection.)

PLATE XXXIII.

No. 1 Cup of crystal and silver-gilt, 1554–5. H. 11 in. — Baron Bruno Schröder.
No. 2 Ewer of crystal and silver-gilt. H. 10 in. 1597–8. — Baron Bruno Schröder.
No. 3 Cup of glass and silver-gilt, 1566–7. H. 16½ in. — Earl of Jersey.

PLATE XXXIV.

No. 1 Tankard, 1680–1. H. 6¼ in. — Emmanuel College, Cambridge.
No. 2 Plain tankard, 1722–3. — Manchester Art Gallery.
No. 3 Tankard, c. 1560. H. 7¾ in. — Viscount Lee of Fareham.
No. 4 Peg tankard, by John Plummer, of York, 1659–60. H. 6¼ in.
No. 5 Tankard, decorated in "Chinese" style, 1689–90. H. 6¼ in.
No. 6 Tankard, 1673–4. H. 6 in.
No. 7 Tankard, 1571–2. H. 6¼ in. — Corpus Christi College, Cambridge.

(Nos. 4–6 were in the collection of the late J. Pierpont Morgan, Esq.)

OLD SILVER OF EUROPE AND AMERICA

PLATE XXXV.
No. 1 Bellows, Charles II.   Earl of Dysart.
No. 2 Large plain wine cistern, by Philip Rolles, 1701–2. L. 46 in. W. 36 in. H. 17 in.   Earl Spencer.
No. 3 Wine fountain, by Paul Lamerie, 1720–1. H. 28 in.   Winter Palace, Petrograd.
No. 4 Large wine cistern, by Philip Rolles, c. 1718. L. 46 in. W. 33 in. H. 27 in. Wt. 3,690 oz.   Marquess of Exeter.
No. 5 One of a pair of andirons, by Benjamin Pyne, 1697–8. H. 21¼ in.   Messrs. Crichton Bros.
No. 6 Wine cistern, by Pierre Harache, 1701–2. L. 27 in., W. 19¼ in., H. 11¼ in.   Earl Spencer.
No. 7 Large wine-bottle (one of a pair), possibly by John Goode, 1701–2. H. 23⅞ in.   Earl Spencer.

PLATE XXXVI.
No. 1 Cup and cover, by John Swift, 1756–7. H. 12 in.   Owner, Mrs. J. C. Warren.
No. 2 Plain mug, 1714–15.
No. 3 Caudle cup, 1660–1. H. 7¼ in.   Emmanuel College, Cambridge.
No. 4 Plain mug, 1704–5.
No. 5 Caudle cup, 1696–7.
No. 6 Tazza, plain, with gadrooned edge, 1694–5.
No. 7 Caudle cup, 1691–2.
No. 8 Cup and cover, c. 1710. H. 13⅜ in.   New York Historical Society.
No. 9 The "Paca" mug, 1767–8. Owner, Miss Joanna Peter, of Lexington, Kentucky.
No. 10 Cup and cover, by George Wickes, 1744–5. H. 13¼ in. Viscount Lee of Fareham.

(Nos. 2, 4 and 6 are in the Manchester Art Gallery.)

PLATE XXXVII.
No. 1 Tall candlestick, clustered column, 1775–6. H. 12 in.
No. 2 Tall "Corinthian" candlestick, 1759–60. H. 22¼ in.   Clare College, Cambridge.
No. 3 Candlestick, 1701–2. H. 8 in.
No. 4 Candlestick, 1685–6. H. 8 in.
Nos. 5 & 7 Pair of candlesticks, by Paul Lamerie, 1737–8. H. 9¼ in.   Lord Swaythling collection.
No. 6 Candelabrum, by Paul Lamerie, 1731–2. H. 12¼ in.   Same collection.
Nos. 8 & 9 Pair of candlesticks, by John Cam, 1741–2. H. 8 in.   Owner, George Tucker Bispham, Esq.
No. 10 Plain octagonal candlestick, 1716–7. H. 7¼ in.   Queens' College, Cambridge.
No. 11 Rococo candlestick (one of four), by Paul Lamerie, 1740–1. H. 9 in.   Collection of the late J. Pierpont Morgan, Esq.
No. 12 Plain toilet service, by Daniel Garnier, 1696–7.   From the collection of Lord Northbourne.

(Nos. 1, 3 and 4 are in the Manchester Art Gallery.)

PLATE XXXVIII.
No. 1 Plain coffee-pot, 1753–4.
No. 2 Plain coffee-pot, 1727–8. H. 10¼ in.   Owner, Mrs. R. B. Drane, of Edenton, North Carolina.
No. 3 Coffee-pot, rococo, by John Swift, 1762–3. Owner, Miss Carrie Coke, of Edenton.

ENGLAND

PLATE XXXVIII (continued)
No. 4 Chocolate-pot, by Paul Lamerie, 1738–9. H. 11 in.   Lord Swaythling collection.
No. 5 Plain octagonal teapot, by Jonathan Lambe and Thomas Tearle, 1718–9. H. 6¼ in.
No. 6 Tea-urn, by Francis Butty and Nicholas Dumee, 1765–6. H. 19 in.
                    Owner, T. J. Oakley Rhinelander, Esq., New York.
No. 7 Ewer, by Ann Tanqueray, c. 1725. H. 11⅜ in.   Winter Palace, Petrograd.
No. 8 Plain teapot on stand, 1708–9.   Sidney Sussex College, Cambridge.
No. 9 Plain globular teapot, 1719–20.
No. 10 Teapot, 1670–1. H. 13¼ in.
    (Nos. 1, 5 and 10 are in the Victoria and Albert Museum.)

PLATE XXXIX.
No. 1 Plain sweetmeat box, 1670–1.   Senior Common Room, Christ Church, Oxford.
No. 3 Tall kettle stand, c. 1705. H. 28 in.   Colonel Mulliner's collection.
Nos. 2, 5 & 6 Sir William Pepperell's three caddies, 1737–8 and 1738–9.
                    Owner, Lady Augusta Palmer.
No. 4 Kettle, by Peter Archambo, 1727–8.
                    Owner, Mrs. Margaret Donnell Nelson, of North Carolina.
No. 7 Plain inkstand, by Augustin Courtauld, 1721–2. Size 13¼ × 10 in.
                    Messrs. Crichton Bros.

PLATE XL.
No. 1 Large chased salver, by Augustin Courtauld, 1732–3. D. 19¼ in.
                    Collection of the late J. Pierpont Morgan, Esq.
No. 2 Rococo soup tureen, by Paul Lamerie, 1747–8. L. 13½ in., H. 11 in. Lord Dalmeny.
No. 3 Small square salver, by Paul Lamerie, 1722–3, 6 in. square.
                    Collection of the late Lord Swaythling.
No. 4 Plain sauce boat, 1751–2.   Victoria and Albert Museum.
No. 5 Sauce boat, by Paul Lamerie, 1738–9. H. 4 in.
                    Collection of the late Lord Swaythling.
No. 6 Pierced cake basket, by Thomas Heming, 1761–2.   Windsor Castle.
No. 7 Monteith bowl, by John Gibbon, 1707–8. H. 9¼ in., D. 12¼ in.
                    Viscount Lee of Fareham.
No. 8 Epergne, 1777–8.   Clare College, Cambridge.

ALL the books and articles ever written fail to convey a true picture of the progress of the goldsmith's art in England from the Norman conquest to the death of George III, so vast has been the destruction, at three periods in English history, of precious objects, both sacred and secular. The first period is the Wars of the Roses, when the plate of the barons was sacrificed. As Pascal said, men never do wrong more cheerfully or more thoroughly than when acting in the name of religion, an observation which may be applied to the iconoclastic zeal of the Reformation, and the consequent loss of priceless treasures. Within a century, the Civil War completed the ruin of the Royal collection of gold and silver plate, which was regarded as the most precious in Europe in Tudor times.

Nothing has survived the wreckage in the great Norman cathedrals. A mere glimpse of the skill of the Anglo-Norman metal worker is afforded by the famous Gloucester candlestick of 1107–1113 in the Victoria and Albert Museum. This escaped sacrifice because it is not of pure silver.

Another twelfth-century object is the famous Coronation spoon in the Tower of London, the bowl of which was re-fashioned in 1660.

In the thirteenth century the arts and crafts and the architecture of England reached a high level. The celebrated Syon cope in the Victoria and Albert Museum, and others on the Continent, are evidence of the undoubted skill of English needleworkers. Nothing has survived of the genius of William Torel, the London goldsmith, but his recumbent figure of Henry III, of gilt metal, in Westminster Abbey.

Incredibly rich in silver as were the Colleges of Oxford before the conflict between Charles I and Cromwell, only some 34 pieces (exclusive of spoons), dating from about 1350 to 1554, have escaped destruction. The treasures saved include the crozier of William of Wykeham, founder of New College, regarded as the finest example of English Gothic silver extant. A later crozier and a chalice and paten of gold, dated 1507–8, have survived at Corpus Christi College. Cambridge cannot claim more than 20 pieces of the same period, and these are all domestic. As the more puritan University of the two, it allowed all the pre-Reformation vessels of the College chapels to go to the mint of Charles I, whereas Oxford succeeded in saving many sacred vessels, including those just mentioned.

The most common of all old English drinking vessels from about the year 1200 to the sixteenth century was the mazer bowl, a circular vessel made of wood, preferably the maple. From them "celestial nectar" was quaffed by the rollicking monks. The earliest examples were probably of plain wood, unadorned with metal; but, later, plain mounts of silver and even of gold were added, while later still the width of the band increased in size, and was

ENGLAND

embellished with an inscription in Gothic characters. Although so common before the Reformation, only about sixty have survived.

One of the most famous is the great mazer of 1398 (restored in 1622 and 1669) in York Minster, inscribed with grants from Archbishop Scrope and another Bishop of forty days' pardon " On to all tho that drinkis of this cope."

Unique is John Northwode's mazer of the late fourteenth century, at Corpus Christi College, Cambridge. Fixed inside the centre of the bowl is an hexagonal pillar with a battlemented top, upon which rests a swan. Inside this pillar is a hollow tube, open at both ends, so adapted that the bowl cannot be filled with wine above the top of the tube, as on reaching that height the wine begins to flow out, escaping through the end in the bottom of the bowl until empty. The short foot with egg and tongue moulding is an addition to the bowl by an Elizabethan goldsmith (Plate XXVII, No. 2).

The Latin inscription on the mazer of about 1470 at Oriel College, Oxford, has been rendered into English thus :

> Man in thy draughts let reason be thy guide,
> And not the craving of perverted lust ;
> So honest nourishment will be supplied
> And strife of tongue be trampled in the dust.

A mazer in the British Museum is inscribed in Latin and Greek :

> " May the Holy One bless us and our drink."

An interesting inscription on one mazer of about 1490 is :

> " In the name of the Tirnitie [Trinity] fille the cup and drinke to me."

Pepys, on his visit to the old almshouses at Saffron Walden, took a draught of drink "in a brown bowl, tipt with silver, which I drank off, and at the bottom was a picture of the Virgin with the Child, in her arms, done in silver "—a mazer which, happily, is still preserved there. The " picture " mentioned by Pepys refers to a medallion of sacred subjects, to be found in the bottom of almost every mazer.

Inscriptions such as the above recall Dekker's drinking song, "Troll the bowl, the jolly nut-brown bowl"; and the passage in Sir Walter Scott's *Lord of the Isles*, where Bruce celebrates the recovery of his ancestral castle of Turnberry:

> Bring here (he said) the mazers four,
> My noble fathers loved of yore.
> Thrice let them circle round the board,
> The pledge, fair Scotland's rights restored !

To an ingenious and imaginative craftsman, nothing was more simple than to add a high silver stem and foot to the mazer bowl, hence the two "standing mazers" of about 1450 and 1490, at Pembroke College and Corpus Christi College, Cambridge, (Plate XXVII, No. 1), and the one of 1529–30 at All Souls College, Oxford. The original mazer bowl of the cup at Pembroke College, just mentioned, has been replaced by one of silver, leaving intact the original mount on the lip and the inscription :

> sayn denes y^t es me dere
> for hes lof drenk and mak gud cher

(Saint Denis that is my dear, for his love drink and make good cheer).

On the stem is the inscription :

> God help at ne|e|d.

The Rochester mazer with the name of Robert Peacham, in the British Museum, has the London date-letter for 1532–3 (Plate XXVII, No. 4).

The mazer lost much of its popularity upon the introduction of new and more convenient forms of silver cups in the reign of Elizabeth, and indeed ceased to be made.

Some of the inscriptions call to mind the Greek inscription on a glass vessel from Cologne, ascribed to the fourth to the sixth century, in the British Museum : "Drink and Prosper."

Drinking vessels of the horn of the ox or buffalo in its natural state were in common use in remote ages. The medieval goldsmith, realising its potentialities for the exercise of his skill, began to mount the horn of these animals in silver. Two important examples of the first half of the fourteenth century have, happily, survived at Oxford and Cambridge, and are the earliest pieces of plate at either University. A later horn belongs to Christ's Hospital, Horsham.

The horn of Queen's College, Oxford, is interesting, apart from other merits, because of the inscribed word "Wacceyl," repeated three times, indicating that it was intended for use for drinking spiced ale on festive occasions, such as the commemorative feast of the founder of the College and donor of the horn, Robert Eglesfield. The Corpus Christi horn originally belonged to the guild of Corpus Christi at Cambridge, but has belonged to the College of that name since 1352, and is used on feast days as a *poculum caritatis*, with appropriate ceremony (Plate XXVII, No. 6). Like the Oxford horn, it has suffered some alteration in the passage of time.

Horns had another use in England, having served the same purpose as a charter for lands in the Middle Ages. The Pusey horn is said to have been given by Canute to an ancestor of the Pusey family, as is confirmed by the inscription : I Kyng Knoude geue Wyllyam Pewse thys horne to holde by thy Lond." Others are of ivory, such as the celebrated Tutbury horn, mounted with a plate of the arms of John of Gaunt ; and the Bruce horn* of the period of Edward III, an heirloom of the Marquess of Ailesbury, which is beautifully decorated with enamels.

Thanks to the munificence of Mr. Harvey Hadden, the Victoria and Albert Museum is now in possession of the remarkably beautiful silver-gilt bowl of the late fourteenth century, one of the glories of early English work, from Studley Church. A mere glance is enough to reveal the fine proportions and the high technical skill of the chased and engraved decoration of a black-letter alphabet, interspersed with and springing from foliage (Plate XXVII, No. 5).

---

* The above three horns are illustrated and fully described in Sir C. J. Jackson's *History of English Plate*, pp. 589–594.

Although ecclesiastical, the English incense boat and censer of the fourteenth century, in the same Museum, deserve notice.

The fashioning of drinking vessels was one of the chief delights of the English goldsmith from early medieval times, as has been traced in the sketch of the mazer bowl. Milton may have remembered the noble cups of his *alma mater*, Christ's College, Cambridge, when he sang:

> their flowing cups
> With pleasant liquors crown'd

First in point of date of extant English standing cups is the one belonging to the Corporation of King's Lynn; this is decorated with enamelled figures, and is of the reign of Edward III—the third quarter of the fourteenth century (Plate XXVIII, No. 7). Unfortunately, there is no evidence to connect it with the enamelled silver cup made in 1370 for this King by one Walsh and one Chichester, goldsmiths of London. English illuminated manuscripts of this period are very uncommon and, therefore, no useful comparisons can be made between the figures and decoration. Not a dozen cups anterior to 1525 have survived, exclusive of the "standing mazers" already mentioned and cocoanut cups. One of these is the famous "Anathema" cup of 1481–2, at Pembroke College, Cambridge, so-called from the appropriate curse, QUI ALIENAVERIT ANATHEMA SIT, inscribed by order of the donor, Thomas Langton, Bishop of Winchester. The entire absence of ornament and the marked resemblance in the form of this historic vessel to Venetian glass cups of the end of the fifteenth century suggest that it may have been copied from one of these cups. Another interesting fact is that it is the first instance of secular plate stamped with the London date-letter, just as the Nettlecombe chalice of the previous year is the earliest extant piece of ecclesiastical silver so marked.

The most conspicuous of the other early cups are one of about 1460 at New College, Oxford; the Leigh and Richmond cups of 1499–1500 and about 1510, of the Mercers and Armourers Companies, respectively; and the "Election" cup of about

1520 at Winchester College, all of which are illustrated in the *History of Old English Plate*.*

Famous among drinking cups is the cup of 1435-40, which formed a part of the precious gift of the Countess of Richmond and Derby, mother of Henry VII, to her foundation of Christ's College, Cambridge, with the beaker-shaped cup of 1507-8, which is chased with a portcullis and a rose in lozenge-shaped panels. The gems are now missing from the foot of the last cup. In the same college is another rare cup of 1520-1, covered with scale work, not unlike that on the font-shaped cup of 1521-2, mentioned later.

Three more domestic cups of the second half of the fifteenth century, all illustrated on Plate XXVIII, are conveniently included here, namely, the small plain cup in Marston Church, Oxon, which has three feet fashioned like hounds, intended to represent the original owner's crest or to commemorate a favourite dog, as was done in old English church brasses. The second is the well-known " Rodney " cup, covered with lobes, and derived from a German shape of cup, which was formerly in Lord Swaythling's collection, while the third is in the church of Lacock, Wiltshire. (Nos. 4, 5 and 2, respectively, on the Plate).

The sale of Lord Methuen's silver at Christie's in February, 1920, brought to light a unique English cup, only seven inches high, dating from about 1450. The shallow plain bowl has a domed cover, surmounted by a crystal ball and a silver-gilt serpent, symbolical of Eternity. It is supported on a stem of crystal, octagonal in shape, encircled by a silver band. Incised around the cover and the bowl, in lettering of the time, are the words :

> If that thou hast a friend of long
> Suppose he sumtimes do thee wrong
> Oppress him not but have in mind
> The kindness that afor has been.

---

* The author of this valuable book, which is frequently mentioned in this chapter, was the late Sir C. J. Jackson.

At thy board when thou art set
Think on the poor standing at thy gate
Love God, do law, keep charity
Sua. Sal. All grace abundant be.

Engraved on the foot is the Latin motto : QUIDQUID AGAS, SAPIENTER AGAS ET RESPICE FINEM.
This delightful piece of late Gothic silversmiths' work was sold for £3,200 to Messrs. Crichton Bros. (Plate XXVIII, No. 1).

A great cup of 1523-4, surmounted by the Tudor arms, was a gift from Henry VIII to the Barber Surgeons Company. The original bowl of wood, like a mazer bowl, has been replaced by one of silver. Four small bells are suspended from the straps, "which every man is to ring by shaking after he hath drunk up the whole cup," as related by Pepys when a guest of the Company.

In medieval times, and especially during the Renaissance, certain objects of no intrinsic value were richly mounted as cups by the English goldsmiths. As early as 1259, a cocoanut cup is mentioned in Durham wills. Their rarity was no doubt the chief and only reason for so mounting them. The cocoanut was more extensively mounted in this way than any other object. Two such cups, of the second half of the fifteenth century, belong to Gonville and Caius College, Cambridge, and were there during the residence of Thomas Lynch, one of the signatories to the famous Declaration of American Independence. The pointed ornaments on the stem of one (Plate XXIX, No. 5), have some resemblance to those on the " Election " cup at Winchester College. A third cup, a little later in date (with a modern foot), is at Corpus Christi College, Cambridge. Oxford can boast of six cocoanut cups : two of the fifteenth century and one of 1584-5 at New College ; one of the late fifteenth century at Oriel ; and two of the early sixteenth century at Exeter and Queen's, all of which are illustrated in Mr. H. C. Moffatt's book on the Oxford plate. Another, of about 1510, is at Eton College.

The little known cocoanut cup of about 1500 (with a new

ENGLAND

wooden stem and foot) at St. Augustine's College, Canterbury, is engraved with the hospitable and charitable injunction:

> Velcom ze be Dryng for Charite
> (Welcome ye be, Drink for Charity).

It is illustrated in *Country Life* for December 2, 1922.

Several of the old Livery Companies of the City of London have cocoanut cups—the Ironmongers, Vintners, Armourers and Saddlers. In the Victoria and Albert Museum is one of 1578-9, and the Marquess of Sligo has one of 1582-3. Some of the Elizabethan cups are carved with Scriptural and other subjects in the manner of German cocoanut cups of the sixteenth century. The London silversmith would seem to have ceased to regard the nut as a curiosity worthy of his skill after the reign of James I, though two specimens of later date are illustrated in *The History of English Plate*, 1641 (Norwich make) and 1670.* For some unexplained reason the fashion was revived after about 1770, when large numbers of nuts were mounted as cups with silver lips, linings and feet, a fashion which continued into the early years of the nineteenth century.

In England, far rarer than the cocoanut cup is the ostrich-egg cup. One of these, dated 1592-3, at Corpus Christi College, Cambridge, was the gift of Richard Fletcher, Bishop of Worcester at that time. The silver garnishings comprise a stem fashioned like the twisted trunk of a tree, in the manner of some German cups, and like the English gourd-shaped cups described on another page. Two other examples are one of 1610-11, at Exeter College, Oxford; and the later cup of 1623-4, recently sold from Lord Swaythling's collection (Plate XXIX, No. 1). Another ostrich-cup with a plain baluster stem, dated 1589-90, is illustrated in Christie's sale catalogue of the Earl of Home's collection in June, 1919.

To these may be added the rare ostrich-egg tankard on a high stem, mounted in 1609-10, now in the British Museum. Of equal rarity is the ewer formed of an ostrich-egg, richly mounted and

---

* A late example, mounted by a York silversmith in 1683-4, was exhibited at St. James's Court in 1902.

decorated with acanthus leaves about 1670, in the collection of the Earl of Yarborough. The large ostrich-egg pot, garnished with enamelled gold, with a gold cover and a handle fashioned like a serpent and enamelled in green, in the collection of Charles I, has perished.

The egg of the ostrich was regarded as worthy of the skill of the artificer in classical times (as in the reign of Queen Elizabeth), as is proved by the recent discovery by the Swedish archæological expedition in Greece of a vase made of this bird's egg, with ornamentation in gold, silver and bronze, among the treasure of golden cups in a Mycenæan tomb. In the British Museum are five carved ostrich eggs from a tomb in Etruria, about 611 B.C.

The nautilus-shell cup, so popular among the German goldsmiths of the sixteenth and seventeenth centuries, and mounted also in the Netherlands and at Vienna, never appealed in the same degree to contemporary English silversmiths. Only one shell cup is known to have survived, although the destructible character of the shell may account for the loss of other examples. This is the cup, in the form of a melon shell, mounted as a monster of the sea, supported by four dolphins on a circular base, by a London silversmith of 1577–8, which was in the collection of the late Mr. Alfred de Rothschild, and is illustrated in the *History of English Plate*. A nautilus-shell cup by a goldsmith of Edinburgh is illustrated on Plate LXXXVI (No. 4).

A beaker-shaped cup with a cover was made in England as early as the fourteenth century, which is the date of one at Trinity Hall, Cambridge, the College of the Rev. Robert Hunt, chaplain to the expedition to Virginia in 1607 (Plate XXVII, No. 3).

Between 1500 and 1575, a small font-shaped cup, usually without a cover, was made in England, of which several examples have been illustrated in books on plate. First in date is the well-known cup of 1500–1, from Lord Swaythling's collection, bearing the same inscription as a cup of the same shape in Wymeswold Church in Leicestershire: SOLI DEO HONOR ET GLORIA. It is followed by one of the treasures of the Goldsmiths' Company, the plain covered cup, made in 1503–4 for John Cressener, who

PLATE XXVII

PLATE XXVIII

ENGLAND

was knighted in 1513 for his gallantry at the siege of Tournai. Another important piece is the "Bodkin" cup of 1525-6, inscribed: SI DEVS NOBISCVM QUIS CONTRA NOS, in the possession of the Corporation of Portsmouth. Better known than all is the cup of 1521-2, with the inscription, BENE DICTVS DEVS IM DONA SVIS AME, which reached the high price of £4,100 at Christie's in 1902, and was sold again in the same rooms in July, 1924, for £3,800. The scales and flutes on this cup are similar to those on a standing cup of the previous year at Christ's College, Cambridge, on Plate XXVIII (No. 3). A cup in the Kremlin at Moscow is dated 1557-8.

In this group may be included the priceless cup of ivory and silver of the Duke of Norfolk, dated 1525-6, familiar from illustrations and remarkable for its Gothic and Renaissance ornament. It is delightfully inscribed in Latin: DRINK THY WINE WITH JOY.

Closely allied to the font-shaped cup are the small cup or bowl of 1525-6, from the collection of the late Mr. J. Pierpont Morgan (Plate XXVIII, No. 6); and the earlier small cup of 1496-7, affixed with ten ribs, perhaps intended to make the holding of the cup easier for the wine bibber; this is illustrated in Mr. J. Starkie Gardner's *Old Silver Work*, 1902 (Plate 37).

The earliest surviving form of salt—one of the most important objects of secular plate in the Middle Ages—is fashioned like an hour-glass, and may be regarded as entirely English. Probably not more than ten examples are known, beginning with the pair of about 1500, and a smaller and plainer one of 1507-8, all at Christ's College, Cambridge. These are of the same shape as the plainer salt of 1508-9, bought at the Ashburnham sale at Christie's in 1914, by Messrs. Crichton Bros. (Plate XXX, No. 11). Older than either is the famous Warden's salt of about 1490, at New College, Oxford, familiar from oft-repeated illustrations. Corpus Christi College, Oxford, claims the possession of an hour-glass salt of hexagonal shape and of about the same date, the gift of its founder, Bishop Foxe. Two others without their original covers, dated 1518-9 and 1522-3, belong to the Ironmongers' Company, and an octagonal one of 1522-3 belongs to the Goldsmiths' Company. It would, therefore, seem from the extant specimens that such salts were made only between about 1490 and 1523. The shape was revived later in the salts made for the coronation banquet of Charles II, to be seen in the Tower of London.

Drum-shaped salts came into fashion towards the middle of the sixteenth century, and are more common than the other forms. A plain one, dated 1550–1 and made in the short reign of Edward VI, is in the possession of the Earl of Ancaster. Later, in Elizabeth's reign, they became more ornamented and are frequently of large size. Several of this cylindrical variety are known, including one of 1577–8 in the Wallace Collection; another of 1581–2, formerly in the collection of the late Mr. Alfred de Rothschild; a third, of great size, dated 1586–7, in the Victoria and Albert Museum; and one of 1584–5 in the collection of the late Mr. J. Pierpont Morgan. Finest of all is the richly decorated "Queen Elizabeth's salt" of 1572–3 (Plate XXX, No. 8), in the Tower of London, which reveals in the panels of symbolical figures the influence of the German designer, Peter Flötner (died 1546), as does the Vintners' salt mentioned later.

The cylindrical salt of 1567–8, of the Corporation of Norwich, deserves more than a bare record, in that it is one of the few important pieces of Elizabethan plate, still extant, which were made in that city. Peter Peterson, son of a Dutch settler, was probably the maker. Another example made outside London was the small cylindrical salt of about 1582, by C. Eston, a conspicuous silversmith in Exeter, which was sold in Lord Swaythling's collection at Christie's, and is illustrated in the sale catalogue.

A scarcer form is square shaped and is represented by the highly important salt of 1569–70, of the Vintners' Company, already mentioned as revealing in the panels the influence of Flötner. The little salt of crystal and silver, dated 1577–8, in Mr. J. A. Holms's collection, is unusual. But more curious is a covered salt of the same date, decorated with crystals, in the collection of Sir John H. B. Noble, Bart. Two rare examples of the square shape in the collections of the Tsars of Russia and the late Mr. Leopold de Rothschild, are dated 1594–5 and 1583–4 respectively, and are illustrated in the present author's books on those collections. Fortunately, the Victoria and Albert Museum has recently acquired* a square-shaped salt of the highest importance and rarity, dating from 1592–3. Its interest lies not only in the workmanship, but also in the panels of *verre eglomisé* (glass decorated with gold and silver leaf and colour) bearing designs and motives adapted from Geoffrey Whitney's *Choice of Emblemes*, published in 1586; similar medallions on the cover show heads of heroes of antiquity. The decoration consists of masks, fruit and cartouches of conventional Elizabethan character; it stands on four lions and the finial is a figure of Justice (Plate XXX, No. 9).

At Goldsmiths' Hall is the "Gibbon" salt of crystal, with a finely wrought frame of architectural form, dated 1576–7, of which no similar piece is known.

The third type of Elizabethan salt retains the cylindrical shape but has a different cover, which is supported on scrolls and has a " steeple " finial in the manner of the well-known " steeple "cups, with which it appears to have been first made at the end of the sixteenth century. A notable example, of 1614-15, belongs to the Innholders' Company. Lord Swaythling had one of 1626-7 (Plate XXX, No. 4).

Between about 1580 and 1613 was made a " bell-shaped " salt of three tiers, generally with a perforated finial for pepper. It was plain or more usually chased with conventional straps and floral ornament, like the early example of 1599–1600 in the late Lord Swaythling's collection (Plate XXX, No. 5).

Although revived for the coronation banquet of Charles II, the standing salt proper virtually came to an end with his death. There are, however, the remarkable and beautiful "Seymour" salt of about 1662 of the Goldsmiths' Company; the curious salt fashioned like the Eddystone lighthouse, by Rowe, of Plymouth, about 1698; and the state salt of the City of London, 1730–1, all illustrated in the *History of English Plate*. The more ornate standing salt was supplanted by a plain salt, circular, octagonal or square in shape and

---

* By the generosity of the Goldsmiths' Company, the National Art-Collections Fund and Mr. Edmund A. Phillips.

generally fitted with three or four scrolls, intended to hold a napkin. Such scrolls were evidently regarded as novel in 1632, when the Barber Surgeons Company bought a "faire silver salt white with scroules of the new fashion." Among the earliest of the circular salts with scrolls is one of 1638–9, a gift of Sir John Dethick to the Mercers' Company. At Harvard College is a salt of the same shape, dating probably from 1629–30, which is of historic interest, having belonged to the Rev. Jose Glover, who had taken it with him when he set sail from London in 1638, accompanied by his devoted wife, Elizabeth, with the object of setting up the first printing press in America, at Cambridge, Massachusetts. One of these salts, dated 1661–2, belonging to the Saddlers' Company, is illustrated on Plate XXX (No. 12). The circular salt with scrolls was made of Lambeth Delft ware in the seventeenth century. One of the octagonal salts, like that of 1686–7 of the Saddlers' Company, (Plate XXX, No. 10), served as a model for two American salts, described on page 28. The square-shaped salts with scrolls appear to date mainly from the time of Charles II, as do the octagonal shape, and are to be found among the plate of the old City Companies.

Trencher salts had made a fitful appearance early in the seventeenth century. One of triangular shape, 1629–30, has been recorded, and a small circular salt, only $2\frac{1}{4}$ inches in diameter, 1603–4, was in Lord Swaythling's sale and is illustrated in Christie's catalogue. A third circular salt, $2\frac{1}{2}$ inches in diameter, dated 1639–40, is in the Victoria and Albert Museum.

The next step in the evolution of the trencher salt is the solid circular form, boldly gadrooned or fluted, found within the last decade of the seventeenth and the early eighteenth centuries. Salts of octagonal and circular shapes were common early in the eighteenth century. Between about 1740 and 1780 a circular salt on three feet was popular, many of the feet having lions' heads in the style of those on mahogany chairs and furniture of 1740–60. Oval salts with pierced sides on four feet, fitted with blue glass linings, were also common in the second half of the century. Several varieties of the trencher salt, some of which were copied by the early American silversmiths, are shown on Plate XXX.

ENGLAND

The erroneous belief that an indignity was cast upon any guest "sitting below the salt," as it has been called, arose from the custom of reserving all the more costly salts, with the other finer plate, for the high table in the halls of princes, colleges and corporations.

While not forgetting the ewers of gold in the inventory of Sir John Fastolfe in 1459 and the earliest extant rose-water dishes, those of 1493-4 and 1514-5 at Corpus Christi College, Oxford, the date of the oldest complete pair—ewer and dish—is 1545-6. These are the unique pair given to Corpus Christi College, Cambridge, by its *alumnus* and benefactor, Archbishop Parker (Plate XXXI, Nos. 5 and 6). The ewer is of the earliest form known in England, where its introduction was perhaps due to Hans Holbein, the younger, who was designer of plate as well as painter to the Court of Henry VIII. Among his designs is a ewer not unlike the Corpus Christi ewer.

A fifteenth-century treatise, called "For to serve a Lord," describes the manner of using silver ewers and dishes thus:

"The principall servitours moste take in ij handys basyns and ewers and towell . . . to serve water with the principal basyn and ewer, unto the principall soverayne, ij principal servitours to hold the towell under the basyn in lengt before the soverayne and after that the soverayne hath washe, to geve thenne water unto such as ben ordeyned to sit at the soverayneis messe."

The next stage in the progress of the ewer occurs in the reign of Elizabeth, when the foot becomes higher, while the body is drum-shaped, widening at the lip and base, and fitted with a long tapering spout, as in the ewer of 1567-8, the gift to the Corporation of Guildford by Bishop John Parkhurst* (Plate XXXI, No. 4). The decoration of these ewers is typically Elizabethan. Two others have been recorded, namely, one of 1562-3, with its companion dish, at Winchester College; and the other, of 1574-5 (with a dish of 1556-7), which has been acquired recently from Lord Newton of Lyme by the Goldsmiths' Company.

But the most popular of the later Elizabethan and Jacobean ewers

---

* The Bishop's Flemish dish, given at the same time, is illustrated on Plate XIX.

are those with tall and graceful vase-shaped bodies introduced into all the chief European countries during the Renaissance. Several specimens (with their basins) are known and have been illustrated from time to time, including those at Windsor Castle, Sidney Sussex College, Cambridge, and in the collections of the late Mr. J. Pierpont Morgan and Lord Swaythling. Unmatched in some respects is the ewer of the Duke of Rutland, which, with its dish, 1581-2, is set with agates, a most unusual feature in English plate. A pair, dated 1610-11, of the same date and by the same maker as the similar pair at Eton College, were sold in the Sneyd heirlooms at Christie's for £2,991, on June 24, 1924, and are illustrated in the catalogue. None of these surpass in decoration the ewer with dish, dated 1617-18, of the Corporation of Norwich. An unusual pair, decorated with friezes of animals, dated 1586-7, are in the Rijks Museum, Amsterdam (Plate XXXI, Nos. 1 and 3).

Just as the Elizabethan tradition in literature was extended for some years into the reign of James I, even beyond 1611, the date of Shakespeare's retirement, so, too, was the conventional ornament of the Elizabethan goldsmiths continued by their Jacobean successors on these ewers and dishes and other plate.

As may be inferred from the fifteenth-century treatise, already mentioned, and from the date of Sir John Fastolfe's gold rose-water ewers, such vessels, with their dishes or basins, have a long history in England and were familiar to Shakespeare :

> Let one attend with a silver bason
> Full of rose-water and bestrew'd with flowers ;
> Another bear the ewer, the third a diaper.
> *Taming of the Shrew*, Act II, Scene I.

Foreign travellers in England in the reign, luxurious as it was, of Charles II, were wont to remark on the absence of silver forks from the table at meals and the presence before each person of a beaker, into which he dipped his napkin at the end of the meal, not only to wash his hands but—an objective more upright than companionable—to clean his teeth as well. But more general in the houses of the great than the beaker here mentioned were a silver dish and ewer for rose-water, which were passed along in front of the guests, in the manner prevailing to this day at the high table and at feasts at some colleges at Oxford and Cambridge.

The ewers of Charles I are very different in shape from those of his predecessor, and, like most of the plate of his reign, are quite plain. They have deep, beaker-shaped bodies, a scrolled handle and a long spout reaching almost to the bottom, and a spool-shaped stem on a trumpet-shaped foot, like one of 1635-6 at Trinity College, Cambridge. The long spout, though not entirely discarded, gives way, in the reign of Charles II, to a mere indentation in the lip, as may be seen in the Earl of Kent's ewer of 1662-3 at the same college. Three specimens of historic interest are preserved in Cambridge colleges. Some have square-shaped handles and others have scrolled and harp-shaped handles. A popular form of decoration is the "cut-card" work, which prevailed on English plate for several years from 1660. Ewers of this later Charles II form were also made in Paris, as may be seen from the illustration on Plate XLII of one of a pair, by Charles Petit in 1674-5, in the collection of Earl Spencer, who owns an English ewer of similar form, dated 1668-9. The Earl of Clarendon has inherited the fourth Earl of Rochester's ewer (with its basin) of 1677-8, almost identical with Lord Spencer's French ewer, just mentioned.

To the Huguenot refugee goldsmiths may be attributed the introduction into England of the familiar ewers with bodies shaped like inverted helmets, of which the Duke of Devonshire's ewer by Pierre Harache, 1697-8, is probably the earliest. No fewer than six are at Cambridge. One of the earliest and finest is at Queens' College—the Earl of Jersey's ewer of 1699-1700, by David Willaume, a most successful craftsman among the refugees, and the maker in 1739-40 of what is perhaps the finest, as it is the latest, of the Cambridge ewers—the Earl of Lincoln's gift to Clare College. The terminal figure handles of many of these ewers, the strap-work decoration, and the masks under the spouts, are noteworthy features of many of the more highly decorated specimens. Unique in gold is the helmet-shaped ewer of 1701-2, by Pierre Platel, in the collection of the Duke of Devonshire, which has been illustrated in several books. The two great ewers of 1701-2 of the first Duke of Marlborough, inherited by Earl Spencer, are noble specimens.

A notable ewer of this form, by Paul Lamerie, 1726-7, richly decorated in his best manner (and much other plate, including the tureen on Plate XL), was made with a dish for Lord Anson, the celebrated admiral. The pair were acquired by the late Mr. J. Pierpont Morgan some years ago.

One pair of 1718-9, by Philip Rolles, were made for George I and were bought from the Duke of Cumberland's collection by Messrs. Crichton Bros. (Plate XXXI, No. 2).

Rose-water dishes and ewers were rarely made after the middle of the eighteenth century.

As has just been mentioned, English silversmiths of the sixteenth and seventeenth centuries indulged but little in the taste of their contemporary German craftsmen for the exaggerated embellishment of such trifles as cocoanuts, ostrich eggs and other objects of no intrinsic value. But it would seem from the numerous examples which have survived the vicissitudes inseparable from domestic life for over three centuries that the English silversmiths were not averse from displaying their skill on the mounts of the stoneware flagons or jugs which were imported into England from Germany, mostly from Cologne, as early as the reign of Henry VIII.

Some of these silversmiths doubtless regarded as unworthy the exercise of so much skilled labour and material wealth upon such inartistic and clumsy objects as these foreign jugs, but were restrained from revolt by the power of their guilds or by the fear of the loss of support of their powerful patrons.

To those who regard it as almost a duty to familiarise themselves with the movements of prices for old English silver, the disposal at Christie's of the West Malling jug in 1903 for the large sum of 1,500 guineas remains fixed in their memories. But there is one fact which is often overlooked by the *habitué* of Christie's, namely, that the West Malling jug is of mottled green, orange and purple earthenware, whereas most of the other jugs have mottled surfaces of varying degrees of "tiger" or "leopard" markings—hence the title of "tiger-ware" often applied to these jugs of German origin.

ENGLAND

Another feature in the West Malling jug which is absent from most of the other jugs is the application of four vertical straps embellished with female terminal figures. In this feature this jug recalls Colonel Fearon Tipping's specimen of seven years earlier (1574–5), which is conspicuous in having a gold medal of the Emperor Charles V inserted in the cover.

The decoration of the silver covers, neck-bands and bases of these jugs consists in the main of the familiar Elizabethan cartouches enclosing masks, fruit or flowers, groups of fruit and other ornamentation in relief, peculiar to that period. In the early examples the neck-bands are inclined to be narrow. A gradual widening is observable during Elizabeth's reign. Many jugs have neck-bands engraved with the conventional Elizabethan interlaced strap-work and arabesque foliage, while the covers are seen to have the relief decoration just mentioned. The silver mounts on the bases of some are devoid of ornamentation or may have a border of cut foliage.

For proof of the German origin of many of these jugs the presence of a German shield of arms is adduced. This occurs on a jug, bearing the London date-letter for 1562–3, in the collection of the late Sir C. J. Jackson, the owner of a rare jug with an impressed ornamentation on the stoneware body which is repeated on the silver neck-band. This jug has the London hall-mark for 1589–90.

The National Museums, if sadly deficient in examples of English silver drinking vessels as of furniture and other specimens of native art, are able to show several of these silver-mounted German stoneware jugs. Several are in the Victoria and Albert Museum, beginning with one of 1556–7. Two specimens are in the Franks collection in the British Museum and are dated 1549–50 and 1584–5.

It need scarcely be said that stoneware jugs have crossed the Atlantic, the late Mr. J. Pierpont Morgan having in his lifetime acquired specimens, including one with mounts by that rare Exeter goldsmith, John Eydes. Exeter goldsmiths, it should be remembered, were particularly partial to the mounting of these jugs, for it is estimated that of the recorded examples ten per cent. were garnished (as the old books pleasantly have it) with silver by the craftsmen of that old city. One from Lord Swaythling's collection was mounted about 1590 in characteristic Elizabethan fashion by C. Eston of Exeter (Plate XXXII, No. 7).

One pottery jug of historic interest was taken over the Atlantic nearly three hundred years ago by the first Governor of Massachusetts Bay, John Winthrop, whose silver cup is also preserved there.* Its history may be traced to that worthy's father, Adam Winthrop of Groton Manor, Suffolk, to whom it had been given by his sister, Lady Mildmay. It is now in the possession of the American Antiquarian Society, of Worcester, Massachusetts (Plate XXXII, No. 5).

In the ancient colleges of Oxford and Cambridge, where almost every conceivable kind of English silver drinking vessel, from medieval times until the nineteenth century, is preserved, it is curious that not one of these stoneware jugs can be found.

For some unaccountable reason the mounting of these stoneware jugs, which had been so popular during the Elizabethan period, went out of fashion shortly after the accession of James I.

In addition to the flagons of Rhenish stoneware, just described, the London goldsmiths mounted other "curious" things in silver in the sixteenth and early seventeenth centuries. Ranking first in date is a small bowl of Céladon porcelain, mounted early in the sixteenth century, said to have been a gift of Archbishop Warham to New College, Oxford. It is illustrated in Mr. H. C. Moffatt's book on the Oxford plate.

A few choice things are in the Victoria and Albert Museum, beginning with a cup of agate, with an elaborate silver-gilt stem and foot, dated 1567-8. Next comes an octagonal flagon of Chinese porcelain, mounted in 1585-6 by an Elizabethan goldsmith who executed the mounts of a jug of white Siegburg stoneware in the same Museum. He also mounted the imposing set of three bowls and a large bottle of Wan Li porcelain (1573-1619), acquired by the late Mr. J. Pierpont Morgan from the Burghley House collection, which is illustrated in the catalogue. Another Chinese flagon in the British Museum is of the same period as the last set, the

---

* See page 123.

silver mounts being undated. A tankard of serpentine marble was mounted about 1620 by the maker of the silver-gilt mounts of the " Dyneley " casket of alabaster in the Victoria and Albert Museum. Here also is a serpentine tankard of about 1630 by a silversmith who copied his thumbpiece from the silver tankards of the period. The British Museum contains a few important specimens of wares mounted in silver, by English and foreign silversmiths.

Nothing finer is known than the ewer of Wan-Li porcelain, 11½ inches high, with Elizabethan silver-gilt garnishings, in the collection of Baron Bruno Schröder, who is also the owner of a small bowl of the same porcelain, mounted in London about 1585.

The large bowl, probably of Chinese porcelain, in the collection of Viscount Lee of Fareham, has " cut-card " and cut acanthus mounts of silver, characteristic of the time of Charles II, and is a rare piece.

An account of some Chinese porcelain mounted in silver by Elizabethan goldsmiths, written by Dr. S. W. Bushell and the present author, was published in the *Burlington Magazine* for August, 1908.

English, as well as Dutch and German, silversmiths mounted other materials into domestic vessels. Here is a flagon of Rhodian faience, mounted in silver-gilt by a London goldsmith in 1586–7, from the collection of Lord Swaythling (Plate XXXII, No. 6).

Cups and drinking vessels of crystal, richly mounted in the Renaissance and earlier periods not only in England but also in other countries, were apparently made under the common belief expressed by Sir John Davies in " A Contention " (1602) that

" The crystal glass that will no venom hold."

James Howell, in his *Familiar Letters* (1622), expressed the current view thus : " Such a diaphanous pellucid body as you see a crystal glass is, which hath this property above gold or silver, or any other minerals, to admit no poison." The German sixteenth-century tankard with a crystal body at Clare College (Plate LII, No. 6), has retained its title of " Poison Cup " from the date of the gift in 1618 to this day. But the belief in the merits of crystal to detect the presence of poison was not general among the Elizabethan and Jacobean goldsmiths, for never in the history of England were so many great cups of silver made than in those times.

One of the most magnificent of all English crystal cups is the well-known "Bowes" cup of 1554–5 (wrought in the short reign of Queen Mary), belonging to the Goldsmiths' Company, from which Queen Elizabeth quaffed wine at her coronation. It is of the same form as the ornate and finely executed cup, attributed to the German goldsmith, Wenzel Jamnitzer, in the collection of Baron Bruno Schröder (Plate LIV, No. 3). Another important and lavishly decorated cup of this form, dated 1566–7, is in the possession of the Earl of Jersey. In this the body is of glass and probably replaces the original crystal, perhaps at the restoration and regilding of the cup as a gift from the great Duke of Wellington to his god-daughter, Lady Clementina Villiers (Plate XXXIII, No. 3). It bears a maker's mark, a bird, similar to that on the superb crystal cup and cover, of the same date as the above "Bowes" cup, which has been acquired from the so-called "Green Vaults" in Dresden by Baron Bruno Schröder (Plate XXXIII, No. 1). The silver cover of this Dresden cup is fluted in the same manner as that of the elegant "Boleyn" cup of 1535–6 in Cirencester church—a cup which has derived its shape from some such design as that of Hans Brosamer, mentioned on page 61.

Baron Bruno Schröder is also the fortunate owner of another treasure in English plate, dated 1597–8: a little crystal ewer of globular form, slightly carved with marguerites and supported by four silver-gilt straps fashioned like caryatids, set with lion masks and fruit. The handle is a serpent and the other decoration consists of lion masks, fruit and straps (Plate XXXIII, No. 2).

In the Shropshire church of Tong is a crystal cup of about 1610, decorated with scrolls and foliage, which is illustrated in the *Burlington Magazine* for December, 1921. The decoration is similar to that on the great cup and cover of 1611–12 at Christ's College, Cambridge.

The Christ's College cup just mentioned is conspicuous among

ENGLAND

Jacobean cups. It was sold for £4,500 at Christie's with the Plomer-Ward heirlooms and was presented by Mr. J. Pierpont Morgan to the College in 1920 (Plate XXIX, No. 6). The bands of vines and scrolls, worked in relief, are similar to those on the Tong cup, previously described, while the vessel itself and its decoration have a close resemblance to the cup of the same date in the Victoria and Albert Museum. The latter is, however, engraved with hunting scenes on the body and the finial is different.

Dr. Johnson's Dictionary, quoting Ben Jonson's "Hath this tankard touched your brain?" describes a tankard as a "large vessel for strong drink."

The tankard enjoyed greater popularity than any other form of personal drinking cup in Northern Europe from the sixteenth to the eighteenth centuries, and in America from the end of the seventeenth century. It was never made, except as a "freak" piece, in the wine-drinking Latin countries.

In England the evolution of the tankard may be followed throughout the changes in shape and decoration for 200 years by the help of the notable specimens preserved in the ancient Colleges of Oxford and Cambridge, and in the old City Companies and the Corporations, where they are conspicuous objects at commemorative feasts.

For the purpose of this brief survey the tall Elizabethan and Jacobean flagons, such as those in the unrivalled collection of the Tsars of Russia, are excluded, though they were doubtless used for drinking beer on ceremonial occasions.

The earliest tankard has a short globular body, like one of 1556-7 from Lord Swaythling's collection (Plate XXXII, No. 8), and one of 1567-8, of the Armourers' Company of London. Historically and intrinsically interesting is one of 1571-2, in the Patriarch's Treasury at Moscow, illustrated in *Country Life* for February 18, 1911. A plainer and later one of 1614-15 is at Winchester College. Their forms were probably suggested by some such pottery vessels as the Winthrop jug, mentioned above, and one with silver mounts of 1550-1, illustrated in Mr. J. Starkie Gardner's *Old Silver Work*, 1902, Plate 48. It is a tankard of this shape that is depicted in Caxton's engraving of Chaucer's pilgrims seated round a table at the Tabard Inn in Southwark, in the second edition of the *Canterbury Tales*, 1484.

> "With bred and chese and good ale in a jubbe
> Sufficing right ynow as for a day."
>
> *(Chaucer.)*

The second and most popular of the early English tankards has a small tapering body, decorated in different styles. One variety would seem to have been in vogue between the years 1570 and 1618, and is represented by at least fifteen specimens. Three are preserved in two Cambridge Colleges, the gifts* of that great bibliophile but destroyer of pre-Reformation plate, Matthew Parker, first Archbishop of Canterbury after the Reformation (Plate XXXIV, No. 7). One only is at Oxford and is in the Ashmolean Museum. A specimen of 1587-8 in the collection of Lord Rochdale is illustrated in *Country Life* for June 7, 1919. Another of 1607-8, from the Church of St. Benet Fink, has been acquired by the Victoria and Albert Museum.

Viscount Lee of Fareham is the fortunate owner of a unique example of an Elizabethan tankard, decorated on the drum with three applied cartouches enclosing shell cameos of heads (restored). The unusually fine cartouches of figures, volutes, straps and fruit recall the French school of Ducerceau and Delaulne, of the sixteenth century, while the other details are English (Plate XXXIV, No. 3).

A slight departure from the small tapering kind is to be seen at Christ's College, Cambridge, in a tankard dated 1597-8, of the same form as the Elizabethan tankard of marble and silver from Lord Swaythling's collection, recently dispersed (Plate XXXII, No. 4). Tankards, both of the cylindrical and tapering forms, were made in the sixteenth and early seventeenth centuries, of horn, glass, marble and serpentine, mounted in silver.

The great Lord Burghley's small narrow tankard of glass and silver-gilt, with arms and crest in enamel, of about 1570, in the British Museum, is in the nature of a curiosity.

---

* An interesting fact is that the arabesques on these tankards are not unlike those on bindings attributed to the Archbishop's own binder.

ENGLAND

For the next stage in the development of the English silver tankard, the small one of 1635-6 at Trinity Hall, Cambridge, is an excellent example of a very rare variety, in outline exactly like the scarce Norwich spout cup mentioned on page 26. The body is short and tapering and the moulded lip and base, inseparable from later tankards, are absent; the cover is quite flat and the wide scrolled thumb-piece is like that of contemporary flagons. An earlier specimen was given to the Corporation of Kendal in 1629.

This type was succeeded in the Commonwealth by a large plain tankard. The low flat-topped cover is in two stages, while the base is wide and splayed, like those of the tall flagons of the reign of Charles I. One of 1649-50 was sold at Christie's for £413 5s. 0d. on March 24, 1909. The Carpenters' Company has a small one of 1653-4, and the Innholders' Company one of average size, dated 1656-7. An interesting example, dated 1655-6, which once graced Barnard's Inn in London before its dissolution, is now in the collection of the Earl of Rosebery; it is illustrated in the *History of English Plate* (Fig. 988). A late one of 1660-1 has been recorded.

When the " second Charles assum'd the sway " in 1660, followed by settled conditions of the country, the London silversmiths of this luxurious period were busily engaged in making tankards, not only for nobles but also for the guilds and institutions already mentioned. In shape the tankard followed the Cromwellian type, just described; some were quite plain, others were embossed along the base with acanthus and palm leaves, while some were engraved with birds, figures and plants in the Chinese taste, first seen about 1665 and popular on English plate between 1670 and 1695 and especially between 1680 and 1690 (Plate XXXIV, No. 5). The thumb-pieces occasionally took the form of the owners' crests, while some were fitted with three feet in the shape of lions. The tops remained flat for about 50 years from 1660, and occasionally a cover may be seen decorated with foliage. In the Charles II tankards the bases are moulded and shorter than those of the Commonwealth.

One of the most interesting plain tankards of this type is one of 1673-4 in the great collection of old plate formed by the late Mr. J. Pierpont Morgan (Plate XXXIV, No. 6). It is somewhat crudely engraved with the royal arms of Charles II and two panels depicting the Plague of London and the Fire of London, and is a copy of one presented by that King in 1666 to Sir Edmund Bery Godfrey for his self-sacrificing services during the Plague. Other copies are extant. A tankard with the above-mentioned embossed acanthus and palm leaves, is shown on Plate XXXIV (No. 1).

In the same American collection is another rare example of an old English tankard, in the " peg " tankard wrought by John Plummer, of York, in 1659–60 (Plate XXXIV, No. 4). Oddly enough, most of the extant specimens of " peg " tankards were made at York between 1657 and 1685, having been introduced probably through the port of Hull from Denmark, where the " peg " tankard was highly popular in the seventeenth century, as will be noticed in the chapter on Danish plate. Both this and the similar tankard at Windsor Castle have thumb-pieces and feet formed of pomegranates, which are essentially Danish features (see Plate XXV).

The title of " peg " tankard is derived from the old expression " taking (down) a peg." These tankards and the drinking customs associated with them are well described by Dr. Pegge, the antiquary, in his *Anonymiana*: " They have in the inside a row of eight pins, one above another, from top to bottom ; the tankards hold two quarts, so that there will be a gill of ale, i.e., half a pint of Winchester measure between each pin. The first person that drank was to empty the tankard to the first peg or pin ; the second was to empty to the next pin, etc., by which means the pins were so many measures to the compotators, making them all drink alike the same quantity ; and as the distance of the pins was such as to contain a large draught of liquor, the company would be very liable by this method to get drunk, especially when, if they drank short of the pin, or beyond it, they were obliged to drink again." The English silver tankards are smaller than those described by the learned antiquary, holding about a quart, and are fitted with four, five or six pegs inside.

Hull has been mentioned as the probable port of entry for those Danish " peg " tankards. A few were made there, including one by Thomas Hebden in 1689–90, which belongs to the borough of

PLATE XXIX

PLATE XXX

ENGLAND

Hedon, in Yorkshire. Another place where they were made, though rarely, was Newcastle, where John Dowthwayte is known to have made one about 1670.

A third English tankard in the Pierpont Morgan collection (all of which are illustrated in the present author's catalogue of that collection) deserves notice from the fact that it is one of the largest known, and was given by Queen Mary to Simon Janszen for safely conveying her husband, William III, to The Hague in 1691. It is inscribed in Dutch:

> When Simon fills this cup with wine,
> Her Majesty's brilliance in it doth shine;
> And as he the cup to his lips doth lift
> He remembers full well the Royal gift.

The maker, in 1692–3, was George Garthorne, whose work is represented in two American churches by sacred vessels in St. Anne's, Annapolis, Maryland, and Whitechapel Church, Virginia.

Towards the end of the seventeenth century, the lower part of the tankard was occasionally spirally fluted, like the contemporary caudle cups. The plain flat-topped tankard continued in vogue for a few years after the accession of Queen Anne, when it was succeeded by a plain tankard of the same shape with a domed cover, which had, however, made its appearance about 1695. This variety was highly popular for about a quarter of a century, from 1710 to 1735, though it did not wholly pass out of fashion until about 1765. Another variety shows a plain body with a fluted base and a fluted shoulder on the cover, which came into fashion at the end of the seventeenth century. The body just above the base was frequently encircled with a plain ring moulding. The thumb-pieces of the English tankards from 1655 to 1715 were formed of two semi-globular or cupped discs flanking a pear-shaped hollow, spiral scrolls, diverging spirals, interlaced straps, and, more rarely, crossed dolphins. The use of owners' crests, already referred to, was less common. Nowhere can the old English tankard and other drinking vessels be so well studied as in the old colleges of Oxford and Cambridge. A common plain tankard is that of 1722–3 (Plate XXXIV, No. 2).

In the middle of the eighteenth century, a tankard with a plain "bellied" or bulbous body with a domed cover and a high moulded foot, with and without a moulding on the body, had become popular, and was especially common in the third quarter of that century.

These, in brief, are the main features in the development of the English tankard for over 200 years. Here and there are tankards of different shapes and decoration, but they are not characteristic specimens.

Here it may be convenient to dispel a long-cherished delusion—that the ends of the handles of old English silver tankards were constructed for use as "whistles," when a servitor was required to replenish the empty vessels with wine or beer for the good trenchermen of inn, home, or college. The holes at the handle ends were, as a fact, intended for the inlet of cold air during the process of fabrication. Without them the air within the handle, expanded by the heat of the solder used in affixing it to the body, would contract in cooling and cause unsightly depressions. Another purpose of these holes was to prevent fraud by silversmiths, who might be tempted to fill the handles with iron and thereby add to the ostensibly intrinsic worth of the vessel. Moreover, the supposed intention to make whistles of the handles is contradicted by the fact that most of the handles of the silver flagons of English cathedrals and large parish churches from 1660 are similarly constructed; in the event of a shortage of wine for the Sacrament it is improbable that the celebrant would resort to the irreverent device of "whistling" for more wine to the verger at such a solemn moment.

Closely associated with tankards are the tall Elizabethan and Jacobean flagons, both of cylindrical and globular form, intended for ceremonial purposes and for pouring out wine at feasts—the original purpose of one is unmistakable, for it is decorated with vines.

The finest specimens of both varieties are in the famous collections of the Tsars of Russia* and the Patriarchs of Moscow. In the former are six globular flagons, two late Elizabethan and four

---

* All are illustrated in E. Alfred Jones's *Old English Plate of the Emperor of Russia*.

ENGLAND

Jacobean; and seven of the cylindrical form, dated between 1585 and 1617, including one of 1613–14, the personal flagon of Eudokia Lopukhina, first wife of Peter the Great, before she was forced by him into a convent (Plate XXXII, No. 1). In the Treasury of the Patriarch are three globular, dated 1596–7 and 1606–7, and also one cylindrical, 1611–12, which is exactly like, and by the same maker as, the above flagon of the Tsarina Eudokia Lopukhina. All these are illustrated in *Country Life* for February 18, 1911.

Lord Dalmeny is the owner of a pair of the globular flagons chased in the flat with conventional straps, Tudor roses and foliage, made in 1604–5 (Plate XXXII, Nos. 2 and 3). A pair of 1607–8 at Trinity College, Cambridge, are decorated with the panels of sea monsters, so prominent a feature of English plate between 1580 and 1620, and sprays of foliage.

In the collection of the late Sir Ernest Cassel was a large cylindrical flagon decorated with similar panels, unusually late in date, 1633–4. Globular flagons with and without spouts were known in England much earlier than any surviving examples, as is shown in the wonderful wall painting of about 1310 in Croughton Church, Northamptonshire, and in the picture of the meeting of Henry VIII and Francis I on the Field of the Cloth of Gold.

An exceedingly rare flagon with a long spout appears to be represented by only two specimens, both in churches: one dated 1606–7, at All Saints', Oxford; and the other, 1609–10, at St. Mary's, Hadley Monken, Middlesex. They are very similar to a flagon in a "Still Life" picture by Willem K. Heda, in the National Gallery, in London. The first flagon is illustrated in *Country Life* for November 15, 1924.

Not one of the many presents of gold and silver plate offered to Queen Elizabeth on her progresses has been handed down. Gold cups were not unusual gifts from her hosts at the different houses where she refreshed herself or stopped the night. Nor can a single cup or any other piece of plate be identified which was made in accordance with an edict of the Goldsmiths' Company in 1571, compelling young silversmiths to make a "masterpiece" before establishing themselves as master craftsmen, as was done in Germany.

The order had fallen into abeyance, but was re-enacted in 1607, in the following terms:—

"Of late times, through the negligence and want of industry in most of the workmen of the Goldsmiths' Company, the true practice of the art and mystery of the goldsmith is not only fallen into great decay but also few workmen are able to finish and perfect a piece of plate throughout, with all the garnishings and parts thereof, without the help of many and several hands. The idler craftsmen betake themselves to the sole exercise of one slight and easy part of the said mystery—some are mere hammermen, others work upon nothing but bell salts or bells; some grave and chase, while others are spoon-makers, whereas in truth every perfect workman ought to be skilful in all and be able to begin and end his own work himself, as in times past. By such negligence all good workmanship will surely decay. Henceforth all craftsmen were required to make within the workshop newly erected in Goldsmiths' Hall a complete piece of work, called a masterpiece, to be begun and finished by himself." (*Memorials of the Goldsmiths' Company*, ii, 363.)

This is an interesting commentary on the state of the craft and confirms the author's contention on a later page that all the plate bearing certain maker's stamps was not wrought wholly by him.

Among the rare things in Elizabethan plate are the following: the banqueting service of 22 plain dishes and plates, made between 1581 and 1601 and buried at Dartmoor in 1645 to avoid seizure by Cromwell's troops. This was sold at Christie's in June, 1911. Twelve plates, engraved with the "Labours of Hercules," and dated 1567–8, are illustrated in the *History of English Plate*.

Evidence of the importation of Venetian wine-glasses into England in the sixteenth century is forthcoming from various sources, not the least interesting of which is the comment of William Harrison, the Elizabethan historian, who says that as gold and silver plate most aboundeth, "our gentility, as loathing those metals (because of the plenty) do now generally choose rather the Venice glasses, both for our wine and beer, than any of those metals or stone wherein before time we have been accustomed to drink." One outcome of the introduction of Venetian glasses was the inspiration to

PLATE XXXI

PLATE XXXII

ENGLAND

the goldsmith to copy them in silver, as may be observed from extant examples, including the domestic silver cup of 1583-4 in Longworth Church, Berkshire (illustrated in *Country Life* for November 15, 1925).

Many of the tall and elegant cups on slender baluster stems, both plain and decorated, of James I and Charles I, have escaped the furnace. One of these tall plain cups, dated 1626-7, was taken out to New England by an early emigrant, Atherton Hough, mayor of Boston, Lincolnshire, and was left by him to the First Church in Boston, Massachusetts, where it now reposes with Governor Winthrop's old English cup. Their plain successors in the latter reign were much shorter, with larger bowls and thicker baluster stems, and were made until the reign of Charles II, when they passed out of fashion. Several are in use as Communion cups in English churches, and one of the year 1631-2 was given or left for the same sacred purpose to an American church, by its owner the Rev. Samuel Newman, first pastor of Rehoboth Church, Rhode Island.

Wine-bottles first appear in England in the reign of Elizabeth, or perhaps it would be more correct to say that none are extant of older date, such as the example shown in Holbein's sketch of Sir Thomas More's family at Bâle. The silversmith was probably prompted in adopting them for use and ornament for the table by the bottles carried by " pilgrims " of the middle ages.

While five tall vase-shaped bottles, with heavy chains, are in the collections of the Tsars of Russia, dated 1580-1, 1606-7 and 1619-20, the gifts of English sovereigns to the Russian Court, not a single specimen has survived in England itself. It is also interesting to remember that a pair of 1579-80 were in the Royal Palace in Berlin when last seen by the writer, and another bottle, of 1598-9, is also recorded in Germany.

In most countries in the sixteenth century the popular shape for bottles of silver, majolica, and other materials was apparently flat and oval, but not one is to be found in England earlier than 1663, the date of a pair, embossed with the familiar animals and birds of that period, which were presented by Charles II to the Tsar Alexis of Russia. This and the earlier bottles mentioned above are illustrated in the present author's book on the Russian collection.

As the century advanced such bottles became more common, though many from the Royal collection of England and elsewhere have been consigned to the melting-pot. A massive and stately pair, dated 1699–1700, 20½ inches high, by Pierre Harache, the *doyen* of the Huguenot refugees, ornately decorated in the style of Louis XIV and unsurpassed in magnificence by any English bottles of the time, are in a private collection. One of the largest and most massive pairs are dated 1701–2 and belonged to the first Duke of Marlborough, and are now exhibited by Earl Spencer in the Victoria and Albert Museum (Plate XXXV, No. 7), with a smaller and plainer French pair, also part of the Duke's plate. The splendid bottle of the Duke's brother, General Charles Churchill, made about 1702 by Pierre Platel and engraved with his arms, is in the possession of Captain C. D. Rotch.

A popular piece of plate in most European countries in the sixteenth century was the tazza. As the name implies, Italy was the country of origin, whence it spread rapidly to Germany, France (where it was extensively made in Limoges enamel, as well as in silver and in the faience known as " Henri Deux "), the Low Countries, Spain and England. At Augsburg and Nuremberg, as is shown in a later chapter, it was made in large numbers, even in sets of twelve or more.

First in date among English tazze is the covered pair of 1528–9, originally intended for secular use, in Rochester Cathedral. The Elizabethan tazza is simpler in decoration than the German, and rarely consists of more than an embossed bust of a male or female in Roman dress, in the manner of those on carved woodwork of the Tudor period, with conventional straps and arabesques engraved on the bowl. The stems are divided by a compressed knop and the circular bases are usually decorated with fruit in escutcheons, repoussé and chased in the formal style of Elizabethan plate.

Examples of tazze with uncommon features are at Christ's College, Cambridge, where there is one of 1572–3 with a later copy of 1609–10, the bowl punched with a beaded diaper pattern and

ENGLAND

supported on a fluted vase-shaped stem and a circular foot. Plainer than usual is the tazza of 1594–5, without the bust inside, at Winchester College. Another unusual tazza, dating from 1606–7, is preserved at Corpus Christi College, Cambridge, where an engraved male bust is substituted for the more usual embossed bust inside the bowl, while the stem is formed of three scrolled dragons on a high pedestal. Other specimens have survived in churches, as gifts of pious donors. Most of the extant English tazze date from 1564–5 to 1583–4, though one is known as late as 1617–18 in the Church of St. Giles, Cripplegate. The Elizabethan tazza of the Goldsmiths' Company is unusual in having a cover.

Only one pair are known, namely, those of 1582–3, part of the old treasure of the Corporation of Boston in Lincolnshire, dispersed at Christie's. A tazza of 1577–8, in the collection of the late Mr. J. Pierpont Morgan, is illustrated in the catalogue.

The direct influence of formal designs of the goldsmiths of the German Renaissance is apparent in the decoration of much Elizabethan plate. Whole cups were made in imitation of the German. First is the gourd-shaped cup, supported on a stem in the form of a tree-trunk, frequently set with figures of woodmen, which is similar to the designs of Hans Brosamer, Georg Wechter (1570–1630), Hans Sibmacher, c. 1590, and others. In England the cups were made perhaps by German settlers, as well as by native silversmiths. An early specimen, marked in London in 1585–6, belonged to the Troitsa monastery in Russia, and another, of 1601–2, inscribed with the name of the Patriarch Joseph, was in the Treasury of the Patriarch at Moscow when last seen by the author. The "Berry" cup, 1608–9, of the Corporation of Portsmouth, is of this form, and several others are known. Several of these cups have another German characteristic—the cut leaves spreading out under the bowls and over the feet. Two such German cups of about 1575, in the collection of the Baroness James de Rothschild, are mentioned in the chapter on German plate. The stem of the English ostrich-egg cup of 1592–3 at Corpus Christi College, Cambridge, is fashioned like a tree-trunk, in the manner of the gourd-shaped cups just mentioned.

The melon-shaped cup on a twisted tree stem of 1563–4, in the Hall of the Inner Temple, is a rare thing in English plate, under German influence.

Not only were German cups copied by London goldsmiths, or made by Germans in London, but a large quantity of German plate was imported and stamped with the London hall-mark in the sixteenth and early seventeenth centuries. One of the most interesting examples is the pine-shaped cup in the Winter Palace, which has German marks and the London date-letter for 1607–8. The author has made some observations on this aspect in the *Burlington Magazine* for February, 1913. In support of his conclusions, the *Memorials of the Goldsmiths' Company* may be cited. A London goldsmith was fined by the Company for selling Nuremberg plate, and a complaint was made against another that he had "soldered up a piece of Nuremberg plate which had been cut." Three cups in the Kremlin are, in the opinion of the author, of German origin, with London marks for 1613–14, 1618–19, and 1619–20.

The potent influence of the German goldsmiths is apparent in another cup, namely, the cup fashioned in the form of a pineapple, though in one example, dated 1612–13, in the Essex church of Farnham, the tall baluster stem and the decorated splayed foot are characteristically English. The finial is a ringed serpent. An illustration is in the Guide to the Church Congress at Southend, 1920. A similar and earlier cup, 1608–9, showing a woodman on the tree-stem, is in the possession of Earl Spencer, while a third, dated 1610–11, was recently on loan at the Victoria and Albert Museum.

The third form of cup has a tall body inspired by German models, like two at Cambridge—at Corpus Christi and St. John's Colleges—and one of 1619–20 from Lord Swaythling's collection (Plate XXIX, No. 3).

The German cups, fashioned like stags, lions, bears, and other animals, were never made in England. Nor were birds ever popular. Two specimens belonging to the Skinners' Company are in the form of a cock standing on a tortoise and were made in 1605–6 for William Cockayne as a rebus on his name. Similarly, the cup shaped like a peahen with three chicks was made in 1642 as a rebus

ENGLAND

on the name of James Peacock, a Master of the same Company, whose wife presented it. In this connection the "pelican in her piety," dated 1579–80, now on loan at the Victoria and Albert Museum from Mr. H. N. Gladstone, of Hawarden Castle, should be mentioned (Plate XXIX, No. 2). It may be compared with the German cup on Plate LV (No. 3).

The introduction of the beaker is probably due to traders between this country and the Low Countries or to the Protestant refugees who sought refuge here in the sixteenth century, just as it had reached Scotland by the means of traders and was adopted as a Sacramental cup in the north-east of that country. The beaker has been found, like other kinds of secular vessels, in use for sacred purposes in many English churches; for example, the beaker of 1591–2 in Kirk German Church in the Isle of Man, has served as a model in form, though not in decoration, for ten other beakers in this small island. Included in the collection of plate in St. Giles's Church, Cripplegate, are three beakers, dated 1591–2, 1602–3 and 1608–9, with a fourth beaker made of horn and mounted in silver-gilt in 1573–4. At least two of these beakers in this historic church represent the fines imposed upon certain persons for their release from offices in the ward, and were not intended for sacred purposes.

As a good specimen of the common type of beaker with conventional interlaced straps and arabesques, a somewhat late example of 1637–8 may be cited. This is doubly interesting from the fact that it was made at Norwich, and that it originally came from the New Meeting Chapel at Great Yarmouth before it had passed into the collection of the late Mr. J. Pierpont Morgan, in whose catalogue it is illustrated.

None are of greater historical interest than the plain set of six, belonging to the old Congregational Church at Great Yarmouth, a church which is intimately associated with Puritan history, for Ironsides and regicides were of the congregation, as was Daniel Bradford, a kinsman of Governor Bradford. Their date is 1654–5.

Sufficient has been said to show how a purely secular cup has been adopted for sacred purposes, not only in England, but also in Holland, Scotland and America.

No English cup was as popular in the few years of its heyday than the " steeple " cup, introduced within about five years of the death of Queen Elizabeth. It is exclusively English, and is not found on the Continent of Europe. The name is derived from the high obelisk, or pyramid, crowning the cover, which was copied from a conspicuous feature of Elizabethan and Jacobean architecture and of tombs in churches. Not one appears to be known earlier than 1599–1600, which is the date of two of them given subsequently as Communion cups to Charing Church in Kent and Buckland Filleigh in Devon (the steeple has disappeared from the second). Of over seventy noted more than half were made between 1604 and 1615. The remarkable collection of English plate in the Kremlin at Moscow* is richer in these cups than any other collection, and next to this comes Cambridge†, where there are six. Four belong to the Carpenters' Company. The well-known set of three in Lord Swaythling's collection, dated 1611–12 (previously in Lord Acton's collection), was sold at Christie's in 1924, and is familiar from frequent illustrations.

The marked partiality for this kind of cup, said to have been shown by James I, may have prompted the Inner and Middle Temples to present him with one of solid gold in 1609, " adorned with a fabric fashioned like a pyramid, whereon standeth the statue of a military person leaning with the left hand upon a Roman fashioned shield or target." The statue here mentioned may be seen crowning the "steeple" of several cups, as on the cup of 1628–9 at Christ's College, Cambridge. The steeples are perforated or solid, and the decoration of the bowls consists of acanthus leaves and fruit, straps and scrolls, trefoils and roses, scallops and fleurs-de-lis, vines and tulips, fluting and other ornament. Panels of sea monsters, as seen on English plate between 1580 and 1620, and animals, were least frequently introduced. The stems are baluster-shaped, supported by brackets (a few have no brackets), and the feet generally are high and bell-shaped. Scarcer than this general type is a cup with a tall baluster stem on a low foot.

---

* E. Alfred Jones, *The Old English Plate of the Emperor of Russia*, 1909.
† *The Old Plate of the Cambridge Colleges*, 1910.

ENGLAND

None is more precious among historical cups than the cup of John Winthrop, first Governor of Massachusetts, which he took with him to his new home across the Atlantic, and is now one of the treasures of the First Church in Boston. This has, however, lost its cover. A second historic cup (bereft of its steeple) is also in America—the cup made in 1604–5 from Queen Elizabeth's great seal of Ireland, which was sold at Christie's in 1902 for £4,000, and passed into the late Mr. J. Pierpont Morgan's collection.

The cup of 1605–6 in the possession of Lord Dalmeny is decorated with large inverted sprays (Plate XXIX, No. 4).

Happily, the national collection in the Victoria and Albert Museum is now spared the long-standing reproach of not having one of these characteristic cups, thanks to the generous gift by the Ven. D. Tait, Archdeacon of Rochester, of a cup of 1627–8. The unusual decoration of dolphins swimming in the sea, on the three parts of this cup, was doubtless regarded by the designer as an appropriate gift to one Richard Godfrey, a member of Parliament for the town of Romney, one of the Cinque Ports. In an official account it has been described as meant for ornament on a sideboard rather than for actual use; but there is ample evidence, from the inscription on the "steeple" cup of St. Ives, quoted below, and from other sources, that such vessels have been used as "loving cups" or "grace cups," though they may have graced the sideboard when not in use:

> If any discord 'twixt my friends arise
> Within the Borough of beloved St. Ives
> It is desyred that this my cuppe of love
> To everie one a peace maker may prove.

In the same Museum is another "steeple" cup, dated 1625–6, which was a gift to the Corporation of Trinity House from Captain Richard Chester, Master of that Corporation.

One of the largest "steeple" cups known, 29 inches high, was sold at Christie's for £1,200 on June 12, 1923. The bowl is chased with formal flowers and fruit, and the finial is surmounted by a warrior holding a spear and a shield.

A silversmith using as his punch a monogram of the initials F. T., perhaps for Fred Terry, made a good many of these cups, including Captain Chester's cup, mentioned above. Would that he had left some record for his choice of this form of cup on which to exercise his skill. Four cups with this mark are in the great collection at Moscow.

A third and rarer variety of "steeple" cup has a larger bowl, hemispherical in shape. The cup of 1615–6 of this shape at Trinity College, Cambridge—the *alma mater* of Governor Winthrop—has lost its cover. Of the small number of these cups in existence, two are in the priceless collection at Moscow, dated 1605–6 and 1608–9.

The "steeple" is also found on salts, and, more rarely, on a gourd-shaped cup of 1608–9 at Armourers' Hall (illustrated in the *History of English Plate*, Fig. 874).

Some other cups of the sixteenth century should not be overlooked in this brief survey—namely, the Vice-Chancellor's cup of the University of Cambridge, dated 1592–3—a gift from Queen Elizabeth's favourite, the Earl of Essex. Then there are the three covered cups made in 1573–4 from the great seal of Queen Mary for Sir Nicholas Bacon, one of which is in the British Museum.

From the time of Charles I, through the Commonwealth into the reign of Charles II, some great standing cups were made for the Livery Companies of the City of London. Two cups of Charles II period deserve notice—the curious "Royal Oak" cup of 1676–7, belonging to the Barber Surgeons' Company, and the ornate cup of 1677, presented by the immortal Pepys to the Clothworkers' Company.

What is perhaps the latest of the great standing cups is dated 1692–3, and is in the highly important collection of Sir John H. B. Noble, Bart. It is not only late in date, but is also unique in having as a stem a figure of Atlas.

The so-called bleeding bowl was introduced in the second quarter of the seventeenth century, and continued to be made for nearly a century in small numbers. The author gives his reasons on page 23 for his suggestion that they were probably intended as wine-tasters,

PLATE XXXIII

PLATE XXXIV

especially as many of them are too small for holding any quantity of blood. A "bleeding bowl" of 1685-6 was used as a stirrup-cup at Fordoun, the seat of Viscount Arbuthnot, according to Christie's sale catalogue for December 14, 1920.

A large covered bowl with two handles, midway in size between the caudle cup or porringer and the punch bowl, was made for spiced drink in the second half of the seventeenth century. Many of these adorn the high tables of Oxford and Cambridge colleges. The fine and early bowl of 1669-70, embellished with the "cut-card" work introduced only nine years previously into English plate—the gift of Lord Norreys to Magdalene College, Cambridge—is interesting for the application of the donor's crest as handles. This bowl is about a year later than the visit of the immortal Pepys to this, his college, when he drank beer in the Buttery, "which pleased him as the best he had ever drunk." Another important specimen is the Bishop of Bristol's bowl of 1677-8, decorated with the conventional acanthus and palm leaves, in the Cathedral of St. John the Divine, New York, which is illustrated on Plate 105 in *The Old Silver of the American Churches*. This is almost identical with the noble bowl in Lord Rochdale's collection, only a year later in date, which was a gift to Judge Sir William Dolben by the Corporation of London in 1679 for his services in protecting their privileges (illustrated in *Country Life*, June 28, 1919). Another bowl of similar size and decoration, dated 1682-3, was a gift of the Marquess of Winchester to Winchester College. Lord Kenyon is the owner of a fine plain one, decorated with "cut-card" work, undated, but perhaps by Ralph Leeke.

One unique cup of solid gold in this fashion was made in 1675-6, and was in the possession of the late Countess of Yarborough (Baroness Fauconberg and Conyers). An attempt was made to introduce a large cup of this fashion into the American Colonies by Edward Winslow, one of the most skilled silversmiths, and maker of the fine cup on Plate XI.

The silver caudle cup or porringer for possets and hot drinks, so dear to Englishmen of 200 to 250 years ago, is a two-handled vessel of English growth. Most of the early pieces were gourd-shaped, and were a development from the higher plain cups with two plain ring handles, such as the well-known examples of 1616-17 of the Mercers' Company. These in their turn appear to have been a development from the more ornate two-handled cups, like one of 1555-6 at Corpus Christi College, Cambridge, and the earlier one of 1533-4 at the Oxford College of the same name. But at Gonville and Caius College, Cambridge, are a covered pair of 1659-60 with upright sides, decorated with the acanthus leaves popular between 1675 and 1695—the gift of Francis Glisson, the great physiologist—which are among the earliest examples of this shape and decoration.

Three specimens are shown on Plate XXXVI, namely, one of 1660-1, at Emmanuel College, Cambridge (No. 3), and two fluted, 1696-7 (No. 5) and 1691-2 (No. 7). The two last patterns were copied by American silversmiths.

The decoration of these cups is as varied as that of contemporary tankards.

Two quotations from English literature suffice to record the custom of drinking caudle—a warm drink composed of thin gruel mixed with wine or ale and sweetened and spiced. Anthony à Wood, the antiquary, states that on Shrove Tuesday in 1648 the freshmen of Merton College, Oxford, entertained the other undergraduates to a brass pot "full of cawdel," and that "every freshman, according to seniority, was to pluck off his gowne and band and if possible to make himself look like a scoundrell. This done, they conducted each other to the high table, and there made to stand on a forme placed thereon ; from whence they were to speak their speech with an audible voice to the company ; which if well done, the person that spoke it was to have a cup of cawdle and no salted drink ; if indifferently, some cawdle and some salted drink ; but if dull, nothing was given to him but salted drink or salt put in college beere, with tucks to boot." The other quotation is from Pepys's Diary for 1659-60, where he says that he " went to bed and got a caudle made for me and slept upon it very well."

More sumptuous are the cups provided with salvers on high feet.

ENGLAND

A remarkably fine specimen has recently been acquired by the Victoria and Albert Museum. It bears the London date-letter for 1673-4, and, according to the inscription added in the eighteenth century, it was a gift from Charles II to Richard Sterne, Archbishop of York, great-grandfather of Laurence Sterne, author of *Tristram Shandy*. The touch of the "Van Vianen" decoration* in the grotesque faces is not its least interesting feature.

It may be conjectured that it was from some such vessel as these—possibly from his own silver caudle cup, which is still preserved—that Pepys drank his lamb's wool, a beverage made of ale, mixed with sugar, nutmeg and the pulp of roasted apples.

Caudle cups and porringers ceased to be made in the first half of the eighteenth century, not before the fashion had been copied by the earliest American silversmiths, as is stated on page 22. The English porringer is different from the American vessel of this name, described on pages 23-26.

Bowls with short notched edges to hang glasses in, but without handles, were wrought for the first time at the end of the reign of Charles II, and may be regarded as a development from the large two-handled bowls for spiced drinks, just described. One of the earliest, made in 1685-6, the first year of James II's short reign, was in the collection of the late Mr. J. Pierpont Morgan, and is chased with the novel Chinese decoration first seen on English plate about 1665, and common between 1670 and 1690. Two others of the same date belong to the Skinners' Company. An earlier one of 1684-5 is known.

As the fashion advanced the size increased, and some of the scalloped and notched edges were decorated with cherubs' heads. In many of the later bowls the rims are removable, with the glasses hanging therefrom. The decoration consists mainly of hollow flutings, as in Viscount Lee of Fareham's bowl by John Gibbon, 1707-8 (Plate XL, No. 7), embossed and hollow scrolls, strapwork and similar ornamentation, with the addition of two jointed handles,

---

* This same decoration may be observed in the silver shield presented by Charles II to the Queen of Pamunkeys in Virginia, in possession of the Virginia Historical Society, which is illustrated in the *Connoisseur*, Sept. 1921.

usually attached to large lions' masks, and occasionally to other masks. In the bowl of 1718–19, given to the Clothworkers' Company by Sir John Bull, the handles are fixed to bulls' heads as a compliment to the donor.

Bowls of this kind were apparently not intended originally for punch, but, according to the antiquary, Anthony à Wood, in 1683, were to be used as "a vessel or bason notched at the brims to let drinking glasses hang there by the foot, so that the body or drinking place might hang in the water to coole them." "Such a bason was called a 'Monteigh,' from a fantastical Scot called 'Monsieur Monteigh,' who at that time or a little before wore the bottome of his cloake or coate so notched."

Oval bowls with notched rims were made of Sèvres porcelain and of silver in France, and one such bowl, with wine glasses hanging inside from the rim, may be seen in an engraving of Le Souper Fin, by Helman, from a design by J. M. Moreau le Jeune (1783).

Lord Mostyn's "Monteith" of 1697–8 (illustrated in the *Burlington Magazine* for May, 1907), is accompanied by a most unusual, if not unique, feature in a small circular cup with a handle, attachable to the bowl by a hook and doubtless intended as a ladle.

Sir John Harpur's "Monteith" of 1700–1, at Magdalen College, Oxford, has been immortalised in Holman Hunt's picture, "May Morning on Magdalen Tower." The "Monteith" was produced in increasing numbers between 1690 and 1700, especially in the last three years of the century. Although there is the very late one, dated 1722–3, of Viscount Parker at Clare College, Cambridge, it virtually disappeared about 1720 in favour of a plain bowl, like the early example of 1717–18, presented by Lord Craven to St. John's College, Cambridge. One of the largest known is Sir Watkin Williams Wynn's bowl of 1726–7 at Jesus College, Oxford, where, according to an old tradition, any member of the College who could encircle the bowl with his arms and drain it of the liquor might proudly carry it away in triumph as his own property.

A small plain punch bowl, made in London in 1768–9, is, like the cup mentioned on page 150, of great interest in the history of horse-racing in America, having been won by the horse Tryall,

PLATE XXXV

PLATE XXXVI

ENGLAND

the property of William Allston, Esq., at Newmarket, near Charleston, South Carolina, in 1768. It is illustrated and fully described in the *Connoisseur* for December, 1919; July, 1921, pp. 164–5; and July, 1922, p. 164.

Four old American punch bowls are described on pages 29–30.

A word must be said about the punch ladles of silver, and others of whalebone and silver, made in great numbers in the eighteenth century. The latter were intended mostly for ladling punch from the bowls of earthenware and porcelain.

Writers on old English plate have long been puzzled by the decoration on a certain piece of silver—the little sweetmeat dish which first came into vogue in the reign of Charles I, and remained a fairly popular ornament of the table until the early years of his son and successor on the throne. Much has been written on this vessel, but no theory has so far been advanced for the origin of the unusual decoration. A second characteristic of this dish is its flimsiness, which is in marked contrast with the massiveness of most English plate of the time. The present writer ventures to suggest that the source from which the Carolean silversmiths derived the little punched flowers, rosettes and other ornament and the small pearl-like beads was the contemporary book covers.

Large and richly decorated silver jars with covers owe their introduction into England to that luxury-loving monarch, Charles II. Emulating the extravagance of his contemporary, Louis XIV, he furnished not only his own palaces with all manner of ornaments and furniture in silver, but also (according to Evelyn's well-known comments) the apartments of his mistresses. The form of these jars was inspired by those of Chinese porcelain, which had been imported in large numbers by the Dutch from the East. The surviving examples of these decorative pieces of plate are to be found in the great houses of England—at Welbeck, Belvoir, Knole and elsewhere. Some were made in sets of five and three. A pair of about 1665, with three richly decorated beakers, from the Earl of Home's collection, were sold at Christie's in June, 1919, and are illustrated in the sale catalogue.

In the collection of plate at Windsor Castle are several silver sconces of Charles II and William and Mary, illustrated in *The Gold and Silver of Windsor Castle*. Sconces for the wall have a long history in England, as may be observed from the inventories of the Tudor period, though none have survived. Those of Charles I were converted into coin in the Civil War, with other priceless treasures. Unfortunately, there was not in the seventeenth century, as in Holland, a great school of English painters of interiors to hand down to posterity authentic pictures of the internal decoration and of the sumptuous furniture of the house of a nobleman in this, the reign of Charles II, the most extravagant period in English history: " Golden sconces to hang upon the walls, to light the costly suppers and the balls."—(Dryden.)

Among many notable silver sconces are the superb sets of twelve of 1685–6, and another set of about the same date, at Knole. A set of eight, part of the plate of William III, date about 1700, was sold for £965 10s. at Christie's on May 24, 1924.

Charles II himself had no doubt become familiar, during his exile in the Low Countries, with many silver vessels, almost unknown in England. Among these were silver sconces, like the four shown in a picture at Windsor Castle, by Hieronymus Janssens (1624–93), a Flemish painter, depicting a ball given at The Hague by Charles's widowed sister, Mary, Princess of Orange, in celebration of his restoration to the English throne, when he was surrounded by relatives, including his aunt Elizabeth, Queen of Bohemia, whose silver ewer and dish and cup are illustrated later.

The fashion of lighting rooms by means of sconces waned after the accession of Queen Anne, though here and there a pair may be seen of later date, as, for example, those of 1703–4 in the Victoria and Albert Museum, and a set of six, decorated with classical subjects, made in 1730–1 by Peter Archambo and bequeathed to Lady Grey, of Enville Hall, by the Earl of Stamford and Warrington.

The history of English andirons or fire-dogs runs almost parallel with that of sconces. All that now remain of the great collection formerly at Windsor Castle are two pairs, dating from the reigns of Charles II and William III. No English examples in silver earlier than the reign of Charles II, have survived, though made of that metal in or before the time of Shakespeare, who refers to the andirons in Imogen's chamber as two winking cupids of silver. The shape of the English andirons of Charles II was probably derived from the fire-dogs of brass, to be seen in every house of moderate comfort in the Holland of Rembrandt, Franz Hals and Vermeer and other painters of the seventeenth century, and as may be seen in one of Pieter de Hooch's interiors in the National Gallery in London.

The Duke of Buccleuch is not only the fortunate possessor of a valuable collection of Charles II silver sconces, but also a great number of silver fire-dogs of that luxurious period. One of the finest pairs are surmounted by figures of Cleopatra. A later and simpler pair, with large plain ball tops on scrolled feet, of the short reign of James II, bear some resemblance to those in the designs of the French artist, François Poilly (1622–93). Knole, famous for its silver furniture and other artistic and historic treasures, contains five pairs, including a pair surmounted by figures of the young Bacchus and enriched with female busts in front, not unlike those on the contemporary sconces at Windsor Castle. Other fire-dogs of silver are described in the introduction to *The Gold and Silver of Windsor Castle*.

A pair, by Benjamin Pyne, 1697–8, have passed through the hands of Messrs. Crichton Bros. (Plate XXXV, No. 5).

Some silver andirons at Windsor Castle were the innocent cause of the discontinuance of the drawing lessons given to George IV in boyhood by a Mr. Elliott. His royal father had been dissatisfied with certain drawings submitted to him, and promised the young prince a day's holiday in Windsor forest if he could make a good drawing of these andirons. The work, however, proved to be unsatisfactory and the future King's lessons came to an abrupt end.

Of the plate of the Charles II period—introduced, however, two or three years before 1660—none is more characteristic than a large tazza, or salver on a foot, about 25 in. in diameter, embossed on the wide rim with a lion, unicorn, a hound and a stag amid large embossed flowers, like one at Windsor Castle and four of about 1662–3 sent by Charles II to the Tsar Alexis of Russia, which are now in the Kremlin. Several others are known, including one of

1662–3, decorated with amorini among tulips on the wide rim, and engraved with the arms of the great Earl of Clarendon ; this historic piece of domestic plate is in St. Martin's Church, Salisbury. In other branches of contemporary English art the same animals and birds amid monstrous blossoms—perhaps introduced as a compliment to the King's fondness for zoological specimens, especially birds—were employed, for example, in the needlework pictures.

Towards the end of the seventeenth century a smaller tazza had become common ; it was mostly plain, with gadrooned edges,* and was used as a salver for serving a glass of wine, in the manner shown in the engraving of the sixth apartment at Versailles by Antoine Trouvain, 1698. The reign of this vessel was of short duration, having been superseded by the small salvers. An example of the year 1694–5 is illustrated on Plate XXXVI (No. 6).

Silver warming-pans are great rarities in England. Although records have come down of such things of the reign of Charles II, to wit, the " noble warming-pan " presented to Pepys by Captain Beckford, the only example of that period known to the author is one of 1662–3, now in America. The only other extant specimen in silver of any period is one made by Seth Lofthouse in 1715–16, which belonged to Queen Caroline and afterwards to Queen Charlotte, and is at Buckingham Palace.

Of great rarity also are silver bellows, probably not more than two being known. One of these is in the possession of the Earl of Dysart (Plate XXXV, No. 1). There is, however, a rare example of a bellows at Windsor Castle, made of marqueterie and silver, traditionally associated with Nell Gwynn and bearing the cipher and crown of Charles II.

For the ladies of fashion in the luxurious age of Charles II there were the toilet services, but few have survived in a complete condition. Others have gone into the furnace with the " great looking-glass and toilet of beaten and massive gold " belonging to the Queen herself. One is the richly decorated Calverley service of 1683–4 in the Victoria and Albert Museum. The late Lord Swayth-

---

* See pages 38–40.

ENGLAND

ling's service of the same date, chased in the "Chinese" taste, is well known.

If toilet services of the luxurious period of Charles II are rare, more than one may be mentioned of the reign of William III. Three were made by one silversmith alone, Daniel Garnier, one of the Huguenot refugees. One of these, in the possession of the Earl of Ilchester, is superbly decorated and is of such fine workmanship that it has been regarded as French. His plain service of 1696–7 is in marked contrast and illustrates the reaction against over-indulgence in ornament characteristic of much Charles II. plate. This was sold as Lord Northbourne's property at Sotheby's in July, 1923, and is shown on Plate XXXVII (No. 12). The third service by this accomplished craftsman, of the year 1696–7, is equally plain and dignified and is in a private collection of choice English plate.

A toilet service of sixteen pieces, by another Huguenot silversmith, Anthony Nelme, dated 1711–12, is illustrated in the *Connoisseur* for December, 1920.

Later toilet services include two by that skilled Huguenot silversmith, David Willaume. One was made in 1725–6 and is decorated with straps and other features characteristic of the Anglo-French school. It was sold as from the collection of the Tsar Alexander I of Russia at Christie's in February, 1723, for £3,700. Willaume's second service belonged to the Duke of Leinster and was sold in the same rooms in May, 1926.

The high price of £6,100 was realised for a plain service of 1719–20 by Benjamin Pyne in the celebrated Ashburnham sale at Christie's in March, 1914.

Paul Lamerie's masterpiece is probably the superb toilet service of 1724–5, now in a private collection.

Other objects of luxury in the reign of Charles II were the silver sweetmeat boxes, of which a few have survived. One of the earliest in date is that of the Ironmongers' Company, namely, 1664–5; it is plain and oval and enriched with the familiar "cut-card" work of Charles II plate. Others of this reign are known. Plain boxes of this kind had, however, been made earlier, as may be seen in the example of 1652–3, illustrated on Plate 33 of the *Plate of the*

Goldsmiths' Company (1926). Some of the later examples, such as that of 1683–4, in the Victoria and Albert Museum, are decorated in the Chinese taste.

The specimen of 1670–1, illustrated on Plate XXXIX, (No. 1), is plain and simple, and was a gift to the Senior Common Room at Christ Church, Oxford, by Mrs. Randal Casson, in memory of her only son who was killed in the Great War.

Sweetmeat boxes were also made by American silversmiths after English models. One is illustrated on Plate VI.

What is perhaps the oldest surviving inkstand in silver is one dated 1630–1, illustrated in the *History of English Plate*, Fig. 1178.

Inkstands (or standishes, as they were called) of the reign of Charles II are fashioned like large plain rectangular boxes with two flat covers and a handle in the middle, like some of 1685–6 in the Treasury and the Privy Council Office. Sir John H. B. Noble has a square inkstand with flat covers of the early date, 1682–3. One of Paul Lamerie's inkstands is regal in its massive proportions, and belonged to the Duke of Cumberland, fifth son of George III, whose resounding motto, " Suscipere et finire," is engraved upon it. Another large plain inkstand, in a private collection, by Samuel Courtauld, 1748–9, has a sliding drawer underneath for pens, like the one of 1721–2 by Augustin Courtauld illustrated on Plate XXXIX (No. 7), which was bought by Messrs. Crichton Bros.

Sir Joshua Reynolds introduced what was probably his own personal inkstand, of rectangular shape with pierced sides, into many of his portraits.

A large cistern containing water for cooling wine was known as early as 1508–11, as is shown in a woodcut, ascribed to the German artist Michael Wolgemut (1439–1519), representing Solomon and his wives at a state banquet.

Although no English silver cistern earlier than 1674 is perhaps extant to-day, there is evidence of its use in England in the reign of Charles I, not only from Inigo Jones's drawing of one in Whitehall Palace, but also from the picture at Hampton Court Palace by Bartelmees van Bassen, who flourished 1613–50, representing the King and Henrietta Maria dining in public. An ornate fluted cistern may there be seen, while another of the same design is in the companion picture of the King of Bohemia at dinner. But it was not until the time of Charles II, when silver was employed in larger vessels than at any other period in the history of English goldsmiths, that silver wine cisterns became common in the great houses of England. The King had no doubt been familiar with their use during his exile in Flanders, if the evidence of the picture in the Groothuis at Bruges, by Jan van Meunincxhove, 1671, may be accepted. This picture represents the banquet given to Charles by his brother, Henry, Duke of Gloucester, at Bruges in 1656, and shows a gilt cistern containing a bottle and ewer. There is a beautiful metal cistern in a picture at Chatsworth, painted by the Dutch artist, Pieter Roestraeten, after his arrival in England in the time of Charles II.

Two early records of English wine cisterns are in the inventory of James, Duke of Lenox and Richmond, at Cobham Hall, where a brass cistern and fountain are mentioned; and in a royal warrant for a silver cistern of 1,000 ounces for Louise Renée de Querouaille (afterwards Duchess of Portsmouth), mistress of Charles II. This has shared the same fate as the other precious plate of the Duchess, having long since been consigned to the melting-pot.

The Earl of Rosebery is the owner of the earliest and one of the latest English silver cisterns. The former is a large and fine piece, dated 1674–5, with a fluted body supported on four dolphin feet. Another cistern of great size, made in 1681–2, is in the possession of the Duke of Rutland and is followed by one of a year later, the property of the Duke of Portland.

Not one of the four silver cisterns wrought for William III in 1689 has survived, nor is there one of any date at Windsor Castle.

Several small cisterns dating from about 1690 to the early Georgian period have been recorded. An immense cistern, with two horse handles, weighing 2,056 ounces, the work of Benjamin Pyne in 1702–3, has descended to the Duke of Buccleuch. The Duke of Devonshire has a large example of 1718–19, and the Marquess of Exeter a finely wrought cistern of about the same date (Plate XXXV, No. 4). In the plate inherited by Earl Spencer from the first Duke of Marlborough is a great cistern of 1701–2 by Philip Rolles, and a smaller one of the same date by Pierre Harache (Plate XXXV, Nos. 2 and 6). The larger cistern was several times filled and emptied of the punch provided for the guests at the marriage of John Spencer's son at Althorp in 1755.

The Earl of Home's cistern by Philip Rolles, 1712–13, with two horse-head handles, is illustrated in Christie's sale catalogue for June 17, 1919. Another, decorated in a different manner, with scroll and mask handles, by Gabriel Sleath, 1720–1, realised £1,934 6s. at the Ashburnham sale in March, 1914, and is illustrated in the same firm's catalogue.

The Earl of Rosebery has a singularly interesting cistern of 1773–4, made by Daniel Smith and Robert Sharp, which is decorated in the style of Robert Adam, and perhaps intended, like the silver candelabra of 1774–5 at Osterley, to match some of his furniture. That the great architect appreciated the decorative value of such cisterns is confirmed by the inclusion of Lord Scarsdale's two cisterns of 1698–9 by Ralph Leeke in his original designs, at Kedleston, for the dining-room there, and from his other designs showing wine coolers of wood underneath sideboards. No finer wooden wine-coolers exist than the one of rosewood designed by Adam and made by Chippendale for the Earl of Harewood. The exquisite metal ornaments are not inferior to the best French work of the time, and are not unworthy of Gouthière himself.

Once again the admirer of old English plate is directed to the remarkable collection of English plate in Russia, this time for illustrations of four noteworthy examples of these cisterns. First in date is a large one of about 1705, embellished with the arms of Evelyn Pierrepont, fifth Earl and first Duke of Kingston, which was in all probability taken to St. Petersburg in 1777 by the notorious Elizabeth Chudleigh, Countess of Bristol, the bigamous wife of the second Duke. The Empress Catherine II paid marked attention to the " Duchess," and this cistern is supposed to have been a parting gift to the Empress for her hospitality and protection.

The second and third cisterns were made in 1712–13 and 1726–7 by Lewis Mettayer and Paul Lamerie, respectively. Both these and the previous cistern are illustrated in the author's book on the collection in Russia. The fourth and largest of these great vessels is the well-known example of English rococo work, completed in 1734-5 by Charles Kandler from a design by Henry Jernegan. It was originally disposed of in a lottery, authorised by Parliament, to provide funds for a new bridge over the Thames at Westminster. No record can be traced of its sale, but most probably it was bought by that omnivorous collector, Catherine II, with many other pieces of English and foreign plate. No description or illustration of this great cistern, weighing 8,000 ounces and holding 60 gallons, can be as satisfactory as the electrotype in the Victoria and Albert Museum.

In the first 35 years of the eighteenth century some of the cisterns were accompanied by tall and massive vase-shaped wine-fountains. Among the earliest known are two of the year 1700-1, in the possession of the Duke of Buccleuch; and another of the same date, part of the first Duke of Marlborough's plate inherited by Earl Spencer. The fountain illustrated is by Paul Lamerie, 1720-1, and belonged to the old Imperial collection of Russia (Plate XXXV, No. 3). Such vessels were rarely made outside England, though certain examples are mentioned in other chapters.

William III, a few years before his death in 1702, had witnessed the introduction by the Huguenot refugee silversmiths of a new fashion of wine cooler, or ice-pail, just large enough to hold a single bottle and intended to stand on the dining-table. David Willaume in 1698-9 made a handsome ice-pail of this new fashion, enriched with straps, for the first Duke of Devonshire, which is illustrated by Sir C. J. Jackson. The Queen Anne pair in solid gold of the first Duke of Marlborough, in the possession of Earl Spencer, are of the same form and are unique in gold. A singularly handsome pair, enriched with decorative features in the style of Louis XIV, were made in 1713-14 by Lewis Mettayer as part of the official plate of Sir Thomas Hanmer, Bart., Speaker of the House of Commons, and are now in a private collection. Another important pair, octagonal in shape and decorated in contemporary taste, by William Lukin, 1716-17, were sold for £3,684 in the Ashburnham sale at Christie's in March, 1914, and are illustrated in the sale catalogue.

The fashion was, however, of short duration and died with George I, to be revived in the third quarter of the eighteenth century, as is illustated in the ornate example of 1770-1 in the collection of the Earl of Yarborough (Fig. 1026 in the *History of English Plate*), and in another, dated 1783-4, in the possession of the Duke of Rutland (Fig. 1027 in the same work).

Such ice-pails were wrought in large numbers between 1800 and 1820 in Sheffield plate as well as silver, as may be observed from Mr. Frederick Bradbury's excellent book on that subject. Lord Nelson's silver pair of 1801-2 are in the United Service Institution. Another pair, 1817-18, by Paul Storr, the most skilled of the early nineteenth-century silversmiths, are illustrated in the catalogue of the late Mr. J. Pierpont Morgan's collection. Several others, of 1803-4 and 1808-9, and four of 1827-8, made after the designs of John Flaxman, are at Windsor Castle and are illustrated in the present author's book on that Royal collection.

Inventories of domestic plate anterior to Charles II contain many references to silver candlesticks, but the extant specimens earlier than that reign may be "counted on the fingers of one's hand." One of the earliest known is a small candlestick of silver and rock crystal, which may be Elizabethan or early Jacobean. It is figured in the *History of English Plate* and was offered for sale at Sotheby's in June, 1921. A few years only separates it from the curious candlestick of 1618-19 on a tripod, exhibited by Sir Samuel Montagu (afterwards Lord Swaythling) at St. James's Court in 1902 and illustrated in the catalogue.

In the luxurious time of Charles II silver candlesticks were not uncommon. Rare among them are the pair on wide trumpet-shaped bases, embossed with animals and birds, a gift to the Tsar Alexis of Russia by Charles II in 1663. The same shape was made of plain brass, like a specimen in York Minster, and of Lambeth Delft ware. An early shape of this reign has a clustered column on a square base, the precursor of the unique American candlestick by Jeremiah Dummer, of Boston, illustrated (Fig. 3). Candlesticks of this form were also made in France and Sweden. A curious pair of 1673-4 in a private collection have bases formed of four large escallop shells.

ENGLAND

Shortly before the death of Charles II the clustered columns give way to conventional pillars of classical form, borrowed from the architecture of Sir Christopher Wren, on square, hexagonal or octagonal bases, sometimes plain or gadrooned. Candlesticks such as these were described in 1689 as "candlesticks of the monumental fashion" and continued to be made with slight variation until the reign of Queen Anne. Meanwhile, a new shape had been evolved as early as 1683-4, with a plain baluster stem on a circular or octagonal foot, the date of a set by Pierre Harache. Pepys discloses the interesting fact in his Diary for December 15, 1664, that he began to burn wax candles, to see whether "the smoke offends like that of tallow candles."

During the reigns of Queen Anne and George I, plain and octagonal and hexagonal cast candlesticks were made in large numbers, followed by the decorated cast and chased candlesticks of the Anglo-French school. The introduction of writing cabinets with slides to hold two candlesticks and card tables for four candlesticks provided the silversmiths with new outlets for their work.

As with cups, so, too, with candlesticks, an increasing height and massiveness is noticeable for about twenty-five years before 1755. Tall pillars of the Ionic and Corinthian orders on square bases, with gadrooned edges, had just come into fashion about 1763, perhaps under the impulse of Robert Adam, who was then designing chimney-pieces with classical pillars.

The festoons and rosettes of the "Adam" style in candlesticks were particularly popular among the Sheffield silversmiths of the fourth quarter of the eighteenth century, so much so that London goldsmiths had no scruple in sending candlesticks with the Sheffield hall-marks to Goldsmiths' Hall to be stamped with the London marks, as is described in the last chapter.

Solid cast candlesticks were rarely made after 1755, a new plan having been evolved of making them of thinner silver, filled with wax. Several candlesticks are illustrated on Plate XXXVII, including a pair of 1741-2, which belonged to the conspicuous New England loyalist, Godfrey Malbone, now the property of Mr. George Tucker Bispham.

No hand candlesticks earlier than the last quarter of the seventeenth century are known. In late Georgian times every great house in England was provided with large numbers for bedroom use.

The small taper candlesticks follow the fashions of the larger candlesticks.

Small candelabra are excessively rare before about 1735 and were not made in any numbers until later in the century, when they were produced largely, and of great height, both in silver and Sheffield plate.

Snuffers are a natural accompaniment of candlesticks. The earliest in silver known to the author is the plain pair of about 1510 (in the British Museum), enamelled with the arms of Henry VIII and Cardinal Bainbridge, a worthy gift from the King to the ecclesiastic. Those with trays do not appear until the reign of Charles II, when an occasional example was made. Towards the end of the seventeenth and early in the eighteenth centuries snuffers fitted on stands fashioned like the lower members of the contemporary candlesticks, were made. Snuffers and trays, both in silver and Old Sheffield plate, were common in later Georgian times. Some of the trays have since been converted into inkstands by the addition of inkpots.

Chandeliers in silver are rare. One of the earliest on record was made in England in 1630 for the Cathedral of the Assumption at Moscow—the historic spot where the Tsars and Emperors of Russia have been crowned—but this was melted down during the invasion of Napoleon's troops. Not the least important of the larger plate of Charles II were chandeliers, though none of his reign have survived in the Royal collection. A magnificent and rare chandelier of this period is in the possession of the Duke of Buccleuch. In harmony with its noble surroundings in Hampton Court Palace is the chandelier of thirteen branches, by George Garthorne, goldsmith to William III. A specimen of the reign of Queen Anne was sold in the Sneyd heirlooms at Christie's for £1,292, in June, 1924, and is illustrated in the sale catalogue. No plate displays better the characteristics of Paul Lamerie than the two magnificent chandeliers wrought by him in 1734-5,

ENGLAND

and acquired by the Russian Court, both of which are illustrated in *The Old English Plate of the Emperor of Russia*.

A drinking vessel, essentially English in character, is the small tumbler cup—so called because the rounded bottom will not permit it to tumble over on its side, thereby compelling the would-be drinker either to put it down warily on the table or consume the contents at one draught. The earliest date from the time of Charles II. In the collection of the late Mr. J. Pierpont Morgan are three interesting examples, illustrated in the catalogue. The first is early in date and was made at York in 1684–5 by John Thompson, and the second was wrought in 1715–16 at Chester, where many were made in the eighteenth century. Like other English customs, the tumbler crossed the Atlantic, and an important American-made cup is illustrated on Plate XV (No. 2).

The cup fashioned like a woman's figure, in imitation of the *Jungfrauenbecher* of the Germans, was made in the reign of Charles II, but only three or four are known, the most familiar being one of the Vintners' Company. Goldsmiths of George IV revived the pattern in a limited number.

Shaving dishes, accompanied by ewers, would seem to have been introduced into England under William III. A dish made by Francis Garthorne in 1689–90 for that king is in the collection of the Earl of Rosebery; another, with its oval ewer, by John Diggle, 1691–2, is illustrated in Christie's sale catalogue of the Earl of Home's silver in June, 1919.

The first silver mugs of the late seventeenth century are merely tankards without covers. From that time onwards until the death of George III they were made in great numbers and continued to follow, in reduced sizes, the shapes of contemporary tankards. American silversmiths copied the same shapes, as will be observed in the first chapter. Such was their popularity as beer-drinking vessels that at several Oxford and Cambridge colleges some of the older gifts of plate were converted into mugs, thus lending some support to Victor Hugo's dictum that fashions have done more mischief than revolutions. One melancholy case of this nature occurs at Queen's College, Oxford, where a piece of plate given in 1658 by John Lee, a native of Virginia, was converted in 1745–6 into a mug of the same shape as Governor Paca's on Plate XXXVI, (No. 9), and a copy of the original inscription engraved upon it.

Matthew Prior voices the prevailing custom of melting down old plate thus:

> Yet wisely melted down my Plate,
> On modern models to be wrought.

Two more typical mugs are shown on Plate XXXVI. No. 2 is 1714–5, and No. 4 is a late example (1704–5) of a type dating from the later part of the seventeenth century. All three shapes were copied by the early American silversmiths.

The earliest English silver teapot is dated 1670–1, and is in the Victoria and Albert Museum (Plate XXXVIII, No. 10). Indeed, but for the fact that it is described in the original inscription as a teapot, presented in 1670 to the East India Company by George, Lord Berkeley, "a true and hearty lover" of that company, it might be mistaken for a coffee-pot. In shape and size it is similar to a coffee-pot of 1681–2 in the same Museum, but differs in that the spout is at right angles to the handle.

This early teapot is separated in date by twelve years from the next specimen, which is hexagonal in shape and is decorated with birds, flowers and foliage in low relief, in the Chinese manner; this is illustrated in the *History of English Plate* (Fig. 1,260). A gap of several years occurs before the arrival of the next known examples in the early eighteenth century. These are pyriform or globular, octagonal or hexagonal (Plate XXXVIII, Nos. 5 and 9). Many of these early shapes were copied in Astbury, Whieldon and other English wares, as were also coffee-pots.

A few of the early eighteenth-century teapots were fitted with stands and spirit lamps, like one of 1708–9 at Sidney Sussex College, Cambridge (Plate XXXVIII, No. 8), and the earlier one of similar shape, with the spout at right angles to the handle, by Simon Pantin, 1705–6, in the Victoria and Albert Museum.

The next step in the history of the English teapot is the introduction of the pear-shaped body, like those of kettles of the middle

ENGLAND

of the eighteenth century, which were copied by American silversmiths (see Plates XII and XXXVIII).

The countless teapots of silver and Old Sheffield plate of the late eighteenth and early nineteenth centuries are too well known for a detailed description. Many of these formed models for the American silversmiths.

No earlier coffee-pot is known than that of 1681–2, mentioned above. It is similar to one of 1689–90 (formerly in the possession of William and Mary) in the personal collection of His Majesty the King, which is illustrated in the *History of English Plate* (Fig. 1,261). This royal coffee-pot differs, however, in one respect, that the spout is at right angles to the handle, like the early teapot of 1670–1, just described. In a private collection is another early example, dated 1696–7, probably by John Penfold, with the spout immediately in front of the handle; and a second one, by Andrew Raven, 1700–1, of the same shape as the above-mentioned early teapot, with the addition of "cut-card" work around the handle-sockets. Examples of plain cylindrical coffee-pots with high domed covers and with spouts in different positions may be mentioned, namely, one of 1714–15, in the Manchester Art Gallery; and the second one, of 1719–20, with heptagonal spout, at Corpus Christi College, Cambridge, where it was perhaps used by James de Lancey during his membership of the college before attaining to the dignified position of Governor of New York, and by his son of the same name. In the same college is a cylindrical coffee-pot with a low cover and a decorated spout at right angles to the handle, made by Paul Lamerie in 1722–3. The third example is of the year 1727–8, and when examined by the author in 1912 was in the possession of Mrs. R. B. Drane, of Edenton, North Carolina (Plate XXXVIII, No. 2). In outline it resembles the pot by Zachariah Brigden (1734–87), of Boston, illustrated by Mr. Bigelow (No. 266).

The silver "Argyles," supposed to have been named after John, fifth Duke of Argyll, but apparently first used by his son, the sixth Duke, were much in use for hot gravy after 1775. Many of these have been converted in recent years into coffee-pots and teapots, just as the contemporary pap bowls have been turned into cream ewers by the addition of feet and handles.

Here a slight digression must be made to remind the reader of the great popularity of many household things in silver, hammered into an octagonal—most persistent about 1718—and in a smaller degree an hexagonal, shape for about 35 years in the first half of the eighteenth century.

Chocolate pots are not distinguishable from coffee-pots, except in those examples which have a covered hole in the cover for inserting a swizzle-stick to stir the contents. An imposing chocolate-pot, by John Fawdery, 1704-5, the property of Colonel Fearon Tipping, is of precisely the same shape as one by the early American silversmith, Edward Winslow, on Plate XIII. Paul Crespin made an unusual plain pot in 1738-9, now in a private collection, with its swizzle-stick.

The next stage in the development of the English coffee-pot may be seen in one of 1753-4, in the Victoria and Albert Museum (Plate XXXVIII, No. 1), which was copied, with slight variations in the spout and finial, by American silversmiths, Paul Revere and others, as was also the shape, without the decoration, of the example of 1762-3, by John Swift, once the property of Governor Samuel Johnston, of North Carolina, and now owned by Miss Carrie Coke, of Edenton, in that State (Plate XXXVIII, No. 3). It is by the same maker as the English cup, also in America, mentioned on pages 150-151.

A rococo chocolate-pot or hot-water jug, from Lord Swaythling's collection, was made by Paul Lamerie in 1738-9 (Plate XXXVIII, No. 4). Illustrated with it (No. 7), is a somewhat rare ewer by Ann Tanqueray, about 1725, in the Winter Palace, Petrograd.

As with teapots, so with coffee-pots, a large number of plates would be needed to illustrate the forms of those of the late eighteenth and early nineteenth centuries, which were also made in Old Sheffield plate.

The forms of the little silver cream jugs, introduced early in the eighteenth century, and others of later date, follow in the main those of teapots. A cream vessel fashioned like a cow was made both of

PLATE XXXVII

PLATE XXXVIII

silver and Staffordshire ware soon after the accession of George III. Many of those in silver are, however, spurious.

The growing habit of tea-drinking, mentioned by Horace Walpole in his Journal for 1743,* had already tempted the London silversmiths to introduce caddies for tea early in the eighteenth century. So precious was the leaf that sets of three with a sugar basin were made and enclosed in shagreen cases, fitted with lock and key. The earlier caddies were octagonal or rectangular and plain, while later examples often followed the shapes and decoration of teapots. As tea became cheaper later in the eighteenth century, single caddies were made of various woods of different shapes, as well as of ivory, pearl, tortoiseshell, and overlaid shell and Sheffield plate.

Of great historic interest is the set of three silver caddies (two for tea and one for sugar) of 1737-8 and 1738-9, by John Newton and another London goldsmith, which was a gift to the New England hero of Louisburg, Sir William Pepperell, by his partner in the victory, Admiral Sir Peter Warren. The set is contained in the original leather-covered case with a silver plate recording the gift, and is an heirloom of Lady Augusta Palmer (Plate XXXIX, Nos. 2, 5 and 6).

The first reference to a silver kettle, known to the author, is in a royal warrant for 1687, for one weighing 47 ounces at 7s. 8d. an ounce, but no example of this early date has survived. A kettle on a brazier-like stand with a spirit lamp, by David Willaume, 1706-7, sold by Christie's on May 12, 1926, and illustrated in their sale catalogue, is probably the earliest example extant to-day. Next to it in date is the Duke of Portland's plain kettle of pyriform shape, by Anthony Nelme, 1709-10, illustrated on page 974 of the *History of English Plate*. One of the most massive known is Paul Lamerie's superb kettle of 1713-14, of great size, in a notable private collection. Later kettles are globular, like the interesting example of 1727-8, by Peter Archambo, belonging to Mrs. M. D. Nelson, at New Bern, in North Carolina, which is said to have come

---

* Ed. by Mrs. Paget Toynbee, I, 319.

from the old palace built there in 1766 by William Tryon, Governor of that colony before the Revolution (Plate XXXIX, No. 4). The American silversmith, Jacob Hurd, copied a kettle of this shape, as is mentioned on page 37. The next stage in the progress of the kettle is marked by the introduction of a pear-shaped body, similar to that of the teapots of the time, and is usually decorated in the rococo manner. Specimens of 1742 and 1754 are known. Occasionally a melon-shaped kettle appears, with a triangular tray, like that of 1732–3 at Windsor Castle.

Christie's sold a most unusual kettle on a tripod stand, in April, 1917, described as chased with architectural ornaments, vases and branches of flowers, the spout chased with a male mask and the handle with two female busts. It is unusual in having the name of the designer inscribed: JOHANNES UDE, SCULP[T]. William Cripps was the maker in 1752–3.

These, then, are the main shapes of the English kettle.

Before the death of Queen Anne, some kettles were provided with high pedestals for standing on the floor, like one, made for John, sixth Earl of Exeter, in the collection of the late Colonel Mulliner, illustrated and described in his book, *The Decorative Arts in England, 1660–1780* (Plate XXXIX, No. 3). This is said to be the only example known, but one or two others have been seen by the author. The manner of using these pedestals is shown in Hogarth's picture of a " Musical Party," in the Fitzwilliam Museum, Cambridge.

Large tea urns superseded kettles and stands about 1760, and are perhaps a development from the wine fountains discussed earlier. Many were made towards the end of the eighteenth and the beginning of the nineteenth centuries, and are hardly distinguishable in shape from the large cups of the time. An unusually fine urn, decorated with rosettes and festoons, suspended from lions' and human masks, in the " Adam " style, dated 1773–4, is in the Metropolitan Museum, New York. Of historic importance is the urn made in London in 1765–6, by Francis Butty and Nicholas Dumee, as a gift from the citizens of Bristol to the American, Henry Cruger, one of their representatives in Parliament, for his services in promoting the repeal of the famous American " Stamp

Act" in 1766. Henry Cruger was the well-known son of a prominent New York merchant, who lies buried in Bristol Cathedral. The urn is in the possession of Mr. T. J. Oakley Rhinelander, of New York (Plate XXXVIII, No. 6).

Unique among English urns is that of the Earl of Orford, which was made in 1786–7 by John Wakelin and William Taylor for the old Falconers' Club; it is illustrated in the *Connoisseur* for May, 1908.

Tea urns were also made by American silversmiths, as is mentioned on page 37.

Early in the eighteenth century a salver on short feet made its appearance, to the gradual exclusion of the tazza mentioned on page 132. The first are square, with incurved corners; rarer are those of octofoil and multifoil outline. Later in the century circular salvers, with or without shaped edges, were made in great numbers in many sizes, plain and decorated, on three or more scrolled feet. Some of these are of the same pattern as the tops of Chippendale tables. Allied to salvers are trays. Many important trays and salvers were made by the Anglo-French school of silversmiths before 1750. Two good examples of salvers are shown on Plate XL. The first is finely chased and was made by Augustin Courtauld in 1732–3 (No. 1). The second is a characteristic specimen of 1738–9 by Paul Lamerie (No. 3).

Equally indispensable on the dining table of the great houses of England in the eighteenth and nineteenth centuries was the soup tureen (the *soupière* of the French), which is well represented at Windsor Castle by thirteen pairs, beginning with the date 1761–2. When first made in London, early in the eighteenth century, at about the time of the Hanoverian succession, soup tureens were oval in shape, with conventional decoration. For example, the applied strap-work, which is a conspicuous feature of some Queen Anne and early Georgian plate by the Anglo-French silversmiths, was the sole adornment of a George I tureen by Simon Pantin, part of the service of English plate belonging to the Empress Elizabeth of Russia. One of the finest is the Earl of Ilchester's oval tureen, by Paul Lamerie, 1736–7, with handles formed of cast boars' heads. An eccentric tureen, fashioned like a turtle, was made by this same goldsmith in 1750–1. Both are illustrated in the *History of English Plate*. A pair of most elaborate tureens, with heavy rococo decoration, suggestive of the influence of the designs of Juste Aurèle Meissonier in the eagle and game on the cover, were made in 1747–8 by Paul Lamerie for the celebrated admiral, Lord Anson. One of these is now in the possession of Lord Dalmeny (Plate XL, No. 2), and the other is illustrated in the catalogue of plate of the late Mr. J. Pierpont Morgan. Nicholas Sprimont's original design of about 1750 for a soup tureen for the Earl of Leicester is in the Victoria and Albert Museum.

Many of the Oxford and Cambridge colleges have their soup tureens, in some cases unfortunately transformed from plate of an earlier generation. On historical grounds, the most interesting is one at Pembroke College, Cambridge, made in 1778–9 by John Wakelin and William Taylor, and presented in 1784 by its great *alumnus*, William Pitt, when Chancellor of the Exchequer and First Lord of the Treasury. One feature in the Pitt tureen may be noticed, namely, the influence of Robert Adam in the decoration.

The work of Paul Storr may be seen in two finely wrought pairs, of 1803–4 and 1805–6, at Windsor Castle, decorated with "Egyptian" subjects and fitted with large stands, directly copied from the French.

Sauce boats in their decoration follow the prevailing fashions, from the plain to the florid rococo. The earliest shape has a low plain oval body, with two spouts and two handles, on a low moulded foot, and was introduced at the end of the seventeenth century. One such pair was made in 1698–9 by William Scarlett. As will be observed on Plate XLIII, the same shape was made by French goldsmiths. These were discarded in the second quarter of the following century for boats on three feet, which often took the form of lions' masks, like those on contemporary chairs and on silver salts. Such boats were popular throughout the eighteenth century, until the introduction of large sauce tureens of the same shape as soup tureens. Sauce boats were made after silver models in Whieldon, salt glaze and other English wares.

ENGLAND

Two examples in silver are illustrated on Plate XL. No. 4 is of the common type just mentioned, and was copied by American silversmiths. The second (No. 5) is a rare pattern of 1738–9 by Paul Lamerie from Lord Swaythling's sale.

Throughout the first half of the eighteenth century the predominant type of cup, presumed to have been introduced, or more probably developed, by the Huguenot refugee goldsmiths in London, was large and massive, and fitted with two handles as a loving cup and as an ornament for the table. The Anglo-French craftsmen vied with each other in the adornment of these cups with the ornate straps and other ornament borrowed from the French school of late Louis XIV. In most cups the upper part of the body above the moulding is plain, while the domed cover and the lower part of the body are effectively enriched with the straps already mentioned and other varieties of ornament. The handles remain much the same throughout the history of this cup, and usually have a large leaf, turned up at the end to act as a thumbpiece. In other examples the handles are harp-shaped.

One of these cups is in America, and is one of the greatest treasures of the New York Historical Society. It is of interest for its own sake as an imposing and regal specimen, and none the less as a gift from Queen Anne to Colonel Peter Schuyler in 1710 for his services in effecting the alliance with the Iroquois Indians (Plate XXXVI, No. 8). The cup and its history are fully described by Miss C. Louise Avery in the Society's Bulletin for April, 1921. Another English cup of the same form, but decorated with plainer straps, is also preserved in America, and was a gift to Christ Church, Hartford, Connecticut, the maker having been one of the Anglo-French silversmiths, Isaac Riboulau, in 1726–7; it is illustrated in the present author's book on old American church silver. In the Methuen collection sold at Christie's in 1920 were an unusual pair with handles of rare shape, by Philip Rolles, 1714–15, which were bought for the high figure of £2,879 12s. 6d. by Messrs. S. J. Phillips.

Paul Lamerie was the maker of some important cups of this shape, including three dated 1720–1, 1723–4, and 1736–7, in an important private collection of silver by the Anglo-French school. Lamerie's own taste would seem to have been in favour of richly ornamented plate, but whether in deference to the desires of his patrons, or from personal inclination, he occasionally indulged in hammering out plain objects. Charles Townshend's decorated cup of this type at Clare College, Cambridge, is mentioned and illustrated in a new book commemorating the sexcentenary of the College.

The only example in solid gold is the Godolphin cup by David Willaume, 1732–3, with handles formed like dolphins, representing the family crest; this was in the possession of the late Countess of Yarborough (Baroness Fauconberg and Conyers), and has been frequently illustrated.

A different variety of cup had appeared just previously, in which the harp-shaped handles are borrowed from French or English ewers. In this the covers and feet are lower and the moulding is absent from the centre of the body, which is decorated with straps of different patterns and vertical leaves. Three imposing specimens are by two Huguenot refugees, John Chartier and Pierre Platel, dated 1699–1700 and 1705–6.

Many sub-varieties of the two-handled cup, plain or decorated in the rococo manner, were made in the first half of the eighteenth century. Two such cups, in the rococo style of ornament, dated 1739–40 and 1742–3, were exhibited by Earl Cowper at St. James's Court in 1902, and are illustrated in the catalogue, Plates 106 and 107. Another cup, decorated with leaves and foliated scrolls in relief, by George Wickes, 1744–5, is the property of Viscount Lee of Fareham (Plate XXXVI, No. 10). In the second half of the century there was a marked tendency towards larger two-handled cups, many of them decorated with motives in the style associated with Robert Adam, himself a designer of plate and of interior decoration as well as architect.

One plain two-handled cup of considerable interest must not be forgotten (Plate XXXVI, No. 1). It was won as a prize at some horse races held at Pembroke, somewhere in America, by a horse named *Sparrow* in 1754 (as inscribed), though the cup was not made until 1756–7 by John Swift, the maker of a coffee-pot, also in America, mentioned on page 144. Mrs. J. C. Warren, of North Carolina, is the present owner.

The plain cup of the second Viscount Palmerston, dated 1761–2, at Clare College, and the similar cup given to the Joiners' Company in 1772 by the Rev. Dr. Wilson (illustrated in the *Connoisseur*, Vol. 14), are examples of the larger cups referred to. Many others are preserved at Oxford and Cambridge and in the Corporations of England.

Among the new table silver of the eighteenth century is the centre-piece or epergne. The earliest have massive low stands and solid dishes, like one by Paul Lamerie, 1743–4, in the Victoria and Albert Museum, and the earlier and larger specimen, of 1734–5, by the same craftsman, labelled on the electrotype in this Museum as the property of Count Bobrinsky. This has six casters, a centre dish, side dishes, and four candle-brackets. Later examples exhibit a lighter and higher frame, with delicately pierced dishes for fruit and sweetmeats. In one epergne, dated 1764–5, the "pagoda" illustrates the influence of the Chinese style prevailing both in English furniture and silver about the middle of the eighteenth century. This epergne is illustrated in the catalogue of the late Mr. Pierpont Morgan's collection.

The second example is lighter and is fitted with nine baskets, all exhibiting in the festoons and rosettes the influence of Robert Adam. It is dated 1777–8, and belongs to Clare College, Cambridge (Plate XL, No. 8).

Many of the later epergnes, both in silver and Sheffield plate, have cut-glass dishes.

The large centre-pieces of the eighteenth century are represented at Windsor Castle by two specimens. First in point of rarity and impressiveness of size is one, of 1741–2, by the Anglo-French silversmith, Augustin Courtauld, which is largely decorated in the rocaille style. The origin of such large pieces of plate is traceable to France, where they were made with casters and other things by Claude Ballin, the younger, early in the eighteenth century, as may be observed in those of 1723 and 1728 in the Winter Palace at Petrograd. The best of the English centre-pieces never reached the same high state of craftsmanship as is displayed in Ballin's works.

Baskets for bread or cake first become common in English plate shortly after the publication of Gay's *Beggar's Opera* in 1728, though an earlier one of the seventeenth century has been recorded. The first examples are massive and are pierced with various patterns and are fitted with two small handles at the ends. Within ten years a large single, jointed handle in the centre had taken the place of the small side handles.

Towards the middle of the eighteenth century a number of baskets were made in the form of a large shell on dolphin feet, like one of 1751–2 at Windsor Castle and two of 1746–7 and 1747–8 in another English collection. Some shell-shaped baskets of this pattern are spurious, having been transformed from other pieces of plate with the original marks left almost intact. Paul Lamerie's work is represented by a rare basket of a " wicker-work " pattern, 1733–4, in the late Lord Swaythling's collection, and by no fewer than seven baskets dated between 1731 and 1747 in another. Three have the pair of small handles, already mentioned.

Later baskets are lighter in weight and have the single, jointed handle in the middle, such as one of 1761–2 by Thomas Heming at Windsor Castle (Plate XL, No. 6). The influence of Robert Adam is observable in the festoons and rosettes of many baskets shortly before and about 1775. Among the baskets composed of open wickerwork is one of 1791–2 at King's College, Cambridge.

Small and delicately pierced baskets for sweetmeats, like miniature cake or bread baskets, were popular features of the table in the middle of the eighteenth century.

The Anglo-French silversmiths met with marked hostility from the native London craftsmen. In 1703 John Bodington, John Brace, Isaac Deighton, William Fawdery, Richard Syng and Joseph Ward, all prominent silversmiths, petitioned the Master and Wardens of the Goldsmiths' Company to " use their endeavours to prevent certain Frenchmen becoming free of the city." Furthermore, they appear to have sold their plate below the current rates of the English goldsmiths, some of whom had been guilty of buying it and taking it to Goldsmiths' Hall to be assayed and touched with their own marks. Despite the order of the Goldsmiths' Company, forbidding this despicable practice of some London goldsmiths in buying and selling the wares of the " necessitious strangers whose desperate fortunes obliged them to work at miserable rates," the practice continued until 1711, when certain London silversmiths were moved to make a protest (*Memorials of the Goldsmiths' Company*, ii, 181, 186–7). On this evidence the assumption may be made that a good deal of the plate wrought in London by the refugee goldsmiths between 1685 and 1711 is masquerading under the marks of native London craftsmen.

Notwithstanding the first of these protests, the Huguenot refugees were protected and patronised by three successive sovereigns, William III, Queen Anne, and George I, and their plate bought by peers of the realm and other persons of quality.

The goldsmiths were not alone in incurring opposition. French refugee pewterers also suffered. Jonas Durand, the maker in 1699 of some pewter dishes in the French Episcopal Church of the Savoy (now in Shaftesbury Avenue), was forbidden to add to his touch the words " Nephew of Taudin," his uncle, James Taudin, a naturalised Frenchman, having been Master of the Pewterers' Company in 1679. Mark Henry Chabroles was another French refugee pewterer who was not allowed to exercise his craft (Welch, *Hist. of the Pewterers' Company*).

The glamour of Paul Lamerie's name as the " greatest " goldsmith of the eighteenth century has reached the ends of the earth, wherever the English language is spoken and the subject of old English silver discussed. That this Anglo-French goldsmith could execute plain plate, devoid of all ornament whatsoever, has been observed on an earlier page. Several of his most notable works in plain silver are in a private collection, beginning with a pair of octagonal salts, wrought by him in 1712–13, the year in which he registered his first mark as a London goldsmith and the first year of the apprenticeship of Hogarth to Ellis Gamble, the goldsmith. Lamerie's *chef d'œuvre* in plain plate is a noble and unique punch bowl of 1723, the year of Wren's death and the birth of Sir Joshua

Reynolds. This is finely engraved with two scenes, representing members of the Newfoundland Fisheries embarking on board vessels bound for that colony, accompanied by their supporters to the quay in a dignified procession, and a convivial gathering of the same personages, executed in a manner not unworthy of Hogarth himself.

A small coffee-pot of 1725–6 is one of his happiest works in his plain manner, improved by delicate chasing on the seven-sided spout. His decorated masterpiece is the superb toilet service of 28 pieces made by him in 1724–5 for the marriage of George Treby, one of the supporters of the Newfoundland Fisheries just mentioned. Lamerie's charges for this set are as follows : for the silver, at the rate of 6s. 2d. an ounce ; for the fashioning, 5s. an ounce ; and for engraving the arms, 6 guineas.

Worthy of record among Lamerie's works are Sir John Astley's richly decorated bowl of 1724–5 and two oil and vinegar cruets of 1725 and 1727–8, while a cruet with three casters of 1735–6 is noticeable for the rich decoration. Noteworthy also is a set of seven dessert dishes of 1734–5, made by Lamerie while Hogarth was painting his " Rake's Progress."

Captain Paul de Lamerie, as he is described in Sir W. Prideaux's *Memorials of the Goldsmiths' Company*, died in 1751, and in his will he requests that his two journeymen, Frederick Knopfell and Samuel Collins, should be employed to make ready for sale all the unfinished plate in his workshop at the time of his death. This will is an interesting revelation that all the plate bearing Lamerie's marks was not executed entirely by his own hands. Knopfell himself afterwards registered his name as a master goldsmith. The elaborate kettle sold at Christie's on May 11, 1927, for £237 15s., and bearing the mark of Lamerie for 1751–2, was doubtless finished by these journeymen.

Such are the vagaries of some collectors that they would rather buy a piece of Lamerie's work at a high price than acquire the work of his equally skilled contemporaries of the same school at lower figures.

Disappointment will be felt at the small quantity of plate at Windsor Castle executed by the Anglo-French school, numbering as it does only twenty pieces. Although William III afforded every

ENGLAND

protection to the Huguenot exiles in London, yet not a single piece of that King's plate at Windsor was wrought by one of these refugee goldsmiths. Many have gone to the melting-pot, and others have strayed away, like the porringer and cover of 1685-6 and the gold tazza of 1691-2, both by the *doyen* of the Huguenot refugees, Pierre Harache, which accompanied one of the Georges to Hanover with other important plate from the royal collection of England. Some of this royal plate has been recently sold by the Duke of Cumberland, with 36 plain dinner plates of 1718-21, eight trencher salts, 1718-19, and a remarkable set of twelve two-handled cups, 1719-20, all by Nicholas Clausen, the maker of the silver throne in the Winter Palace at Petrograd. In addition to these important pieces, there was the toilet service by Benjamin Pyne, 1711-12, formerly in the possession of Princess Augusta Sophia, second daughter of George III, and 24 round trencher salts, by Pierre Platel, 1717-18.

Of the plate at Windsor, twelve pieces are by Nicholas Sprimont, who was not only a goldsmith but also a potter, and was the proprietor of the celebrated Chelsea porcelain factory. These pieces include two large salts in the form of crabs and two others, fashioned like lobsters and large shells, all dated 1742-3; and four sauce boats with seated figures of Venus and Adonis, supported on large dolphins, rocks and shells, dated 1743-4 and 1744-5, evidently inspired by the designs of Juste-Aurèle Meissonier (1675-1750). All are illustrated in *The Gold and Silver of Windsor Castle*. By Sprimont is a rare silver kettle and stand of 1745-6, decorated in the Chinese taste favoured by him in the early productions of his porcelain; this is in the Winter Palace at Petrograd. Some few pieces of his porcelain are fashioned under the influence of his silver, such as craw-fish salts and other vessels, covered with the shells, coral and seaweed beloved by him.

The other pieces by the Anglo-French silversmiths at Windsor are a large table ornament, by Augustin Courtauld, 1741-2; an octagonal caster by Samuel Margas, 1713-14; two rare spice boxes by Nicholas Clausen, 1721-2; and four salvers by Simon le Sage, 1755-6.

One of many eighteenth-century objects in silver, which owes its origin to that desire for novelty which was as potent then as it is to-day, is the cruet frame of two bottles and three silver casters, wrought most extensively between 1760 and 1770. Later cruets have oval or circular sides of pierced silver—a mode of decoration which was particularly common in English plate between 1750 and 1790—and are fitted with several bottles, while other cruets have solid sides and wooden bottoms.

These large cruets had been preceded earlier in the eighteenth century by smaller frames, containing two silver-mounted bottles for oil and vinegar, in the French fashion. An occasional example has a silver caster. Several have appeared in auction sales, by Paul Lamerie and other silversmiths of the Anglo-French school.

Casters were first made in England in the reign of Charles II and were cylindrical in form, like the French example of 1630–50 on Plate XLIII. Sets of three are not infrequent from 1685. Sir John H. B. Noble, Bart., has a pair of glass, mounted in ornate pierced silver, by Pierre Harache about 1700, which must be very rare if not unique. Octagonal casters run parallel in date with other plate of this shape. Vase-shaped casters of various sizes were in use throughout the eighteenth century. Some American casters are illustrated on Plate XIV.

Scallop shells were a favourite decorative motive in English mahogany furniture and appear in a design for a table by William Jones in 1739. They were made of silver as early as 1733-4, the date of a set by Paul Lamerie, who made several, including one of 1748–9 in the collection of Earl Spencer. A set of four, dated 1768–9, has been noted, as have several single ones between 1760 and 1770. Four of the year 1814–15 are among the latest.

Reference has been made to the fashion of decorating silver in the flat with Chinese subjects between about 1665 and 1690. The fashion was revived about 1745, and lasted for less than 25 years, coinciding in date with the " Chinese " lacquer and other " Chinese " decoration in English furniture. All the objects were, however, decorated in repoussé. A kettle of 1745–6 by that master of the rococo style, Nicholas Sprimont, and a tea and coffee set, by Fuller White,

ENGLAND

1756-8, are illustrated in *The Old English Plate of the Emperor of Russia*. Among the latest things under the "Chinese" influence is the tea-urn of 1767-8 in the Victoria and Albert Museum (Plate 51 in the catalogue). The late Mr. J. Pierpont Morgan's epergne is mentioned on page 151.

Despite notable gaps, English plate decorated in the "Adam" style is represented at the Victoria and Albert Museum by an excellent group, dating from 1770 to 1790, which would harmonise well with the decoration and furniture designed by Robert Adam and made by Chippendale and the "Adam" furniture painted by Pergolesi. One of the best works is a chocolate pot of 1777-8. Among the candlesticks are some by silversmiths of Sheffield, who displayed a marked preference for the "Adam" decoration.

Pitt's soup tureen of 1778-9 at Pembroke College, Cambridge, and the epergne of 1777-8 at Clare College, Cambridge (Plate XL), are decorated in this style.

Robert Adam not only designed furniture but also silver plate for household use, and among his original designs are an epergne for Lord Lisburne; a cup and cover for the Duke of Roxburghe in 1775; and things for other noblemen, as well as a cup for Richmond races in 1770, as disclosed in Mr. A. T. Bolton's book on Adam. The present author has, however, failed to identify any of the actual silver.

As prosperity increased in the second half of the eighteenth century plate became heavier and heavier, and such large things as dinner services were made. Soup tureens and sauce tureens, entrée dishes and large centre-pieces were added to the list or increased in size towards the close of the long reign of George III. Great silver trays and massive candelabra were not uncommon in the great houses of the land. Tea and coffee services grew in size. Indeed, bulk was the fashion in most of the plate made before the death of George IV. Large cruets, of four and eight bottles, were common in the early nineteenth century, as were large cups of classical form for prizes for horse races.

During the late Georgian period interesting comparisons may be made between the fashions and designs of old silver and Sheffield plate, as illustrated in Mr. Frederick Bradbury's standard work on Sheffield plate.

Despised as they are by the collector of older pieces of English plate, many " collectable " pieces of late Georgian silver of no mean merit may be found to-day.

The new classical spirit exerted profound influence in the arts throughout Europe. In England the fashion for everything in the style of the antique is visible in many public buildings. The Elgin marbles, brought to England in 1801–3, did as much as anything to direct the public taste into classical channels. English collectors acquired Greek and Roman statuary and other antique objects, and it was at that time that many of the celebrated collections were formed. Porcelain and other arts were affected by the prevailing classicism. John Flaxman, Blake's " dear sculptor of eternity," was strongly influenced by classical art, as is apparent in his sculpture and also in his earlier designs for Wedgwood ware. After his long sojourn in Italy Flaxman was engaged to design silver plate for the Court goldsmiths, Rundell, Bridge, and Rundell. His great influence in effecting a change in the design of English plate is apparent from a superficial glance at any collection of family plate in the great houses of England. Indeed, many " old-fashioned " silver things of the utmost interest in the historical sequence of English plate were ignominiously cast aside and melted and the metal remade into objects in the new classical taste. Windsor Castle is rich in great pieces of goldsmiths' work displaying the influence of Flaxman when not actually designed by him. At least eight pieces in the royal collection were designed by him, including a cup of 1812–13, which is an attempt to reconstruct the famous cup in the first Idyll of Theocritus, and eight ice-pails. One well-known object designed by him is the " Trafalgar " vase of 1805–6, in the Victoria and Albert Museum.

The style of the " First Empire " spread its tentacles over Europe, and even to America, in silver and decoration.

Silver coasters or bottle-stands in silver and Sheffield plate are familiar objects. The earliest specimen recorded by the author is a chased pair by Paul Crespin, 1742–3, in a private collection. There is, however, an exceedingly rare stand of oval shape for a wine bottle, 1723–4, by Augustin Courtauld, known to the author. It was not until the end of the eighteenth century that the usual circular form, with pierced or solid sides, came into general use, in pairs, sets of four, and, more rarely, of eight.

Sir Edward Thomason is credited with the invention of pairs of bottle-stands on wheels, for running along the table, as is suggested in his letter stating that Lord Rolle had been asked by George IV to call upon him (Thomason) in Birmingham, in the hope that he might invent a bottle-stand to obviate the necessity of guests at table rising from their seats to pass round the bottle. Thomason told Lord Rolle that he had 40 of the dies of medals commemorating the victories over Napoleon, which he proposed to fit into two bottle waggons of silver-gilt. These were afterwards given by George IV to the Duke of Wellington and are now at Apsley House. This letter, unfortunately, is undated (Sir E. Thomason's *Memoirs*, 1845, pp. 327–8). Bottle-stands on wheels were, however, made as early as 1790. Earl Spencer has a pair dated 1816–17.

Complementary to the coaster is the wine-strainer, without which no house where port was consumed was regarded as decently equipped. All manner of silver wine-labels were also made, inscribed or pierced with names unfamiliar to the wine-bibber of to-day. A comprehensive collection of these labels is in the London Museum.

A small group of old silver at Clare College, Cambridge, illustrated in the new history of the college, deserves notice because of the association with America of the donors, and because one of these and the older treasures must have been familiar objects to six American-born members of the College: William Allen, Chief Justice of Pennsylvania; Daniel Dulany, the greatest lawyer of Colonial America, and his son, Lloyd Dulany; Charles Carroll and John Brice, both lawyers and partisans of the American Revolution; and Alexander Lawson, who, like Allen and the two Dulanys, was active on the other side in that great conflict. This group includes a two-handled cup which is a late example of the English cups so popular in the first half of the eighteenth century and is decorated with the ornate straps inseparable from many of these cups mentioned on page 149. It was made by Thomas Farrer in 1750–1 and was the gift of Charles Townshend, Chancellor of the Exchequer, before he had achieved fame from the imposition of his taxes in America. Lord Cornwallis, when a member of Clare College as Viscount Brome, presented some tall silver candlesticks, made in 1754–5.

The question of the collaboration between the actual worker and decorator of English plate and the engraver of the heraldry and mantling upon it has not received that consideration in books on old plate which the subject demands and deserves. In many cases there is no doubt that an heraldic engraver, most probably an engraver of bookplates, was engaged to add the arms. There is a hint of this procedure in the accounts for royal plate and in those of English and American silversmiths, where separate charges are made for the engraving. But there is more definite evidence of collaboration between silversmith and engraver in two pieces of plate at St. John's College, Oxford, where the arms of the college and of the donors in 1685–6 and 1689–90 are signed by the engraver, L. King. Further authentic evidence of the same combination between two craftsmen, though not in this instance of contemporary date, is apparent in an historical gold tobacco-box of the second Duke of Argyll, known to the author. The box itself was made in London by Humphrey Payne, in 1741–2, while the inscribed panel inside the cover, which was added after the Duke's death, was executed and signed by the engraver, J. Ellis.

Collaboration between American silversmiths and engravers is noted on pages 45–46.

Collaboration was not unknown in other crafts, for example, in English memorial brasses, in what is regarded as the most perfect of monumental effigies, that of Richard Beauchamp, Earl of Warwick (died 1439), in the Beauchamp Chapel in St. Mary's Church, Warwick. At least four craftsmen were employed upon it, including one Bartholomew Lambrespring, a Dutchman and goldsmith, of London. The engraving of the memorial brass to a lady, c. 1630,

PLATE XXXIX

PLATE XL

ENGLAND

in St. Mary Magdalen's, Launceston, and the "Chiverton" brass of 1631 at Quethiock, in Cornwall, are attributed to a silversmith of Launceston (Macklin, *Brasses of England*, p. 298).

So, too, the arms and other devices on old English wine glasses were often executed in diamond point by engravers, as distinct from the glassblowers themselves.

If the zeal for collecting persists, the conjecture may be made that some of the work of Paul Storr will in future ages be regarded by collectors with the same awe and admiration as that of Paul Lamerie to-day in England or Paul Revere in America. (It is an odd coincidence that these three conspicuous silversmiths should be named Paul.) Much of Storr's work is over-elaborated, as is a good deal of Lamerie's; but he was capable of making many things in excellent taste and of fine workmanship. That he could work in plain, as well as over-decorated silver, is evident from the interesting cheese dish of Earl Spencer and from other things. A pair of silver-gilt candlesticks, cast and chased, made by him in 1814-15 for Rundell, Bridge and Rundell, are interesting examples of his skill; these were the gift of Mr. Lionel A. Crichton to the Victoria and Albert Museum. A good deal of his finest work is in the royal collection and is illustrated in *The Gold and Silver of Windsor Castle*.

In addition to the illustrated books mentioned in the text, the following may be consulted: *Old English Silver*, by W. W. Watts, 1924; Catalogue of English Silver at the Victoria and Albert Museum; *Works of Art of the Livery Companies*, published by the same Museum, 1927; the *Plate of the Worshipful Company of Goldsmiths*, by J. B. Carrington and G. R. Hughes, 1926; and several books by the present author.

FRANCE

PLATE XLI.

No. 1 Ewer of sardonyx and enamelled gold, probably executed in Paris, c. 1570. H. 10¼ in.
Imperial Museum, Vienna.
No. 2 Salt, late 16th century, set with two Limoges enamel plaques. H. 9¼ in.
Wallace Collection, London.

PLATE XLII.

No. 1 One of a pair of bottles, Paris, 1682–3. H. 13⅞ in.   Earl Spencer.
No. 2 Perfume-burner, c. 1680. H. 9 in.   Viscount Lee of Fareham.
No. 3 One of a pair of ewers, probably by Charles Petit, of Paris, 1674–5. H. 8⅞ in.
Earl Spencer.

PLATE XLIII.

Nos. 1 & 3   Pair of candlesticks, Paris, 1682; No. 2, Caster, 1630–50; No. 4, Bedwarmer, by Charles Petit, of Paris, 1661; No. 5, Plain tureen, by Jean Baptiste Petit-Boulogne, 1765; and plain oval dish, by Guillaume Loir, 1730; No. 6, Plain sauce-boat, by Jacques Roettiers, 1734; No. 7, Sauce-boat and dish, by François Martin Michelin, Provins, 1760; No. 8, Plain sauce-boat, by Jacques Roettiers, 1734.
(All in the collection of M. Puiforcat.)

PLATE XLIV.

No. 1 Ewer; No. 2, Salt; No. 3, Samovar; No. 4, Pierced basket; No. 5, Double salt; No. 6, Ice-pail, by Robert Joseph Auguste, 1778–9; No. 7, Chocolate-pot.
Nos. 1–5 and 7 by François Thomas Germain, c. 1758.   Royal collection of Portugal.

PLATE XLV.

No. 1 Rococo ewer, by Antoine Sébastien Durand, c. 1735.   National Art Museum, Lisbon.
No. 2 Ewer, of avanturine and gold, 1734–5. H. 12½ in.   Baroness James de Rothschild.
No. 3 Gold chocolate-pot, with stand and spirit-lamp, 1703–13.   Mme. Martin Le Roy.
No. 4 Frame, for oil and vinegar bottles, by Robert Joseph Auguste, 1782.
Messrs. Cartier, of Paris and London.

PLATE XLVI.

Nos. 1 & 2   Candelabra, by François Thomas Germain, c. 1758.
Royal collection of Portugal.
No. 3 Écuelle (with dish, spoon, knife and fork), by Jean Jacques Kirstein, of Strassburg, 1785.   Mme. Martin Le Roy.

PLATE XLVII.

No. 1 Gold wine-taster, c. 1790; No. 2, Small gold coffee-pot, by Jean François Garand, 1759; No. 3, Plain octagonal frame for oil and vinegar bottles, by Remy Chatria, 1733; No. 4, Oil and vinegar stand, by Pierre Germain II, 1774; No. 5, Small gold coffee-pot, by

FRANCE 163

PLATE XLVII (continued)

Jean François Garand, 1756; No. 6, Caster, 1707, attributed to Gilles Gouel; No. 7, Plain shaving dish and ewer, by Marc Antoine Leroy, 1780; No. 8, Caster, 1726; No. 9, Plain teapot, Bordeaux, first half of the 18th century; No. 10, Plain kettle, by Jean-Louis Outrebon, 1785; No. 11, Teapot, first half of the 18th century, probably made at Poitiers.

(All in the collection of M. Puiforcat.)

PLATE XLVIII.

No. 1 Three candelabra, by Robert Joseph Auguste, 1776–83; No. 2, Large tureen and stand, by François Thomas Germain, 1758–9.

(Winter Palace, Petrograd.)

FRANCE has suffered losses in domestic plate of immeasurable value. The treasure of Charles V alone contained about 25 gold cups of great size and 36 gold hanaps of smaller size. Of these many were enamelled and enriched with pearls and gems. In addition there were many goblets, salts, ewers and basins and five great nefs, all of solid gold. Even washing basins were of this precious metal and richly enamelled. Ecclesiastical plate is not included in this brief summary of this great collection. Nothing of it now remains, for Louis XIV completed the destruction of the royal plate of France by converting it into coin for the prosecution of his wars.

One of the few examples of secular plate of later medieval times is the magnificent gold and enamelled cup, decorated with scenes from the life of St. Agnes, known as the cup of the Kings of France and England, one of the great treasures of the British Museum. It was probably made in Paris in 1380 for the Duc de Berry by a goldsmith and enameller, unsurpassed in technical skill by any modern craftsman. In 1391 the Duke presented it to his nephew, Charles VI, and at the death of this King in 1422 it passed into the possession of John, Duke of Bedford, Regent of France and England, and was sent to England in 1434. Henry VI, a nephew of the Duke, inherited it and it remained in possession of English sovereigns until 1604, when James I presented it to Don Juan Fernandez de Velasco, Duke of Frias and Constable of Castile, head of the embassy sent by Philip III of Spain to negotiate peace with

England. It then went to a convent at Medina de Pomar, where it remained for more than 250 years.

The cup has undergone several alterations and losses of parts during its long and romantic history. The knop or finial and a cresting of pearls from the lower edge of the cover, corresponding to that on the foot, have gone. In the time of Henry VIII the stem was lengthened by the addition of the section ornamented with Tudor roses, and again in 1610 by the second section, added in Spain, bearing a Latin inscription recording the gift to De Velasco. Thus the goldsmiths of three countries, France, England and Spain, have had some part in converting this precious cup into its present form.

The attribution to a goldsmith-enameller in Paris is supported not only by the recorded history but also by the similarity of the figures and other motives in the "Life of St. Agnes," enamelled on the cup, to those of contemporary illuminated manuscripts of Charles V or the Duc de Berry, attributed to Hennequin du Vivier or Jacquemart de Hesdin.

A brochure, by Mr. O. M. Dalton, with an illustration in colour and line illustrations, was published by the British Museum in 1924.

An interesting event in the history of the cup is that when offered to several connoisseurs in France by the priestly envoy from the Abbess of the convent at Medina it was rejected as spurious, and it was only at the last moment, just as the priest was about to return to Spain, that the well-known French collector, Baron Jerome Pichon, changed his mind and acquired the cup for a small sum.

Not a single piece survives of the plate shown on the miniature symbolical of the month of January in the priceless Book of Hours at Chantilly, executed for the Duc de Berry by the three brothers, Pol, Herman and Jehannequin van Limburg, in 1410–16. In this miniature the Duke himself is seen at dinner, and the plate displayed includes a great nef and a cup, in shape not unlike the famous gold cup in the British Museum, just described.

The remarkable covered beaker, bearing the Paris mark for 1462–3, at Oriel College, Oxford, is familiar from the illustration in Mr. H. C. Moffatt's book on the Oxford plate.

PLATE XLI

PLATE XLII

FRANCE

The very few pieces of domestic plate of the sixteenth century comprise the pair of massive ewers with their dishes, the pair of covered cups and the oval wine bottle, all conspicuous for their massiveness and absence of ornament, which are now in the Louvre. They had formed part of a service of the date 1581-2 from the Chapel of the Order of St. Esprit.

The same Museum contains the magnificent enamelled gold shield and morion, wrought for Charles IX of France between 1560 and 1574. No others in gold of this or any other period can be seen in any collection. It is a misfortune that the name of the highly skilled craftsman remains anonymous to this day.

Of the end of the sixteenth century is the little French silver-gilt salt in the Wallace Collection in London, which may be described as unique in having plaques of Limoges enamel set in two of the square sides. One plaque represents "Dives in Torment," and was the work of Jean Penicaud II; the other is "Cupid Triumphant," and was executed by the later enameller, François Limousin. Decorating the other two sides of the salt are busts of Vespasian and Flavia Domitilla in silver-gilt (Plate XLI, No. 2).

It is difficult to identify the craftsmen of the vessels and cups of crystal, jasper and other stones in the sixteenth century, owing to the absence of marks, or other means of identification, in the enamelled gold and silver garnishings of these objects. There can be no doubt that more than one craftsman collaborated in the execution, carvers in crystal and goldsmiths and enamellers. That some of the great collection of these princely objects in the Louvre were executed by goldsmiths in Paris, possibly in some cases by resident Italians, is almost certain. Indeed, the gifted artist of the enamelled gold shield and morion mentioned above may have executed some of this work.

The present author ventures to attribute the beautiful sardonyx and gold ewer—in the old Imperial collection of Austria—to a craftsman working in Paris (Plate XLI, No. 1). It was sent as a gift, with Benvenuto Cellini's golden salt, from Charles IX of France to Ferdinand of Tirol in 1570, and in some details bears a close resemblance to a gold mounted sardonyx cup in the Louvre.

Within living memory all such vessels were attributed to Italian artists. But more recent researches have restored many precious objects to their rightful creators, the craftsmen of Southern Germany, Bohemia, France and Vienna.

The fluted covered-beaker in the beautiful portrait of Mary Tudor, Queen of France, of the French school, in the National Gallery in London, has disappeared with other historic vessels. The fact that it occurs in this portrait suggests that it was a favourite drinking cup of the Queen, just as the cups shown in the portraits (mentioned on page 62) were probably the personal drinking vessels of Ægidius and Lady Jane Grey.

If the medallic art of France took the lead in the seventeenth century, but few pieces of plate survive to-day, for reasons already given, to show the accomplishments of the French goldsmiths of that period. No single example is known of the work of Claude Ballin, the elder, except a design for an enamelled gold plate, destined for his royal master, Louis XIV, which is illustrated by M. Henry Nocq in *Le Poinçon de Paris*, vol. 1 (1926).

The exhibition of over 1,000 pieces of French *orfèvrerie* at the Musée des Arts Décoratifs in Paris in April and May, 1926, was a notable achievement of the organisers, and afforded an opportunity to study the subject as had never occurred before. Yet withal it contained nothing of the seventeenth century except the rare bed-warmer by Charles Petit, 1661; a caster of 1630–50; and a pair of candlesticks of 1682, all illustrated on Plate XLIII; and a gold cup and a second pair of candlesticks; and a *coquetier*; all exhibited by M. Puiforcat. Some candlesticks by Guillaume Lucas, 1675, with three other pairs by unknown goldsmiths; and an écuelle by Sébastien le Blond, complete the list, exclusive of five pieces by provincial goldsmiths and seven of uncertain *provenance*.

There was nothing there to surpass in interest the massive pair of plain ewers, made in Paris in 1674–5, probably by the above-mentioned Charles Petit, or the fine pair of bottles* by an un-

---

* Silver bottles of this shape were made by London goldsmiths. (See pages 117-118).

PLATE XLIII

PLATE XLIV

identified Paris goldsmith of 1682–3, both acquired in France by the Earl (afterwards first Duke) of Marlborough, and now in the possession of Earl Spencer (Plate XLII, Nos. 3 and 1). Nor could anything be seen to rival the small écuelle (from Lord Swaythling's collection) and a ewer and dish (from Colonel Tipping's collection), dated 1674–5 and probably made by the above Charles Petit and now in a private collection in London. Furthermore, there was no object superior in quality to the exquisite silver-gilt perfume burner of about 1680, belonging to Viscount Lee of Fareham (Plate XLII, No. 2). Both the body and the cover of the latter are elaborately pierced and engraved with flowers interspersed with birds and with a cypher and a coronet, the whole resting on four eagle feet. The cover is fashioned like a French royal crown of fleurs-de-lis with four arches. The pierced work resembles that of watch cases of the period and recalls the design of Jean Vauquer of Blois, whose book of designs for goldsmiths and engravers was published about 1680, a *fac simile* of which was issued by Quaritch in 1888.

Nor were there any toilet services to compare with that of Frances Stewart, Duchess of Richmond, the beauty of the Court of Charles II, which bears the Paris mark for 1672–80. This was exhibited by Mr. W. A. Baird at St. James's Court in 1902 and is illustrated in the catalogue.

The little écuelle or bowl of 1674–5, just mentioned, is not only interesting as a rarity, but also because similar bowls were made by English goldsmiths. One example may be cited—the covered bowl of 1670–1 at Queen's College, Oxford, which is embellished with almost identical " cut-card " work. The only great difference is in the handles, which are solid cast scrolls, while those of the French piece are serpents.

Rare indeed is a French silver tazza, or salver on a foot, like that shown in Claude's picture of the Marriage of Isaac and Rebecca, dated 1648, in the National Gallery in London, or like the octagonal example, holding a glass wine decanter and two glasses, in a picture by Jean-Baptiste Oudry (1696–1755), in the Wallace Collection, or, again, like the one in a " Still Life " picture by A. F. Desportes (1661–1743). A tazza of decagonal shape, with a gadrooned edge, by a Paris goldsmith of about 1740, was examined by the author in the Royal Silberkammer at Munich some years ago. Vessels of this kind were made of faience in France for those whose purses were not deep enough for silver.

It may be assumed that domestic silver candlesticks were almost as abundant in France as in England in the eighteenth century, and consequently their scarcity to-day appears to be surprising, despite the ravages of the Revolution. In design they doubtless resembled the candlesticks of gilt bronze, executed by the well-known metal worker, Caffieri, and others.

The exhibition in Paris revealed an early pair of about 1655–70 (in the collection of Mr. Junius S. Morgan), similar to an English pair of 1660–1, illustrated in the *Connoisseur* for November, 1906. The same shape was made in pewter and faience in France. Another early pair of a different form, with short baluster stems on moulded octagonal feet, by an unknown Paris goldsmith of 1682, in the Puiforcat collection, are illustrated on Plate XLIII. Candlesticks of octagonal shape, plain and decorated, were made in France and England early in the eighteenth century, and a few have survived the wreckage of the French Revolution, including a plain pair in the possession of Lord Mostyn, illustrated in the *Burlington Magazine* for May, 1907. A small group of silver candlesticks with several coffee-pots and beakers, may be seen in the Musée des Arts Décoratifs in Paris.

Two candelabra by François Thomas Germain, from the Royal collection of Portugal, are illustrated on Plate XLVI. The stem of the shorter specimen is very similar to those of 1758 by the same skilled goldsmith, illustrated on Plate 25 of the catalogue of the silver in the Winter Palace, Petrograd. Illustrated here on Plate XLVIII are three great candelabra by Robert Joseph Auguste, in the Winter Palace.

Whether the two ornate candelabra of gold, designed by Thomas Germain and shown in Bapst's *Etudes sur l'Orfèvrerie Française du XVIII siècle*, were ever made, cannot be determined.

Important pieces of old French plate have been found in England from time to time. The gold cup of the Kings of France and

FRANCE

England in the British Museum and the superb beaker, stamped with the Paris mark for 1462–3, at Oriel College, Oxford, have already been noticed. The collection in the Victoria and Albert Museum is small and contains no specimens of unusual interest. It includes some of the coarsely and flimsily wrought things for the table of the last quarter of the eighteenth century, which in point of workmanship are not superior to the pierced work of contemporary English silversmiths. A silver-gilt frame for a portrait, of fine workmanship, by a goldsmith of Paris, 1672–80, is in the Jones collection of superb French furniture and *objets d'art* in the same Museum.

A rare and important toilet service and Earl Spencer's ewers and bottles and Viscount Lee of Fareham's perfume burner have just been described, as have a dish and ewer and an écuelle.

In the Marquess of Exeter's collection are a pair of early Louis XIV sconces by the same maker as the pair of large silver mirrors with candle-branches at Knole. The former recall the many dozens of silver sconces, including twelve " in the style of Roberdet," goldsmith to Cardinal Mazarin, which were part of the destroyed treasure of Louis XIV.

Rare French plate occurs occasionally in the sales at Christie's. Within the past few years the following objects have been sold in those well-known auction rooms :—a silver casket, described as French and said to have conveyed the letters between Mary, Queen of Scots, and Bothwell, which realised the large sum of £2,835 in November, 1919. In the same sale was a rose-water ewer with its dish of 1738, by Louis Renart, of Paris, sold for £720 ; and an " Empire " service of sixteen pieces by Biennais, which reached £2,400. At the sale of the Bateman-Hanbury heirlooms on July 7, 1926, a dinner service made by a goldsmith of Paris in 1723 for the first Viscount Bateman, was acquired for £1,785 by Mr. S. J. Phillips, who also bought some candlesticks and condiment boxes of the same date.

Collector as Charles II of England was of French plate and of French tapestry and furniture—he sent French silver by the Earl of Carlisle as a gift to the Tsar Alexis of Russia in 1663—old French silver at Windsor Castle is represented by only seven pieces, and not one of these is earlier than Louis XV. One is a plain écuelle with a cover and plate, stamped with the Paris date-letter for 1762-3 and the mark of the silversmith, Simon Bourguet, with that of the farmer-general, Jean Jacques Prevost. It is engraved with the initial of Napoleon, crowned, and is one of the Napoleonic relics at Windsor Castle, and according to the inscription was taken at Waterloo. Here, it may be noted parenthetically, that in the old collection of the Kings of Bavaria in the Silberkammer at Munich is another écuelle and cover, bearing the same maker's marks.

Second in date are a pair of massive and elaborate soup tureens on stands in the Louis XVI style, wrought in 1787 by that unfortunate goldsmith, Henri Auguste. They were bought by George III at the sale of the effects of the Neapolitan Ambassador to the Court of St. James, and are illustrated in the present author's book on the royal collection with the above écuelle.

The next pieces of plate are five objects by Jean Baptiste Claude Odiot (1763-1850), of Paris, the well-known goldsmith of Napoleon I. Three of these, which should be classified as ornaments rather than as plate, are statuettes and groups of Perseus, Silenus, Pan and a nymph, and Hercules and the bull, and were no doubt executed chiefly by one of the several sculptors who designed for and collaborated with Odiot in his great undertakings for the Court of Napoleon. One of the other Odiot pieces is a small stand in the form of a satyr holding a wreath in his uplifted hands and containing a plain loose bowl in the form of a woman's breast, which is modelled after that of Pauline Borghese, Napoleon's sister-in-law. The last piece is a pair of small salt-cellars in the shape of a donkey carrying double baskets. All these are illustrated in the above book on the plate at Windsor Castle. There are copies of the two last objects in the same collection, made by Paul Storr in 1816-17 and 1810-11, respectively.

Odiot came of a family of silversmiths established in Paris as early as 1690. His long and successful career began with his appointment as goldsmith to Napoleon Bonaparte, after the downfall of Robert Joseph Auguste, the celebrated silversmith to the Court

PLATE XLV

PLATE XLVI

of Louis XVI, whose models, designs and tools he purchased. Odiot was assisted in the designs for much of his silver work by many prominent artists—Moreau, Prud'hon, Lafitte, Garneray and Cavillier, while some models were executed by such well-known men as Chaudet, Dumont and Roguier. The gifted *ciseleur*, Thomire, was one of Odiot's chief collaborators. Among the chief works from Odiot's atelier were the silver-gilt service, begun by Robert Joseph Auguste, which was presented to the Emperor by the city of Paris; the toilet service of the Empress Marie Louise; and the cradle for the King of Rome, executed with the assistance of Prud'hon. Odiot's fame as the maker of the popular "Empire" style spread over Europe, and there was hardly a court where some of his silver was not to be seen. Russian and Austrian nobles were among the most extensive purchasers of his work. Names famous in English military history, such as those of the Duke of Wellington and Lord Combermere, and English diplomatists, such as Lord Stewart, Ambassador at Vienna, appear in Odiot's original account books, preserved intact by his successors in the business in Paris. The "Iron Duke," when British Ambassador in Paris, was a frequent visitor to Odiot's atelier, and bought in November, 1815, a large pair of candelabra for 8,584 francs. Lord Lucan in 1816 purchased a toilet set (apparently similar to one sold in 1818 to Lady Vernon), an oval teapot, a chocolate-pot and other things. Lord Stewart's purchases included two small soup tureens in August, 1819. It would be impossible to enumerate even briefly within these necessarily short notes the great number of pieces of "Empire" plate by Odiot seen by the present writer, scattered in European collections. But a few pieces may be mentioned: the large service of the King of Bavaria at Munich; and a charming chocolate service, presented by Napoleon to the Prince de Wagram, on his marriage, which is, or was, in the collection of Monsieur G. Sortais. Of pathetic interest are Napoleon's silver-gilt toilet basin and ewer, from Odiot's atelier, which, in the words of the Earl of Rosebery, displayed an uncongenial splendour amid the general squalor of his bedroom at St. Helena. These were last recorded as in the possession of Prince Murat.

In the Musée des Arts Décoratifs in Paris is a case of models of silver by Odiot, from designs by Prud'hon, Moreau, Garneray and Cavillier, and from models by Chaudet, Dumont and Roguier.

A large cup of historic interest, executed in the Empire style, is in the Royal United Service Institution. It was a gift in 1816 to Lieut-General Sir Hudson Lowe by the Municipal Council of Marseilles for his services in saving the city from pillage in July, 1815, shortly before he was given the custody of Napoleon. It is signed " Charles Cahier, orfèvre du Roi, Paris."

The écuelle is a vessel as peculiar to France as is the quaich to Scotland, the porringer to America and the tankard to Northern Europe and Colonial America, and was a favourite piece of plate in the Regency and rococo periods. Of the fifty or more shown in the Exhibition in Paris in 1926, about half were made between 1714 and 1770. Outside Paris the écuelle was made in large numbers by the goldsmiths of Strassburg, where one of the earliest known, dating from 1680, was exhibited. Next in date came one from the Louvre, the work in 1690-1 of Sébastien Le Blond, of Paris, and adorned with the arms of the Grand Dauphin. Of the six objects from the famous atelier of Thomas Germain, master in 1720, two were écuelles, one of which was the finely wrought piece made in 1733-4 for, and enriched with the arms of, Cardinal Motta e Silva, now in the Louvre. They include also a charming pair of candlesticks, 1734, in Mr. Junius S. Morgan's collection.

It would seem that the earlier écuelles had flat covers, with a handle on top, while in the eighteenth century the covers were mostly domed, and surmounted by finials. Two handles are invariably fixed to the sides, in the manner of the Scottish quaich and the single handle of the American porringer. Most examples have dishes.

A superb Louis XVI example with its dish, spoon, knife and fork and original leather case, is in the possession of Mme. Martin Le Roy, of Paris, by whose courtesy it is illustrated (Plate XLVI). The maker was Jean Jacques Kirstein, a flourishing goldsmith of Strassburg, in 1785.

Outside France the following écuelles have been noted : one,

PLATE XLVII

PLATE XLVIII

FRANCE

described as made at Perpignan in 1680-4, in the Victoria and Albert Museum ; Napoleon's écuelle at Windsor Castle, by Simon Bourguet, 1762-3, the maker of another in the Royal Silberkammer at Munich ; one by a goldsmith of Bordeaux, in the possession of Earl Spencer ; and some seen by the author in Quebec, in Canada.

The écuelle was also made of faience and pewter in France.

Rarely was this household vessel made in other countries. German goldsmiths made a few, such as the one by a Munich craftsman of about 1740, which is in the Silberkammer at Munich. Others by the Augsburg silversmith, Johann Engelbrecht (died in 1748) have been noted by the author. The écuelle was never popular in England, notwithstanding the flourishing school of Anglo-French goldsmiths in London between 1685 and 1750. One example of English work was, however, in the collection of the Duke of Cumberland, made by Thomas Heming, goldsmith to George III, and inscribed as the gift of Queen Charlotte to Mrs. Louisa Cheveley. An earlier one, by the Huguenot refugee goldsmith, Daniel Garnier, 1694, is in the collection of Sir John H. B. Noble, Bart. A late écuelle by a goldsmith of Naples is on loan at the Victoria and Albert Museum.

Just as the finest Sèvres porcelain is to be found outside the country of origin, namely, in England and Russia, so, too, the fact is undeniable that no single collection of French eighteenth-century silver, in France itself, whether public or private, can rival in splendour and in extent the old Imperial collection of Russia and the collection of the Kings of Portugal at Lisbon. Happily, the *chefs-d'œuvre* in Russia, acquired for the most part by that insatiable collector, Catherine II, are accessible for study and comparison in the illustrations in Baron A. de Foelkersam's catalogue. In date they begin with three splendid *surtouts-de-table* by Claude Ballin, the younger, wrought between 1723 and 1728. Soup tureens on stands, of unsurpassed splendour, are in the collection, by such masters of the goldsmith's craft in Paris as Paul Charvel and Louis Lenhendrick, all executed in 1769-70, and others by Robert Joseph Auguste in 1776-8 and Antoine Boullier in 1782-4, the last of whom was the author in 1778 of a superb toilet service, illustrated on page 168 of M. Henry Nocq's book. Great tureens, candlesticks and other objects of great importance and technical skill, by François Thomas Germain, 1750-62, are also illustrated, together with three charming *surtouts-de-table*, representing Bacchus et Amour, Le Réveil de l'Amour, and L'Enfance de la Comédie, also by the same master.

The collection is rich in candelabra and candlesticks of characteristic French style and workmanship, by Lenhendrick, 1769-70, and Jacques Röettiers, 1770, the second of whom is represented also by a soup tureen, on Plate 31 in the catalogue, and by some ice-pails and other vessels. Edme Pierre Balzac—the skilled craftsman of the rococo *soupière* in 1763-4, shown on page 60 of M. Nocq's book—was the maker of a quantity of dinner plates in solid silver. Illustrations are also included by Baron de Foelkersam of specimens of exquisite Louis XVI dessert knives, spoons and forks, executed in Paris in 1778-9 by Claude Augustus Aubry for the celebrated service of Sèvres porcelain of Catherine II. Robert Joseph Auguste furnished the Empress with no fewer than four table services during the years 1776-1783, named the "Catherine II," "Nijni-Novgorod," "Kazan" and "Moscow." The first and third were partly from his own hands and partly by Louis Lenhendrick and Charles Sprimann, while the second and fourth were by Auguste himself. The three great candelabra of 1776-83 on Plate XLVIII bear the mark of Auguste.

Silver in the style of the First Empire is richly represented in the Russian collection by the chief exponents of that style in Paris—Martin Guillaume Biennais and Jean Baptiste-Claude Odiot.

By French provincial goldsmiths are an écuelle from Marseilles, of the date 1760, and four candelabra by a craftsman of Dijon in 1785.

Not the least interesting features of the collection in the Winter Palace are the great vessels in Louis XVI style, executed by the German goldsmiths, members of the family of Drentwett, Gottlieb Mentzel and Joh. Ph. Heckenauer, all of Augsburg, and those inspired by some of François Thomas Germain's works, made by J. F. Köpping, of St. Petersburg, in 1769. Just Nicolaus Lundt, also of St. Petersburg, executed plate in Louis XVI style for Catherine II in 1783.

It is convenient here to digress by referring to the dinner service executed by Biennais for the Court of Bavaria, preserved in part at Munich, with copies of some of the vessels by the Munich goldsmith, Weishaupt.

The author is privileged to add a few illustrations on Plate XLIV of choice specimens from the great collection of the Crown of Portugal, some of which are already familiar from Bapst's book on the subject. These include a fluted salt, and a salt formed of two cupids, by François Thomas Germain, and candelabra by the same master, the pillars of which are similar to those of some candlesticks of 1758 by the same goldsmith, shown on Plate 25 of Baron de Foelkersam's catalogue of the collection in the Winter Palace. The ice-pail by Robert Joseph Auguste is almost identical with those of 1778-9 from his atelier, in the Winter Palace.

Some of the French plate was lost in the flight of the Portuguese royal family to Rio de Janeiro in 1808, from the threatened invasion of Portugal by Napoleon.

Bapst in his book on the superb French collection of the Crown of Portugal had attributed all the pieces to François Thomas Germain. It now appears from the marks, disclosed by the careful examination by M. de Figueiredo and M. Luis Keil, that this skilful goldsmith cannot be credited with many important specimens. Furthermore, the sixteen small silver-gilt statuettes, so typically French in style and workmanship, are attributed by the Marquis de Foz in his monograph upon the same Royal collection, to one Edme-François Godin, who was only the intermediary for their acquisition. The marks stamped upon them include the initials, A.N.C., believed to be those of Ambroise-Nicolas Cousinet, by whom only one piece was shown in the exhibition in Paris in 1926, namely, a *cabaret à chocolat*, dated 1775-6. Bapst was mistaken in giving some candelabra to Germain, for the marks indicate the maker as Louis Thomas Lenhendrick in 1757-8.

One interesting point in the splendid toilet service by François Thomas Germain at Lisbon is that the snuffers bear the marks of

Pierre Germain and of an unknown goldsmith with the initials, A.D.

A few other interesting pieces of the eighteenth century, the great age of French furniture and decoration, may be noticed. The Baroness James de Rothschild's ewer of avanturine mounted in solid gold in the rococo style by a goldsmith of Paris in 1734-5, stands alone (Plate XLV, No. 2). Exhibited with it in Paris in 1926 was a drawing of the cover, handle and foot, by Boucher *fils*. The ewer was sold in the celebrated Hamilton Palace sale in 1882 for the high price of £2,467 10s. Of great interest, too, are Marie Antoinette's ewer and basin of crystal, mounted in gold by the Paris goldsmith, Jean Ecosse, in 1731-2, which are now in the Louvre. Another vessel of crystal with mounts of gold is the small tankard of 1767-8, in the Wallace Collection in London, stamped with the maker's initials, perhaps those of Antoine Victor Joseph de Vaast.

Gold plate is rare enough in all countries to arouse more than a fleeting interest. Two small coffee pots of 1759 and 1756, both by Jean François Garand, of Paris; and a wine taster, in the collection of M. Puiforcat are noteworthy (Plate XLVII, Nos. 2, 5 and 1). In the same collection is a gold ewer and a *soupière* of silver, both of 1790, by Henri Auguste, the maker of the soup tureens at Windsor Castle, already mentioned, and of a charming little soap box in the Metropolitan Museum, New York. Auguste was unfortunate and was obliged to flee in 1809 to England and thence to Jamaica, where he died in 1816. Meanwhile, in 1810, he had been condemned to six years' punishment in irons and to prison. Rare, too, is an escallop shell of gold in the Germain service at Lisbon.

Yet another important piece of gold plate finds a place here, the chocolate pot on a stand, made between 1703 and 1713, which has passed through the well-known collections of Pichon, Demidoff, Eudel, Montgermont and Doistau, into the possession of Mme. Martin Le Roy (Plate XLV, No. 3).

One of the most conspicuous, and certainly the most prolific, of the Paris goldsmiths in the eighteenth century was Robert Joseph Auguste—a pupil of Thomas Germain—goldsmith to the Court of

Louis XVI. The author has seen silver from his atelier in Vienna, Petrograd, Lisbon and elsewhere on the Continent.

He was the maker in 1782 of a superb dinner service for George III, which was exhibited at the Musée des Arts Décoratifs, in Paris, in 1926, by Messrs. Cartier, jewellers, of Paris and London. Space can be found for an illustration of only one piece, the oil and vinegar frame on Plate XLV (No. 4).

Auguste appears to have sold the work of other goldsmiths, as is proved by the exquisite service of fruit spoons and forks, in the possession of Earl Spencer, all of which (except one piece) bear the mark of Jean Etienne Langlois for 1786, while inside the original case of the service is the card of Auguste and his bill dated 1786.

In the above-mentioned exhibition in Paris were several important pieces by him, described in the catalogue. These included two tureens, given by Louis XV. to Count Boehme, Danish ambassador; a tureen on a plateau; and candlesticks (part of a dozen), forming portions of a service made in 1775-6, with reliefs representing allegorical scenes from the life of Gustavus III of Sweden, for the Count G. Creutz, Swedish ambassador in Paris, and now the property of the King of Sweden. The toilet service of 1776 given by this Swedish King to his daughter on her marriage to the Prince of Oldenburg was also exhibited.

In the eighteenth century in France, Spain and Portugal, and but rarely in other countries, were made a silver ewer and dish for ablutions at the toilet, called *aiguière avec sa cuvette*, which were fashionable products of the goldsmiths' ateliers of Paris between 1720 and 1765. Illustrations of designs for a fluted pair by François Thomas Germain are in Bapst's *Etudes sur L'Orfèvrerie Française au XVIII siècle* (1887). A superb ewer (with its dish) by Antoine-Sébastien Durand, of Paris, is in the National Museum in Lisbon and is illustrated here (Plate XLV, No. 1). Examples may be seen in the plain pair in the Victoria and Albert Museum and a pair by Robert Joseph Auguste 1784, engraved with the arms of Portugal, in the Musée des Arts Décoratifs in Paris. As might be expected from the connection of the city with France from 1697, domestic vessels in the French style were wrought by the silversmiths of

Strassburg in the eighteenth century. By the well-known craftsman, Johann Ludwig Imlin, the younger, are a pair of these ewers and dishes, of about 1750, in the Royal Silberkammer at Munich, where there is also a covered bowl with its dish by him.

Vessels of this kind, of French faience and Sèvres porcelain, are familiar objects in collections.

Some choice pieces from the notable collection of M. Puiforcat are illustrated on Plates XLIII and XLVII. They comprise two oil and vinegar frames, one of which is a charming example executed by Remy Chatria in the same year, 1733, that Nattier painted his portrait of Mlle. de Clermont, in the Wallace Collection. The second frame was made in 1774 and is of interest if for no other fact than that its maker was Pierre Germain II, of Paris. One of the three casters was wrought in 1630-50 and is interesting as the precursor of the English casters of Charles II, both in shape and in the decoration of "cut-card" work, which does not appear in English plate earlier than the Restoration of that monarch in 1660.

Three sauce boats also deserve notice, as do the rare pieces of gold plate noticed on a previous page.

Among the few important examples of French plate, illustrated in the first volume of M. Henry Nocq's indispensable work on the goldsmiths of Paris (to be completed in four volumes) are an oil and vinegar frame by Jean François Balzac, 1748-9; an exquisite double spice-box, with escallop-shaped covers, by Claude Antoine Charvet, 1761-2; and a finely chiselled *soupière* on a dish, by Jean Baptiste Cheret.

Outside France, the work of François Joubert, of Paris, is represented by a small tea and coffee service of about 1778, in the old Imperial Museum in Vienna.

In the eighteenth, and particularly in the nineteenth, century, every vintner had his little silver "wine taster" fitted with a single handle. In M. Puiforcat's collection is an example, chased with vines, in solid gold (Plate XLVII, No. 1). The author has seen one of silver on the other side of the Atlantic, in the Archbishop's Palace in Quebec. Many of the specimens imported into England to satisfy the demand for them as bon-bon dishes are spurious.

FRANCE

From the end of the seventeenth century French beakers were made in the shape of inverted bells, like those in two pictures by Chardin, "Le panier de raisins" and "Gobelet d'argent." The decoration consists mostly of the conventional Louis XIV straps. Later beakers are plain or chased.

In this short sketch some mention must be made of the influence upon French applied art of Jules Aurèle Meissonier (1659-1750), a most prolific and original designer, not only of furniture and ornaments, but also of snuff-boxes and sword handles and other objects. His designs include two great shell-shaped tureens in 1735 for the second Duke of Kingston, whose bigamous marriage with the notorious Countess of Bristol was one of the scandals of the eighteenth century.

Exhibited in Paris in 1926 were examples by silversmiths of Aix-en-Provence, Amiens, Angers, Bayonne, Besançon, Béziers, Bordeaux, Caen, Dijon, Lille, Lyons, Macon ou Chalon-sur-Saône, Marseilles, Metz, Montpellier, Nîmes, Orléans, Pau, Perpignan, Poitiers, Reims (probably), Rennes, La Rochelle, Rouen, St. Omer, Strassburg, Toulouse, Toulon, Tours and Troyes, all of the eighteenth century.

Exhibited also were designs for silver by Le Brun, Pineau, Duplessis, Delafosse, Forty, Auguste, Odiot and Oertel.

The exquisite gold and enamelled boxes of the eighteenth century, especially between the years 1750 and 1780, for which French craftsmen are justly famous, must for reasons of space remain outside the present survey.

The following sources of information are recommended :—

Eléments d'Orfèvrerie, by Pierre Germain, 1748 ; Eudel, 60 *Planches d'Orfèvrerie*, 1884 ; the writings of Labarte, de Laborde, Lacroix, Lasteyrie and Pichon ; H. Bouilhet, *L'Orfèvrerie Française* (1908-13) ; H. Bouilhet, *Orfèvreries de style Empire exécutées par Claude Odiot* ; Cripps's *Old French Plate* ; and the works mentioned in the text. The attributions in Havard's *Histoire de l'Orfèvrerie Française* must be accepted with caution, for not all the objects are of French origin. A recent work is *Orfèvrerie Civile Française*, by Henry Nocq, Paul Alfassa and J. Guérin.

GERMANY

PLATE XLIX.

No. 1 Covered beaker, c. 1500. H. 11¼ in. Collection of the late J. Pierpont Morgan, Esq.
No. 2 Beaker, decorated in niello, c. 1480. H. 10¼ in. British Museum.
No. 3 "Master" cup, probably by Martin Rehlein, of Nuremberg, master in 1566.
H. 8¼ in. Victoria and Albert Museum.
No. 4 Gold and enamelled beaker, c. 1610. H. 7½ in.
Collection of the late J. Pierpont Morgan, Esq.

PLATE L.

No. 1 Large centrepiece, by Wenzel Jamnitzer, of Nuremberg, 1549. H. 39⅜ in.
Baroness James de Rothschild.
No. 2 Triangular salt, 16th century. British Museum.
No. 3 Triangular salt (one of a pair), c. 1520. H. 3¼ in. Width, 7¼ in.
Collection of the late J. Pierpont Morgan, Esq,

PLATE LI.

No. 1 "Martin Luther's cup" (see page 197). H. 17¾ in. University of Greifswald.
No. 2 Cup, given by Queen Elizabeth to Heinrich Bullinger in 1561. H. 10 in.
National Museum, Zurich.
No. 3 Pine-apple cup. Nuremberg, c. 1650. H. 23½ in.
No. 4 Double cup, late 16th century. H. 16¾ in.
No. 5 Cup and cover. Augsburg, c. 1610. H. 20 in.
No. 6 Cup of pearl and silver, by Christoph Jamnitzer, of Nuremberg, c. 1595. H. 14¼ in.
Messrs. Crichton Bros.
(Nos. 3, 4 and 5 are from the collection of the late Leopold de Rothschild, Esq.)

PLATE LII.

No. 1 Small tankard, c. 1600. Imperial Museum, Vienna.
No. 2 Large tankard, c. 1650. From Christ Church, Oxford.
No. 3 Small tankard, covered with "diamond" work, Augsburg, c. 1635. H. 5¼ in.
Metropolitan Museum, New York.
No. 4 Tankard, 16th century. Collection of Dr. Alfred Pringsheim, Munich.
No. 5 Small tankard, covered with granulated work, Augsburg, c. 1670. H. 4½ in.
Metropolitan Museum, New York.
No. 6 "Poison" tankard, c. 1560. H. 7 in. Clare College, Cambridge.

PLATE LIII.

No. 1 Covered tazza, decorated in niello, c. 1585. H. 7¼ in. D. 6⅞ in. The Louvre.
No. 2 Small cup, by Sebald Bühel, of Nuremberg, c. 1575. H. 3½ in.
Collection of the late Leopold de Rothschild, Esq.
No. 3 Large tazza, c. 1590. Total ht. 15¼ in. D. 15 in.
Collection of the late J. Pierpont Morgan, Esq.

PLATE XLIX

PLATE L

GERMANY

PLATE LIV.

No. 1 Standing cup of crystal and silver gilt, Cologne, c. 1555. H. 12¼ in.
Viscount Lee of Fareham.
No. 2 Double cup of crystal, c. 1485. H. 9⅝ in. Imperial Museum, Vienna.
No. 3 Large cup of crystal and silver gilt, attributed to Wenzel Jamnitzer, of Nuremberg, c. 1550. H. 18¾ in. Baron Bruno Schröder.

PLATE LV.

No. 1 Gold celestial globe, by Urban Schneeweis, of Dresden (1536–1600). H. 9 in.
Collection of the late J. Pierpont Morgan, Esq.
No. 2 Tall nautilus cup, c. 1680. H. 17¼ in. Same collection as No. 1.
No. 3 "Pelican in her piety," Ulm, 1583. H. 23 in.
No. 4 Ostrich-egg cup, c. 1610. H. 22⅜ in.
No. 5 Carved cocoanut cup, mounted in enamelled silver gilt, c. 1610.
No. 6 "Jungfrauenbecher," c. 1610. H. 10⅜ in. Baroness James de Rothschild.
(Nos. 3, 4 and 5 are in the Imperial Museum, Vienna.)

PLATE LVI.

Nos. 1 and 2 Dish and ewer, by Jacob or Johann Jäger, of Augsburg, c. 1645.
Lord Clifford of Chudleigh.
No. 3 Tall ewer, by Kornelius Erb, of Augsburg, c. 1580. H. 15 in. Pitti Palace, Florence.
No. 4 Basin, by Paul Hübner, of Augsburg, c. 1590. D. 24 in. Pitti Palace, Florence.

PLATE LVII.

No. 1 Diana on the Stag, by Mathaeus Wallbaum, of Augsburg, c. 1600. H. 13¾ in.
Kunstgewerbe Museum, Berlin.
No. 2 Statuette, probably Charles I, Augsburg, late 17th century. H. 17 in.
Kremlin, Moscow.
No. 3 "Cannon" cup, c. 1600. Nuremberg Museum.

PLATE LVIII.

No. 1 Gold and enamelled cup, 17th century. H. 9 in. Duke of Portland.
No. 2 Ship on wheels, perhaps by Esais zur Linden, of Nuremberg, c. 1620. H. 7½ in.
Baroness James de Rothschild.
No. 3 Large ship, Strassburg, late 16th century. H. 20 in. L. 16 in. Baron Bruno Schröder.
No. 4 Tall standing cup, 1598. Municipality of Emden.

PLATE LIX.

Large jewel casket of ebony and silver, by Boas Ulrich, of Augsburg, c. 1590.
H. 16¼ in., L. 14¼ in., W. 12¼ in. Baroness James de Rothschild.

PLATE LX.

No. 1 Small enamelled gold bowl, by a member of the Dinglinger family, of Dresden, early 18th century.
No. 2 Enamelled gold teapot, set with enamelled miniatures, by Johann Melchior Dinglinger, of Dresden, c. 1700.

PLATE LX (continued).

No. 3   Tall crystal cup, set with gems, of Frederick Augustus I. of Saxony (1694–1733).
(These three objects are in the " Green Vaults," Dresden.)
No. 4   Helmet-shaped ewer (H. 10¾ in.), and companion basin (D. 21¼ in.), by Daniel Schaeffler, of Augsburg, c. 1710.   Viscount Lee of Fareham.

THIS work is not concerned with ecclesiastical vessels and ornaments, tempting as it is to dwell upon the riches in the churches of the Rhineland.

As a fragment of early secular plate, a recent acquisition of the Fitzwilliam Museum at Cambridge may be mentioned. This is part of a gold cup of about 1200, originally enriched with precious stones, of which two remain, and decorated with figures having some affinity with those on the celebrated shrine of Charlemagne at Aix-la-Chapelle.

The " Kaiserpokal " of Osnabrück, attributed to the thirteenth century, is unique; it is decorated on the bowl with medallions of the Virtues and Vices and enriched with champlevé enamel. The stem and the finial are, however, of a later date. It is illustrated by Lessing in *Gold und Silber* (1907).

Two of the few early pieces of German secular silver are the well-known ewer of Goslar (1477) and the celebrated Lüneburg horn of ivory and silver (1486). This tall ewer has a neck of twisted lobes or flutes, encircled by winged figures playing musical instruments, all applied in relief. A dragon forms the handle, the high cover being of Gothic arches. The large lobes or flutes which form the main ornament appear to have crossed the Alps from Italy, where they were used as decoration as early as 1431, the date of the monstrance at Guardiagrele by a famous Italian goldsmith, Nicola di Andrea da Guardiagrele. The ewer is illustrated on page 61 of Lessing's *Gold und Silber*, where also may be seen a large ewer of a different shape, slightly later in date.

The influence of the Renaissance in Germany is apparent in goldsmiths' work earlier than in any other craft, and may be observed groping its way as early as the last decade of the fifteenth century until about 1520, when it had firmly established itself. But the assumption must not be made that all Gothic forms and ornament in plate were instantly cast aside with ignominy in favour of the new fashion, for the crucifix in the celebrated service of ecclesiastical plate by that most talented goldsmith, Anton Eisenhoidt of Warburg (c. 1554-1603), shows signs of Gothic influence at the late date of 1589. It is illustrated by Lessing in his brochure (1879) on this service. Eisenhoidt was originally an engraver and worked as such in Rome from about 1572 to 1581, when he settled at Warburg. Similarly, reminiscences of Gothic survive in the most surprising manner in some church buildings of a much later date.

In plate, as in German architecture of the Renaissance, the general tendency is to exuberance of ornamental detail. Although figures of saints were largely displaced by the spirit of the Reformation, certain Biblical scenes and characters were retained on drinking and other vessels.

The two chief centres of the goldsmith's art in Southern Germany in the sixteenth century were, it is superfluous to add, Augsburg and Nuremberg. Here the crafts, of the goldsmith particularly, were stimulated by the accumulating wealth of the patricians of those international cities, as well as by the patronage of ecclesiastics, princes and nobles, just as German medallic art of the first half of the century rose to great perfection under the same stimulus.

The garnishing of horns by goldsmiths has a long history in Germany as it has in England. Indeed, so long ago as Cæsar's time it was observed that the Germans drank at their sumptuous feasts from the horns of the urus or bison, tipped with silver. Several important specimens are known. There is the celebrated Oldenburg horn, executed for the Danish Court in 1455, now in Rosenborg Castle; and the Lüneburg horn of ivory, already mentioned. Two early horns are in the collection of the Grand Duke of Baden and are illustrated in Dr. Marc Rosenberg's catalogue of the exhibition at Karlsruhe in 1881. Of the sixteenth and seventeenth centuries several horns may be seen in collections.

Wenzel Jamnitzer (1508-85), born in Vienna—the Benvenuto Cellini of Germany, as he has been called—dominates the literature of the goldsmith's art at Nuremberg from the date of his migration there in 1534. Admiration for his technical skill must not be withheld, overcrowded as much of his work is with minute ornament. His realistic imitations of lizards and insects and serpents recall those of Palissy pottery.

His most conspicuous objects include the great centrepiece of 1549, over 39 inches high, in the collection of the Baroness James de Rothschild (Plate L), which is a remarkable example of his exuberant style and of his love of the exact reproduction of natural forms. Several parts are enamelled, notably the vase containing flowers. The interior of the bowl is also enamelled with medallions of arabesques and cornucopiæ and decorated in relief with masks, amorini, trophies of arms and birds on an enamelled ground. Supporting the bowl are three amorini and three enamelled eagles. The stem is in the form of a figure of Ceres, standing amid plants, interspersed with lizards and lobsters. A long inscription in Latin in praise of the goddess is enamelled on escutcheons. Dr. Marc Rosenberg, in his important book (1920) on the Jamnitzer family of Nuremberg goldsmiths, illustrates the model for the figure of Ceres and a design for the centrepiece itself, which differs in some particulars from the finished work. He also mentions most of the other works by Wenzel, including the celebrated cup in the Schloss at Berlin.

To him is attributed the great cup of crystal and silver-gilt in the collection of Baron Bruno Schröder (Plate LIV, No. 3). The five other members of the Jamnitzer family include Albrecht, who became master of the Nuremberg guild in 1550 and survived for only five years. His fame rests on a cup of crystal and silver in the Kremlin. To Hans Jamnitzer is attributed the elaborate silver bell in the Waddesdon collection in the British Museum.

Bartl Jamnitzer is remembered for his charming and rare little silver figure of Cupid, executed in 1576, which is illustrated in the catalogue of the Baroness James de Rothschild's collection. Nautilus-shell cups appear to have been highly favoured by him, for as many as three were mounted in his workshop. To Abraham Jamnitzer is given a curious writing cabinet of ebony and silver.

Christoph Jamnitzer's works include the great silver-gilt eagle

GERMANY

of 1595 in the Kremlin; a pair of cups, fashioned of strips of pearl and silver, acquired by Messrs. Crichton Bros., from the Duke of Cumberland's collection (Plate LI, No. 6); and two globe cups, celestial and terrestrial, in collaboration with Jeremias Ritter and the engraver, Johann Hauer (1620), both of Nuremberg, which are in the Historical Museum, Stockholm.

Beakers in the precious metals, with and without covers, are displayed in pictures of the early German and Flemish schools. These vessels were popular in Germany throughout the sixteenth and two following centuries, especially as guild cups.

Not the least interesting are the beakers of silver made in the seventeenth century in imitation of the German wine glasses. One of these by a goldsmith of Nuremberg—the birthplace of Dürer, himself a goldsmith in early life—belongs to Dr. Pringsheim.

A highly important group of six covered beakers in the Imperial Museum in Vienna comprises two of the late fifteenth century enamelled in grisaille with animals and birds after the "Master of the Playing Cards"; one of crystal and enamelled silver-gilt, the beaker of the Emperor Frederick III; and two others. These early beakers stand on feet fashioned like animals or figures.

Two early specimens are in the British Museum. The first is of silver-gilt and is engraved with designs after the "Master of 1466," by a goldsmith of Lübeck. The second is decorated in niello with subjects in the style of the engraver, known as the "Master E S and the Master of the Playing Cards," by a goldsmith of about 1480 (Plate XLIX, No. 2).

The beaker of about 1500, covered with plain bosses, on Plate XLIX (No. 1), is characteristically German and is first seen in this form in the second half of the fifteenth century. It rests on three kneeling figures in the form of jesters and was in the collection of the late Mr. J. Pierpont Morgan. In the same collection was a costly example of a covered beaker of gold, about 1610, richly decorated in enamel with designs almost identical with those published in 1594 by Corwinian Saur, engraver and goldsmith of Augsburg and Nuremberg (Plate XLIX, No. 4).

A typical German beaker of the second half of the seventeenth century and the early eighteenth century, with or without a cover, is usually heavily embossed, or decorated with spiral fluting, and stands on three large ball feet. The fashion spread to Scandinavia, and a Danish example is shown on Plate XXVI.

Drinking vessels form the major part of German plate in the sixteenth and seventeenth centuries and all the skill of the goldsmiths was lavished upon them in the decoration of Scriptural, Classical, and other subjects.

The German tankard proper runs parallel in date with that in England. Most of those of the sixteenth century had small tapering bodies, similar in outline to the contemporary English tankard. One such tankard, designed by Georg Wechter of Nuremberg, is characteristic of the type mentioned; the body is decorated with conventional flat scrolls and clusters of fruit, while the centre is occupied by a large mask, also a familiar feature of much German plate of the Renaissance.

One of these small tankards, only five inches high, decorated with conventional strapwork and arabesques and set with three medallions of masks in relief, was sold in the Earl of Home's sale at Christie's in 1919 for £900 and is now in Baron Bruno Schröder's collection. The maker was Ulrich Moringer, or Michel Ludwig, of Augsburg, about 1565; in shape it is similar to Wechter's design mentioned above. Pewter tankards of the same early shape were also made in Germany.

These small tankards were succeeded about the middle of the seventeenth century by others of larger capacity, as in contemporary England, and much might be written on the variety of their decoration, from chasing and engraving on the flat to the bold repoussé subjects from classical mythology, so much favoured by German goldsmiths, such as those by Hamburg goldsmiths in the Tower of London.* The bases of many of the Hamburg tankards are decorated with large grotesque faces, which suggest the influence of the Dutch goldsmith, Adam van Vianen, mentioned in a later

---

* E. Alfred Jones, *The Old Royal Plate in the Tower of London.*

chapter. One popular variety, by a craftsman of Nuremberg, is represented at Worcester College, Oxford: it has on the body the wide vandyke ornaments characteristic of Germany, as may be seen in the illustration on Plate 96 of Mr. H. C. Moffatt's book on the Oxford plate. Bacchanalian subjects, worked in high relief, were also popular in the middle of the seventeenth century. One such tankard, the gift of Viscount Ascott to Christ Church, Oxford, is illustrated on Plate LII (No. 2), having been sold by the College about 1730. Tankards set with coins, carved ivory tankards and those covered with "diamond" work, are mentioned separately.

The bodies of some seventeenth-century tankards have a wide band of granulated work, as in the specimen on Plate LII (No. 5), to be observed also in American, Danish and English plate.

Other tankards were made of German stoneware, mostly with pewter covers; some were of serpentine and other natural products, mounted in silver. In North Germany tankards of carved amber, which is found in East Prussia, were executed and garnished in silver-gilt. One of these amber tankards, by Joachim Wessel of Königsberg, about 1610, is illustrated in Schürmann and Luthmer's book on the plate of the Grand Duke of Hesse. Two examples are in England—namely, one with gilt-metal mounts, 1659, from North Mimms Church, now on loan at the British Museum, and the other, mounted in silver-gilt, in the Waddesdon collection in the same Museum.

Goldsmiths of Northern Germany introduced at the end of the sixteenth century a tall flagon-like tankard with a cylindrical body, known as the "Baltic" type, which was made until about 1630. Many specimens are extant; there is one in the British Museum, and another, from the Pierpont Morgan collection, is in the Metropolitan Museum, New York (see pages 53–54).

What is one of the most curious among German tankards of the sixteenth century is the type with a crystal or glass body of cylindrical form, enclosed in a delicate filigree frame of Italian origin, like the well-known example at Clare College, Cambridge (Plate LII, No. 6). Not more than eleven have been recorded.

In the Figdor collection* is an example, where the important features are friezes of children at the top and bottom of the frame, skilfully modelled in relief from a design by Peter Flötner.

Tankards and cups set with coins were much favoured in Germany, especially by Berlin goldsmiths of the seventeenth and eighteenth centuries. Although medallions of celebrated personages or family connections may frequently be found set in the foot of cups of the sixteenth and seventeenth centuries, the custom of covering the whole surface of tankards, beakers and cups with coins did not become common until after about 1650. An unusually early cup of 1536 set with coins is in the Lüneburg treasure at Berlin.

Double cups are intimately identified with Germany, and became increasingly common from the end of the fifteenth century. The early form, like the important cup of crystal (in the Imperial Museum, Vienna) with Gothic silver cresting and silver foot of about 1485, on Plate LIV. (No. 2), frequently appears of wood and silver.

Depicted in the *Chronique de Nuremberg*, published in 1492, is a double cup covered with the familiar bosses, which the King of Bohemia is presenting to an emperor, probably Maximilian I.

Later double cups were designed by Hans Brosamer and Paul Flindt. The most common of these cups in the sixteenth and early seventeenth centuries are covered with the large bosses (*buckeln*), characteristic of German plate. A most ornate example, with decorated bosses of 1538, similar in outline to one in Brosamer's designs, is in the Lüneburg treasure.

The top cup is often of a smaller size than the lower cup, and was intended for the exclusive use of the bride or the mistress of the house. Others have both halves of equal size, forming a tun. By Hannss Beutmüller,† who migrated from Venice to Nuremberg (master in 1588), are two double cups, covered with bosses, in the

---

* Dr. Marc Rosenberg, *Studien über Goldschmiedekunst in der Sammlung Figdor*, 1911.

† Georg Beutmüller, presumably his son, used the same maker's mark between 1619 and 1622, and continued to do so after the death of Hannss in 1622.

PLATE LI

PLATE LII

collections of Earl Spencer and the Baroness James de Rothschild. An example of a somewhat more simple character, by a Nuremberg goldsmith of about 1590, from the collection of the late Mr. Leopold de Rothschild, is shown on Plate LI (No. 4).

Many others of divers shapes and sizes, decorated in the Renaissance style, may be studied in several collections. Hans Petzolt, conspicuous among Nuremberg goldsmiths (1551–1633), made several double cups. Such cups were rarely made after the middle of the seventeenth century.

There are many manifestations of the liking of German goldsmiths for the large *buckeln*, just mentioned, from the second half of the fifteenth century to the eighteenth century. Cups so embellished include the large specimen, known as the "Pokal mit Christophorus," $26\frac{3}{4}$ inches high, dating from 1486, and made probably by Hermann Kolmann, of Lüneburg, part of the old treasure of that city. This is very similar in form to the "Matthias Corvinus" cup, on Plate XVI (No. 4), the shape of which prevailed for more than a century.

One feature to be observed in these early cups is the cut Gothic foliage suspended from the bottom of the body over the top of the stem (which was continued on cups into the early years of the seventeenth century), and the finials of the same foliage. This conventional foliage is supposed to have been derived from the holy milk-thistle, the venation of which had become white through the spilling upon its leaves of a drop of the Virgin's blood. Drawings of such foliage, by M. Schongauer (died 1486) and others, are illustrated by Wessely in *Das Ornament*.

Some of the more ornate cups of a century later, while retaining a similar outline in the bowl, show a departure in the shape of the bosses, which are inclined to be more circular and larger and are separated by foliage and other ornament. One of the best known and most impressive examples of these highly decorated cups is the great "Diana pokal," by Hans Petzolt, which is in the Schloss in Berlin. Petzolt appears to have achieved distinction for making elaborate cups of this fashion, and repeated one example more than once. By him is a much-decorated cup of similar outline, introducing plain and decorated bosses, illustrated on Plate 5 of the Baroness James de Rothschild's catalogue. Christoph Jamnitzer's cup in the Kremlin at Moscow is a notable example of these cups.

The first of two cups, both of the same form and embellished with these conventional bosses, at Windsor Castle, is of historical associations, having been bequeathed in 1596 to the city of Würzburg by its burgomaster, Henry Wilhelm. Lost for 28 years, it was recovered and was presented to the city by Christian Baur, its then burgomaster. Friedrich Hildebrand, of Nuremberg (master 1580, died 1608), was the maker. The second cup was also made at Nuremberg, some twenty years later, by Michel Haussner. According to tradition it was given by Charles I, when holding his Parliament at Oxford, to one of the high officers of the University.

In All Saints' Church, Fulham, is an interesting cup, decorated with large bosses, which is one of many practical illustrations of the gift of personal drinking cups for sacred purposes. The maker was Tobias Wolff, of Nuremberg, master in 1604. A curious feature is the "steeple" finial, added to match those on two English cups of 1615-6 in this church, probably at the time of the gift in 1689. It is shown in Freshfield's book on the plate in the Churches in the County of London, 1895.

One other point should be observed in the bosses of later German cups is that many are decorated with flowers or foliage in relief.

The gourd-shaped cup first became popular from the designs of Hans Brosamer (working c. 1520-54), Virgil Solis (1541), and Georg Wechter. A rare example of the sixteenth century, decorated with interlaced strapwork in niello, is in the Museum at Nuremberg; the finial is a seated monkey, and the stem is a figure of a woodman. In the Louvre is an ornate specimen by a goldsmith of Strassburg. Two of about 1575 are in the Baroness James de Rothschild's collection. Dr. Alfred Pringsheim is the owner of one, with terminal figures, fruit and other formal decoration, repoussé and chased, and with a vase of flowers as a finial—a favourite type of finial for German cups; it is dated 1613, and was made at Augsburg.

GERMANY

This form of cup was copied by English goldsmiths, as is recorded on page 119.

An eccentric cup for wine was made from the skull of St. Nantwein (S. Antbinus, or Antwein), who was condemned to death in 1286. It was mounted in silver by Abraham Zeggin, of Munich, in 1609, and was sold for 210 guineas in the Wyndham Cook collection at Christie's.

Characteristic of the German Renaissance are the tall standing cups with covers, of the same shape as the cup, presented to the City of Emden by the English Merchant Adventurers in 1598 (Plate LVIII, No. 4), and of Wenzel Jamnitzer's cup at Berlin, already mentioned. The goldsmiths lavished all their skill on some of these cups. Two cups of crystal of the same form are illustrated on Plate LIV. The same shape of cup was made by English and Dutch goldsmiths of the Renaissance.

Chief among these cups (now bereft of its cover) is that which was acquired by the late Mr. J. Pierpont Morgan from Warwick Castle, where it had long occupied a place of honour as the "Cellini" cup. The whole of the decoration is finely executed. It is illustrated on Plate 68 of the catalogue.

Another popular form of cup evolved late in the sixteenth century, and common for the first quarter of the next century, has a deep beaker-shaped bowl with or without a cover, on a short vase-shaped stem frequently supported by three scrolled brackets, on a low foot. Georg Wechter and Hans Sibmacher designed cups of this fashion. In the great Spitzer collection was a rare cup of this shape, decorated in niello. One characteristic example of about 1610 in the collection of the late Mr. Leopold de Rothschild is illustrated on Plate LI (No. 5). Two more are in the possession of the Duke of Buccleuch and two others belong to Lord Dalmeny. Many more are extant.

The German alone among the goldsmiths of Europe appears to have made the standing cups and covers of great height, appropriately called *Riesenpokal*, intended for display rather than actual use. Familiar from the electrotype copy in the Victoria and Albert Museum is one of silver-gilt and enamel, 40 inches high, probably by Hans Schaller, of Augsburg (died 1573), now in the Kunstgewerbe Museum Joanneum in Graz. A pair of these "giant cups," Nuremberg work of the seventeenth century, in the remarkable collection in the Kremlin, are over 60 inches high, and are probably the largest extant. Of the same form are the two cups, 32¼ inches high, ordered to be made in 1571 by a reigning Prince of Hesse—one for himself and the other for the Prince of Anhalt—to celebrate a wager made over the rules of card playing. Lessing in *Gold und Silber* (p. 78) shows one of these cups, called the "*Hessische Willkomm.*"

Cups and other domestic objects of niello and silver are exceedingly rare. One of the most important is the glandiform cup and cover, entirely covered with geometric and arabesque patterns, skilfully executed in niello, recalling the ornament of Peter Flötner, supported on a tree-trunk on the back of a female peasant, by a goldsmith of Augsburg about 1585; it is illustrated on Plate 14 of the catalogue of the Gutmann collection acquired by the late Mr. J. Pierpont Morgan, and is now in the Metropolitan Museum, New York. The unidentified master was skilled in niello work, and wrought another cup, at one time in the collection of the late Baron Carl von Rothschild. A gourd-shaped cup is mentioned on another page, as is a niello cup from the Spitzer sale.

As a highly important example of silver enriched with niello decoration is the large covered tazza, of the late sixteenth century, now in the Louvre (Plate LIII, No. 1). Earlier than either is the rare beaker in the British Museum, already described.

Dr. Marc Rosenberg has published an excellent illustrated book on niello.

The small German cup known as *häufebecher, setzbecher* and *monatsbecher* was first introduced about the middle of the sixteenth century, and popularised by the designs of Virgil Solis (1514–62), and would seem virtually to have passed out of fashion before 1650. Later examples may, occasionally, be seen.

Nests of twelve and six, as well as pairs and single cups, were made, and fitted into each other as far as the mouldings encircling the centre of the cups, hence the title of *häufebecher*. They were

PLATE LIII

PLATE LIV

GERMANY

thus rendered convenient for the use of monarchs and princes on their hunting expeditions and on the battlefield. The engraved or embossed subjects introduced on the cups are Scriptural and allegorical, feasting and hunting, and symbols of the months. The bowls are generally circular in shape on short stems and circular feet.

An example of these little cups in solid gold, dating from about 1575, embossed and chased with boar and stag hunts, was exhibited at the Burlington Fine Arts Club in 1906.

In the Salting collection in the Victoria and Albert Museum is an unusual example by a goldsmith of Salzburg, the lower half of the body being enclosed in pierced enamelled work and the upper half engraved with arabesques.

The following specimens may be mentioned: a set of twelve, ornamented with hunting scenes in relief, made at Ulm about 1610, which are illustrated on Plate 24 of Stockbauer's work on the collection in the Reiche Kapelle at Munich. In the Royal Museum at Cassel is a set of eight, with a cover, by a goldsmith of Speier. To these may be added eight cups illustrated in the catalogue of the Gutmann collection acquired by the late Mr. J. Pierpont Morgan; and a set of four, decorated with hunting scenes, by Sebald Bühel, of Nuremberg, in the collection of the late Mr. Leopold de Rothschild (Plate LIII, No. 2). In the Ashburnham sale at Christie's, in 1914, a nest of six, by Andreas Oettinger, of Nuremberg, master in 1613, realised 1,050 guineas; and another set of six, by a goldsmith of the same guild, believed to be Heinrich Straub, master in 1608, reached 680 guineas.

In height they vary from $3\frac{1}{4}$ to $4\frac{1}{2}$ inches, while the usual diameter of the mouth is about 3 to $3\frac{1}{2}$ inches.

Dr. Rosenberg* records more examples by Nuremberg than by Augsburg goldsmiths.

Cups introducing the figure of Bacchus in some part of the vessel were rarely, if ever, made in England, but were common in the Germany of the late Renaissance and the seventeenth century.

---

* In *Der Goldschmiede Merkzeichen*, which is the book mentioned throughout this chapter under his name, unless otherwise indicated.

To these may be added the contemporary cups fashioned like tuns.

There was hardly a goldsmiths' guild which did not make a pine-apple cup (*ananaspokal*), which is as distinctive of Germany as the "steeple" cup is of England. Introduced somewhat late in the sixteenth century, the period of greatest popularity was between about 1600 and 1650. From that date fewer and fewer were made, until at last, in the eighteenth century, the cup passed out of fashion. More were apparently made at Nuremberg than at Augsburg. One Nuremberg goldsmith, Paulus Bair, who became master in 1613, is recorded as the maker of eleven, including a pair in the "Green Vaults," in Dresden. Hans Petzolt, a member of the same guild and a specialist in cups covered with the characteristic German lobes or bosses, was the maker of the pine-apple cup, called the "Kaiserbecher," which is illustrated by Lessing in *Gold und Silber* (p. 59).

The stems are of different forms; some are trunks of trees, upright or twisted, with or without a woodman, others are figures. They are of different heights, one being 30 inches, and others are considerably smaller. Some have finials of flowers in a vase, others of human or symbolical figures.

Rare specimens are those with a cluster of four pine-apples, like one supported by enamelled figures of Adam and Eve, by a goldsmith of Osterode in 1649, formerly in the collection of the Duke of Cumberland. Another rare cup has three pine-apples, by Andreas Michel, of Nuremberg, master in 1615, illustrated in the catalogue of the Baroness James de Rothschild's collection, which contains two other pine-apple cups.

Illustrated on Plate LI (No. 3) is an example, $23\frac{1}{2}$ inches high, from the late Mr. Leopold de Rothschild's collection, by a Nuremberg goldsmith of about 1650, the maker of another *ananaspokal* with a different stem and base, in the same collection.

The pine-apple cup is rare in English plate, not more than six having been recorded. These were made perhaps by German goldsmiths in London, or copied direct from German models, in the reign of James I. Mention is made on p. 120 of the cup in the Winter Palace which has German and English marks.

It was the rule that apprentices should make what are called "Master cups" upon their admission to the rank of master craftsman in the great goldsmiths' guild of Nuremberg. In the second half of the sixteenth century a certain form of cup, resembling a columbine flower, appears to have been adopted there, and is called a *Becher in Glockenblumenform (Agley)*, or *Ackleybecher*. One in the Victoria and Albert Museum is decorated with figures of goddesses, and is believed to have been made by Martin Rehlein, of Nuremberg (master in 1566), as his model for a trial work (Plate XLIX, No. 3). There are other cups of the same type, but differently decorated, in the British Museum, the Gewerbe Museum at Nuremberg, and the Hungarian National Museum at Budapest. An example realised the high price of £3,244 10s. in the celebrated Hamilton Palace sale at Christie's.

Only one piece is known by Paul Flindt, the younger, of Nuremberg (master in 1601); this is a dish in the Kremlin. He executed the chasing of a "masterpiece" cup by Hans Röttenbock, in 1631, as recorded by Dr. Rosenberg.

The cup made in 1670 by Balthasar Lauch, of Leipzig, as his "masterpiece" is a variation of the same form as the above Rehlein cup; it is in the Kunstgewerbe Museum in Leipzig.

German goldsmiths were ever inventing new fashions in cups. One of their inventions in the sixteenth century were those in the form of globes, celestial and terrestrial, of which some were fitted with mechanism, to enable them to circulate round the table for the diversion of guests.

The only example in gold is probably the celestial globe by Urban Schneeweis (1536–1600), of Dresden, acquired by the late Mr. J. Pierpont Morgan (Plate LV, No. 1).

The globes are for the most part carefully engraved with the newest geographical discoveries, whether in all cases by an engraver as distinct from the goldsmith cannot be determined. Collaboration between goldsmith and engraver occurs in two globe-cups in the "Green Vaults" at Dresden, which were wrought by a goldsmith of Augsburg, while the engraving was executed, about 1640, by Johannis Schmidt, also of Augsburg. In the Schloss at Berlin are two terrestrial globe cups. The engraving of the first was executed by one Wilhelm Jansson Blaeu in 1667, while the cup itself was made by a goldsmith of Magdeburg. It was a gift to the Elector of Brandenburg by the Burgomaster of that town, who was no less a person than Otto von Guericke, well known as a geographer. The other was wrought probably by Lorenz Biller II of Augsburg, and engraved by Christoph Schmidt, of the same place, in 1696.

An earlier case of collaboration in globe cups is mentioned on page 185.

The historic globe cup by Hans Jacob Stampfer, the celebrated goldsmith and medallist, of Zurich, is illustrated on Plate XCVI (No. 4).

Of the German-made cups with English historical associations, none are more interesting than that which was bestowed by Queen Elizabeth upon the celebrated Swiss reformer, Heinrich Bullinger, in 1561, as a token of her appreciation of his hospitality towards the Bishops of Salisbury, Winchester and Norwich, and other English exiles at Zurich. The cup is inscribed in Latin to the effect that a church in Zurich had cherished the exiled English in the reign of Mary : this fact Elizabeth piously recognised and rewarded Bullinger with this gift of a cup. The reformer's arms are engraved upon it (Plate LI, No. 2).

It appears paradoxical that the Queen of England should select a piece of German plate for the gift when there were goldsmiths in her own country who were capable of executing a cup worthy of their monarch ; but here, as in many other instances, money was probably sent by the donor for the purchase of plate in the place of residence of the recipient. For example, the three above Bishops sent money to Zurich with a request that cups be bought to commemorate the hospitality of their hosts in their exile.

This cup is in the National Museum at Zurich and was made by a goldsmith of Strassburg, who made another piece of German plate with English associations : a small circular bowl covered with

PLATE LV

PLATE LVI

characteristic bosses and set in the middle with a later medallion, which is at Peterhouse, Cambridge.

A standing cup of about 1575 decorated with Scriptural subjects, by Jacob Fröhlich, of Nuremberg, is in the possession of the Broderers' Company in London and was a gift from John Parr, embroiderer to Queen Elizabeth and James I. The "Queen Mary" cup at St John's Church, Perth, is a secular German cup, as is the early seventeenth-century cup by a Nuremberg goldsmith in the same church. The first has a cover restored by the Dundee goldsmith, Robert Gairdyne. Both are illustrated in Burns's *Old Scottish Communion Plate*.

Conspicuous among historic cups is the "Luther" cup, now in the possession of the University of Greifswald (Plate LI, No. 1). According to the inscription, it was a gift from the once famous University of Wittenberg (now united with Greifswald) to Martin Luther on his marriage to Kethe von Bore in 1525. But stamped upon it is the mark of Augsburg, with a maker's mark assigned by Dr. Marc Rosenberg to Nikolaus Leiss (Losse), who died in 1623, but more probably to Nikolas Leucker, who died in 1595. These marks would seem to indicate a date of about fifty years later for the cup than the time of the gift. The discrepancy cannot at the moment be explained.

To the cups associated with German Universities must be added those which were executed by Paul Birckenholtz, of Frankfurt-am-Main, to celebrate the centenary of Marburg University in 1629. One now belongs to the University of Giessen and the other is in the Kunstgewerbe Museum in Berlin.

The Lüneburg treasure includes the *Interimsbecher*, a tall standing cup, presented to the town of Lüneburg by its citizens to commemorate the abrogation of the well-known religious compromise or covenant of 1548, called the "Augsburg Interim." It is suitably embellished with figures and scenes associated with that event, and is illustrated in Lessing's *Gold u. Silber*, p. 79.

Some cups were made to commemorate mining, for various guilds from the sixteenth to the eighteenth centuries. First in importance is the great cup, in the Bavarian Royal collection at

Munich, executed in 1543 by Georg Kobenhaupt, of Strassburg, from silver obtained from the mines of Markirch, which had been working from 1527. More celebrated is the cup of 1625 by the well-known goldsmith, David Winckler, of Friburg in Saxony, now in the "Green Vaults" at Dresden, which is illustrated in great detail by Dr. Marc Rosenberg in *Geschichte der Goldschmiede Kunst*, 1908.

It was the custom in the sixteenth and seventeenth centuries to celebrate any civic or domestic event of importance by the gift of a cup. This little book might be filled with German inscriptions, moral, bibulous and amatory, from cups and other vessels. Likewise, much might be written on the old ceremonial drinking customs associated with many historic cups still preserved.

The German goldsmiths of the sixteenth and seventeenth centuries were unceasing in introducing new and often fantastic cups or decoration. One of their most curious conceits is a decoration in imitation of facetted diamonds (*diamant-buckeln*) on tankards and cups, as may be seen on a small tankard and beaker in the Metropolitan Museum, New York, the former of which is illustrated on Plate LII (No. 3). Dr. Rosenberg records many other specimens of this curious taste in decoration, in which an Augsburg silversmith, using as his distinctive mark the initials I F, appears to have specialised in the early seventeenth century.

No country can show such diversity of guild cups as Germany, whether in silver or pewter. Every craft had its guild and its cups, especially in the seventeenth and eighteenth centuries, and more space than can be spared here would be necessary even for a short history of these cups. Some are topical, as, for example, a cup fashioned like a bull, for a butchers' guild. A rare cup, in the form of a cannon, was formerly in the possession of the Nuremberg Artillery about 1600 (Plate LVII, No. 3).

These cups were displayed at convivial gatherings of the guilds, as is the custom with the splendid plate of the old guilds of the City of London, and were passed round as "loving cups" in accordance with ancient ritual.

One of the rarest among ceremonial drinking vessels is the large

GERMANY

silver-gilt waggon and tun running on four wheels, given to the Mercers Company of London by one William Burde, a merchant in the foreign trade, of which there is an electrotype copy in the Victoria and Albert Museum. Jeronimus Orth, of Breslau, was the maker between 1554 and 1584.

The nautilus shell was prized as a rare and curious natural product and found great favour among German goldsmiths for about a century between 1550 and 1650 and was regarded, as Sir Walter Scott said, as a "fairy cup, made out of a nautilus shell."

Most important in the number and variety of the cups and other ornaments for the sideboard and the table mounted from this shell is the collection in the Kremlin at Moscow, which contains about fifteen. Others are in the treasure of the Kingdom of Bavaria at Munich. Swans, ostriches and cocks were fashioned from the shell.

Of great diversity are the silver-gilt mounts and stems, the stems including the appropriate mermaid and merman and Bacchus and his tun, with Neptune and Jonah and the whale as popular finials. So precious was a gift of a nautilus-shell cup regarded that some are set with gems. Enamel forms part of the decoration of several, such as the important cup, by Steffan Kipffenberger, of Augsburg (died 1541), illustrated by Von Drach on Plate 8 of *Silberarbeiten Cassel*, 1888.

The iridiscent and strongly turbinated Trochus shell was also mounted frequently as a cup. One with a lion stem and a figure of Neptune as a finial, by a Nuremberg silversmith of the early seventeenth century, is in the Jones collection in the Victoria and Albert Museum.

In the "Green Vaults" at Dresden is one of the latest, mounted by Bernhard Quippe, of Berlin, in 1689, probably after a design by Balthasar Permoser (1651-1732), sculptor and ivory carver; it is illustrated in the third edition of Dr. Marc Rosenberg's book on marks. This is only about nine years later than one in the late Mr. Pierpont Morgan's collection (Plate LV, No. 2).

The nautilus shell was introduced whole or in strips into other vessels—ewers, ships and basins—by German goldsmiths, to their manifest delight.

Of the great number recorded by Dr. Marc Rosenberg in his second edition, 25 were executed at Augsburg and 15 at Nuremberg.

A long list of these cups with their various features might be compiled. Paul Flindt, the designer of plate, was not (as had been supposed) the first inventor of the nautilus-shell cup, for it had been in fashion for several years before the publication of his designs in 1618.

At Windsor Castle is one of the finest, by the prominent Nuremberg goldsmith, Nicolaus Schmidt (about 1582–1608), the maker of a great silver ewer and basin, embellished with shell, in the Imperial Museum at Vienna, and of other objects similarly decorated. This cup was greatly admired by no less an artist than John Flaxman, who pronounced it as the work of Benvenuto Cellini! It is illustrated in *The Gold and Silver of Windsor Castle*.

Bellekin, a Dutch artist of the seventeenth century, had a fancy for engraving nautilus shells with marine and other subjects, leaving the mounting of them as cups to goldsmiths. By him is the specimen engraved with figures of Neptune and Amphitrite and mounted by a German goldsmith, described as in the possession of Lady Theodora Guest and illustrated in the *Connoisseur* (Vol. XI, p. 178). It was sold in the Fonthill sale in 1823 for £69 6s. One of his shells, finely engraved with scenes, symbolical of Peace and War, was mounted by a goldsmith of Breslau early in the eighteenth century; it is illustrated on Plate 20 of the present author's catalogue of the late Mr. J. Pierpont Morgan's collection (formerly Gutmann).

Friedrich Hildebrand, of Nuremberg (died 1608), was perhaps the most conspicuous of those who favoured this exotic ornament. By him is a remarkable set of eight double cups made up from bits of shell, set in their centres with small silver rosettes, partially enamelled. This set is in the Imperial Museum, Vienna, and a specimen was illustrated in the *Connoisseur* for July 1919. Another pair of double cups of a different form are in the same great collection. A cup by him, in the Royal Museum at Cassel, is covered with pieces of shell, which is very similar to a cup of about 1600, by Jörg Ruel, of Nuremberg, in Lady Rothschild's

GERMANY

collection. These do not, however, exhaust the list of pieces made by Hildebrand. An ornate nautilus-shell cup by him, supported on a figure of Apollo, is one of the treasures of Baron Bruno Schröder.

Georg Barst (Parst), master of the same guild in 1627, was the maker of a cup with a pointed bowl fashioned from strips of pearl, which are set with silver ornaments of cherubs' heads and scrolls; this is in the Imperial Museum at Vienna.

The cocoanut was the second natural product which was mounted by German goldsmiths as cups and garnished with elaborate silver-gilt fittings, sometimes enamelled. Some nuts are carved with sacred or mythological subjects. None appears to date from medieval times, as in England, the earliest being of the sixteenth century.

Hans Brosamer executed a design for a cocoanut or ostrich-egg cup, the lip of which is decorated with medallions. A long list of these cups might be compiled. The stems are various; they might be vase-like, with brackets, in the popular fancy for cup-stems of the German Renaissance, or they might be standing figures, like the enamelled Nubian archer on the carved cocoanut cup, with enamelled straps and lip, in the Imperial Museum, Vienna (Plate LV, No. 5).

Another nut, doubtless regarded with more wonder than the cocoanut, was mounted by German goldsmiths. This is the great Seychelles nut, of which the ewer by Anthoni Schweinberger, of Augsburg, goldsmith to the Court of Rudolph II (1587–c.1603), in the same Vienna Museum; and the large fountain of about 1600, in the Waddesdon collection in the British Museum, are notable examples of these rare objects.

But more popular was the contemporary ostrich-egg cup, which is said to have been regarded as the egg of the phœnix or the griffin. In some rare and remarkable examples the egg is painted with divers subjects, the finial being an ostrich. One example is mounted as an ostrich and another as a pelican, the egg forming the bodies. Appropriately, the stem of many cups is an ostrich and in one case three ostriches. An unusual example of about 1610 is illustrated on Plate LV (No. 4), where the egg is supported by an ostrich standing on a base fashioned of tree trunks and branches, while the finial is the popular sprig of coral* of German cups; this is in the Imperial Museum, Vienna. Several ostrich-egg cups are in the Kremlin.

The fashion of mounting ostrich eggs virtually ceased about 1650, though occasionally found of a later date.

Of all the German cups none is more engaging than the wedding gift in the form of a maiden holding in her uplifted arms a smaller cup on a swivel, called *Jungfrauenbecher*. In the ceremonial use of this cup at a wedding feast, both receptacles were filled with wine and the bridegroom first drank the contents of the larger cup; he was afterwards expected to turn the figure right side up without spilling any of the wine in the smaller cup, and so present it to his bride, to the accompaniment of jests. Cups of this fashion have been called "wager cups" from the wagers said to have been made at the festive board in wine-drinking bouts when the competitors were supposed to quaff all the wine from both receptacles without spilling a drop—no mean task, since the smaller cup revolves on a swivel.

Similar customs prevailed in Holland, as is mentioned on a later page. All new members of the Vintners Company in London were required to go through a similar ceremony from the rare Charles II silver cup of this form—borrowed from German cups—in the possession of that company, which is one of the very few of English workmanship.

The *Jungfrauenbecher* first appears about 1565 and was made in large numbers, especially at Nuremberg, early in the seventeenth century, when one Meinrad Bauch, the elder, of that city, made several before his death in 1623. He was the maker of one in the late Mr. J. Pierpont Morgan's collection. A specimen of about 1610, in the Baroness James de Rothschild's collection, is shown on Plate LV (No. 6). Three unusual examples are the one with an enamelled face, in the National Museum at Munich; another, partially enamelled; and the third of the exceptional

---

* Coral was worn as a charm in medieval times and is familiar from the representations of the Infant Saviour wearing it in Early Italian and Flemish pictures.

GERMANY

height of 17½ inches, in the "Green Vaults" at Dresden, which is decorated with nautilus shell, by Friedrich Hildebrand, of Nuremberg.

They vary in height from 5¾ to 10 inches, mostly about 8½ inches.

A second variety of cup is shaped like a woman without the little cup on a swivel, doubtless based on the designs of Sibmacher and Paul Flindt.

Among the thousand and one fantastic conceits of the German goldsmiths in drinking vessels and ornaments, from the sixteenth to the eighteenth centuries, none are more interesting than those fashioned like animals and birds. In animals the lion and the stag take precedence in numbers, followed by the horse. The stag is seen in many attitudes, leaping over crudely-fashioned trees of silver-gilt and branches of coral. One stag of 1589 stands on an oval pedestal worked like natural ground, embossed with reptiles and snails. Another is in the act of running on "ground" similarly embossed with rabbits, a hound, a lizard and two cows, all coloured, about 1610. The unicorn was also popular and was similarly treated.

The lion as a cup or ornament may have been suggested by the medieval aquamanile of bronze, in the form of this beast, which was used, not as a drinking vessel, but for washing hands. In the Lüneburg treasure is one of the earliest German silver lions, called a *gusskanne*, made by a goldsmith of Lüneburg in 1540. (See Lessing, *Gold und Silber*, p. 103).

German plate of solid gold is almost as rare as English plate in this precious metal, and consequently the gold lion of 1635 in the collection of the late Mr. Leopold de Rothschild calls for more than a passing thought. Both it and a silver-gilt lion are illustrated in the catalogue of that collection.

The bull was the appropriate symbol of butchers' guilds. Many drinking flasks fashioned in the shape of this animal are known.

Bears are represented by the interesting piece, enriched with precious stones and enamel, by a goldsmith of Augsburg, about 1600, in the old Imperial collection at Vienna, which is illustrated in the *Connoisseur* for July 1919.

Lady Rothschild's collection contains a curious small elephant with a castellated top enclosing six figures in the act of shooting, and a small man riding in front, by Wolff Christoff Ritter, master of the Nuremberg guild in 1617—a piece which recalls the elephant fountain by the Nuremberg goldsmith, Christoph Jamnitzer (1563-1618), in the Kunstgewerbe Museum in Berlin.

Camels were also made, and one, ridden by a young negro, by a Dantzig goldsmith, Salomon von der Renne(n), about 1650, is in the Kremlin.

Sixteen species of animals, at least, were fashioned into cups—the fox and the hare, the hound and the chamois, the cat and the panther, and the two fabulous animals, the dragon and griffin.

It is supposed that some of these animal cups or flasks were prizes to huntsmen and sportsmen, as well as guild cups or fantastic drinking vessels for the diversion of guests on suitable occasions.

The fish must not be overlooked in this brief survey. As may be surmised, the cups thus fashioned were destined for the use of fishermen's guilds, like the specimen mentioned in the chapter on Swiss silver.

Among birds the most popular was the owl, which was made not only of silver, but also of German faience, like the specimen in the collection of the Grand Duke of Baden. Some owls have bells on their feet. A Swiss owl of historic interest is described in a later chapter. Imitations of these old silver owls have been made and foisted upon collectors as originals.

The ostrich was also highly favoured and was made of silver throughout, or with the egg of the bird introduced as the body for the cup. Some have the right foot raised and clutching a stone, symbolical of the ancient fable that cranes keep watch perched on one foot, so that if they should fall asleep, the fall of the stone would awake them to their duty of renewing their watch. One tall ostrich cup, of about 1625, is of silver. In its beak is a horse-shoe and encircling the neck is an enamelled collar set with rubies, the pedestal being worked in imitation of natural ground and with two lizards. Another has a body of nautilus shell, painted with birds on festoons.

PLATE LVII

PLATE LVIII

GERMANY

The partridge was not despised. That the bird should be ornamental as well as useful, the German goldsmith conceived the quaint device of cutting up bits of nautilus shells into the shape of feathers and forming them into a partridge. Two elaborate and costly examples by Nuremberg goldsmiths may be singled out for notice. The first, in the National Museum at Copenhagen, was probably executed by Meinrad Bauch, the elder (master in 1575), and is illustrated in the catalogue; the second, set with emeralds and garnets, was made by Jörg Ruel (master in 1598), and is shown in the catalogue of the late Mr. Leopold de Rothschild's collection.

But more popular than the partridge was the swan, the queen of aquatic birds, and in this the nautilus shell frequently forms the body, like the important specimen (in the collection of Lady Rothschild), richly mounted and set with precious stones, by the same Jörg Ruel, the maker of another swan in the Kremlin.

Once again the nautilus must be observed as the body of a bird, this time a domestic hen, standing in a pen, wrought about 1590 by Samuel Becker, of Brunswick, which is illustrated in the catalogue of the old royal collection at Cassel. The cock, too, was a picturesque object of the table or sideboard on festive occasions, and the great one, by Friedrich Hildebrand, of Nuremberg, in the Hermitage Museum at Petrograd, doubtless found a place at the feasts of Tsars of Russia.

The eagle was not so favoured as might be supposed. An impressive and regal example, standing 20 inches, was made in 1595 by the well-known Nuremberg goldsmith, Christoph Jamnitzer, and is illustrated in Mr. F. R. Martin's book on the gifts of plate from Christian IV of Denmark to the Court of Russia.

The German fashion for cups in the likeness of birds and animals was at its zenith between 1575 and 1650.

Illustrated on Plate LV (No. 3), is a pelican in her piety, by a goldsmith of Ulm, 1583, in the Imperial Museum, Vienna.

More imposing and costly are the figures of Diana on the Stag.

"Queen and huntress, chaste and fair."

Some of these groups are fitted with clockwork contrivances for moving along the polished tables. They were wound up and despatched on their journey, and the guest opposite whom the vessel stopped was compelled by an honoured custom to consume the wine contained in the body of the goddess, on pain of a forfeit, to the accompaniment of great merriment. The specimen illustrated on Plate LVII (No. 1) is in the Kunstgewerbe Museum in Berlin. The maker was the well-known Augsburg goldsmith, Mathaeus Wallbaum (1554-c.1630), the maker of one of these groups in the Historical Museum at Stockholm. A few other groups of Diana on the Stag are preserved, including an important specimen, 1605-10, by Joachim Friess, of Augsburg, now in the Metropolitan Museum at New York. By the same craftsman are three others—in the Kremlin, in the Grand Ducal Museum at Darmstadt, and in the collection of the late Baron Carl von Rothschild, a collection which contained another example by a different maker, Jacob Miller, the elder, of Augsburg (1548-1618), which is illustrated on Plate 48 of Luthmer's catalogue, and is now in the possession of Lady Rothschild. Two such figures by anonymous goldsmiths, in the Royal Museum at Gotha, are of historic interest, having been tilting prizes at the tournament held in honour of the election of the Emperor Matthias at Frankfurt-am-Main, in 1612. Some few others have been recorded.

With these may be associated the groups of St. George and the Dragon of about the date 1600–20, fitted with similar clockwork in their pedestals. An imposing specimen by the above Jacob Miller, of Augsburg, is in the Grand Ducal Museum at Darmstadt, and a fellow, by the same master, is illustrated in the late Mr. Alfred de Rothschild's catalogue. The bridle and trappings of the second are set with gems, and the dragon is enamelled in red and green, while the octagonal pedestal is set with scorpions, toads, spiders and lizards, in the manner of Wenzel Jamnitzer and other German masters. A third, by an Augsburg craftsman, is in the "Green Vaults" at Dresden, where there is a figure of Diana riding a centaur.

As will be observed, all these early groups of Diana and the Stag and St. George and the Dragon were executed by goldsmiths of

Augsburg, and it would seem that they were rarely, if ever, produced at Nuremberg.

Later groups of Diana on the Stag, of the second half of the seventeenth century, are fixed on high pedestals without clockwork, like those of some equestrian statuettes and other objects. A silver centaur, with a figure of Diana astride, stands on a pedestal of ebony and silver, which is fitted with mechanism to move along the table; it was executed by an Augsburg goldsmith and is illustrated in colour in Ilg's book on some of the treasures of the Imperial Museum at Vienna.

In the same category are such things as the immense Europa on a bull on a high oval pedestal, of the seventeenth century, in Lady Rothschild's collection.

In this long catalogue of fantastic cups notice must be taken of those in the form of vintagers and other human figures, both male and female, carrying barrels on their backs. Some are wholly of silver, and others of carved wood and silver, and are enriched with symbols of vintagers.

In the collection of the late Mr. Leopold de Rothschild is a figure of a huntsman, possibly by Christoph Erhard, of Augsburg, between 1568 and 1604. Lady Rothschild has a figure of a blacksmith, of the early seventeenth century, and her sister, Baroness James de Rothschild, has a large wine flask, formed of a figure of Vulcan at his forge, by a member of the Augsburg family of Biller about 1690, both probably cups of blacksmiths' guilds.

German goldsmiths from the end of the fifteenth century displayed a liking for mounting vessels for the table and sideboard from the colourless variety of rock crystal, found chiefly in the Alps from Dauphiné to Tyrol and in Hungary. Upon these they lavished all their skill in goldsmiths' work, combined with brightly coloured enamel mingled in many objects with precious stones. The supposed power of crystal to reveal the presence of poison has been mentioned on pages 107–108.

Only within recent years have the gold and silver garnishings of some of the finest vessels, of crystal, jasper, agate and other stones, been assigned to the goldsmiths of Southern Germany.

Previously all, without exception, had been assumed to be the work of Italian craftsmen. A notable case in point is the celebrated "Gabbitas" biberon in the form of a monster of carved rock-crystal, mounted in enamelled gold of about 1550 (illustrated in colour in the *Connoisseur*, Vol. xiii, p. 56), which was described as Italian when sold for 15,000 guineas in 1905, but in the sale at Christie's in July, 1910, it was correctly catalogued as German, with the added information that the vessel was considered to be the work of Daniel Mignot, of Augsburg, some of whose engraved designs for enamelled work are well known. But this artist appears to have been solely a designer, and no example of plate from his hands is extant.

Standing cups fashioned in part from rock crystal were, as might be expected, greatly favoured in the German Renaissance. Two important specimens find a place here, in addition to the earlier double cup already mentioned. The first is a remarkably fine piece mounted in silver-gilt, elaborately chased and repoussé, by a Cologne goldsmith of about 1555, in the collection of Viscount Lee of Fareham (Plate LIV, No. 1). The second, in Baron Bruno Schröder's collection, is just over six inches higher and is richly decorated. No marks have been discovered on the elaborate silver-gilt mounts, but the maker is thought to be Wenzel Jamnitzer (Plate LIV, No. 3). Two facts connected with the cup deserve recognition—namely, that it bears a close resemblance in form to the celebrated "Bowes" cup, with London marks for 1554-5, of the Goldsmiths Company, and that it was sent to Hanover by George II in 1740; it was recently sold by the Duke of Cumberland.

Graceful vase-shaped ewers, accompanied by their basins, were highly prized in the Germany of the Renaissance and in England and other countries. The designs of Virgil Solis (1541), of Nuremberg, and of the "Master of 1551," of Hans Sibmacher (c. 1590), of Georg Wechter, and of Paul Flindt (published in 1618) show ewers of this shape with characteristic decoration, which were copied with slight modifications by the goldsmiths of Augsburg, Nuremberg and elsewhere.

PLATE LIX

GERMANY

The Duke of Buccleuch is the owner of an important example with its basin, bearing the mark of an Augsburg goldsmith, possibly Hannss Miller (died 1599), or Hans Ment (died 1604). One of the finest pairs, by Franz Dotte, master in the Nuremberg guild in 1592, are illustrated on Plate 84 of the present author's catalogue of the late Mr. J. Pierpont Morgan's collection. Of superior quality are the vase-shaped ewer and its basin, decorated in relief with Biblical subjects, which were wrought early in the seventeenth century and are shown on Plates 11 and 12 in the late Mr. Leopold de Rothschild's catalogue.

In the Pitti Palace at Florence—a collection rich in German plate, which the author has heard described by guides as the work of Benvenuto Cellini—are two ewers of this shape, with their basins, by goldsmiths of Augsburg. One pair were executed between 1583 and 1614 by Paul Hübner, the maker of some tazze in the same collection and of a little tankard in the possession of the Duke of Buccleuch. The basin is decorated with scenes of Orpheus charming wild animals with his music (Plate LVI, No. 4.) The second pair are of more than usual interest from the fact that the maker has been identified by Dr. Marc Rosenberg as Kornelius Erb, who migrated from Genoa to Augsburg, where he died in 1618 (Plate LVI, No. 3, for the ewer).

Noticeable on account of the absence of ornament are the ewer and basin by Reinhard Dietmar, master in the Strassburg guild in 1582, belonging to the City of Emden.

Of the same graceful shape as the ewers just described is the well-known pewter ewer made with a basin by François Briot about 1580, which was imitated in the same metal by Caspar Enderlein, of Nuremberg, and reproduced in Palissy ware in France.

Some other important ewers with their basins must not be overlooked in this brief survey, chiefly because of their exuberant decoration. There are the remarkable enamelled pair, by Christoph Jamnitzer, of Nuremberg (1563–1618), in the Imperial Museum, Vienna, which are illustrated in the *Connoisseur* for July 1919. In the same museum are the extraordinary large ewer and basin, conspicuous by reason of the inlaid pieces of mother-of-pearl, by the

Nuremberg goldsmith, Nicolaus Schmidt, who favoured this exotic decoration in plate. Here also is a large basin by Christoph Lencker, of Augsburg, which is illustrated with the Schmidt ewer in the same article.

English ewers and basins of the Elizabethan and Jacobean periods are more restrained in their decoration than the contemporary German. The ceremonial use of these vessels in England is explained on pages 101–3. Doubtless similar customs prevailed in Germany.

Ewers of the same shape as that on Plate LVI (No. 2), were introduced in Germany early in the seventeenth century. It is repoussé with Scriptural subjects of the Virgin and St. Elizabeth and the birth of St. John. Supporting the hemispherical body is a group of three figures, illustrative of the Murder of the Innocents. The border of the dish is decorated in relief with angels bearing baskets of fruit and floriated ornaments. In the centre is an elaborate composition of the Holy Family and St. John at a fountain, chased and repoussé, from an engraving after Sebastian Bourdon (1616–71). Johann or Jacob Jäger, of Augsburg, was the maker about 1650.

This pair of vessels are in the possession of Lord Clifford of Chudleigh, to whom they have passed by descent from Thomas Clifford, first Lord Clifford, Treasurer of England, one of the members of the famous Cabal. To him they had been a gift by Ferdinand II, Grand Duke of Tuscany (Plate LVI, Nos. 1 and 2).

With these may be mentioned the well-known Augsburg ewer and dish of about the same date, but of different forms, at St. John's College, Cambridge.

Another variety of ewer is represented (with its basin) by that of Lucas Neisser, of Augsburg, the property of Earl Annesley, illustrated in the *Connoisseur* for June 1906, which is of the same shape as one shown in the catalogue of the Ashburnham sale at Christie's in 1914.

Early in the eighteenth century ewers of a modified helmet-shape were popular in Germany as in contemporary England. An important example is in the collection of Viscount Lee of Fareham. It is plain, save for the fluting. With it is a handsome

GERMANY

plain basin gadrooned at the edge. Daniel Schaeffler, of Augsburg, was the maker of both vessels (Plate LX, No. 4).

A short outline has already been given of the history of English and French silver wine-bottles. They have a long history in Germany, though but few have survived. The bottles (*Kettenflaschen*) of the sixteenth century would seem to have been flat and oval, with heavy chains. Of this shape is the exceedingly rare little bottle of solid gold, decorated with translucent enamel of great richness and colouring, and with the arms of Wolf Dietrich von Raitenau (1559-1617), the splendour-loving Prince-Archbishop of Salzburg; this is now in the Pitti Palace in Florence and was for long ascribed to Benvenuto Cellini. With it are three two-handled gold cups, also richly enamelled, one of which is embellished with the same arms. The handles of two resemble Le Blon's designs for toothpicks. These four pieces of German plate are described and illustrated in an article by the present author in the *Connoisseur* for May 1907.

German silver bottles of the seventeenth century include several in the former royal collection in Berlin, beginning with a pair engraved with figures and flowers and made probably by Georg Ernst, of Augsburg, before his death in 1651, and including a massive pair by the Prussian Court goldsmith, Daniel Männlich, the elder, of Berlin, 1696. Four more heavy bottles in the same collection (now in the Schloss at Berlin) are fluted, and were made at Augsburg in 1698.

Lady Rothschild is the owner of a charming little bottle, only 7½ inches high, probably wrought by Johann Christoph Treffler, of Augsburg, about 1695. Square bottles are unusual, but several by goldsmiths of Hanover towards the end of the seventeenth century were in the collection of the Duke of Cumberland. Unusual, too, are the examples enclosed in a silver box, made in 1715, with an oval wine cooler, for Maximilian, Elector of Bavaria, by Johann Georg Oxner, of Munich, which were in the Silberkammer at Munich when examined some years ago by the author.

Silver bottles or flasks of this description were seldom made after about 1725.

A popular piece of plate in almost all European countries in the sixteenth century was the tazza. In Venice it was made of glass, and in France of Limoges enamel and in the faience known as "Henri Deux," as well as in silver. One of the most important examples, from the Pierpont Morgan collection, is illustrated on Plate LIII (No. 3). In the interior of the bowl are four scenes from the life of Vespasian, worked in low relief. Standing in the middle is a figure of the Emperor. It was originally part of the Aldobrandini set of twelve, containing similar statuettes of the Cæsars, made by an anonymous German goldsmith about 1590.

German goldsmiths made several sets of the tazza, of twelve and more. There are more than fifty in the Pitti Palace in Florence, several of which were wrought between 1583 and 1614 by Paul Hübner, of Augsburg, the maker of a set of twelve in the Waddesdon collection in the British Museum. The decoration in the interior of the bowls comprises symbols of the months, subjects from classical mythology and other scenes, chased in relief.

Rarer than these is the late sixteenth-century tazza with a cover, like the piece decorated in niello, in the Louvre (Plate LIII, No. 1). One such covered tazza was made probably by Isaac de Voghelaer, of Emden, and belongs to the municipal plate of that city.

In the Pierpont Morgan collection was a model in carved boxwood for a silver tazza.

The most remarkable of all covered tazze is that by Jonas Silber, of Nuremberg, 1589, supposed to have been made for the Emperor Rudolph II. The stem is formed of a Gothic temple, symbolical of the heavenly Jerusalem, supported on the tree of Paradise, with figures of Adam and Eve and the serpent. On the exterior of the bowl, in relief, are figures of the Emperor, the Electors and 97 shields of arms of the Imperial estates. Inside is the map of Europe fashioned in the form of a maiden, while in the interior of the cover are twelve figures, after models by Peter Flötner, representing the twelve ancestors of the German people. It is illustrated by Dr. Marc Rosenberg in *Der Goldschmiede Merkzeichen* (third edition).

The silver salt never attained the same degree of importance in Germany as it did in England from medieval times to the seventeenth century. The "Huntsman" salt of the early sixteenth century at All Souls' College, Oxford, is unique in German plate.

While most English standing salts of the sixteenth century are conspicuous for their height, those of Germany in the same period are low and inconspicuous. The one illustrated on Plate L (No. 3) is triangular in shape, enriched with Gothic foliage, and is one of a pair of the early sixteenth century in the collection of the late Mr. J. Pierpont Morgan. The scarcity of examples before about 1650 is proved by the fact that Dr. Marc Rosenberg enumerates not more than fifteen. Of these, three are in the Victoria and Albert Museum, the earliest of which is triangular and was made at Memmingen about 1550. The second is circular, with three receptacles for salt, and bears the town-mark of Straubing of a few years later, while the third came from the hands of a goldsmith of Ulm, about 1600.

A small circular salt, standing on three cherubs' heads, of the late sixteenth century, is in the collection of Dr. A. Figdor in Vienna, and another of a different design of the same date, both made at Augsburg, is in the Kunstgewerbe Museum in Berlin. Three rare little salts, examined by the author in Dr. Alfred Pringsheim's collection, were by Augsburg goldsmiths of the sixteenth century. One is hexagonal and is decorated on the sides with animals in relief. The second is triangular, and the third is round and flat.

In the British Museum is an excellent example of German Renaissance work in the triangular salt (Plate L, No. 2), of the same form as the pottery salt made at Urbino by Francesco Xanto in 1532, in the same museum. Of this form is a salt by an Augsburg goldsmith of the end of the sixteenth century, acquired by Baron Bruno Schröder from Lord Swaythling's sale. It has three circular cavities for the salt and three lion feet. In the centre is a standing figure in classical armour.

From about the middle of the seventeenth century most of the few German salts that were made took the form of circular pedestals, narrowed in the middle, not unlike the bases of silver equestrian statuettes and other German figures, and not dissimilar to the Swiss salt illustrated here. A salt of this fashion by the Hamburg goldsmith, Heinrich Eickhoff, was in the Patriarch's Treasury in Moscow. Salts of similar shape are familiar objects in Dutch " Still Life " pictures of the seventeenth century.

The author has seen several small plain salts of octagonal shape, evidently copied from English models by a Munich goldsmith of the eighteenth century, and other copies of the same form by C. Weishaupt, of Munich, about 1825, all in the Royal Silberkammer at Munich—a collection which contains a pair of spice boxes by an Augsburg goldsmith of 1705, very similar in shape to an English example of about 1700 at Windsor Castle.

A remarkable salt of silver-gilt and enamel was sold in the Holford collection at Christie's in July 1927. The octagonal base is fitted with small drawers chased with masks and strapwork on a background of blue and green enamel. Encircling the centre is an enamelled frieze of scenes from the Life of Christ. The enamelled cover, over the receptacle for the salt, represents the Crucifixion, the maker was Christoff Ritter (le), of Nuremberg, master in 1547, or the later goldsmith of the same name, master in 1577 ; it is illustrated in the sale catalogue.

Nowhere else except Germany have great silver caskets been made. One of the finest is the rectangular casket set with plaques of mother-of-pearl and lapis lazuli, the latter having symbols of the planets in silver fixed upon them. The maker was probably Hannss Straub, of Nuremberg, about 1580 ; it is in the Kunstgewerbe Museum at Berlin. Another is the remarkable enamelled casket, by Hans Lencker, the elder, of Nuremberg (died in 1585) and Elias Lencker (died in 1591).

Wenzel Jamnitzer's sumptuous cabinet is in the Silberkammer at Munich, while the original drawing for it is in the Kunstgewerbe Museum at Berlin.

The most conspicuous cabinet is the great Pomeranian *Kunstschrank* of architectural form in the above Berlin Museum. Several Augsburg craftsmen were employed in its completion about 1617. One Ulrich Baumgartner made the ebony frame, and Mathaeus Wallbaum wrought some of the silver work, while David Altenstetter executed the enamel. Painters were invited to decorate the

GERMANY

interior of the door. The fittings comprise a complete outfit for a prince—a little table service of plates, knives, spoons and other requisites, a medicine chest and articles for the toilet—the whole ingeniously fitted into their several places. A separate brochure would be needed to explain the cabinet in detail, with the names of the many artificers engaged upon it. The reader is directed to Lessing and Brüning's illustrated publication upon it.

Mathaeus Wallbaum (1554-1630), of Kiel and (from 1582) of Augsburg, was the craftsman of many devotional objects, such as triptychs of ebony or black wood mounted in silver. Many of these from his own workshop, and others by his contemporaries, are in the Geistliche Schatzkammer in Vienna. One characteristic feature of these are the little silver ornaments, sometimes enamelled, like those of some German Renaissance jewellery, with which they are studded. One painter who collaborated with him in some of these triptychs was Anton Mozart. A triptych by Wallbaum, with paintings of Scriptural subjects by this artist in 1598, from the Pierpont Morgan collection, is in the Metropolitan Museum, New York.

But he did not confine himself to devotional works: he made ebony and silver caskets for secular purposes, like one in the Waddesdon collection in the British Museum and others. Nor did he neglect silver work proper, for he was the maker of the Diana on the Stag on Plate LVII, and was one of the craftsmen of parts of the Pomeranian *Kunstschrank* just mentioned.

A second Augsburg goldsmith who made ebony and silver caskets in this manner was Boas Ulrich (1550-1624), the maker of a notable example, decorated with silver figures of Charity, Love and Truth, in the Baroness James de Rothschild's collection (Plate LIX).

Almost unknown outside Germany are the little ships of several varieties (a development from the nef of the Middle Ages), which first appear about 1550. They were intended on occasions to act as drinking vessels and were offered to the parting guest as symbols of good wishes for his journey by sea or land. Many sizes were made, some as cups and ornaments combined.

One Nuremberg silversmith, perhaps Esais zur Linden, master

in 1609, specialised in this kind of vessel and was the maker of many specimens extant to-day in museums and private collections, including the Baroness James de Rothschild's (Plate LVIII, No. 2). Another considerable maker of ships was Heinrich Winterstein, of Augsburg (c. 1553-1634).

Some of these little ships have four wheels for running along the table in front of the guests, others are supported on high stems of various shapes, such as a figure of Neptune. The human figures in the ships are frequently enamelled in colours.

A large and impressive specimen (formerly in the Londesborough collection), by a silversmith of Strassburg about 1590, was sold at Christie's in July 1919, and has passed into the important collection of Baron Bruno Schröder. In this are 24 galley slaves rowing 19 soldiers and other figures, while under a canopy are five figures at a repast, all the figures being enamelled in colours. Delicately engraved on the body are sea deities and monsters. It stands on a vase-shaped stem on a circular foot, chased with conventional fruit, shells and strapwork (Plate LVIII, No. 3).

The German fashion of making ships ceased in the eighteenth century.

Enamelled work on the precious metals is a subject which deserves separate treatment, solely because the enamellers were often distinct from the goldsmiths proper. Benvenuto Cellini is a striking example of a craftsman who took up enamelling later in his picturesque career, as he relates in his Memoirs.

David Altenstetter (Attemstetter), of Augsburg (died 1617), provides an interesting case of a craftsman who specialised in enamel on silver. One of his choicest things in enamel is the silver case of a little clock, in the Imperial Museum at Vienna, probably made shortly before the death of Rudolph II, for whose crown he is supposed to have executed the enamel work in 1602. Here is definite proof of collaboration between a goldsmith and an enameller, for this case has the marks of a member of the Grosz family of Augsburg goldsmiths and of Altenstetter himself. Likewise a part of the above-mentioned Pomeranian cabinet is stamped with these two craftsmen's marks.

GERMANY

The enamelled work of Altenstetter is recognised from the repetition of the designs, apart from his individual mark stamped upon it. The author has seen one or two enamelled pieces which might be attributed to him or to a follower, including a cup in Baron Bruno Schröder's collection.

In Germany, as in England and Holland, vessels of glass and porcelain, as well as rock crystal and other natural products, already mentioned, were lavishly mounted in silver-gilt by goldsmiths of the sixteenth and seventeenth centuries. These can only be studied in detail by visits to the great collections in Dresden, Paris, Munich, Vienna and elsewhere.

Chinese porcelain is represented by the ewer, mounted by Georg Berger, of Erfurt, about 1570, illustrated on page 94 of Lessing's *Gold und Silber*; and a bottle, mounted by Hieronymus Bang, of Nuremberg, about 1600, in the collection of the Baroness James de Rothschild.

Venetian glass was also brought into the goldsmiths' workshops to be mounted in precious metal. Two important specimens of *latticinio* glass, richly garnished by goldsmiths, are illustrated in the catalogue of the Baroness James de Rothschild's collection. A beaker of this glass, with German silver-gilt mounts of about 1600, is illustrated on Plate 86 of the present writer's catalogue of the late Mr. J. Pierpont Morgan's plate.

The art of the goldsmith was closely allied to that of the armourer, the former often working "parade armour," as for example, the iron shield of the second half of the sixteenth century, signed by Jörg Sikmann, silversmith of Augsburg, which is in the Victoria and Albert Museum. A sword by Desiderius Colman, of Augsburg, 1562, is in the Königliche Zeughaus in Berlin. Two other members of the Colman family of armourers, Lorenz and Koloman, executed "parade armour" in the manner of goldsmiths' work, as did Anton Peffenhauser of Augsburg, the maker of the ornate suit of that romantic figure, King Sebastian of Portugal, now in the Royal Armoury at Madrid.

The silver suit of armour ordered in 1516 by the Emperor Maximilian from Koloman Colman and completed in 1519 after the Emperor's death, has perished. Four drawings by Albrecht Dürer (two at Vienna and two at Berlin) are supposed to show parts of it. The armourers of Augsburg of the sixteenth century used the same pine-cone mark as the goldsmiths, as may be observed on the armour by Lorenz Colman, about 1540, in the Wallace Collection.

During the Thirty Years' War (1618-48) poetic zeal was quenched and art in Germany languished. The goldsmith's craft, however, was not wholly stagnant, for many important objects were made in that unsettled period. Pillage and plunder were inevitable accompaniments of the war, and many precious objects in gold and silver, ecclesiastical and secular, perished.

The art of carving in ivory practised in the old towns of the Rhine between the tenth and twelfth centuries fell into decay and was not revived in Germany for objects of secular use until the seventeenth century.

Little or nothing is known regarding the history of the carvers of the many ivory tankards mounted by German silversmiths in the seventeenth and eighteenth centuries. One name, however, has been recovered, namely, that of Bernard Strauss, of Augsburg, the author of the signed tankard of the second half of the seventeenth century, carved with a Bacchanalian subject and with a Centaur and Lapith on the cover, which is in the Victoria and Albert Museum. A tall cup and cover, carved with Olympic gods, also signed by him, is in the splendid collection of ivories in the old Imperial Museum at Vienna. No drinking vessels by the chief of the German workers in ivory of the seventeenth century, Christoph Angermair, can be ascribed to him.

One of the most prolific mounters of carved ivory cups and tankards was an Augsburg silversmith, supposed to be Andreas Wickhart, one of two men of this name. Several pieces stamped with the Wickhart mark are recorded, but no proof has been adduced that he (or they) was the carver as well as the mounter.

Two cups carved by the Scandinavian ivory worker, Magnus Berg, are at Windsor Castle (see page 82).

Statuettes, in the form of figures on horseback, designed both

GERMANY

as wine flasks and as ornaments for the table or sideboard, were highly popular in Germany in the middle of the seventeenth century, the idea having been derived, it is supposed, from the great equestrian portraits of Rubens and Vandyck, rather than from large bronze statues. Contemporary or earlier figures prominent in European history were chosen as suitable subjects for commemoration in this manner; and the most popular of all, judging from the number extant to-day, was Gustavus Adolphus of Sweden, the hero of the Thirty Years' War, of whom several silver statuettes remain. One of these, inherited by Lord Dalmeny from his maternal grandfather, Baron Mayer de Rothschild, was fitted by the silversmith, with engaging impartiality, with interchangeable heads, one being Gustaphus Adolphus and the other Wallenstein. The maker was an unknown Augsburg goldsmith, who made the supposed statuette of Charles I. of England, in the Kremlin at Moscow (Plate LVII, No. 2). At Windsor Castle is a later statuette of another personage, wrought at Augsburg, probably by Heinrich Mannlich, which differs from the others in having medallions of Socrates and Hippocrates on the high pedestal. No fewer than eight statuettes are in the Kremlin, including the gifts of Charles XI and Charles XII, of Sweden, to the Russian Court. One interesting fact is that most of these statuettes were made at Augsburg and that they were seldom favoured by the goldsmiths of Nuremberg.

Different from either of these is the silver group (in Rosenborg Castle) of Christian IV of Denmark tilting, made at Brunswick in 1595-6.

From about 1640 German goldsmiths wrought many dishes of great size, both oval and circular, for ostentatious display on sideboards rather than for practical use, as conspicuous in size as the German *Riesenpokal*, already described. Three dishes of this character are at Windsor Castle and are illustrated in the present author's book on that collection. Dishes with medallions of Roman Emperors on the rims abound in collections of German plate. One such vessel, with Tiberius and Augustus, Julius Cæsar and Caligula, the gift of Charles XII of Sweden to the Court of Russia, is in the Kremlin, while another, adorned with busts of

Cicero and Seneca, is in the Rijks Museum at Amsterdam. Biblical and classical subjects are the chief decorative features of the centre.

Some dishes have tulips and other flowers—similar to those in the designs of Johannes Thünckel (1664)—foliage, birds and other motives, repoussé and chased on the borders; others show traces in the grotesque faces of the influence of Adam van Vianen, especially in those by Hamburg goldsmiths.

In one collection alone—the vast treasure of the Emperors of Russia in the Kremlin—there are at least nineteen great dishes, and of these no fewer than fourteen were wrought at Augsburg and the others at Hamburg. Some large dishes have come under the author's notice in England, in addition to those at Windsor Castle. One, in the possession of the Earl of Derby, was made by Gottlieb Mentzel, of Augsburg (died 1757), and is chiefly interesting from the engraved arms of the Duke of Buckingham.

None are more conspicuous among the cups introduced in the seventeenth century, not earlier than about 1625, than those with shell-shaped bowls, like the richly decorated cup of enamelled gold in the possession of the Duke of Portland (Plate LVIII, No. 1). This has a stem in the form of two lovers, vigorously modelled by a master craftsman, while at the back is a figure of Pan, with Cupid as bride. In the unfortunate absence of marks, the creator of this notable piece of German goldsmith's work must remain unidentified.

Many cups with shell-like bowls may be seen in collections. Six with figure stems are illustrated in Filimonov's catalogue of the great collection of German and other plate in the Kremlin. One with the mark probably of Mateus or Markus Wolff, of Augsburg, is in the Waddesdon collection in the British Museum.

One of the most interesting pieces of the second half of the seventeenth century is a large fruit stand, set inside with a plaque representing a battle, supported by a figure of Judith holding the head of Holofernes. The foot is repoussé with four panels containing various animals, symbolical of Asia, Africa, America, and Europe. The maker was Johann Jacob Wolrab (1633–90), silversmith and medallist, of Nuremberg, who made mechanical figures for Louis XIV and other monarchs. It is illustrated in the catalogue of the late Mr. Leopold de Rothschild's collection.

Canisters of large size were made in Germany between about 1650 and 1725, both in silver and pewter. They are of several shapes, hexagonal and octagonal, circular and pear-shaped.

Domestic silver candlesticks are by no means common in Germany. Not until the middle of the seventeenth century do they appear in any number. A favourite pattern from 1650 to about 1700 was a twisted pillar, plain or chased with flowers (derived no doubt from the legs of contemporary furniture), which was supported on a wide spreading circular base with or without ball feet. The same shape was made by silversmiths of Holland and Sweden, as are illustrated on Plates LXVII and XCII.

A second pattern has classical figures as stems—Venus, Juno, Minerva and others, on high circular bases. Of this type are the candlesticks by a goldsmith of Hamburg, given by Charles X of Sweden to the Court of Russia in 1655, which are illustrated in Mr. F. R. Martin's book on these gifts. Candelabra of this style were also made.

In the collection of the Kings of Saxony at Dresden are some silver-gilt candelabra by the above Gottlieb Mentzel, the maker of several candlesticks in the royal collection at Darmstadt.

The author has seen some plain silver candlesticks of octagonal shape, copied from English models by goldsmiths of Hanover early in the eighteenth century.

Designs for silver chandeliers were executed by Johann Michael Hoppenhaupt, of Berlin, in the middle of the eighteenth century.

German silver sconces were not made before the seventeenth century, and are generally more elaborate than those by English goldsmiths. One of the few collections is that in the Kremlin at Moscow, where there are several ornate examples of Augsburg workmanship of about 1650–75. Others are in the old royal collections of Germany.

Designs for sconces were executed by Abraham Drentwett in the Louis XIV taste, and by Leonhard Heckenhauer shortly before 1700. One other designer was Hieronymus Bölmann, of

Nuremberg. Georg Lorenz Gaap, of Augsburg (1669–1745), executed sconces with horses, after designs by Riedinger, a well-known animal artist.

Gueridons of silver were only made for princes. Two by Gerhardt Oberdieck, of Magdeburg, in 1681, are in the Schloss at Berlin. Several others by members of the well-known Biller family of Augsburg are at Dresden and Rosenborg Castle.

Silver andirons also were fit objects for the palaces of princes. Specimens by Augsburg silversmiths of the seventeenth century are in the Kremlin.

German silver furniture includes two tables by a member of the Biller family, four chairs of wood covered with silver, and two large wall mirrors, all of the first half of the eighteenth century, and all in the collection of the Duke of Cumberland when examined by the author in 1910. To these may be added the ornate silver table, by an Augsburg goldsmith, in possession of Prince Esterhazy.

Johann Andreas Thelot, of Augsburg (1654–1734), was skilled in repoussé work, and executed many silver plaques of Scriptural and mythological subjects. For about three years he was in Rome, and signed one of his works *Roma*, with the date 1687.

Towards the end of the seventeenth century German goldsmiths, with the collaboration of enamellers, introduced some domestic vessels decorated with painted enamels. One such enameller was Johann Jakob Priester, of Augsburg, who flourished at the end of the seventeenth and the beginning of the eighteenth centuries. He was the enameller of six little beakers, only $2\frac{1}{8}$ inches high, with wide bands of the Zodiac and subjects symbolical of the months, doubtless originally part of a set of twelve, in the Baroness James de Rothschild's collection. In the same collection are several other pieces of silver-gilt plate, decorated with painted enamels of the early eighteenth century: a teapot by an unknown Augsburg goldsmith; a small vase; a small beaker by Elias Adam, of Augsburg, who made enamelled objects in collaboration with Priester; two small cups; two small plates and a box. All these are illustrated on Plates 84 and 85 in the catalogue of this collection.

GERMANY

Two beakers by Philipp Stenglin, of Augsburg, about 1720, were in the collection of the late Baroness Salomon de Rothschild, of Paris, which also contained a liquor stand with a bottle and six cups of painted enamel, by the above Elias Adam.

The use of wine-coolers on the floor of the dining hall or chamber was not unknown in Germany at the end of the fifteenth century, as is proved by a woodcut, ascribed to Michael Wolgemut (1434-1519), showing Solomon and his wives at a banquet. The flagon and bottle standing in the cooler were doubtless intended to be silver or even gold.

Such coolers in silver were comparatively common in the first half of the eighteenth century, and several are in the late collection of the German Emperor, now displayed in the Schloss at Berlin. Others by Johan Jacob Bruglocher, the elder, of Augsburg, are in the Royal collection at Gotha. By him is one in the Winter Palace at Petrograd, which is illustrated in Baron de Foelkersam's catalogue of that collection, and another in the old royal collection at Dresden. An example by Oxner, of Munich, 1715, is in the royal collection at Munich, and another, by Salomon Dreyer, of Augsburg, about 1740, is in the royal castle at Weimar.

Sir John Ramsden, Bart., is the owner of a great wine cooler by a member of the Drentwett family of goldsmiths of Augsburg, early in the eighteenth century, probably the maker of another, shown on Plate 97 of the late Mr. J. Pierpont Morgan's catalogue.

An occasional cooler is accompanied by a large wine-fountain, as was the case in England. One notable example, decorated in Louis XIV style, by Johann Jakob Biller, of Augsburg (1716-9), is illustrated in the above catalogue by Baron de Foelkersam.

The windmill cup (mühlenbecher) of the Dutch (Plate LXIII) was also made occasionally by German goldsmiths, as were the cups called "Hansel im Keller" and "vexier pokal" (puzzle cup).

From the early years of the eighteenth century much of the German plate is markedly under the influence of French decoration.

Designs in Louis XIV taste were made and published by such men as Abraham Drentwett, of Augsburg (1647-1729), and Johann Leonhard Eysler, of Nuremberg (died 1733), a practical goldsmith as well as designer, many of whose works are illustrated in Dr. P. Jessen's book on designers.

Johann Erhard Heuglin II, of Augsburg (master in 1717), was not only a designer, as is seen in his published prints of table plate, introducing in many cases his favourite motive of human busts in medallions, but he was also a practical goldsmith. Several pieces from his hands are recorded by Dr. Rosenberg, including a rare toilet-set of Saxe enamel inlaid with gold, in the Schatzkammer at Munich.

Members of the prominent Biller family of Augsburg goldsmiths were skilful, if not always successful, imitators of French designs. To Johann Ludwig Biller is attributed a great centrepiece in the Winter Palace at Petrograd, wrought in emulation of some such French centrepiece as that of 1727–8 by Claude Ballin, the younger, in the same collection, both of which are illustrated in Baron de Foelkersam's catalogue. Shown in the same book is a large toilet-set decorated in Louis XIV taste by the same goldsmith in 1730, and other important German plate of the eighteenth century.

Joh. Jac. Baumgartner, of Augsburg, published in 1727 some details of ornament in the French manner for ecclesiastical and secular vessels.

A gold toilet-set of about fifty pieces by a member of the Biller family is in the Hermitage Museum at Petrograd.

The enthusiasm evoked among German princes and other noble patrons for French manners and art and for the rococo (called in German *muschelwerk* and *Neueste Art*) led to exaggerated extravagance in many crafts, not only in silver but also in other metal work, and in furniture, porcelain and pottery.

Among the designers of silver in the rococo style were Martin Engelbrecht (1684–1756) and Caspar Gottlieb Eissler, of Nuremberg, about 1750, some of whose designs are illustrated by Wessely in *Das Ornament*. Ecclesiastical goldsmiths' work was also affected by the new taste.

Bernhard Heinrich Weye, of Augsburg, was the maker in 1751–2 of a large centrepiece in the most extravagant phase of the rococo, as may be observed from the illustration in the third edition of Dr. Rosenberg's book on marks. He also made in 1761–3 three curious centrepieces containing many figures of

GERMANY

musicians playing divers instruments, which were in the collection of the Duke of Cumberland.

Contrasted with the remains of French goldsmith's art of the eighteenth century, much domestic plate of Germany in that century often appears bizarre and crude in conception and execution, and, like some of the plate of the seventeenth century, is marred by over-elaboration of detail. Between 1700 and the introduction of the rococo style some plate of excellent workmanship was, however, executed.

Ecuelles, with or without their dishes, in the French fashion already described, were made by German goldsmiths shortly before 1750. Several examples are in the Industrial Art Museum in Vienna. One of these was made by Johann Engelbrecht, of Augsburg, before his death in 1748. A charming specimen, with its cover and dish, decorated with Louis XIV ornament, by Thomas Dankelmair, or Theodor Dassdorf, of Augsburg, early in the eighteenth century, is in the collection of Baron Bruno Schröder.

The fact is not surprising, in view of the dynastic connection between Hanover and England, that English plate was copied by Hanoverian goldsmiths in the eighteenth century. The collection of the Duke of Cumberland contained octagonal salts and casters in the English style, and double sauce-boats, by Behrns, and others by John Ludwig Selle (master in 1724), of Hanover, where also were made some other sauce-boats by Bunsen, the maker of several candelabra, inspired by French models, in the same collection. Here also were some barrel-shaped ice-pails by G. Hossauer, of Berlin, copied from English models of about the year 1800. Some other plate of English style by Hanoverian goldsmiths has been observed elsewhere by the author.

The Dinglinger family, goldsmiths and jewellers to the Court of Saxony, must not be forgotten in this survey, brief as it is. The "Green Vaults" at Dresden contains their most precious works, including a gold and enamelled tea or coffee service by Johann Melchior Dinglinger, of which the teapot, made about 1700, is illustrated on Plate LX (No. 2).

Several artists executed designs for goldsmiths, many of which were published in the second half of the sixteenth century. Albrecht Altdorfer (c. 1480–1538) was a designer of cups. Peter Flötner's ornaments, as shown in his *Kunstbuch* of 1549, had a marked influence in Germany, and was not unknown to English goldsmiths (see page 98). Seven other designers are well known from their published engravings: Hans Brosamer (worked c. 1520–54); Virgil Solis (1514–62); the anonymous Nuremberg designer of c. 1570–80; Bernard Zan (worked 1580–1); Hans Sibmacher (fl. 1555–95); Georg Wechter; and Paul Flindt.

Besides engravings of ornament, wooden models of vessels were occasionally used, while lead casts of the figures and of the most popular decorative motives were kept for use. Several of these casts are in German museums.

The books of Dr. P. Jessen should be studied on this subject, as well as Wessely's *Das Ornament*.

In this brief survey of German domestic plate it is impossible to sketch the historic sequence of the subject in adequate detail. Visits to the great collections would be necessary to appreciate the full extent of the subject. The Kremlin contains perhaps the most important collection of seventeenth-century plate. The treasure of the kingdoms and principalities of Germany must be seen to be understood—Dresden, Munich, Gotha, Cassel, Darmstadt, and others—likewise the public museums. The Imperial Museum in Vienna is rich in rare specimens. The magnificent municipal plate of the old city of Lüneberg is in the Kunstgewerbe Museum at Berlin. In London there are the British Museum and the Victoria and Albert Museum. The Louvre has a few pieces. At Windsor Castle are twenty-four pieces. Some important specimens are in the Metropolitan Museum, New York.

Dr. Marc Rosenberg's indispensable work, *Der Goldschmiede Merkzeichen* (third edition), includes references to many catalogues of, and writings on, German plate. For illustrations of more examples, the following additional works, by the present author, may be consulted: the catalogues of the collections of the late Mr. J. Pierpont Morgan, the late Mr. Leopold de Rothschild, the Baroness James de Rothschild, and of Windsor Castle.

PLATE LX

PLATE LXI

HOLLAND

PLATE LXI.

No. 1 Silver horn of St. George's guild, 1566. H. 18¾ in. Rijks Museum, Amsterdam.
No. 2 Dish, by Hans Christiaans, of Leeuwarden, 1632. D. 7⅞ in.
On loan at the Friesch Museum, Leeuwarden.
No. 3 Queen of Bohemia's cup, by Hans Coenraet Brechtel, of The Hague, 1641. H. 31⅛ in.
Stedelyk Museum, Leyden.
No. 4 Silver-mounted horn, 1397. Friesch Museum, Leeuwarden.

PLATE LXII.

No. 1 Basin, by Adam van Vianen I, 1614. D. 20¾ in.
No. 2 Ewer, companion to No. 1, by the same maker. H. 15¼ in.
No. 3 Basin, by Johannes Lutma, the elder, of Amsterdam, 1647. D. 27⅛ in.
No. 4 Ewer, companion to No. 3, by the same maker. H. 19⅞ in.
No. 5 Ewer (H. 8¼ in.) and basin (D. 23⅞ in.), by Johannes Lutma, the elder, 1655.
(All in the Rijks Museum, Amsterdam.)

PLATE LXIII.

No. 1 Windmill cup, Dordrecht, c. 1610. H. 9 in.
No. 2 Beaker, c. 1675.
No. 3 Gold and enamelled cup of Admiral De Ruyter, 1667. H. 11¾ in.
No. 4 Carved cocoanut cup, Utrecht, 1610. H. 9½ in.
No. 5 Silver-gilt glass-holder, probably by Leendert Claesz, of Amsterdam, 1609. H. 9¼ in.
(Nos. 1, 3, 4 and 5 are in the Rijks Museum, Amsterdam.)

PLATE LXIV.

No. 1 William the Silent's covered cup of tazza form, c. 1574. Earl of Yarborough.
No. 2 Ewer of jasper and gold, by Paul van Vianen, 1608. Imperial Museum, Vienna.

PLATE LXV.

No. 1 Interior of tazza, by Adam van Vianen, 1620. D. 8¼ in. H. 6¼ in.
Baroness James de Rothschild.
No. 2 Nautilus-shell cup, Utrecht, c. 1580. H. 12 in.
No. 3 Tazza, Utrecht, 17th century. D. 8¼ in. H. 6⅜ in.
(Nos. 2 and 3 in the Victoria and Albert Museum.)

PLATE LXVI.

No. 1 Dish, by Jan Looff, of Middelburg, 1631. D. 18¼ in.
Collection of Mr. A. O. van Kerkwijk.
No. 2 "Bezoar" cup, by Michel Esselbeeck, of Amsterdam, 1647-8. H. 17⅜ in.
National Museum, Copenhagen.

PLATE LXVII.

No. 1 Brandy bowl, c. 1650. D. 4¾ in. H. 3¼ in.
No. 2 One of a pair of candlesticks, by Nicholas Mensma, of Leeuwarden, 1670.
H. 12 in.   Friesch Museum, Leeuwarden.
No. 3 Large wine fountain, The Hague, early 18th century.   Winter Palace, Petrograd.
No. 4 Rococo candlestick, c. 1750.
No. 5 One of a pair of candlesticks, Nijmegen, early 18th century.   Earl Spencer.
No. 6 Candlestick, by Anthony de Rooy, of Amsterdam, 1734. H. 8¼ in.
No. 7 Brandy bowl, by Johannes Lelij, of Leeuwarden, 1725. Total length, 8⅞ in. H. 3 in.

PLATE LXVIII.

No. 1 Tobacco box, by Gabynus Lelij, of Leeuwarden, c. 1735.
No. 2 Kettle, by Johannes Lelij, of Leeuwarden, 1718. H. with handle, 7⅞ in.
                                                                                           Rijks Museum, Amsterdam.
No. 3 Reliquary, by Johannes Lelij, c. 1715, with Italian niello of c. 1490-1510. H. 14¼ in.
                                                                                           Friesch Museum, Leeuwarden.
No. 4 Caster, Dordrecht, 1729. H. 7¼ in.
No. 5 Pierced dish, by Jan Pondt, of Amsterdam, 1733.

IN Holland, as in other countries, serious losses in precious old gold and silver have to be recorded.

The earliest piece to be illustrated here is a silver-mounted drinking-horn, in the Friesch Museum at Leeuwarden—a Museum containing many personal objects in silver and other treasures. Inscribed upon it in Gothic characters is the following : " Desen hoern hebben doen maken de broders va Sinte Antonis ghilde MCCCXCVII." On a silver plate are figures representing St. Peter and St. Anthony. On another piece of silver are the words "Laute Antonis." The horn belonged to the St. Anthony's guild, of Stavoren, a historic town in Friesland, and the residence of Frisian princes in the early Middle Ages, where this interesting old relic is believed to have been mounted by an unknown silversmith (Plate LXI, No. 4).

Two highly interesting horns of silver, relics of two of the old Amsterdam guilds, are deposited in the Rijks Museum. First in date is the horn of the guild of St. Sebastian, 1565, supported on figures representing the martyrdom of that saint. It is painted in B. van der Helst's picture of the heads of the guild in 1653, in the same Museum. The second is the horn, only a year later in date, of the guild of St. George, appropriately crowned with a

PLATE LXII

PLATE LXIII

figure of the saint and decorated on the silver foot and mouth with rich ornament in the manner of the Dutch Renaissance (Plate LXI, No. 1). This actual vessel is commemorated in two pictures, in the Rijks Museum, by B. van der Helst, of the banquet in the hall of the guild in celebration of the Peace of Münster in 1648 and again in the work representing the four heads of the guild of archers in 1656. A finely wrought standing cup and cover of the early seventeenth century of a St. George's guild, is illustrated by Mr. Carel J. A. Begeer.*

Just as it was the custom of the heads of the various Dutch guilds to adorn their halls with portraits and paintings of scenes associated with their history, as mentioned above, so, too, costly cups were frequently presented by members for their convivial gatherings. One piece of guild plate is the horn of crystal and silver of the guild of St. Hubert at Haarlem, executed by Arend Lambertsen from a design by Salomon de Braij, of that picturesque town.

With the Dutch people the beaker was a popular drinking vessel in the sixteenth and seventeenth centuries, not only for domestic purposes, but also after the Reformation as a Sacramental cup. Many old churches in Holland have several of these beakers, some merely engraved with the conventional interlaced band of arabesques from which depend sprays of flowers—perhaps derived from the engraved designs of Balthasar Sylvius (1518–80); others are engraved with sacred subjects, such as the Last Supper, and figures of Faith, Hope and Charity, and with views of churches. These Dutch beakers spread their influence into Scotland and America, as is shown in the chapters on the plate of those countries.

Beakers decorated with the conventional band mentioned above are conspicuous objects in many " Still Life " pictures of the Dutch artists, Pieter Claesz and Willem K. Heda and others.

Seven interesting Dutch beakers are preserved in American churches, five of which were made at Haarlem. One of them, wrought at Amsterdam by an unknown silversmith in 1637, is believed to have been the " silver tunn," bequeathed to the First

---

* Mr. Begeer's brochure, *Inleiding tot de Geschiedenis der Nederlandsche Edelsmeedkunst*, to which frequent mention is made in this chapter.

Church in Boston by the eminent divine, John Cotton. The earliest of the Haarlem beakers is of the year 1638, and the second is 1655 and is in the old Dutch Church at the entrance to " Sleepy Hollow " near Tarrytown, New York, made famous by Washington Irving in his " Legend of Sleepy Hollow." One of these Haarlem beakers, of the year 1660, in the First Reformed Church in Albany, served as a model for one made in 1678 by Ahasuerus Hendricks, the New York silversmith of Dutch antecedents. All these beakers are illustrated in *The Old Silver of the American Churches*.

Among the historic English plate preserved at Gonville and Caius College, Cambridge, is a travelling nest of four plain seventeenth century Dutch beakers, fitted with a cover, and wrought by an unknown silversmith at The Hague. One of the beakers is quaintly inscribed : " Ralph Lord Hopton's Little Kitchen of silver Plate," the owner having been Lord Hopton, Royalist leader under Charles I before his death in exile at Bruges in 1652. The set is illustrated in the present author's book on the old plate of the Cambridge Colleges, with a Dutch flagon described later.

A beaker by a Dordrecht silversmith of the date 1667 is engraved with five medallions of princes of the House of Orange ; it is in the collection of Baron Bruno Schröder.

The Dutch family of Van Vianen is known everywhere as highly skilled goldsmiths.

Adam (c. 1555–1627), born at Utrecht (son of Willem Eernstensz van Vianen), was one of the most talented goldsmiths of his time and is best known, perhaps, for his introduction of a new decorative feature into plate, the grotesque masks, a veritable " art nouveau," which profoundly affected Dutch silversmiths' work for fifty years and spread to England and Germany. To him is attributed the finely executed ewer and basin of 1614, belonging to the City of Amsterdam and now in the Rijks Museum, the former of which still retains a Renaissance shape, but introduces the fantastic decoration already mentioned (Plate LXII, Nos. 1 and 2). He was also the author of a shrine of crystal and enamelled gold, in the late Mr. J. Pierpont Morgan's collection of jewels, which is illustrated in Dr. G. C. Williamson's catalogue ; and of a silver

HOLLAND

tazza in 1620, in the collection of the Baroness James de Rothschild (Plate LXV, No. 1). By him is a fine dish, signed and dated 1624, in the collection of Sir John H. B. Noble, Bart.

Paul van Vianen (c. 1565–c. 1614) brother of Adam, was also highly skilled, and after learning his craft from one Cornelis Elertz, decided, like many painters, to travel to Italy in search of experience, and thence in 1596 to Munich, where he became a master goldsmith in 1599. Five years later this cosmopolitan artist entered the service of that patron of the arts, the Emperor Rudolph II, at Prague. Here he executed, in 1608, his masterpiece, the superb ewer of jasper and gold, now in the Imperial Museum at Vienna (Plate LXIV); and in 1610 the Prince of Wied's gold cup and cover, decorated with mythological subjects, of which an electrotype copy is in the Victoria and Albert Museum.

Adam van Vianen the younger (born 1595), son of the above Adam van Vianen, is chiefly known for his designs for silver work, introducing the grotesque masks of his father in a more exaggerated manner, which were engraved by Th. van Kessel in 1641 and published in facsimile by Nyhoff in 1892. The exuberance of the "Van Vianen" style is nowhere more marked than in the ewer, formerly in the collection of the late Marquess of Sligo and attributed to Adam the younger. It is illustrated in the reproductions by Nyhoff. Many of his works have perished.

Another member of the family, Christian van Vianen,* was in England in 1637 and was employed by Charles I to make the altar vessels for St. George's Chapel, Windsor Castle, which were unfortunately melted in the Civil War, with countless other treasures in plate, both English and foreign. A dish by him of the year 1635 in the Victoria and Albert Museum (a gift of Sir John Ramsden, Bart.) is skilfully decorated with an elaborate design of dolphins. One result of his visit to England was probably the introduction, to the English goldsmiths of Charles II, of the "Van Vianen"

---

* There is some contradiction between the Lexicons of Wurzbach and Kramm as to the parentage of Christian van Vianen. In the former he is stated to have been the son of Adam van Vianen, the younger, and in the latter of Adam van Vianen, the elder.

grotesque masks, as may be observed in the Coronation salts of 1660 in the Tower of London, and in several cups illustrated in an article by Mr. W. W. Watts in the *Burlington Magazine* for June 1918. Other evidence of Dutch influence in the decoration of English silver between 1660 and 1685 is apparent not only in the objects themselves (as in the furniture) but also from the encouragement given by Charles II to foreign craftsmen, as revealed in the petition to him in 1664 lamenting the neglect of the London goldsmiths in favour of "the multitude of strangers" (Dutchmen and others) in London. There is no evidence that Pieter Roestraeten, pupil and son-in-law of Franz Hals, exerted any influence in the designs of silversmiths during his sojourn in England, though he painted silver in some of his pictures.

Christian van Vianen was perhaps the maker of the tazza of 1649 illustrated on page 17 of Mr. Begeer's brochure.

Next to the Van Vianen family, the most prominent Dutch goldsmith of the seventeenth century was Johannes Lutma, the elder, of Amsterdam, a familiar figure from the portrait etched by his friend Rembrandt. Few of his authentic works have survived. His dish and ewer of 1647, decorated with marine subjects in relief, show traces of the "Van Vianen" influence, and are in marked contrast with the simplicity of his ewer and dish of 1655. The dolphin handles on both ewers are alike (Plate LXII, Nos. 3, 4 and 5). The second pair were made by Lutma expressly for the banquet in celebration of the opening of the new Town Hall at Amsterdam, and are deposited with other city treasures in the Rijks Museum, where there is a finely wrought little bowl or cup from his skilful hands.

Ewers like the second specimen would seem to have been common in Holland in the seventeenth century. The similar one of Elizabeth, Queen of Bohemia, preserved with its companion dish at Windsor Castle, is mentioned later. Such ewers and dishes were not only used for rose-water or plain water for ceremonial purposes and for the dining table, but were apparently used for other purposes, as is confirmed by the picture of a lady at her toilet by Jacob Ochterveldt, in the National Gallery in London.

HOLLAND

In discussing Dutch dishes, an example deserving of study, because of the superiority of the repoussé decoration over some Dutch work, is one made in 1661 by Klaes Baardt, a Frisian goldsmith working at Bolsward, who is believed to have improved his technique by his sojourn in France. This is illustrated by Mr. Begeer (No. 39), with the base of a candlestick, showing the excellence of his work. An interesting salver on a stand, embossed and chased on the wide border with scenes from Dutch rural life, by a goldsmith of Delft, is illustrated on Plate 33 of the catalogue of the late Mr. Leopold de Rothschild's collection. It is inscribed : " Ian van der Strate and Jacomiinje van Weemaer. Echtelick ver Vaemt binnen Delft. den 18 Mey 1642 "—the year in which Rembrandt finished his famous " Night Watch."

Four dishes, by Hans Christiaans, the most highly skilled of the Frisian goldsmiths of that time, of Leeuwarden, 1632, repoussé with mythological subjects, are on loan in the Friesch Museum in that town (Plate LXI, No. 2).

Reference has been made in the chapters on English and German plate to the tall and graceful vase-shaped ewers, with their basins, of the sixteenth and early seventeenth centuries. The same shape of ewer found favour among Dutch goldsmiths in the first few years of the seventeenth century, before the introduction of the shorter and wider ewer towards the middle of the century. Adam van Vianen's skilfully executed ewer of 1614 has just been mentioned. One more of a different character, though retaining its Renaissance form (in the Rijks Museum), was made in 1608 by Jacques Bogaert of Amsterdam and is illustrated by Mr. Begeer (No. 26). In this ewer the decoration is engraved and is composed of conventional festoons of fruit and arabesques.

The history, interesting as it must have been, has been lost of the tall vase-shaped silver ewer and basin to which Gerard Dou devoted a whole picture with his usual minute finish, now in the Louvre. The same vessels are repeated in his picture " Le trompette" in the same Gallery. Terborch shows a graceful vase-shaped ewer on a basin in one of his best pictures, in Buckingham Palace.

In form and in some of the decoration most of the few extant standing cups and covers of Holland follow those of Germany of the sixteenth century. One of the finest is the St. Martin cup of 1604 of the old Brewers' guild at Haarlem, by the two Haarlem goldsmiths, Hendrik de Keyser, who executed the figure of the saint on the cover, and Ernst Janszoon van Vianen, the chaser of the four panels of scenes from the life of the saint, after designs of Hendrik Goltzius. While the form is German there is a marked departure from German cups in the workmanship and decoration. Similar in shape is the fine cup of a guild of St. George, already mentioned. Electrotype copies of both cups are in the Victoria and Albert Museum. The decoration of sprays of fruit and other characteristic German ornament suggests that these conventional ornaments were continued somewhat later in Holland than in Germany itself. A third cup of this shape, of about 1600, illustrated on Plate 9 of the catalogue of the Baroness James de Rothschild's collection, has an inscription in Dutch to the effect that it was a gift to the Burgomaster of a town in Holland. Another important cup, illustrated by Mr. Begeer (No. 20), has the conventional German decoration on the vase-shaped stem and foot, while the body is skilfully engraved with subjects in the manner of Crispin van der Passe, the elder (1536–1601). The name of the maker in 1649 is unknown.

Among other standing cups worthy of notice is the unique specimen in the National Museum at Copenhagen, with a body formed of a "Bezoar" stone, supported on a trunk of a tree with figures of Adam and Eve, whose legs are fastened by chains to grotesque animals seated on the foot. Michel Esselbeeck, of Amsterdam, the maker in 1647–8, was influenced in the grotesque faces and wavy decoration of the foot and other parts by the familiar "Van Vianen" manner (Plate LXVI). A touch of the "Van Vianen" style is also apparent in the large and historic silver-gilt cup of Elizabeth, Queen of Bohemia, made in 1641 by H. C. Brechtel at The Hague and presented by her to the City of Leyden upon the departure of her children from Leyden University. The finial is a statuette of the Queen herself, while the stem is a satyr, seated on a high foot, on which is worked in relief a represen-

HOLLAND

tation of the Rape of Amphitrite (Plate LXI, No. 3). The cup is in the Stedelyk Museum at Leyden. The Queen's Dutch ewer and basin are described on page 241.

The originals of the tall cups decorated with the large plain bosses of early seventeenth-century German cups, as seen in the "Still Life" picture by Pieter de Ring (died 1660) in the Wallace Collection and in the "Still Life" by J. D. de Heem in the Louvre, are probably German, as no specimens of Dutch origin are known to have survived.

In the Museum van Oudheden at Arnhem are some guild cups of the seventeenth and eighteenth centuries.

Cups were popular gifts to the naval heroes of Holland in celebration of their successful exploits in the seventeenth century. Two priceless gold and enamelled cups, executed by an unknown Dutch goldsmith and enameller, commemorate the famous descent of the Dutch fleet on the Rivers Thames and Medway in June, 1667. This is not the place for a detailed account of this successful exploit. Sufficient is it to describe the cup which was presented by the Dutch government to Admiral Michael de Ruyter, whose popularity in Holland was as great as that of Nelson in England at a later date, and not only were other gifts bestowed upon him by his admirers and a silver medal struck in his honour by the talented Dutch medallist, Peter van Abeele, but his portrait was painted no fewer than nine times by one artist alone, Ferdinand Bol. To return to a description of the cup: it is $11\frac{3}{4}$ inches high and is engraved with an inscription recording the feats of De Ruyter, and on the painted and coloured enamelled band is a view of notable scenes in the Medway—Dutch and English fleets, the forts of Chatham and Sheerness, the castle and cathedral of Rochester, the castle of Upnor and the Isle of Sheppey and Queenborough. This cup is in the Rijks Museum at Amsterdam (Plate LXIII, No. 3).

The similar cup, presented to Cornelis de Witt, who accompanied the Dutch fleet on the same occasion, has been bequeathed to the City of Paris by Baroness Salomon de Rothschild and was by a curious mistake catalogued, when in the possession of her father, Baron Carl von Rothschild, as of German origin, made in commemoration of the victory of the Roman Catholics over the Huguenots in 1628.

The acanthus and other foliage on these cups are enamelled in black and white. Here again regret must be expressed at the absence of marks indicating the name of the Dutch maker and his town.

Linked indirectly with the same naval exploit are an English silver caudle cup and stand, made in 1668 to commemorate the launching of the new Royal Charles warship to replace the ship of that name captured by De Ruyter. These vessels are in a private collection in England.

A second commemorative gift to a naval commander is one of the typical Dutch beakers, by a Rotterdam silversmith, finely engraved with the conventional straps, fruit and foliage and a view of the River Medway with the Dutch ship, *Pro Patria*, and the warships, *Vrede* and *Funete*, with the name of Captain John Danielszoon van de Rijn as commander of the first ship, to whom it was doubtless a gift. This is also in the Rijks Museum, with a Dutch silver tobacco box, engraved with a representation of the naval engagement between the Dutch and English on the Dogger Bank on August 5, 1781.

Beakers were made in commemoration of more peaceful events and one is illustrated by Mr. Begeer (No. 24) by an unknown Amsterdam silversmith of the seventeenth century. Engraved upon it are three ships and panels representing Justitia, Constantia and Prudentia, with the date 1696 and the names of Claes Jppes and Elles Annes, believed to be two Frisian shippers; this is in the collection of Mr. A. O. van Kerkwijk. The beaker of about 1675 on Plate LXIII (No. 2) is finely engraved with panels of the three Kings in the style of Hendrik Goltzius and other formal ornament.

Unknown by goldsmiths outside Holland are the rare and elegant silver-gilt stands (*bekerschroef*) for holding a wine glass, like the important and well-wrought set, part of the old city plate of Amsterdam, which were made in that city in 1609, probably by Leendert Claesz, and are deposited in the Rijks Museum (Plate LXIII, No. 5). In the collection of Baron Bruno Schröder are an interesting pair in silver-gilt. One such glass holder is in a picture by Jan Steen

PLATE LXIV

PLATE LXV

HOLLAND

at Berlin, and another is in a " Still Life " by Willem van Aelst in the same public gallery.

In the sixteenth century cocoanut cups and nautilus-shell cups crossed the borders from Germany into the Netherlands and were copied there, though not slavishly. Few, however, have survived the ravages of wars and other times of destruction. An example of a carved cocoanut cup, skilfully mounted by an anonymous goldsmith of Utrecht in 1610 (in the Rijks Museum), suggests in some of the decorative features that the Renaissance style survived in Holland to a later date than in Germany (Plate LXIII, No. 4).

Dutch nautilus-shell cups are represented by one by a goldsmith of Utrecht, about 1580, in the Victoria and Albert Museum (Plate LXV, No. 2), while an unusually fine specimen, not improbably made at the same place, is illustrated by Mr. Begeer (No. 10). Nautilus-shell cups are familiar objects in the " Still Life " pictures of Willem Kalf, Beyeren, J. D. de Heem and other Dutch artists of the seventeenth century.

Here it may not be inappropriate to mention the fact that a Dutch artist of the seventeenth century, one Bellekin, specialised in engraving nautilus shells, leaving the mounting of them as cups to goldsmiths. Many of his engraved shells are extant, in addition to three, probably engraved by him, which are in the Natural History Museum, South Kensington. Others are mentioned in the chapter on German plate.

Silver tankards are rare in Holland. A tall flagon-tankard, engraved with festoons of fruit and birds on fruit in a formal manner, dating from the early seventeenth century, is illustrated by Mr. Begeer (No. 30). Of exceeding rarity is a tankard covered on the body, lid and foot with hollow flutes, like those of English plate of the late seventeenth and early eighteenth centuries, and with cut leaves, not unlike those on the New York tankards. This was made at Groningen* in 1706 and is in the collection of Mr. A. O. van Kerkwijk ; it is illustrated by Mr. Begeer (No. 35).

---

* Some silver plate made at Groningen in the eighteenth century is in the Museum there. One piece is a little covered bowl with two handles, decorated with the hollow flutes mentioned above, made in 1726 by Bernardus Pootholt. Another

It is doubtful whether any examples have survived in silver of the pewter tankards or flagons of globular form, with and without the characteristic long spout, which are such conspicuous objects in Dutch "Still Life" pictures, nor has any specimen been recorded of the tall flagon with a globular body on a high foot, with a curved spout, as shown in Willem K. Heda's "Still Life" in the National Gallery in London. Not without interest is the fact that two secular English flagons of this shape, almost identical with Heda's, have been consecrated for sacred purposes in two churches: one dated 1606–7 at All Saints', Oxford, which is illustrated in *Country Life* for November 15, 1924, and the other, three years later in date, at St. Mary's, Hadley Monken, Middlesex.

Interesting survivals of the convivial meetings of the old Dutch guilds and family gatherings of the prosperous burghers occur in the wind-mill cup (*molenbeker*), the form of which was doubtless suggested by that conspicuous feature of the Dutch landscape. Many a wager has been made at festivals and carousals on the attempts of a member or guest to consume the liquid contents in accordance with the prescribed ritual. After filling the cup with wine the would-be drinker must blow through the little tube running parallel with the stairs and by this act causing the wings of the wind-mill to revolve and the figures of the clock to move. The drinker was expected to consume the liquid at one draught before the wings ceased from revolving, otherwise he was penalised by having to drink as many cupfuls as were indicated on the clock at the first attempt. One of these delightful relics of the hard-drinking Dutchmen, wrought at Dordrecht early in the seventeenth century, is in the Rijks Museum (Plate LXIII, No. 1), where there is also a later specimen from the old Millers' guild of Rotterdam. A Danish goldsmith appears to have seen one of these wind-mill cups and to have made one, as is mentioned on page 80.

Another variety of Dutch festive cup of the seventeenth century is in the form of "Hansje in den Kelder" ("Hansel in the cellar")

---

piece is a tall pear-shaped coffee pot on legs, with a spirit lamp underneath, and fitted with a tap, which is characteristic of Groningen province and town. The maker in 1766 was a member of the well-known Van Giffen family of silversmiths in Groningen.

PLATE LXVI

PLATE LXVII

and many of the burgher families could boast the ownership of one, which was proudly brought forth before the assembled guests on the occasion of the expected birth of a child in the family. This is in the form of a tazza, containing in the perforated domed centre the figure of a child, which emerges therefrom upon filling the dish with wine, and the health of the mother is accordingly drunk, to the great content of the onlookers. A specimen is illustrated with a *molenbeker* and other " wager cups " of the seventeenth century in Mr. Begeer's book. One of the plain silver " wager cups " is included in a " Still Life " picture by Joh. van Haensbergen.

Common as were silver salts in the seventeenth century, the student must turn to Dutch " Still Life " pictures for representations of several varieties, by such artists as Willem K. Heda, Pieter Claesz, Jan Steen and others. Of the few extant specimens a pair of unusual form, with large circular bases on ball feet, in the Kremlin at Moscow, are known from the electrotype in the Victoria and Albert Museum. Four interesting salts, by Pieter Verduyn, of The Hague, in 1662, part of the old plate from the ancient Raadhuis at Leyden, are in the Stedelyk Museum in that historic city. A pair, of the same circular form as some German and Swiss salts of the seventeenth century, may be seen in the Victoria and Albert Museum.

Rarer still to-day are Dutch silver casters of the seventeenth century. Here again " Still Life " pictures are evidence of the existence of a plain cylindrical caster, with a gadrooned foot, depicted in a work by J. D. de Heem in the Rijks Museum. A later caster of a form common in other countries, showing a French pattern in the chasing, was made at Dordrecht in 1729 and is illustrated on Plate LXVIII, No. 4.

Dutch candlesticks of the seventeenth century are as rare as salts. A popular shape, found also in Germany and Sweden, has a twisted pillar, suggestive of the legs of Netherlands furniture, but chased with flowers, as in the interesting pair of 1670 by Nicholas Mensma, of Leeuwarden (a pupil of Hillebrandt Brongersma of that town), part of the Popta treasure in the Friesch Museum at Leeuwarden (Plate LXVII, No. 2). The maker had been influenced by the fine example of twenty years earlier by the Dutch goldsmith, known as the "Meester met den Beker," whose finest works, a dish and ewer, decorated with designs after Hendrik Goltzhius, are in the same Museum and are illustrated by Mr. Begeer (Nos. 63 and 64). J. B. Weenix, in a picture of an interior, shows a candlestick with a twisted pillar, as does J. van Streek (c. 1632-78) in his "Still Life" in the Louvre.

Eight tall plain candlesticks, formed of pillars divided into four cylindrical sections on bases of quatrefoil outline, were made by a goldsmith of Leyden about 1660, and were part of the old city plate of Leyden, where they may be seen in the Stedelyk Museum with the four salts mentioned above.

Admirers of old Dutch pictures are familiar with the silver candlestick, perhaps a favourite family possession, which appears over and over again in the pictures of Gerard Terborch. One example only need be quoted—the "Guitar Lesson", in the National Gallery in London. That talented painter, Jan Steen, painted a similar candlestick in his "Physician's Visit," one of his best works, in the collection of the Duke of Wellington, and Brekelenkam shows another of similar shape in one of his pictures. The presumption is probably not rash that silver candlesticks of this shape were not uncommon in Holland about the middle of the seventeenth century, since they are shown in pictures by at least three artists.

Akin to candlesticks are of course the silver sconces, and for specimens of these, as for other Dutch plate of the seventeenth century, the lover of old silver must journey outside Holland to the Kremlin at Moscow, where a set of four are preserved.

Turning to candlesticks of the eighteenth century, an interesting example of the influence of French design may be seen in one by Anthony de Rooy, of Amsterdam, in 1734. This is illustrated with a characteristic candlestick of Dutch rococo of about 1750 and with a plainer and earlier candlestick, wrought at Nijmegen, in the collection of Earl Spencer (Plate LXVII, Nos. 6, 4 and 5 respectively).

In Mr. Begeer's brochure are illustrations of several other Dutch candlesticks.

HOLLAND

Here it may be convenient to note the influence of Daniel Marot, during his exile in Holland, on the designs of Dutch silver, as of other crafts. Other Huguenot craftsmen also fled to Holland from France, but their precise part in the development of silver is not as apparent there as it is in England.

Many rare and historic specimens of old Dutch plate, unmatched in Holland itself, have been preserved in England. Among them is the fine and dignified cup, commemorating the sea fight between the Dutch and the Spanish at Enkhuizen on October 11, 1573, which is adorned with the arms of the Prince of Orange, called William the Silent. The chasing and repoussé work of tritons and sea monsters and appropriate marine subjects with their explanatory inscriptions are of a high order. On the cover is a view of the Zuider Zee, with ships and towns, including Enkhuizen, and surmounting the cover is a standing figure, said to be symbolical of that Dutch town (Plate LXIV). The gifted and anonymous craftsman who wrought this treasure with such skill, probably as a gift for the Prince, has left no trace of his name or place. A full account of the cup and illustrations of details, by Sir Hercules Read, is in *Archæologia*, vol. lix. The present owner, the Earl of Yarborough, has failed to discover any previous history of the cup.

Dutchman as was William III, it cannot be certain that either of the few pieces of Dutch silver at Windsor Castle belonged to him. In fact, two historical vessels, a rose-water dish and ewer of characteristically Dutch forms, which had belonged to the ill-fated Elizabeth, Queen of Bohemia, were purchased by George IV. They were made at The Hague about 1650 during her exile in Holland. It is hardly conceivable that the Queen could have run into further debt by the purchase of these costly vessels at a time when her extreme poverty necessitated—according to the testimony of her daughter Sophia—the disposal of her jewels to provide what Sophia satirically describes as banquets more luxurious than Cleopatra's. The suggestion may not be out of place that these vessels were a gift to the Queen from her loyal friend, the Earl of Craven, who put the whole of his fortune at her disposal. In form the ewer is identical with a decorated one given by Charles XI of Sweden to the Tsar

Alexis of Russia in 1674, now in the Kremlin, and with one by Johannes Lutma the elder, 1655, illustrated on Plate LXII (No. 5).

The third piece of Dutch silver at Windsor is a chalice, by Joannes Bogaert, of Amsterdam, in 1760. Of a more pleasing character is the earlier caudle cup and cover, finely chased with panels representing Jacob receiving Isaac's blessing and the return of Esau from the hunt. This likewise was wrought at Amsterdam, in 1648, by an unknown silversmith. All are illustrated in *The Gold and Silver of Windsor Castle*.

Four fine plain octagonal candlesticks, executed at The Hague late in the seventeenth century, were probably acquired by the first Duke of Marlborough and have been inherited by Earl Spencer with the candlesticks wrought at Nijmegen, previously mentioned.

A rose-water dish and ewer, characteristic of the skill and style of the elder Adam van Vianen, passed into the collection of the Earl of Rosebery from that of the Duke of Sussex. The Duke of Portland is the fortunate owner of some Dutch silver vases, made and embossed by a seventeenth-century goldsmith of The Hague with flowers and acanthus leaves in the same manner as English plate of about 1660-80; these are illustrated in the *Burlington Magazine* for April 1905, with a charcoal burner of the same date and *provenance*, very similar to one in the picture at Chatsworth by Roestraeten, the Dutch artist in England. These rare objects are unmatched in Holland itself.

Historically interesting is the flagon wrought at The Hague about 1675, in the Chapel of Corpus Christi College, Cambridge, the gift of William Stanley, Master of the college and previously tutor to the Princess of Orange, wife of William III of England. This is similar to a pair of flagons of 1682 also made at The Hague— an important centre for silversmithing in the seventeenth century— for the defunct English Church of that city, which are illustrated in an article on old Sacramental vessels in English Churches in Holland, in the *Burlington Magazine* for April, 1908. Of equal historic interest is the nest of plain beakers at Gonville and Caius College, Cambridge, mentioned earlier.

Perhaps unique is the Marquess of Londonderry's oval " Monteith " bowl, by a goldsmith of The Hague ; and of equal rarity is the Duke of Buccleuch's oval and fluted silver wine-cistern, wrought at Amsterdam early in the eighteenth century and recalling in its use the copper wine coolers depicted by the Dutch painters of interiors of the seventeenth century.

A brief reference has just been made above to old Dutch plate in England. The regal silver bedstead, made in 1674 by John Cooqus, a silversmith from the Low Countries in London, for Charles II as a gift to his favourite, Nell Gwynn, has been melted.

Outside Holland and England is the superb ewer of jasper and gold, by Paul van Vianen, already mentioned. The collection of Dutch plate of the seventeenth century in the Kremlin is unequalled in some respects even in Holland; some of this is illustrated in Filimonoff's catalogue. In the Winter Palace at Petrograd is an impressive wine fountain by a goldsmith of The Hague early in the eighteenth century (Plate LXVII, No. 3).

By the courtesy of the owner, Mr. A. O. van Kerkwijk, of The Hague, an illustration is included of an exceedingly rare silver dish, with a curved border of eight points, $18\frac{3}{4}$ inches in diameter—a form which is seen only in the Low Countries. In the sunken centre is a representation of the Biblical story of Hannah and Samuel, while on the edge are four panels of different subjects, separated by scrolled foliage, all finely engraved in 1631 and signed by the talented Dutch medallist, Jan Looff, of Middelburg (working 1627–60), and probably the only known piece of plate from his atelier. The interesting problem arises as to whether he collaborated with a silversmith, who made only the dish, leaving the engraving to Jan Looff (Plate LXVI). A full account of this rarity has been published in a brochure by M. G. A. le Man, *Het Leven en de Werken van Johannes Looff*, 1925.

A dish of the same shape, engraved with arabesques, by Pieter Francke, of Ghent, is in the Victoria and Albert Museum, while a representation of another is in a picture by J. Victor in the Hermitage Museum, Petrograd.

Comparatively scarce as it is to-day, the Dutch silver tazza would seem to have been a common vessel in the seventeenth century, if the popularity may be judged from its frequent representation in " Still Life " pictures by Abraham van Beyeren, Willem K. Heda, Metsu and others. It was used for fruit, as shown in some of De Heem's pictures, and as a drinking vessel in the manner of the Greek kylix, as is confirmed by Dirk Hals's " Convivial Party," in the National Gallery in London, where a jovial burgher is in the act of drinking from a silver-gilt tazza.

A tazza in the Victoria and Albert Museum, decorated with the story of Meleager in repoussé inside the bowl, was wrought by a craftsman of Utrecht in the first half of the seventeenth century (Plate LXV, No. 3).

Other examples of tazze are illustrated in the catalogue of the Leeuwarden exhibition in 1900—including one of 1622 by a goldsmith of Alkmaar—and in Mr. Begeer's brochure.

A characteristic Dutch silver vessel of the seventeenth and eighteenth centuries, as characteristic as the porringer is of Colonial America, is a two-handled oval bowl (*brandewijkom*) which enjoyed a place of honour on the occasion of birthdays, weddings and other intimate family events, when it was filled with raisins steeped in brandy, the fruit being eaten from silver spoons. The handles of some early specimens have human heads on the shoulders, while the later handles are flat and chased. Some are plain and others are embossed and chased with flowers and other motives. The specimen illustrated is by Johannes Lelij, of Leeuwarden, 1704 (Plate LXVII, No. 7). An earlier form of bowl is octagonal and is engraved in typical Dutch fashion with panels of symbolical figures (Plate LXVII, No. 1). These are different from the shallow circular silver bowl with two handles, depicted in a " Still Life " picture by A. van Beyeren (c. 1620-74).

One phase of Dutch silver which followed closely upon the overthrow of the formal embossed and chased decoration of the third quarter of the seventeenth century must not be omitted from this brief survey, namely, the work executed at Leeuwarden by Johannes Lelij at the end of that century and early in the next. His treatment of chased relief ornamentation is executed with great skill, as may be observed in an important kettle (1718) and reliquary

HOLLAND

(Plate LXVIII, Nos. 2 and 3). Mr. Begeer illustrates one of Lelij's masterpieces in an early eighteenth-century teapot, which introduces his favourite motive, the acanthus leaf. The explanation of the superior skill of this Leeuwarden goldsmith is that he, like Klaes Baardt, is said to have improved his technical knowledge by a sojourn in France before settling at the ancient capital of Friesland. By Lelij are a box or caddy in the Baroness James de Rothschild's collection and a tea-caddy in the Victoria and Albert Museum.

Gabynus Lelij, of Leeuwarden, son of Johannes, was a master goldsmith in 1731. One of the few pieces from his workshop is a teapot, 1738, in the Victoria and Albert Museum and the snuff box on Plate LXVIII (No. 1). In the same museum is a brandy bowl by that rare craftsman of Leeuwarden, Johannes Vos, master in 1694.

Throughout the eighteenth century Dutch silversmiths excelled in the execution of pierced work, from the Louis XIV style of decoration—which permeated the arts and crafts—to Louis XVI. Especially charming are the dishes for fruit, bread and sweetmeats, and the stands for oil and vinegar bottles, by craftsmen of Amsterdam, Rotterdam and elsewhere. Several choice specimens of these are illustrated by Mr. Begeer, whose brochure reveals the potent influence of French designs upon Dutch silver in this century. One of these little dishes, by Jan Pondt, of Amsterdam, 1733, is illustrated on Plate LXVIII (No. 5).

As characteristic of Holland as the brandy bowls are the charming little silver marriage caskets, made to contain rings and gifts of coins to the brides.

The subject of old Dutch silver spoons, as of the spoons of other countries, would need a separate book for adequate treatment and illustration. For reasons of space an illustrated history of the evolution of the picturesque silver head-dresses of Dutch women from the sixteenth to the nineteenth centuries is omitted, as is, for the same reason, a sketch of filigree work and book-covers.

Silver was made in at least 34 towns in Holland before the year 1800. The town marks are often taken from the civic arms, notably in the case of Amsterdam.

To those who may desire to study old Dutch plate in greater detail than is possible within the compass of this little book, they are directed to the public collections in Holland, especially the Rijks Museum in Amsterdam. Several important pieces are in the Victoria and Albert Museum.

The following works may be recommended: Dr. A. Pit's illustrated book on the more important plate in the Rijks Museum; the catalogues of the exhibitions at Leeuwarden in 1900 and 1927; and Mr. C. J. A. Begeer's well illustrated brochure, already mentioned. The book of Mr. E. Voet, Jun., on the marks of Amsterdam is indispensable, as doubtless will be his forthcoming book on the marks of Haarlem. Dr. M. Rosenberg has some Dutch marks in *Der Goldschmiede Merkzeichen*. *Friesch Zilver*, by Mr. N. Ottema (1927), contains a history of Frisian goldsmiths.

PLATE LXVIII

PLATE LXIX

HUNGARY

PLATE LXIX.

Tall wine ewer (H. 29 in.) with basin (D. 31¼ in.), 1548.   Prince Esterhazy.

PLATE LXX.

No. 1   Tall cup, early 17th century, a gift to the Church of Miskolcz in 1649. H. 12 in.
No. 2   Crystal wine vessel. Early 16th century. H. 16¼ in.   Count Francis Erlödy.
No. 3   Tall flagon. Early 17th century.

PLATE LXXI.

No. 1   Beaker, dated 1685.
No. 2   Beaker, of sixteenth-century type.
No. 3   Carved crystal tankard, with enamelled mounts, 1645-76. H. 9¾ in.
                                                            Collection of M. Ernst.
No. 4   Cup. Early 16th century. H. 11¾ in.   Museum of Applied Art, Budapest.
No. 5   Beaker. 17th century.
No. 6   Beaker, dated 1654.
No. 7   Beaker, c. 1660.

HUNGARY has witnessed many changes and developments in the art of the goldsmith in the course of centuries, from Byzantine to the Gothic, the Renaissance to the Baroque, and finally to the decline from the middle of the eighteenth century. In the sixteenth and seventeenth centuries the influence of Germany is visible. Oriental elements are noticeable in Transylvania, then in frequent touch with the East, while in the South decoration from Turkish sources prevails. The craft of the goldsmith was, however, in a high state of development in Hungary in the early Middle Ages, as may be observed from the richly decorated silver vessels found in graves in that country, of which a unique collection is in the Hungarian National Museum at Budapest.

    Notices of plate in the thirteenth century indicate the riches in gold and silver plate in Hungary. The daughter of King Andrew II, St. Elizabeth, who married Louis, Margrave of Thuringia, was richly endowed with plate. According to original sources, the church of Veszprém was plundered in 1276 of 15 gold and 20 silver chalices, 20 gold crucifixes, 4 gold and 11 silver reliquaries. During the reign of the Anjou Kings in Hungary in the fourteenth century the goldsmiths enjoyed a position of great importance and dignity and were granted arms of their own. But their works have perished in the furnace at different unsettled periods in the history of the country.

At the death in 1490 of its art-loving ruler, Matthias Corvinus, Hungary was a very large kingdom, and a high standard of culture prevailed. During his long rule of 32 years the churches were furnished with costly vessels in the precious metals, which were often embellished with richly coloured enamelled work. Foreign travellers and diplomatists have recorded the riches in plate and jewellery of his Court. Hungarian noblemen were also in possession of great quantities of plate.

In Hungary, as in some other countries, there was a tenacious insistence on the part of goldsmiths, probably under ecclesiastical instruction, to maintain the Gothic tradition in sacred vessels for some time after the introduction of the Renaissance forms into the country, perhaps by Venetian craftsmen. As late as the middle of the sixteenth century certain Gothic features are found in conjunction with Renaissance ornament, not only in vessels for ecclesiastical purposes, but also occasionally in domestic plate.

Hungarians proudly claim the father of Albrecht Dürer, the celebrated German artist, as one of the early native-born goldsmiths, his birthplace having been Ajtós, but nothing survives to-day as a practical demonstration of his skill.

Some of the most interesting and finely wrought goldsmiths' work was developed in the late Renaissance, in consequence of the great demand for the very characteristic jewellery as worn in the national gala dress of Hungary.

The goldsmiths' guilds were an important means of encouragement of the craft in Hungary, as they were in Germany.

A most conspicuous feature of Hungarian ecclesiastical work, especially on chalices, is to be found in the richly coloured enamel of the second half of the fifteenth century and the first half of the next

HUNGARY

century, the designs of some of which are reproduced at the end of this chapter. The enamels are of floral or foliated designs, executed by a process somewhat resembling cloisonné and outlined in silver, and occasionally of gold, twisted wire, giving the vessels an appearance of richness. The seven colours favoured by the fifteenth-century enamellers were red, white, green, blue, violet, brown and black, while in the next century the same colours were used, except brown and black. About the year 1550 yellow was introduced as a novelty. Venetian goldsmiths are supposed to have introduced this method of enamelled decoration into Hungary. Hungarian goldsmiths of about the same period also practised a minute wire work, or filigree, for their chalices, without enamels.

Enamelled decoration, both for secular and ecclesiastical vessels, by a different process of painted enamel without the wire work, was practised in Hungary in the seventeenth century, an example of which is to be seen on a crystal and silver tankard described later.

One of the finest examples of Hungarian wire-enamel in secular work is the early fifteenth-century historic sword which was presented by King Sigismund of Hungary (1368–1437), Holy Roman Emperor, to Frederick I, known as the Warlike, Elector and Duke of Saxony (1410–1425); this is in the Historisches Museum in Dresden.

A tall ewer for wine in the Hungarian National Museum deserves notice. It is richly decorated in high relief with pears and with Gothic foliage, of a style suggesting the fifteenth century, but perhaps executed early in the following century. An illustration may be seen (No. 91) in the catalogue of electrotype reproductions of the Museum of Applied Art in Budapest, 1908.

Rare among vessels for wine is Count Francis Erlödy's cylindrical shaped vessel of crystal cut into hexagonal sections with a tall silver handle and foot, $16\frac{1}{4}$ inches high, dating from the early sixteenth century. The silver edges are like fleurs-de-lis, but were probably intended by the goldsmith to be a glorified Gothic ornament; it marks the transition between Hungarian Gothic and Renaissance. The cylindrical silver neck is ornamented with imbrications and engraved foliage. Emblazoned on a silver shield affixed to the ends of the crystal barrel is an imperial eagle in translucent blue enamel. No suggestion can be offered regarding the names of the goldsmith and crystal worker who made this interesting vessel, or of their place of residence (Plate LXX, No. 2). It is inscribed on one of the eight lobes of the foot with these initials, C L R D F V C E B D N M, representing Comes Ladislaus Rákoczi De Felsö Vadasz Comitissa Elisabetha Bánffy De Nagy Mihaly, with the inscription and the arms of the noble families of Rákoczi and Bánffy.

One historical and magnificent piece of plate of the Renaissance is the ewer with its companion dish of the date 1548, illustrated on Plate LXIX. The first thought of the author upon seeing the photograph was that these princely vessels were intended for use for rosewater, in the manner of English ewers and dishes from the sixteenth century, as described on earlier pages; but it would seem that the ewer contained sweet spicy wine, which flowed from the little taps at the side, whenever a guest desired to refresh himself. On the ewer is an enamelled inscription in Hungarian, to the effect that it was made for Antony Losonci in 1548. The ewer bears the combined arms of this nobleman and his wife, Clara Bathory, also a member of a noble Hungarian family. The highly skilled maker of these sumptuous vessels is supposed to have hidden his identity in an enamelled monogram of his initials K.F., said to be a goldsmith settled in Northern Hungary. They passed by inheritance in the seventeenth century to the princely house of Esterhazy, and have been deposited by the present representative of the family in the Museum of Applied Art in Budapest. The vessels themselves and several details of the ornamentation, including the supposed mark of the maker, are illustrated in the catalogue (in Hungarian) of the exhibition of goldsmiths' work at Budapest in 1884.

Beakers were as popular in Hungary as in Northern Europe. Some of those with Gothic ornament, dating from the earlier half of the sixteenth century, have been inspired by German models, but with the personal touch of the Hungarian goldsmith imposed upon them. Many beakers were made towards the end of the sixteenth and throughout the seventeenth centuries and are at once identified

PLATE LXX

PLATE LXXI

from those of other countries, not so much from the shapes, but from certain unmistakable features in the decoration. There is a marked partiality for heightening the ornament, whether it be foliage, scrolls or other motives, by gilding, leaving the other parts of the beaker in white silver. These beakers are inclined to have tall and slender bodies, like one illustrated on Plate LXXI (No. 5). In contrast with these is a wider beaker of the same period on a flat bottom. The decoration of this variety may consist of engraved motives and the arms of the owners, or of a series of short wavy lines which are a conspicuous feature peculiar to Hungarian goldsmiths. Five specimens of beakers of the sixteenth and seventeenth centuries are illustrated on Plate LXXI. Illustrations of several characteristic types, with other Hungarian vessels, may be found in the catalogue of electrotype reproductions mentioned above.

Another curious feature of some beakers found in use as Sacramental cups in Protestant churches in Hungary is a flame-like ornament, representing drops of blood or sweat, called *verejtékes pohár* in Hungarian and *Schweissbecher* in German.

One characteristic vessel of the late sixteenth and early seventeenth centuries is a tall flagon or tankard, of hexagonal, octagonal, or cylindrical form, narrowed in the middle of the body and frequently decorated with medallions of Roman heads or masks in relief, a not uncommon feature in other forms of Hungarian domestic plate. A flagon of this kind, dating from the early years of the seventeenth century, hexagonal in shape, is illustrated in the late Mr. J. Pierpont Morgan's catalogue, with a sixteenth-century chalice of conventional design, enamelled in the national style already described. Three specimens are shown in the book of Pulszky, Radisics and Molinier, *Chefs-d'œuvre d'Orfèvrerie à l'Exposition de Budapest*, including a plain one of hexagonal shape, with Gothic-like borders, on feet formed of cherubs' heads. One more flagon—the gift to a church in 1665—may be mentioned. This is cylindrical in shape and is decorated with characteristic ornament below the lip and along the base. Inscribed upon it is the name of the maker, Thomas Sthin (Stin), the elder, with the date 1603. His individual mark of his initials, with the date 1583, is also stamped upon it. This man was a member of a family of goldsmiths of Saxon origin, settled at Nagyszeben in Transylvania. He died in 1589, leaving a son of the same name, who became master of the guild in 1598 and died in 1604. The flagon is illustrated (No. 181) in the above catalogue of electrotype reproductions, with several other flagons.

Although secular in intention, many of these flagons have been found in Protestant churches in the country, the pious gifts of nobles, and are frequently engraved with inscriptions of later dates, recording the benefactions in a permanent form.

The early seventeenth-century flagon illustrated on Plate LXX is octagonal in shape and stands on ball and claw feet. It is very similar (except that cherubs' heads take the place of the claw and ball feet) to No. 128 in the catalogue of electrotype reproductions previously mentioned.

Another characteristic piece of Hungarian plate of the seventeenth century should not be overlooked, namely, a dish of octagonal and hexagonal shape, repoussé on the wide border with flowers.

An early seventeenth-century tall cup covered with the brightly burnished lobes, so characteristic of German cups, is engraved with a later inscription in Hungarian to the effect that it was a gift to the church of Miskolcz by Gregorius Miskolczi in 1649. A second inscription, in Latin, records the restoration of the cup by Joannes Szepesi of Negyes in 1740. This is only one of many instances of the gifts of purely secular plate to churches in Hungary and in other countries, particularly in England and America. No marks are stamped on the cup, but there can be no doubt that it was wrought by a goldsmith in Hungary, with little individual touches of his own, after a German model (Plate LXX, No. 1).

Illustrated on Plate LXXI (No. 4) is another tall cup of German design with Hungarian craftsmanship imposed upon it, dating from the beginning of the sixteenth century, now in the Museum of Applied Art at Budapest.

An interesting vessel illustrated on Plate LXXI (No. 3) is a tankard of crystal, mounted in silver-gilt and enamelled, of the date 1645–76. Carved on the crystal are fantastical representations, it is supposed, of the Hungarian castles of the original owner.

HUNGARY

Engraved inside the cover are the arms of Prince Francis Rakoćzi (1645–76), and it is inscribed as follows :

FRANCISCVS . DEI . GRA . PRINC . RAKOCZI . COM . DE . SAAR . DUX .
MUNK . ET . MAKOV . DOM . PER . DE . SAROSPATAK . REG . EC . SOM.

No maker's or other marks have been found on it, but it is regarded as the work of a Court goldsmith at Rakoćzi in Northern Hungary, in collaboration with a worker in crystal. The tankard was inherited with other relics of the princely family of Rakoćzi by Baron Luzsenszky and is now in the collection of Hungarian plate of M. L. Ernst in Budapest.

Although Nagyszeben is not now in Hungary, it is convenient here to include a short note on the domestic work executed at that Transylvanian town in the sixteenth and seventeenth centuries. Dominated as are some of the tankards and other vessels by German work, there are certain features which reveal a marked departure from German influence.

Sebastian Hann the elder (1644/5–1713), was one of the most successful of these men. Two tankards and a tazza from his workshop are illustrated in the work by Pulszky, Radisics and Molinier. One tankard is inscribed :

> So oft mit Kuhlen Wein die Kanne man wird heben
> Soll Herr Sebastian Hann in Lieb und Lobe leben.
>
> —1697.

Several of this goldsmith's characteristic tankards are in public and private collections, including one with a similar inscription, which is illustrated in the catalogue of the Baroness James de Rothschild's collection. One of his works is a stag of German fashion, now in the Museum of Applied Art at Budapest. A long list of his works is given by Dr. Marc Rosenberg.

One rare and uncommon vessel was made at Nagyszeben in the seventeenth century—namely, a casket for spiced wine, $7\frac{1}{4}$ inches high exclusive of the handle. It is set with a number of barbarous imitations, made in the second century B.C., of Greek coins. Transylvanian silver vessels are often set with such coins, which would seem to have been executed in great numbers in Transylvania. Inscribed upon it in Hungarian are the names of the owners, Count Michael Teleki and his wife, Ver Judit, and the date, 1687. The maker's stamp is GB in a monogram. The present owner, Count Dominic Teleki, has deposited it in the Hungarian National Museum at Budapest.

To appreciate Hungarian metal work, a visit must be made to the churches throughout the country, which are rich in vessels of gold and silver by native goldsmiths. The Hungarian National Museum and the Museum of Applied Art, in Budapest, have goodly collections of Hungarian plate. In the Victoria and Albert Museum is a small collection of electrotypes of silver work, with two or three original specimens of the large and characteristic brooches worn with the national Hungarian dress.

Illustrations of Hungarian work and decorative details, as well as jewels, may be seen in that useful work, *A Magyar Törtéenti Ötvösmü-Kiállitás Lajstroma*, 1884 ; and in Pulszky, Radisics and Molinier, *Chefs-d'œuvre d'Orfèvrerie à l'Exposition de Budapest*, which contains some illustrations in colour and specimens of the *garnitures de corsages* for the Hungarian national costumes of the sixteenth and seventeenth centuries.

Specimens of Hungarian enamels from chalices of the fifteenth and sixteenth centuries.

IRELAND

PLATE LXXII.

No. 1 Cup, by William Williamson, of Dublin, c. 1735. H. 7¾ in.
No. 2 Small cup, by Joseph Walker, of Dublin, 1701. The Earl of Derby.
No. 3 Large two-handled cup and cover, Dublin, 1694.
No. 4 Caudle cup, by Caleb Webb, of Cork, c. 1695. H. 4¾ in.
No. 5 Plain cup, by Joseph Johns, of Limerick, c. 1740. H. 4⅛ in.
No. 6 Plain tankard, by David King, of Dublin, 1714-5. H. 8 in.

(Nos. 1, 4, 5 and 6 are in the National Museum of Ireland, Dublin.)

PLATE LXXIII.

No. 1 Snuff-box, Dublin, 1801.
No. 2 Plain teapot, by John Warner, of Cork, c. 1790.
No. 3 Plain globular teapot, by George Hodder, of Cork, c. 1740.
No. 4 Small plain cup, Youghal, c. 1620. H. 3⅞ in.
No. 5 Sauce boat, by John Nicholson, of Cork, c. 1770.
No. 6 Two candlesticks, Dublin, 1717-8 and 1726-7. H. 7¼ in.
No. 7 Bread basket, by John Lloyd, or John Locker, of Dublin, 1772.

(Nos. 2, 3, 5 and 7 are in the National Museum of Ireland; Nos. 1, 4 and 6 are in the Manchester Art Gallery.)

PLATE LXXIV.

No. 1 Dish ring, by Joseph Jackson, of Dublin, 1788.
No. 2 Dish ring, by Carden Terry, of Cork, 1770-80.
No. 3 Dish ring, by William Townshend, of Dublin, c. 1770.
No. 4 Dish ring, by John Lloyd, of Dublin, c. 1775.
No. 5 Bottle stand, by Charles Townshend, of Dublin, 1770.
No. 6 Dish ring, Dublin, 1732. H. 3⅛ in. D. 14⅞ and 13⅜ in. Charles G. Rupert, Esq.

(Nos. 1-5 are in the National Museum of Ireland.)

REMARKABLE as they are as masterpieces of the early medieval goldsmiths of Ireland, the famous Ardagh chalice and the Tara brooch and some earlier decorative objects of the eighth century, when masterpieces in the art of the goldsmith were common in Ireland, a discussion on such " uncollectable " treasures is out of place in this book.

The author is tempted to illustrate the Ballylongford cross of the date 1479, now in the National Museum of Ireland, because it is signed by the maker, Willialmi Corneli, *i.e.*, William, son of Cornelius, who doubtless made secular as well as ecclesiastical plate. Unfortunately, the limited number of plates will not permit the inclusion of an illustration.

In view of the disturbed state of the country in the sixteenth century, surprise need not be expressed at the scarcity of Irish secular plate of that period, and indeed of the first half of the seventeenth century. The later plate of Ireland, in the main, conforms to that of England, though the so-called "potato rings" are almost exclusively Irish.

Irish tankards after 1660 cannot be distinguished from English, except by the marks. For example, a pair which once belonged to the defunct guild of St. John the Baptist in Dublin, wrought in that city in 1679–80, by Andrew Gregory, in no way differ from contemporary English tankards: the plain drum body and the repoussé and chased acanthus and palm leaves are copied from London tankards of the reign of Charles II. These tankards were acquired by purchase by the Merchant Taylors Company of London, and are illustrated in the *History of English Plate*. Scarcely less English is the plain tankard with a domed cover, by a prosperous Dublin silversmith, David King, 1714–15, in the National Museum of Ireland (Plate LXXII, No. 6).

Goldsmiths were working in Dublin in the twelfth and thirteenth centuries, but 1498 is the earliest mention of an actual company of goldsmiths there. Six years later the Dublin goldsmiths were in possession of a charter. But it was not until 1638 that a definite system of hall-marking was adopted in Dublin, following the grant of a royal charter in 1637, when the crowned harp was registered as the distinctive mark of the guild, combined with a system of date-lettering. The maker's initials were also required to be stamped. In 1730, the figure of Hibernia as a duty mark was added to the marks, which became four in number in 1804 by the addition of the Sovereign's head, twenty years later than in London.

Cork was the most flourishing guild of goldsmiths outside Dublin, while Limerick and Youghal, not to mention other places, provided

PLATE LXXII

PLATE LXXIII

IRELAND

interesting specimens of ecclesiastical and domestic silver in the seventeenth and eighteenth centuries. Although goldsmiths are recorded at Cork in the two previous centuries, no plate earlier than the seventeenth century can be definitely assigned to that place. The plan of marking from 1656 to about 1710, was generally the town mark, combined with the maker's initials; but an exhaustive explanation of the Cork marks, as indeed of other Irish marks, is unnecessary in face of the exact tables in *English Goldsmiths and Their Marks*.

Robert Goble is regarded as the principal Cork silversmith between 1672 and 1722, and was the maker of the finely wrought silver mace of the Cork guilds in 1696, one of the few treasures of Irish silver in the Victoria and Albert Museum. Probably more skilful and experienced was Charles Bekegle, an emigrant from the Netherlands, whose nationality was no barrier to his election as warden of the Cork guild in 1693. He was the maker of a fine two-handled cup in the collection of the late Sir C. J. Jackson, illustrated in the above book. Robert Goble, the younger, was also an excellent craftsman, and was the maker of a helmet-shaped cream ewer with lion-mask feet, about 1720, now in a private collection.

An example of a piece of Youghal work is the small plain cup of about 1620, modelled in a reduced size after an English cup, in the Roberts bequest in the Manchester Art Gallery. The maker was probably John Sharpe (Plate LXXIII, No. 4).

One silversmith's name emerges from Bandon in the seventeenth century, namely, Jo: Moore, who signed his name on the only recorded example of his work, a cup in Cloyne Cathedral. It is interesting as being a copy of an English Communion cup of about 1565–1575; an illustration is in the Rev. C. A. Webster's book on the Church plate of the Diocese of Cork, Cloyne and Ross.

The little cup of the Earl of Derby (whose ancestors were Lords and Kings of Man) is of considerable interest and importance, not only for its own sake as a piece of Irish plate, but also as commemorating the "birth" of horse-racing in the Isle of Man. Engraved upon it are the familiar arms, the "Legs of Man"; a jockey riding a horse; and the legend *Pro Gloria Patri Curro*, with the following inscription :

"To give birth to ye Royal Sport of Horse Racing. This cup was given, run for, and won at Derbyhaven."

Joseph Walker, of Dublin, was the maker in 1701 (Plate LXXII, No. 2).

In shape it resembles the earlier cup with a cover by a Dublin goldsmith of 1694, exhibited some years ago at the Victoria and Albert Museum (Plate LXXII, No. 3).

Irish caudle cups, in the main, conform to those of English goldsmiths. One rare example was sold for the high price of £717 10s. at Christie's on May 11, 1927. It had shaped sides, with a cover, chased in relief with lions and stags—familiar features of Charles II plate—and foliage and formal flowers. The handles were somewhat unusual in having scrolled dragons as thumbpieces. Timothy Blackwood, of Dublin, was the maker in 1679-80. The example by Caleb Webb, of Cork, about 1695 (in the National Museum of Ireland), is decorated along the bottom with acanthus and palm leaves, in the manner of London plate of Charles II, while the body is covered with branches of vine and birds, all in relief (Plate LXXII, No. 4).

The late Sir C. J. Jackson, in his book on marks, pays a tribute to the skill of the Scottish silversmith, Charles Leslie, who attained the important rank of warden in 1732-4, and master in 1735-6, of the Dublin guild of silversmiths, that his work is not inferior to that of Paul Lamerie. Not a single piece of his silver is in the National Museum at Dublin, nor does Sir C. J. Jackson illustrate any specimens in his *History of English Plate*. The present author has failed to find any important pieces of Leslie's work to illustrate here.

Many other household vessels, besides tankards of the seventeenth and eighteenth centuries, follow English fashions, such as candlesticks of the common octagonal shape, like the two of Dublin make, 1717-18 and 1726-7, in the Manchester Art Gallery (Plate LXXIII, No. 6). In the collection of Sir John H. B. Noble, Bart., are a pair of excessively rare if not unique candlesticks,

IRELAND

modelled after a German form by David King of Dublin, in 1699–1700. The stems are twisted and decorated with foliage and hollow flutes and are supported on high circular bases embossed with foliage. They are similar in form to the Dutch candlestick on Plate LXVII (No. 2), which has been inspired by a German example. Salvers of different patterns and other things were copied from English models.

A plain cup of several sizes, with two harp-shaped handles after the fashion of earlier English handles on rose-water ewers, was highly popular among the Dublin goldsmiths throughout the eighteenth century, and was made in such great numbers as to be called an "Irish" cup, though English in inception (Plate LXXII, No. 1). This specimen was made by William Williamson, of Dublin, about 1735. The same shape was also wrought with scrolled handles, like one of about 1740 by Joseph Johns, of Limerick (Plate LXXII, No. 5).

In Baron Bruno Schröder's collection of plate is a somewhat rare two-handled cup and cover, $12\frac{1}{2}$ inches high, with the conventional harp-shaped handles. The rarity lies in the fact that the lower half of the body, the domed cover and the foot are hammered into sixteen wide facets. The maker was John Clifton, junior, of Dublin, in 1714.

The English "Monteith" bowl is a rare thing in Irish, as it is in old Scottish, plate. A fine bowl of this fashion with a fixed rim and two bold grotesque mask handles, dated Dublin 1701–2, is known to the author. In the same private collection is another great rarity: an Irish copy of a Scottish quaich, made by Anthony Stanley, of Dublin, in 1702–3. Two more Irish "Monteith" bowls by Dublin goldsmiths may be mentioned: one of 1717 and the other about 1720, in the collection of Baron Bruno Schröder.

One of the earliest Irish dish-rings (wrongly called potato-rings) was made in Dublin in 1732, and is in America in the possession of Mr. Charles G. Rupert, who has obliged the author with particulars and the photograph (Plate LXXIV, No. 6).

Dish-rings of the pierced type sprang suddenly into prominence about 1760, and were made by Dublin silversmiths for about seventy years. Between 1770 and 1795 they were wrought in such numbers that hardly a house of any size in Ireland was without at least one. The dish-ring proper was, however, first made by an English goldsmith in London, in a different pattern of solid silver and shallower, as is proved by the rare if not unique specimen of 1704-5, by Andrew Raven, in the collection of Sir John H. B. Noble, Bart. They ceased to be made in Ireland about 1820. Four specimens are shown on Plate LXXIV, with a bottle stand of 1770 by Charles Townshend, of Dublin, all in the National Museum of Ireland.

A practical instance of the use of dish-rings is shown in an article by the present writer in the *Connoisseur* for November, 1923, where a specimen in the possession of the Marquess of Sligo, made apparently not later than 1765 by Robert Calderwood, of Dublin, is supporting an old bowl of bog oak, mounted in silver, and of much older date than the ring itself. At an early stage in a dinner they supported bowls of wood and other materials for soups, sauces, vegetables and potatoes, which were replaced later by porcelain and glass bowls for sweets and dessert, and finally, at convivial gatherings of men, by a bowl of silver or porcelain or pottery, for punch. By using these dish-rings as supports for bowls containing hot ingredients, the highly-polished mahogany tables were spared from injury. The dish-ring was also used for another purpose in Irish country houses—to hold a porcelain bowl containing *pot pourri* of rose leaves, and were occasionally covered by frail silver covers of pierced work, embossed and chased in the same manner as the rings, thereby preventing the rose leaves from being blown about the room, while allowing diffusion of their fragrance. Lord Sligo's bowl and ring, just described, show a cover of this kind, made by the same maker as the ring, Robert Calderwood. Sir John H. B. Noble, Bart., has several of these covers.

In the National Museum of Ireland is a very early and interesting specimen, by John Hamilton of Dublin, about 1745, $6\frac{3}{4}$ inches in diameter, recently acquired. An earlier example is known, by Joseph Jackson, of Dublin, in 1720.

IRELAND

The height of dish-rings varies from 3⅜ to 3⅞ inches, and the diameter from 7¾ to 8 inches.

In the collection of Colonel Claude Cane were sixteen of these dish-rings, which realised a total of nearly £2,240 at Christie's, the highest price being £205 for one by John Lloyd, of Dublin.

The popularity of, and the high prices realised for, Irish dish-rings among collectors has stimulated the ingenuity of the forger in foisting false specimens on the buyers, as is mentioned in the last chapter.

The Marquess of Sligo is the owner of four unusually large decanter stands, or coasters, 8½ inches in diameter, made at Dublin in 1818 expressly for the historic cut-glass decanters which were used on board the *Queen Charlotte* on the " Glorious First of June," in 1794, by Admiral Lord Howe, those silent witnesses of many a bumper drunk by the gallant Admiral and his officers in celebration of that memorable naval victory. An illustration of these may be seen in the *Connoisseur* article mentioned above, with a little Irish silver caster of 1704–5.

A few important pieces of silver made in Dublin are in a superb collection of old English plate, mostly of the Anglo-French school, known to the author. These are an imposing octagonal tray, of large size, made in 1706–7–8, and finely engraved with the arms of Tichborne; a tall, plain coffee-pot of hexagonal shape, 1712–14; a very choice and plain octagonal kettle and stand, by Thomas Bolton, of the early date 1714–15; and a plain octagonal sugar basin by John Cuthbert, junior, 1715–16. A large salver by John Hamilton, 1734, is notable for the fine engraving of the mantling in the arms. Robert Calderwood, one of Dublin's premier goldsmiths, is represented by a set of eight imposing candlesticks, copied about 1750 from a pair of 1742–3 by the London silversmith, George Wickes, in the same collection. Of these goldsmiths Thomas Bolton was particularly conspicuous in the early eighteenth century, and was the maker of a handsome two-handled cup and cover of 1704–5–6, and a pair of tazze of 1701–2, in private possession.

The " Adam " style of decoration in silver was practised in

Dublin a few years later than in London, as indeed was the "Chinese" manner of ornament. As an example of late " Chinese " decoration, a small globular teapot, chased and repoussé, by George Wheatley, of Dublin, 1796, in the Victoria and Albert Museum, may be cited; also the dish-ring of about 1770 on Plate LXXIV (No. 3).

As a survival of a piece of plate long after it had ceased to be made by London goldsmiths the sweetmeat box inspired by an English one of the reign of Charles II is interesting. Its maker was Alexander Richardson, of Dublin, in 1750; it is figured in the *History of English Plate*, No. 1077.

Silver toilet services are rare in Irish plate. Sir John H. B. Noble, Bart., is the owner of a casket, two large and two smaller boxes, by a Dublin goldsmith of 1691, with a pair of silver hair-brushes of about 1730.

Among other Dublin plate noted by the author is a plain flat-topped tankard of 1679–80, in the late Sir Ernest Cassel's collection, illustrated in *Country Life* for January 19, 1924; and a two-handled cup, decorated in the rococo manner, of about 1750, in the Ashburnham sale at Christie's in 1914, and illustrated in the sale catalogue. Unusual is the wine urn, formed as a flattened vase for hanging on a wall, the tap fashioned as a monkey and the cover as a coronet, by Robert Calderwood, about 1750, which was sold with the Duke of Leinster's silver at Christie's in May, 1926.

Cork goldsmiths of the eighteenth century would seem to have been busily engaged in making boxes of gold and silver to contain the " freedom " of boroughs bestowed upon persons of distinction. The silver freedom box of the Earl of Shelburne, made by William Reynolds in 1764, is illustrated in the *History of English Plate* (Fig. 1207), as is Admiral Lord Rodney's gold box of 1782, by the same maker. Earlier than this was the silver box presented with the freedom of Cork in 1737 to Dean Swift, who wrote, in characteristic style, to the Mayor and Council thanking them for the honour bestowed on him—" a private man, and a perfect stranger without power or grandeur." So proud was the Dean of the honour that he returned the box to have an inscription engraved upon it, recording the presentation. The Dean's inventory of plate contains many curious pieces, probably of Irish workmanship, since he emphasises two English candlesticks as distinct from others (*Works of Jonathan Swift*, 2nd ed., 1824, xix, 229–230).

In the Frank Smith bequest in the Victoria and Albert Museum is a small but not unimportant group of silver, including three of the typical Irish sugar basins on three feet. Two of these have lion-mask and claw feet, the makers being William Thompson, of Dublin, 1760–70, and Stephen Walsh, of Cork, about ten years later. The third has shell feet, and was made about 1760–70 by Joseph Johns, of Limerick, the maker of the cup on Plate LXXII. One of the best pieces is a charming plain teapot of many sides by an unknown Dublin silversmith of about 1765.

If two instances may be cited as sufficient evidence, it would seem that Dublin goldsmiths were not averse (with the sanction of the Assay Office) from having the Dublin marks stamped upon imported silver. One such case occurs in a German pine-apple cup of the seventeenth century, shown to the author by the late Earl Annesley at Castlewellan, where the Dublin hall-mark for 1811 is stamped upon it. The other case is that of a pair of candlesticks bearing the London hall-mark for 1753–4, and the Dublin mark for about 1760, in a sale at Christie's on April 28, 1919.

The name of one Irish goldsmith of the early eighteenth century has been traced to Philadelphia, namely, Philip Syng, who is believed to have learned his craft in Dublin. His name is not, however, recorded as a member of the Goldsmiths' Company of Dublin, from which it may be concluded that he was a journeyman. In 1712, at the age of 36, he emigrated to that American town, and there wrought the important flagon and dish in Christ Church, mentioned in the chapter on American silver. His son, Philip, was also a silversmith in Philadelphia, and was the maker of the historic silver inkstand used in signing the famous Declaration of American Independence (see Plate XI).

A second link between Dublin and America is provided in the silver snuff-box in the Manchester Art Gallery (Plate LXXIII, No. 1). This is divided into compartments for four different kinds of snuff, inscribed "Lundy," "Scotch," "Rapee" and "Mackoba," and was made in Dublin in 1801. The precise connection between Dublin and America lies in the engraved names of the officers of the 38th Foot (1st Staffordshire Regiment), among whom are two gallant American-born officers, Lieut.-Colonel Spencer Thomas Vassall, who was mortally wounded in the storming of Monte Video in 1807, and Major John Lindall Borland, both members of prominent families in Massachusetts.

The gold boxes, given with the freedom of certain Irish towns to the fourth Duke of Rutland as Lord Lieutenant of Ireland, and those given by several towns to the fourth Duke of Devonshire, while holding the same high office, were doubtless made by Dublin goldsmiths. They are, however, no longer in their original state, having been melted down and the gold made by Paul Storr into a salver and a plateau in 1801–2 and 1813–14, respectively, and are now at Belvoir Castle and Chatsworth. Two gold boxes by an Irish goldsmith in 1780–1, were presented in 1782 to the third Duke of Portland, Lord Lieutenant of Ireland, by the City of Dublin and Trinity College, Dublin, and are now at Welbeck Abbey.

In addition to the pieces already mentioned, the following are illustrated here from the collection in the National Museum of Ireland. By Cork goldsmiths are an early globular teapot, by George Hodder, about 1740; a later oval teapot, by John Warner, about 1790; and a sauce boat, chased with a monkey riding a pig, by John Nicholson, about 1770 (Plate LXXIII, Nos. 3, 2 and 5, respectively). The twisted wire dish-ring, by Carden Terry, of Cork, 1770–80, is somewhat unusual (Plate LXXIV, No. 2). The pierced cake basket by a Dublin goldsmith is of more than usual interest in that it was a gift to Lancelot Sandys by the Dublin Society for reclaiming bog land in 1765–67 (Plate LXXIII, No. 7).

Just as the Victoria and Albert Museum in London is deficient in many characteristic specimens of English plate, such as "Monteiths," tankards and other things, so too is the collection of Irish plate in the National Museum of Ireland singularly unrepresentative of native craftsmen's work.

PLATE LXXIV

PLATE LXXV

ITALY

PLATE LXXV.

Casket of carved crystal and silver-gilt, by Valerio Belli, 1532. Pitti Palace, Florence.

PLATE LXXVI.

No. 1 Travelling service, by L. Valadini, of Rome, c. 1790. Tray, 14 × 10¾ in.
Her Majesty the Queen.
No. 2 Gold Salt, by Benvenuto Cellini, 1543, H. 10½ in. ; greatest width, 12⅜ in.
Imperial Museum, Vienna.

RICH as it is in ecclesiastical vessels in the precious metals, no country has suffered more severe losses in secular plate than Italy. Goldsmiths flocked to the Papal Court as the main source of patronage of their craft. British names are recorded in the goldsmiths' guilds of Lombardy in the early fourteenth century.

Recorded in 1392 is a silver nef on wheels, which suggests in the description the German ships of two centuries later. This has perished with two crystal cups and a nef of gold and silver, which adorned the table of Pope Pius II in 1462, and a slightly later salt in the form of a nef on gilt wheels, drawn by silver horses, one of the treasures of Paul III (1464-71). Nothing now remains of the splendid plate made for the Medici by the great goldsmiths of Florence. With the foregoing have perished a nef of silver-gilt, enamel and niello, executed about 1535 by Giovanni Battista di Mariotti de Marco, of Perugia, from a design by Pietro Christofori, who also designed another nef, ordered to be made in 1513 by Frederico di Francesco, also of Perugia.

The centrepiece, designed by the Florentine painter, Benedetto Luti, for his marriage feast, has perished ; there only remains his original design for it in the Uffizi.

Many of the graceful domestic vessels of majolica ware, now surviving solely because of their intrinsic worthlessness, were doubtless made in gold and silver, as were the forms of metal-gilt candlesticks depicted in Italian pictures.

Under the pontificate of Nicholas V (1447-55) the patronage of letters and of arts really begins, a patronage which virtually ended a little more than a century later. Yet nothing remains in domestic plate of this magnificent period as monuments of the goldsmiths' achievements. Art in Italy, as in other countries, has suffered not only from plunder and pillage, but also from the excessive zeal of successive custodians, who desired to "improve" upon the work of their predecessors by replacing the old by new. Just as Italian architects from Bramante to Bernini rarely treated with reverence the work of their great predecessors, both Christian and pagan, so, too, precious objects in gold and silver were consigned to the crucible without a pang.

The most famous goldsmiths were commissioned to execute the golden roses, bestowed by Popes upon Princes in all countries, but few of more than a century old remain to-day. The earliest surviving example is in the Cluny Museum in Paris, having been sent by Clement V (1305-14) to the Prince Archbishop of Bâle. Giovanni Bartolo, of Siena—the artist of the celebrated reliquary bust of St. Agatha at Catania in 1376—executed at least eleven golden roses between 1365 and 1395. Henry VIII was the recipient of three during his reign.

Papal swords were also lavishly decorated by famous goldsmiths. Angelino di Domenico de Sutri, a celebrated craftsman, was the maker of the sword sent by Julius II to James IV of Scotland in 1507, which survives as part of the Scottish regalia. Three others of the fifteenth century are illustrated by Lessing in *Jahrbuch der K. Preuss. Samml.* xvi, 1895.

It would seem that several goldsmiths of eminence, including Caradosso and Cellini, were not members of the goldsmiths' guild of Rome. In 1628 a candidate for admission to this guild had to prove service for three years as a workman in Rome, and was obliged to give a practical demonstration of his skill by executing a specimen of his work before the consuls. In 1734-40 the guild was limited to 170 master goldsmiths.

ITALY

Florence had statutes for the regulation of goldsmiths as early as 1314. Most of the famous painters of the Florentine school, as is well known, were members of this guild in their early lives, including Andrea Verocchio, the brothers Pollaiuolo, Botticelli and Leonardo da Vinci, none of whose plate, ecclesiastical or secular, has survived.

Siena was famed for its goldsmiths no less than for its sculptors and painters in the Middle Ages.

An important problem arises from the secular vessels of gold and silver in so many pictures of the Italian and other schools as to whether the artists painted them direct from their own designs or from the finished vessels by contemporary goldsmiths. This remark applies to the silver salts in the copy of Leonardo da Vinci's Last Supper, by Marco d'Oggione (c. 1470–1520), in the Diploma Gallery of the Royal Academy; to the pots of ointment in the hands of the Magdalen in many pictures; and to the precious vessels in the Adoration of the Magi by several masters.

The love of luxury had increased with such rapidity in Italy early in the sixteenth century that goldsmiths, who had mainly devoted their skill in the previous century to ecclesiastical objects, now diverted their activities to domestic vessels.

One of the most celebrated goldsmiths of the sixteenth century was Valerio Belli (1468–1546), of Vicenza, who, though a practical goldsmith, is more famed for his skill in carving crystal and in cutting dies for coins and medals. In the Pitti Palace is his most celebrated work, the crystal casket, carved with scenes from the Passion, signed by him in 1532, and bought by Clement VII as a gift to Francis I on his marriage with the Pope's niece (Plate LXXV). To him is ascribed the exquisitely wrought crystal cross of translucent enamel and silver-gilt in the Victoria and Albert Museum, now happily united with (it is supposed) the original pair of candlesticks by the generous gift of Mrs. Leopold de Rothschild. By him also is a notable crystal cross in the Vatican Library. But perhaps more important as an example of secular work is the beautiful cup of rock crystal, mounted in gold and garnished with precious stones, believed to have been made for the coronation of the Emperor Charles V at Bologna; this is in the old Imperial Museum at Vienna.

A second gem engraver and medallist was Giovanni Bernardi, of Castelbolognese (1495–1555), whose collaborators were Pierino del Vaga in the designs, and Mariano, of Florence, in the goldsmith's work. His most celebrated work is the large carved crystal casket in the Museum at Naples.

An interesting fact in the history of the goldsmith's art is that the Italian peasants still retain much of their ancient jewellery and their picturesque costumes—unlike the nobility, who have lost their old plate.

Benvenuto Cellini was apprenticed at the age of fifteen to Antonio di Sandro, familiarly called Marcone, the goldsmith. His diverting memoirs have put him on a higher pinnacle of fame than his achievements have merited, to the neglect of the work of greater men. His sole surviving piece of domestic plate is the famous gold salt at Vienna (Plate LXXVI, No. 2) The silver jug and basin executed by him for Cardinal Ippolito d'Este, of Ferrara, in his workshop in Rome (where he employed many workmen and wrought with their help much gold and silver plate) have disappeared, as have the candlesticks and other objects made by him for the Bishop of Salamanca and the wonderful silver Jupiter and many other pieces mentioned in his fascinating pages. Perished also have the drinking cup, girdle and vases, all of gold, executed after his own designs by Domenico and Gianpagolo Poggini. In these memoirs he speaks of Lucagnolo, a clever goldsmith who made a two-handled silver basin for Pope Clement VII to contain discarded bones and rinds of fruit on the dining table. He also mentions Amerigo, a Florentine enameller of genius, whose marvellous works were so greatly admired by Cellini that he betook himself with energy to the practice of this beautiful art.

The story of the progress of the salt is told vividly, with a wealth of detail, by Cellini, with characteristic self-assurance. It was ordered by Cardinal Ippolito d'Este, of Ferrara, and was first modelled in wax. The figure of Ceres held a cornucopia in her right hand, and a little Ionic temple for pepper in the other hand, while the figure symbolical of the sea held a ship, for the salt, in the left hand. Four figures in more than half-relief, originally enamelled in parts, were affixed along the base. These represented day, night, twilight and dawn, while four other figures symbolised the four chief winds. When shown to Francis I (whose service he had entered in 1540 at the age of forty) the King cried aloud in astonishment. The exquisite enamel, described by Cellini, has now disappeared. Cellini and his friends celebrated the completion in 1543 of the salt, " this child of his own imagining " (as he called it), by dining very merrily, with the salt itself in a place of honour on the table. It is evident that it was not wrought entirely by himself, for he had other helpers. Among the journeymen in his employ in Paris were two boys, Pagolo and Ascanio, and some Germans.

The salt was a gift of Charles IX of France to the Archduke Ferdinand of Tirol on the occasion of the King's marriage to the Archduchess Elizabeth, daughter of the Emperor Maximilian II.

The gem-set morse of gold, executed by Cellini for Clement VII, was one of many treasures of the goldsmith's art surrendered to Napoleon by Pius VI as part of the indemnity. Cellini describes in detail this splendid specimen of the jeweller's art, on which he " had fashioned such wonderful designs " at the age of twenty-nine, when he had in his employ five excellent journeymen. Three illustrations of it, from some old coloured drawings (in the British Museum) are reproduced in an article by the Rev. Herbert Thurston, S.J., in the *Burlington Magazine* for October, 1915. With it is an illustration of the magnificent golden tiara, set with great gems and pearls, executed by the celebrated goldsmith, Caradosso, for Pope Julius II, the patron and friend of Raphael and Michael Angelo, which was also part of Napoleon's plunder. Caradosso, it will be remembered, executed medals of this Pope. Both he and Cellini perfected the modern processes of striking medals.

At the moment of writing there is exhibited in the Victoria and Albert Museum a sumptuous ewer with its companion basin, both of great size, by an unknown goldsmith of Venice in the second half of the sixteenth century.

Illustrated on Plate LXXVI (No. 1) is the silver-gilt travelling service of the Cardinal York. It comprises an oblong tray, with a double condiment box at the back, two steel knives with silver-gilt handles, two forks and two spoons, all decorated in the Louis XVI style transplanted in Italy. Chased in the centre of the tray are the Royal Arms of England, crowned by a Cardinal's hat. It was sold at Christie's in November, 1919, and was added to the Stuart collection at Windsor Castle by Her Majesty the Queen. The maker was L. Valadini, of Rome, about 1790, who wrought some large rectangular trays, 22 inches long, engraved with the cipher of George III and a baron's coronet, which are in the possession of the Marquess of Londonderry.

The "Turin" service in the Winter Palace at Petrograd was apparently made by a goldsmith of Turin. Of this service two soup tureens, an ice-pail and a dish, finely executed in Louis XVI style, are illustrated on Plate 44 of Baron de Foelkersam's catalogue of the collection. Two pairs of silver-gilt candlesticks of the same period by a Turin goldsmith are in the Jones collection in the Victoria and Albert Museum, a museum which contains nothing of importance in Italian secular plate. But it is not alone in this respect, for no museum in Italy itself can show a representative collection, even of the eighteenth century.

The late Mr. S. J. A. Churchill had devoted many years to the study of original documents for the history of Italian goldsmiths, and his valuable researches are embodied in a book,* to which the present author is indebted for much information in this chapter.

---

* *The Goldsmiths of Italy*. . ., compiled by Cyril G. E. Bunt from MSS. of the late S. J. A. Churchill, 1926.

PLATE LXXVI

PLATE LXXVII

NORWAY

PLATE LXXVII.
No. 1 Beaker, c. 1495. H. 5¾ in.   Bergen Museum.
No. 2 Small bowl, by a Bergen silversmith, c. 1660. H. 1¼ in. D. 5 in.
No. 3 Plain tea-caddy, probably by Magnus Bessel, of Bergen, c. 1730. H. 5⅞ in.
No. 4 Bowl, c. 1660. H. 2⅜ in. D. 4⅞ in.
No. 5 Beaker, with granulated body, by Baard Gangolphi Bonsach, of Christiania, 1671.
No. 6 Candlestick, by Micael Hansen Blytt, of Bergen, 1788. H. 9¼ in.
No. 7 Plain octagonal candlestick, by Fridrich Romanussen Möller, c. 1720.
No. 8 Octagonal candlestick, slightly chased, by Mathias Remerdes, of Christiania, c. 1725.
No. 9 Octagonal candlestick, by Niels Haugaard, of Christiania, c. 1762.
No. 10 Small brandy bowl, c. 1700.

PLATE LXXVIII.
No. 1 Tankard, by Albret Groth, of Christiania, 1712.
No. 2 Plain tankard, dated 1641.
No. 3 Tankard, by Johan Slytter, of Bergen, c. 1620. H. to top of cover, 8 in. Bergen Museum.
No. 4 Tankard, by Romanus Fridrichsen Möller, of Christiania, 1662.
No. 5 Tankard, by Berendt Platt, of Christiania, 1681.

PLATE LXXIX.
No. 1 Caster, by Steen Wirtmani Bryggemanns, of Bergen, 1769. H. 6⅞ in.
No. 2 Plain caster, by Albret Groth, of Christiania, c. 1710.
No. 3 Caster, by Torje Landass, of Christiansand, 1791.
No. 4 Small bowl, by Baard Gangolphi Bonsach, of Christiania, c. 1675.
No. 5 Caster, 18th century.
No. 6 Coffee-pot, attributed to Jacob Campbell, of Stavanger and Egersund, 1764-89.
No. 7 Plain caster, by Jacob Andersen Möller (1706-81), of Christiania.

GOLDSMITHS' work is frequently mentioned in Norwegian documents in medieval times, including silver-mounted drinking horns. An English bowl is described as the Bishop of Stavanger's present to a king. Bishop Alf in 1478 was the owner of seven silver bowls, one of which was adorned with a picture of St. Olaf, the national saint, a vague description which was probably intended for an enamelled figure of the saint, recalling the prints of sacred subjects of English medieval mazer bowls.

From 1425 onwards the goldsmith's craft in Norway became more and more important.

Several of the silver-mounted and copper-mounted drinking horns in the National Museum at Copenhagen are of Norwegian origin, as explained on pages 75–6, and as may be observed from the excellent catalogue of that remarkable collection. One of the best examples dates from about 1300 and is decorated with Gothic architectural features and enriched on the mouth with divers shields of arms, including the royal arms. This is illustrated, with two medieval silver chalices of Norwegian workmanship, in Mr. Thor Kielland's *Sætryk av Norsk Kunsthistorie*. Outside the scope of this work as is the subject of ecclesiastical silver, it may not be out of place to mention Mr. Kielland's interesting historical sketch of the development of silver Gothic chalices in Norway, wherein he traces the influence of immigrant goldsmiths probably from Lübeck. Two groups of chalices can, however, be distinguished by their definite local characteristics, one centred in Bergen and the other in Trondhjem. One interesting point emerges from this sketch, namely, that similar ornaments to those on the Trondhjem chalices were introduced into the Norwegian silver bridal crowns and jewellery.

In a more recent and more comprehensive work, *Norsk Guldsmedkunst i Middelalderen* (1927), the same author traces the development of the finely executed Norwegian silver from about 600 to 1550, illustrated with many specimens. Here is shown the influence of medieval English chalices upon those of Norway.

With the exception of seals and jewellery, a few drinking horns are the only things in secular silver now surviving in Norway anterior to the year 1400. From that date a number of horns have survived, skilfully mounted in silver or copper-gilt and decorated with inscriptions, vine leaves and other motives.

A characteristic drinking vessel in silver in Scandinavia is the beaker, and one of the earliest specimens dates probably from the end of the fifteenth century and is in the Bergen Museum (Plate LXXVII, No. 1). In some of these early beakers the cast feet are in

NORWAY

the form of lions, but in this they are fashioned like female busts. The open band of flowers and foliage, encircling the body, is a conspicuous feature of these early Norwegian and Danish beakers, the form of which was probably introduced from Germany. Another early Norwegian beaker of about 1500 is in the Birmingham Art Gallery.

The beaker continued through the Renaissance, when it was very common, and as late as the nineteenth century.

Later Norwegian beakers of the seventeenth and eighteenth centuries are not unlike those of Denmark, in the granulated work like that on the beaker of 1671 by Baard Gangolphi Bonsach, of Christiania (Plate LXXVII, No. 5); and in the large embossed flowers of others, as well as in other respects.

In Norway, as elsewhere in Scandinavia, a little silver bowl with one or two handles was made for brandy and other liquor in the seventeenth and eighteenth centuries, called öreskaal in Norway, orekovsken in Denmark, and dopskål in Sweden. Specimens are illustrated in this chapter.

The most popular of all vessels in Scandinavia in the seventeenth and eighteenth centuries was the tankard, made of silver for the nobility and the prosperous merchants and mostly of wood, and sometimes of silver, for the peasants.

The earlier silver tankards of Norway (as have those of Denmark and Sweden) have tall, narrow cylindrical bodies and were made at Bergen, Christiania and elsewhere from the end of the sixteenth century until about 1650, when they were superseded by the form now about to be described. An early and unusually plain example, eight inches high exclusive of the thumbpiece, by Johan Slytter, of Bergen, about 1620, is one of three of this early type in the Bergen Museum (Plate LXXVIII, No. 3). Another, engraved with cherubs' faces, scrolls and other conventional decoration, made by Jochum Kirseborn, of Stavanger (1618–54), is shown on Plate 8 in the excellent and well-illustrated catalogue of the exhibition at Stavanger, mentioned later. Illustrated on Plate XXV is a Danish tankard of this form.

Meanwhile, there appeared a little plain tankard on a moulded foot, like that on Plate LXXVIII (No. 2), which is dated 1641; but this form is far from common.

Norwegian tankards are usually bolder in design than the Danish, while the late "baroque" tankards of Norway are inclined to be more exaggerated in design and execution. From about 1650 the tankards of the three Scandinavian countries are fitted with three feet, though a rare example may be seen with four feet.

In the next important stage in the development of the Norwegian tankard the plain cylindrical body is comparatively small, and has a flat-topped cover, which is usually somewhat larger in diameter and is often engraved with the owner's arms or initials within a laurel wreath and sometimes set with a medal or coin; the feet and thumbpieces are often in the form of pomegranates, the feet being attached to large acanthus leaves on the bodies. Excellent examples are those by Romanus Fridrichsen Möller, of Christiania, one of whose tankards, dated 1662, is illustrated on Plate LXXVIII (No. 4). His son, Fridrich Romanussen Möller, also of Christiania, was also a skilled maker of tankards. The former was a sound craftsman and was fond of engraving flower stems and chasing conventional "baroque" ornament. His traditional style passed to the above son, who appears to have used some of his old casts in the "baroque" manner. Many of the tankards of the late seventeenth and early eighteenth centuries have ball and claw feet, attached to large embossed flowers on the body. The younger Möller was the maker of the plain octagonal candlestick of about 1720 on Plate LXXVII (No. 7).

Berendt Platt, also of Christiania, had travelled abroad and was the most skilful goldsmith in that town in the seventeenth century, excelling in tankards and beakers covered with embossed decoration of large "baroque" flowers, mingled with figures. One of his tankards, dated 1681, and standing on lion feet, is illustrated on Plate LXXVIII (No. 5). Not far behind in technical skill was Albret Groth (flourishing 1706–17), of Christiania, who displayed a marked partiality for acanthus foliage and "Berainesque" ornament and was skilled in cast work. He was not unfamiliar with English silver and wrought some excellent plain work, like the plain caster derived from an English model of the late seventeenth century (Plate LXXIX, No. 2). He was also the maker of the plain tankard, with a decorated cover and with lion and ball feet, dated 1712, on Plate LXXVIII (No. 1).

Martin Finchenhagen ranks high in technical skill among the goldsmiths of Christiania, though uneven in much of his work. In the silver made by him for prosperous merchants he lavished great care upon the engraving and ornamentation, but was careless in the work destined for peasants, doubtless from economic considerations. He specialised in silver vessels for the Church, but lacked distinction in most of his work for sacred purposes. Like Albret Groth, he wrought some plain silver in the English style of the early eighteenth century.

Mathias Remerdes, of Christiania, was a follower of his contemporaries, Groth and Finchenhagen, and made simple silver tankards for peasants between 1717 and 1730. He was the maker of the octagonal candlestick on Plate LXXVII (No. 8).

Among other goldsmiths of the Norwegian capital were Baard Gangolphi Bonsach (died in 1701), the maker of the beaker and small bowl on Plates LXXVII and LXXIX ; and Jacob A. Möller (1706–81), the maker of the caster of English pattern on Plate LXXIX (No. 7).

The peculiarities of style of the above goldsmiths of Christiania are described in great detail in that admirable book, *Guldsmedhaandverket i Oslo og Kristiania*, by MM. H. Grevenor and T. Kielland, 1924. The finest silver was, however, made by the goldsmiths of Bergen, Skien and Brevig, whose works have not yet been illustrated in book form.

The wooden tankards of the shape just discussed were made for their own use by peasants during the long winter evenings, just as were the wooden quaichs of Scotland. Specimens of these may be seen in the public museums of Denmark, Norway and Sweden.

The later form of the Norwegian silver tankard, with and without pegs inside, persisted into the early nineteenth century. One with pegs, of the year 1820, by a Bergen silversmith, is in the possession of the Earl of Rosebery.

Although mentioned earlier—some years after the impoverishment arising from the Reformation in 1536—it was not until 1593 that the history of the silversmiths of Stavanger begins, with the names and accounts of their lives. In 1621 the suppressed guilds were reintroduced and a certain activity reigned once again. Such was the progress of the craft that in 1685 new ordinances were made and the masterpiece as a test of the technical capacity of budding goldsmiths was re-established.

One of the few successful goldsmiths in Stavanger in the seventeenth century was of Scottish antecedents, and was probably born there of Scottish parents, namely, Jon Feiff or Pfeiff, who flourished from 1660 until his death about thirty years later. A quarrelsome and arrogant man, he brooked no competition, and in 1668 obtained a monopoly for making silver in Stavanger, though there were other goldsmiths in the district. In this year he was elected to the important office of vice-chairman of the City Council. Three years later he occupied the proud position of Burgomaster of Stavanger, and during this time he was dependent upon his faithful apprentice, Peter Dorenfeldt (master in 1690–1709) for the execution, partial or complete, of the silver wrought in his workshop. The hammer marks of this Scoto-Norwegian may be detected in three boxes for ecclesiastical purposes.

One of Peter Dorenfeldt's silver tankards is illustrated on Plate XVI of the catalogue of the exhibition of silver at Stavanger by MM. Thor Kielland and Helge Gjessing (1918).

In the eighteenth century the most prosperous silversmith in Stavanger was Anders Hansen Smith (1742–1803), also of Scottish descent, who received his first instruction in the art from a goldsmith at Bergen. In 1760 he removed to Copenhagen and there worked for Lauritz Nilsen Möller for three years and afterwards for the widow of one Lunte. Having returned to Stavanger in 1766, he instantly established himself as the most flourishing goldsmith and was frequently associated with his colleagues in actions against forgers. Smith succeeded in obtaining a privilege limiting the number of silversmiths in the town to four. In 1786 he was admitted to the goldsmiths' guild at Christiansand, and in 1789 his

PLATE LXXVIII

PLATE LXXIX

name is recorded as the only silversmith in Stavanger. His work is not conspicuous for fine finish: he favoured the rococo, but in his hands it loses any elegance that may be claimed for this style of ornament. One doubtful practice which he shared with some goldsmiths of other countries—Jacob Hurd in America, as is mentioned on page 43; the marking of foreign plate by Dublin silversmiths, as shown on page 263; and the stamping of London marks by London silversmiths on candlesticks made in Sheffield, as related in the last chapter—was in adding his own stamp to the marks of the original makers of old silver, brought to his workshop for repairs. Smith was the maker of a tankard on ball and claw feet, decorated with flowers and foliage and embellished with cast masks on the handle.

Just as the Canadian goldsmith, François Ranvoyze, failed in his attempt to prevent Laurent Amyot from establishing himself as a silversmith in Quebec, and just as the native London goldsmiths unsuccessfully opposed the granting of privileges to Dutch silver smiths in the seventeenth century and the later French Huguenot refugees, so, too, did Smith fail to stop a craftsman from working in Stavanger. This was Jacob Campbell, born in that town in 1742, son of James Campbell, a surgeon, and like Smith a descendant of Scottish settlers in Norway. He was apprenticed in Stavanger but was obliged by the difficult times to remove about 1769 to Egersund, where he continued his craft. As Smith was the only goldsmith in Stavanger at that time, Campbell was tempted to return there. Smith fought hard against his return and supported his opposition by alleging that Campbell had not enrolled himself in the guild at Christiansand. However, Smith was foiled in his malicious attempt by an ordinance of the city elders in 1789 granting Campbell permission to settle there as a silversmith. Campbell's work in spoons and other small things is heavy and massive. In his larger silver he was more careful, and in a little rococo coffee-pot (attributed to him) he reveals a good sense of form and competent workmanship (Plate LXXIX, No. 6).

The coffee-pot just mentioned, and a caster on Plate LXXIX (No. 1), are good examples of the twisted hollow flutes which are distinguishing features of so much Norwegian and Scandinavian plate in the rococo manner. Similarly, a twisted ribbing was much practised on plate of the same time, as may be seen on the caster on Plate LXXIX (No. 5).

The influence of English silver of the eighteenth century upon the goldsmiths of Norway may be observed here and there, including some octagonal candlesticks, like those of about 1720 and 1725 by two craftsmen of Christiania, illustrated on Plate LXXVII. On the same Plate (No. 6) is another candlestick, copied in 1788 by one Micael Hansen Blytt, of Bergen, from an English candlestick of about 25 years earlier. The tea-caddy of about 1730 (Plate LXXVII, No. 3), probably made by Magnus Bessel, of Bergen, also betrays an English influence in the design, as do the plain cylindrical caster by Albret Groth, of Christiania, and the plain vase-shaped caster, by Jacob A. Möller, of the same place, both illustrated on Plate LXXIX. Some Norwegian spoons also show traces of English designs.

Niels Haugaard, of Christiania, departs from the conventional octagonal candlestick in the specimen wrought by him about 1762, mainly by adding a higher and more clumsy foot (Plate LXXVII, No. 9). The coffee-pot submitted by him in 1762 as a "masterpiece" for election to the rank of master goldsmith is still preserved in Christiania (Oslo). One of his best works is a toilet set, which reveals in the execution of the several parts, except in the engraving, the hand of a skilful craftsman; it is illustrated in the book of MM. Grevenor and Kielland, mentioned earlier.

For the names of the private owners of the various pieces of plate here illustrated by their courtesy, the above books must be consulted.

POLAND

PLATE LXXX.

No. 1   Silver cock, 1552. H. 7 in.   National Museum, Warsaw.
No. 2   Tazza, by Andreas Mackensen (Maxson), of Cracow, c. 1648. H. 10¼ in.
        D. 11 in.   Collection of Count Edouard Krasiński.
No. 3   Two cartridge boxes (c. 1700 and 18th century).   National Museum, Warsaw.
No. 4   Ring of crysolite and enamelled gold, c. 1540.   Goldsmiths' Guild of Cracow.
No. 5   Enamelled gold chain and pendant of precious stones. Early 17th century.
                                                                      Goldsmiths' Guild of Cracow.

HERE as elsewhere in the history of precious objects in gold and silver, the destruction has been most deplorable. The ancient insignia of the Kings of Poland, preserved in the Castle at Cracow, the old royal capital, some of which dated from the year 1000, were lost in the division of the country in 1794.

Chalices are the oldest surviving relics of the goldsmith's craft in this country, and of these two are of the Romanesque style, and are at Trzemeszno. One of these is decorated in niello. Both are illustrated in colour in Przezdziecki and Rastawiecki's book on old plate in Poland. Another, with two handles, in the National Museum at Cracow, is assigned to the early date of 1166–1185. Of the thirteenth century are the chalice and paten of Conrad I, Duke of Mazowsze (1230–1238), at Płock, which is decorated with Biblical subjects in niello and engraving, both being illustrated in colour in the above work. After the invasions of the Mongols in 1241, 1259 and 1287 Poland was plundered of many of her historic treasures. Casimir the Great, the greatest personality among the early Kings, revived the arts in his stricken country, and during his reign a series of silver statues of saints and reliquaries were executed by goldsmiths and sculptors for churches. Among the important objects then created were the silver-gilt reliquary bust of St. Sigismund, of the year 1370, in the Cathedral of Płock, to which was added in 1401 a silver-gilt crown set with gems by the goldsmith, Stanislas Zemelka, of Płock; and that of St. Mary Magdalene of the same date in the Church of Stobnica. The above-mentioned book has coloured illustrations of these busts, both of which were the gifts of Casimir. In the convent of the Clarisses at Cracow are several reliquaries from the thirteenth to the eighteenth centuries.

A precious relic in Cracow Cathedral is the Gothic gold cross set with gems—the so-called cross of Casimir the Great. Into this has been introduced the gold from the two royal crowns with which Wladyslas Jagiello and Jadwiga, daughter of Louis of Hungary, were invested at their coronation in 1386.

The dynastic connection between Hungary and Poland was not without its effect upon the arts before the middle of the sixteenth century. The influence is particularly manifest in the Hungarian wire-enamel, described on a previous page, which was also practised by Polish craftsmen and may be observed in such sacred vessels as the chalices from the majestic ruins of the Benedictine Abbey of Tyniec, five miles from Cracow, which are now in the Cathedral of Tarnów, and the chalice of Thomas Strzempiński, Bishop of Cracow (1455–60), in Cracow Cathedral.

A notable specimen of goldsmith's work is the imposing " pacificale " in Sandomierz, richly ornamented and enamelled, probably from the hands of the Cracow goldsmith, Hanusz Glogier, about 1472.

The forms of monstrances in the fifteenth century are dominated by Gothic architecture, and are of great size. Of noble dimensions is the monstrance at Luborzyca, near Cracow, wrought by an unknown goldsmith between 1460 and 1470. Two great monstrances are at Wilno (Vilna) and Wieliczka, the second of which was the work of one Abraham Grochowski. Living in this century was the Cracow goldsmith, one Johannes, who removed to Olmütz (now Olomouc, in Czechoslovakia). Down to the middle of the fifteenth century Bohemian influences prevailed at Cracow, but from that time the art of Nuremberg is dominant. The Painters' Guild of Cracow, organised in 1410, included not only painters but also goldsmiths and other craftsmen.

At the end of the century appears the name of a many-sided artist at Cracow, one Wit Stoss, called Stwosz, who provided designs for goldsmiths of the city, among whom was his brother, Maciej

(Matthew). This brother began his career in 1488, and was goldsmith to the Polish Court before his death in 1540. The Stwosz family exercised great influence in the decoration of ecclesiastical and secular plate, and introduced figures in the manner of the wood carvers into sacred vessels.

One of the most precious objects of Polish goldsmith's work extant to-day is the Gothic reliquary-head of St. Stanislas, executed by Marcian Marcinek of Cracow in 1504 for Queen Elizabeth of Habsburg and her two sons, John Albert and Cardinal Frederick, which is now in the Cathedral there, and is illustrated in colours in the book by Przezdziecki and Rastawiecki, mentioned above.

Throughout the changes effected in artistic taste at the Renaissance and under Baroque influence, many Polish monstrances still retained certain Gothic features, under the guidance of the clergy, who regarded the Gothic as the ecclesiastical style *par excellence*.

Goldsmiths from Italy emigrated to Poland during the Renaissance, including Vicenzo Palumba and Gaspare Castello, and the Milanese, Cesar de Seronis, and other craftsmen, who introduced the new applied art of Italy direct from its original source, and not through the medium of Germany as was Polish painting. Most eminent of all was the Veronese, Gian Jacopo Caraglio, goldsmith to the Polish Court from 1539 to his death in 1560, who, like Cellini, was designer, engraver, goldsmith, enameller and gem-cutter. By him was the cameo portrait of Queen Bona Sforza, wife of Sigismund I (1467–1548), which was set in a golden frame, and when last heard of was in a collection in Paris. To him is also attributed the sword (1540) of Sigismund* in Cracow Cathedral.

The goldsmiths' guild of Cracow has a long history and is still in possession of a beautiful ring of crysolite and enamelled gold (Plate LXXX, No. 4), bequeathed with a house and furniture by one of its honoured members, Gregorz Przybyło, who was working between 1523 and 1547. Another interesting relic of the guild is the enam-

---

* He was the donor of the enamelled reliquary of St. Sigismund to the Cathedral at Cracow, interesting for the dolphins and other Renaissance ornament of a secular character. It is illustrated in colour in Przezdziecki and Rastawiecki's book on old plate in Poland.

elled gold chain and pendant, set with precious stones, of the early seventeenth century, which is worn by the oldest member at times of festivity (Plate LXXX, No. 5).

From the end of the seventeenth century onward Polish monstrances are richly adorned with gems and enamel, often in an extravagant manner. One of the most important is that of Podkamień, dating from 1766 and enamelled with the black and white colours of the Dominicans and decorated with figures of saints of that order. An interesting fact in this monstrance is that the golden bridal wreath of Queen Bona Sforza was offered and accepted as a part of the vessel, in accordance with an old custom of Polish ladies of distinction offering their gold and silver wreaths after their weddings for embellishing monstrances.

Cracow, as the old capital of Poland, attracted vendors of precious stones, and a prosperous trade was carried on from the fifteenth century, if not earlier, between the city and the Orient and Venice. Cameo cutters and seal engravers were much employed, as were the goldsmiths, who specialised in incrusting oriental onyx and turquoises into the hilts of swords and the harness of horses. Such was the fame of Cracow for precious stones that a ruby of 250 carats was exported to England in 1464.

German silversmiths, as well as Italian and Polish, were employed by the Court. In the years 1515–1518 a Nuremberg craftsman executed a reliquary for a chapel in the Church of the Holy Virgin at Cracow. He was possibly Hans Kulmbach, pupil of Albrecht Dürer, whose brother, Andrew Dürer, it is interesting to recall, executed work in the precious metals for the Polish Court and for high ecclesiastics between 1530 and 1534 and again in 1538. To Andrew Dürer's influence is attributed the drinking vessel of a buffalo's horn and silver, supported on a figure of Hercules, which was made as a gift to the guild of salt-miners at Wieliczka, near Cracow, in 1534; and also, two years later, the silver candelabra in the Sigismund Chapel at Cracow. In this same chapel is the famous silver altar of 1538, ordered in Nuremberg by Sigismund I and executed by Melchior Bayr with the help of other artists.

Little has been said of secular work, for the sufficient reason that little has survived the terrible havoc made at the siege of Cracow by the Swedes in 1655 and during the occupations of the city in the eighteenth century by Swedish, Saxon, Russian, and Polish soldiers. Characteristic of Poland from medieval times to the nineteenth century are the silver belts as seen in early Polish portraits. They are of two different types. The first is called " Przeworsk," from the town where it was made ; this is chased with rosettes and other ornament sewn upon morocco leather. The second variety consists mostly of rectangular plaques, generally cast in relief with figure or plant decoration, and date from the fifteenth to the eighteenth centuries. Specimens of each are in the National Museum at Cracow. Equally characteristic of the country is the elaborate harness for horses, a specimen of which, dating from the seventeenth century, is illustrated in colour in the book on Polish silver mentioned earlier.

In the second half of the sixteenth and the beginning of the next century the goldsmiths' guilds of Poland were affected by the introduction of the French taste, by such artists as Pierre Remy, the brothers Blanc, Wilhelm Chefdeville, Jean Herblin, the court goldsmith, Benjamin Lanier, and many other settlers, attracted to the country after the offer of the Polish throne to Henri III. The influence of the French extended also to enamels.

Nothing now remains of the treasures in gold and silver plate wrought under the protecting guidance of the cultured Sigismund III at the end of the sixteenth and the early seventeenth centuries. Not satisfied with the work executed in Poland itself, the nobles and others bought plate from Augsburg, a connection which was severed by the Thirty Years' War. Hauteville, in his glimpse of the life of Polish nobles towards the close of the seventeenth century, refers to the abundance of plate in their houses, adding that all the guests at a feast were expected to bring their own knife, fork and spoon, and recalling the earlier entertaining account of the visit of Jerome Horsey, Ambassador to Russia, to the Court of Nicholas Radziwill at Vilna, when every guest at dinner had his own silver fork.

Mention must be made of the designs for goldsmiths' work by Erasmus Kamyn, of Poznań (Posen), published in 1592.

A set of twelve parcel-gilt tazze, displaying in the bowls portraits of twelve Kings of Poland from Ladislas Jagellon (1386) to Jean Casimir (1648), is in the possession of Count Edouard Krasiński, to whose ancestor, Count Casimir Krasinski (1602–69), and his bride, Countess Anne Andrault de Langeron, it had been given by the King of Poland (Plate LXXX, No. 2). The maker was Andreas Mackensen (Maxson), who migrated to Cracow from Denmark, and was appointed Court goldsmith. Alarmed by the disturbed condition of the country, he removed in 1650 to Dantzig and died there about 1670.

Early in the seventeenth century a native goldsmith, Samuel Piastowski, was prominent. Later in this century is the enamelled chalice of 1680 in the church of Corpus Christi, Cracow, bearing the initials of the maker, S. K., probably Stanislaus Kniper, of Cracow, and of the enameller, L. T., whose name has not been identified.

Three pieces of Polish work are illustrated on Plate LXXX. The first is the silver cock of the shooting guild of Warsaw, dated 1552. The others are cartridge boxes, characteristically Polish. One is of iron, studded with silver, and dates from about 1700; the other is of silver and niello, and is set with pieces of jasper, turquoise and red glass, dating from the eighteenth century. The last is attributed to one of the goldsmiths of Armenian origin, who were numerous in the south-east of Poland. All these are in the National Museum at Warsaw.

In the Victoria and Albert Museum is a most ornate nautilus-shell cup, mounted in gold and set with engraved gems, and signed " I. Martin, fait à Varsovie, le 26 Août 1770."

Old Polish silver spoons are interesting for the humorous poesies in Latin and Polish from the pens of Polish poets, Nicholas Rey and others, inscribed upon them.

Dantzig (Gdańsk) was closely connected with Poland in the sixteenth and early seventeenth centuries, and boys, destined for the life of a goldsmith, were sent to Cracow to learn their craft.

Among other places in Poland where silver was wrought were Lwów (Lemberg) and Wilno (Vilna).

M. Leonard Lepszy's book on Cracow (with an English translation by R. Dyboski, 1912) will be found useful.

PLATE LXXX

PLATE LXXXI

PORTUGAL

PLATE LXXXI.

Ewer (H. 18¼ in.) and basin (D. 20½ in.) (c. 1560-5).   Wallace Collection, London.

PLATE LXXXII.

No. 1 Plateau. 16th century. D. 12¼ in.   Victoria and Albert Museum.
No. 2 Dish (c. 1660-90). D. 16¼ in.
No. 3 Dish (c. 1660-90). D. 16¼ in.
No. 4 Dish (c. 1670-1700). D. 16⅜ in.

PLATE LXXXIII.

No. 1 Dish, Oporto. 18th century. D. 17⅜ in.
No. 2 Ewer. Early 18th century. H. 8⅜ in.
No. 3 Wine taster (c. 1800).
Nos. 4 & 5 Shaving dish (13¾ in. by 12¾ in). and ewer (H. 11¼ in.), 18th century.
No. 6 Pair of candlesticks. 18th century. H. 10 in.

(All except No. 3 are in the Metropolitan Museum, New York.)

ONE of the consequences of the rise of Portugal to the rank of foremost colonising power in Europe in the fifteenth century, as the result of the discoveries by Portuguese mariners, was a marked development in the taste for personal objects of luxury and the adornment of churches with vessels in the precious metals. The ancient and honourable craft of the goldsmith was stimulated by the material prosperity of the country and by the first importation of gold from the East by the famous navigator, Vasco da Gama.

In the reign of Emanuel I (1495–1521), called the Fortunate, Portugal acquired ever-increasing wealth, and it was during this period that the national and florid style in architecture, known as *Arte Manuelina*, a mixture of late Gothic and early Renaissance, was evolved, and spread into Spain. The architecture in question, of which the monastery of Belem is a familiar and conspicuous example, is reflected in certain features and ornaments in the sacred vessels of the Church, such as the chalices in Braga Cathedral and in the Museum of Religious Art at Coimbra, as may be seen in the illustrations of these and other vessels in *Arte Religiosa em Portugal*, and, as a practical example, in the gold and enamelled monstrance of Belem. This celebrated monstrance is highly important as the work of a Lisbon goldsmith, Gil Vicente, executed from a drawing by Garcia de Rezende, to the order of King Emanuel I, early in the sixteenth century, and is made from the gold brought from India as tribute of the King of Quilon, the old capital of Portuguese India. It was a bequest of Emanuel to the monastery of Belem, and is now in the National Museum of Art in Lisbon, with other ecclesiastical goldsmiths' work.

The sixteenth century was the golden age of silversmiths' work in Portugal, as it was of literature, and during the Portuguese Empire, 1499–1580, social life in Lisbon is said to have been hardly less brilliant than that of Rome and to have quickened the development of the arts and crafts.

In consequence of the excessive scarcity of domestic plate of the sixteenth century it is impossible to visualise the influence of Flemish goldsmiths upon the craft in Portugal, though it may be inferred from the intimate trading connection between Antwerp and Lisbon, and from the strongly marked influence of the Flemish masters upon the early Lisbon school of painting, that it was not negligible. Nor is it possible, for the same reason, to offer a description of the silversmiths' work executed by craftsmen from other countries, who were attracted to the Iberian Peninsula by the reports of the vast wealth in the precious metals brought from the East and the New World.

If conclusions may be drawn from the Portuguese plate of the Renaissance it would seem to betray the same tendency to over-elaboration as does that of Spain. The ornate and important rose-water dish (20½ inches in diameter) and ewer (18½ inches high), adorned with the arms of Pius IV, Pope from 1559 until his death in 1565, in the Wallace Collection in London, display in the decoration and in the shape of the ewer and in the decoration of both, in the symbols of the four seasons, sea monsters, in panels, masks and figures, fruit and foliage, repoussé in high relief, the dominating influence of the goldsmiths of Augsburg and Nuremberg, though the

PORTUGAL

workmanship is not German (Plate LXXXI). The maker was perhaps Antonio de Castro, a Portuguese silversmith, to whom is attributed a dish and ewer in 1565 in the Palazzo Coccapani at Modena (M. H. Bernath, in *Kunstchronik für Kunst u. Kunstgewerbe*, January 12, 1912).

One of the most popular objects of domestic plate in the sixteenth century was a shallow dish or plateau, of which several examples are extant. An important specimen of these dishes has been acquired by the Victoria and Albert Museum from Madryn Castle in Carnarvonshire, and is of unusual interest in that it was once the property of Elihu Yale, one of the founders of Yale University, and a family connection of the Madryn family (Plate LXXXII, No. 1). No surprise need be expressed at the possession of old Portuguese silver by Elihu Yale, for he not only had business relations with Portuguese merchants during his life as a merchant at Madras, between 1670 and 1687, and as Governor of the East India Company after 1687, but also from the evidence of some genealogists that one of his Madras mistresses was Mrs. Pavia, a Portuguese Jewess, and that his wife was of Portuguese descent. The decoration consists of trophies of arms, fruit and flowers and hunting scenes. Some more of the Yale Portuguese silver is described later.

Another Portuguese dish of the same period passed from the collection of Baron Albert von Oppenheim to that of the late Mr. J. Pierpont Morgan, and is decorated on the wide border with Biblical and mythological subjects in relief; it is illustrated in the catalogue. A second, identified as Portuguese from the arms of the family of De Mello, is decorated with castellated buildings and martyrdoms and symbolical figures of the seven Arts and Sciences. This is in the collection of the Baroness James de Rothschild, and is illustrated in the present author's catalogue of that collection with another Portuguese dish of the same date and engraved with the same arms. Yet another example, decorated with a representation of the Siege of Troy, formerly in the Wyndham Cook collection, was sold in the Whawell sale of armour at Sotheby's on May 6, 1926. (*Catalogue of Burlington Fine Arts Club*, 1901, No. 11.)

Common as were these dishes in the Iberian Peninsula, and

similar as many are in the workmanship, some difficulty arises in the separation of the Portuguese from the Spanish, in the absence of identifiable marks.

A favourite vessel after the restoration of the Duke of Braganza as John IV in 1640 is a circular dish of thin silver, embossed with tulips and other flowers and birds, recalling in the decoration the luxuriant vegetation of Portugal and suggesting in the thinness of the metal the increasing scarcity of silver or the need for economy. These dishes were made in various sizes, particularly towards the end of the seventeenth century. A good specimen is believed to have belonged to Elihu Yale (Plate LXXXII No. 3); and another, from the important royal collection of Don Fernando, has been acquired by Mr. Ernest A. Sandeman. Characteristic also of this period is the large dish with long and deep flutes on the wide border, such as the specimen from Madryn Castle, also part of the " Yale " collection (Plate LXXXII, No. 2). A dish with similar fluting, dated 1690, and stamped with the mark of Oporto, is in the Church of St. Mary Abbotts, Kensington, the burial place of Colonel Richard Saltonstall, the loyalist exile from Massachusetts, an illustration of which is in Freshfield's *Communion Plate of the County of London*. Illustrated in the same author's work on the church plate in the City of London are two other Portuguese dishes of the same date belonging to the Church of St. Bene't Fink (now destroyed).

Equally characteristic of Portuguese silversmiths' work is the circular dish, embossed with various flowers and a bird in the centre, of about 1670–1700 (Plate LXXXII, No. 4).

A two-handled bowl of the late seventeenth century, now in the American collection of Dr. Theodore S. Woolsey,* is essentially Portuguese, and may be compared with the bowl sold at Christie's on May 21, 1919, and inscribed : " The Guift of John Edwardes & John Bridger to Simon Wellis in Lixborn Anno 1646." Portuguese silversmiths made a characteristic and ornate tazza (*fruteiro*) in the seventeenth and eighteenth centuries, of which

* It is illustrated on page 126 of Mr. Francis H. Bigelow's *Historic Silver of the Colonies*.

PORTUGAL

several specimens are in the old Royal collection of Portugal and in the National Museum of Art at Lisbon.

Shown on Plate LXXXIII are a few pieces of the eighteenth century in the Metropolitan Museum, New York. Silver shaving dishes and ewers, such as the pair illustrated, were wrought in large numbers at Lisbon and Oporto in the eighteenth and early nineteenth centuries, and a small collection has been acquired by the Museum of Fine Arts at Boston, Massachusetts. Others are in the National Museum of Art in Lisbon. A shell-shaped shaving bowl and ewer of the eighteenth century are illustrated in the Bulletin of the Wadsworth Athenæum, Hartford, Connecticut, for April, 1924.

The influence exerted by French decorative motives of the later style of Louis XIV, the rococo of Louis XV and the style of Louis XVI, superimposed on the national decoration, is apparent not only in domestic but also in ecclesiastical silver in Portugal, as in other European countries. Not without interest is the fact that from the date of the Methuen treaty in 1703 and from the close commercial relations between England and Portugal, especially in the late eighteenth and early nineteenth centuries, English plate was copied and wrought in considerable quantities by the silversmiths of Lisbon and Oporto. The author has seen many domestic things, teapots and coffee pots, cream jugs, and sugar basins copied, with slight modifications, from English models and in some cases attempts have been made even to reproduce the English hall-marks. In the National Museum at Lisbon is a plain salver of about 1775, copied from an English piece.

In 1725 a serious destruction of precious plate in the Royal collection occurred, when the extravagant King, John V (1706–50), ordered most of it to be melted. This collection of the House of Braganza originally comprised not only vessels of Portuguese workmanship, but several notable pieces of English silver, probably the gifts of Charles II of England to his bride, Catherine of Braganza, and the later English plate ordered by John V himself, which included an immense wine cistern, "large enough to be called a bath." Much other plate perished in the great earthquake and resulting fires of 1755.

No account of Portuguese plate would be complete without a notice of the characteristic plain silver wine-tasters of the eighteenth and nineteenth centuries of Oporto and Lisbon, which were as common as the contemporary French silver wine-tasters with handles. As will be observed, in the centre is a large dome, round which the wine is circulated, thereby enabling the vintner to test the colour, as well as the flavour, of his wine against the highly polished surface of the metal (Plate LXXXIII, No. 3). Common as they were in Portugal, they are English in origin. An early example, bearing the London mark for 1646–7, is in the collection of Sir John H. B. Noble, Bart. Two others of the same shape, dated 1671–2 and 1673–4, are in Mr. Thomas Taylor's collection at Chipchase Castle, which also contains a French taster of similar form, made at Bordeaux in the eighteenth century.

Mention should be made of the great silver centre-piece, showing a touch of the Empire style, which was made in Lisbon in 1814 from the designs of the well-known artist, Domingos Antonio de Sequeira (1768–1837), and presented by the Prince Regent, afterwards John VI, to the great Duke of Wellington, and now preserved at Apsley House with some old Portuguese silver beakers, brought from Portugal by the Duke after his Peninsular campaigns, and other important presentation plate.

Such luxurious things as bed-warmers, washing basins and ewers and spittoons were made in the country in the eighteenth and nineteenth centuries.

Silver was wrought at several places in Portugal, including Beja, Braga, Evora, Guimarães, Lisbon, Oporto, Setubal, and Coimbra (Laurindo Costa's *As Contrastarias em Portugal*, 1927). At the last of these places a chalice of unusual interest, happily still preserved, is believed to have been made by the goldsmith whose name is inscribed upon it with the date of 1190. Plain, simple spoons, requiring no great skill in hammering out, were doubtless made at many places, other than those mentioned, and an account of these by the present author is in the *Burlington Magazine* for December, 1919.

The street of the goldsmiths (still called "Gold Street") in

PLATE LXXXII

PLATE LXXXIII

PORTUGAL

Lisbon, was known as early as 1382, and the first recorded regulations for the craft appear to date from 1460. In 1551–2 Lisbon could boast of 430 workers in gold and silver.

The earliest known record of assayers at Oporto is 1570, though there were probably older records, now lost. Indentures of apprentices are recorded there from 1667, and such was the increasing demand for silver that the number of assayers was increased from one to two in 1725.

But centuries old as is the art of the goldsmith in Portugal an organised system of marking plate was apparently not inaugurated at Lisbon and Oporto, to name the two principal places, until the eighteenth century.

The National Museum of Art at Lisbon contains an important collection of Portuguese silver, mostly ecclesiastical, and a few specimens are in the Victoria and Albert Museum.

RUSSIA

PLATE LXXXIV.
No. 1   Gold kovsh. 16th century.   "Green Vaults," Dresden.
No. 2   Silver-gilt kovsh, 1635.   Victoria and Albert Museum.

PLATE LXXXV.
Nos. 1 and 2   Enamelled charka. 17th century.   British Museum.
No. 3   Enamelled gold bratina, set with gems, 1632-48. H. 10¼ in.
                                                                                  Imperial Museum, Vienna.

THE history of Russian art is said to date from the time of Vladimir (c. 956–1015), through his marriage with Anne, sister of the Emperor Basil II, who took Byzantine artists with her to Kiev. No names of goldsmiths of the Middle Ages have, however, survived with that of the famous icon painter, Rublëv, whose icon of the Trinity in the Troitska monastery—the Trinity monastery of St. Sergius—was mounted in a golden covering in 1600 by order of Boris Godunov.

The splendour of the gold and silver plate of the Tsars was the theme of travellers and ambassadors to Russia in the sixteenth and seventeenth centuries, though their letters and comments give but little information regarding the plate wrought actually by Russian goldsmiths. Indeed, many of the most striking pieces of those periods are known to be English, German, Dutch and Scandinavian. Samuel Maskievitch in his annals of 1610 testifies, however, to the skill of the Russian craftsmen, as did Olearius, who says that they could imitate whatever object was put into their hands, but that they excelled not in invention.

The most conspicuous of Russian domestic vessels is the bratina (derived from *brat*, brother), a drinking cup not found elsewhere in Europe. Those of the Tsars and members of the Imperial family were of silver-gilt and occasionally of enamelled gold and precious stones. Many of the boyards, or nobles, had their bratini of silver, as did the Patriarchs of the Russian Church and the archimandrite (abbot) of monasteries. From some of the extant specimens the celebrated vintages of the Crimea and Georgia, including the famous Kakhetian wine of Georgia, have doubtless been drunk.

Three bratini of the Tsars in the Kremlin may be mentioned. The first is of silver, and, according to the Slavonic inscription, it belonged to Ivan IV, called "The Terrible," who reigned from 1533 to 1584 (illustrated in Filimonov's catalogue, No. 638, Plate 188). The second, also of decorated silver, is inscribed in niello to the effect that it was the bratina of the Tsar Michael (1613–45), the first of the Romanov line of Russian Tsars, and that it was placed on the coffin of the Tsarevitch Ivan Ivanovitch. From this inscription the assumption may be made that this was the actual drinking vessel used by the Tsar as a memorial of the anniversary of the murder of the Tsarevitch by his father, Ivan the Terrible, in a fit of ungovernable fury in 1580 (Filimonov, No. 694, Plate 187).

So personal was the bratina of the Imperial family that it had in some cases almost a sacred significance after death, as may be gathered from the history of the previous vessel. The custom here mentioned was a survival of an ancient practice of burying the early Russians, especially princes and men of valour, in an open field (*step*) and a mound or hillock made over their graves, on which a solemn memorial feast (*trizna*) was celebrated, and wine drunk in memory of the departed. More recently a memorial service (*Panichida*) was held in the church, and afterwards the mourners and friends adjourned home and drank wine from the loving cup (bratina) in memory of the dead, in accordance with ancient custom. At the death of a prince or princess of royal blood a favourite bratina, as is mentioned above, was placed on his or her tomb in a church and was consecrated for use as an incense burner during and after the memorial service. The gold bratina (with the cover of silver-gilt), decorated with niello and set with emeralds, precious stones and pearls, which was presented by loyal subjects to the Tsar Michael, and by him transferred to the Cathedral of the Annunciation in Moscow, was the personal cup of his wife, the Tsarina Eudokia Lukianovna, and at her death was deposited on her tomb in the Ascension convent, and afterwards used for incense. In the same monastery was the bratina of the Tsarevna Eudokia Michailovna, daughter of the Tsar Michael, in 1637.

One of the most precious of all bratini is in the Imperial Museum at Vienna and is illustrated on Plate LXXXV (No. 3). It is of solid gold and is enriched with large precious stones, sapphires and rubies and rows and circles of pearls on the cover and the bowl, which are divided into sections of pierced work, richly enamelled in characteristic Russian fashion. Surmounting the cover is a finial formed of the King of Poland's arms and monogram, enamelled in colour. This regal relic of the defunct monarchies of Russia and Poland was the gift of the Tsar Michael to Wladislaus IV (1632–48), King of Poland. A more vivid impression of its magnificence may be obtained from the coloured illustration in Dr. A. Ilg's book on the Imperial collection at Vienna. Here and in other typically Russian vessels the absence of a maker's name is regrettable.

The small gold and enamelled bratinka (small bratina) of the Tsarina Eudokia Lukianovna, second wife of the Tsar Michael, would seem to indicate that a smaller vessel was made for the exclusive use of ladies (No. 525, Plate 173, in Filimonov).

A bratina of the seventeenth century in the Henderson bequest in the British Museum is decorated in relief with characteristic Russian foliage, as is seen also on sacerdotal vestments, and is inscribed on the lip in Slavonic: "True love is like a golden cup: it cannot be broken, and if it is bent it can be restored by care." Three others of about the same date, in the Victoria and Albert Museum, are inscribed: "The bratina of the Abbot Ignatius of the town of Serpukov"; "The bratina of the servant of Nikon Ragozin"; and "The bratina of a good man."

The conventional form of the bratina is globular, with a contracted lip, not unlike the ancient plain gold cup (with animal handle) found in a grave in Siberia, one of the treasures of the Hermitage Museum at Petrograd. The lip is usually decorated with an appropriate inscription in interlaced and highly decorative Slavonic lettering, engraved, chased or nielloed. Forming part of some inscriptions is the name of the owner, but, more frequently, a toast or sentiment, or welcome, such as " Bratina of the good man " (from bratini of Tsars).

Bratini, it should be remembered, are with and without covers —some of the latter resembling the familiar pointed domes of Russian churches. They were made of wood and copper for the peasant and the households of princes and nobles. Ten of copper are illustrated in Filimonov (Vol. III, Plate 39). Examples of fourteen bratini and of other Russian vessels, ecclesiastical and secular, may be studied in the electrotypes in the Victoria and Albert Museum, as well as in the three original bratini previously mentioned and the Russian wine bowl of " Stepan Efremov, elder of the Don Force (Cossacks)," dated 1751.

It was probably the bratina which Heberstein had in his mind when writing in 1549 of Russian drinking customs and the manner of proposing toasts: " He who proposes the toast takes his cup and goes into the middle of the room, and, standing with his head uncovered, pronounces in a festive speech the name of him whose health he wishes to drink and what he has to say in his behalf. Then after emptying the cup he turns it upside down over his head so that all may see that he has emptied it and that he sincerely gave the health of the person in honour of whom the toast was drunk." There can be no doubt that the bratina was a familiar object to Anthony Jenkinson, the English merchant, who has left an entertaining account of the royal banquet to which he had been invited on his first visit to Russia in 1557, when the Tsar gave him drink from his own hand, doubtless from one of these " loving cups." Dr. Marc Rosenberg mentions (Nos. 4736 and 1613 in the second edition of his book on marks) some cups in the form of a bratina copied at Amsterdam and Hamburg in the seventeenth century, from the Russian, which are in the Kremlin.

Another popular Russian silver vessel from the sixteenth to the eighteenth centuries was the kovsh, usually with a boat-shaped body and a single handle, used for ladling out the everyday drinks, such as quass or beer—" The Russ drinks quass," as Thomas Heywood has it in his *Rape of Lucrece*, 1608. Some are of simple plain silver and others are decorated. The royal double-headed eagle, seen in the middle of many specimens, indicates generally that they were complimentary gifts from Tsars to faithful boyards (nobles) and others. In some examples the eagle is accompanied by the name and titles of the Tsar in medallions and an account of the gift and recipient in a band of lettering in Slavonic characters, which adds a pleasant touch of ornament to the lips.

One historic kovsh (in the "Green Vaults," Dresden), the supposed gift of Peter the Great to Augustus the Strong of Saxony, is of solid gold, and is set with large sapphires of inferior quality. Its historic past is enshrined in several inscriptions : " By God's grace and by order of the great Tsar and great Prince Basilide . . . Emperor, Lord of Liefland. . . ." Another is to the effect that it was made by order of the Grand Duke of Moscow and Tsar of Muscovy, Vassili III (1505–33) from gold of the town of Polozk, taken in 1512, while another gives the name and title of the Tsar Ivan the Terrible (1530–84), son of Vassili III (Plate LXXXIV, No. 1).

Two excellent specimens of different engraved decoration are in the Victoria and Albert Museum. One is inscribed : " The gift of the Tsar Michael to Ivan Kostyurin, Lord of the Council, as a reward for his military services," which is dated 1635 and engraved inside with the royal eagle and clusters of fruit, attached to festoons (Plate LXXXIV, No. 2). The other bears an inscription indicating that it was a gift of the joint rulers, the Tsars John and Peter (the Great) to Peter Ivanov in 1691. An important kovsh, engraved with a portrait of the Empress Anne of Russia (1730–40), which was her gift to the Don Cossack Timothy Turaberin in 1735, is on view in the same Museum in the loan collection of Mr. F. J. Varley's Russian silver.

The personal kovsh of Boris Godunov is illustrated in the *Antiquities of the Russian Empire*, and a plain one was given to a monastery in Moscow by the Tsar Alexis. Others may be seen illustrated in Filimonov's catalogue of the silver in the Kremlin.

One of great size, dated 1673, in the Treasury of the Patriarch at Moscow, is known from the electrotype in the Victoria and Albert

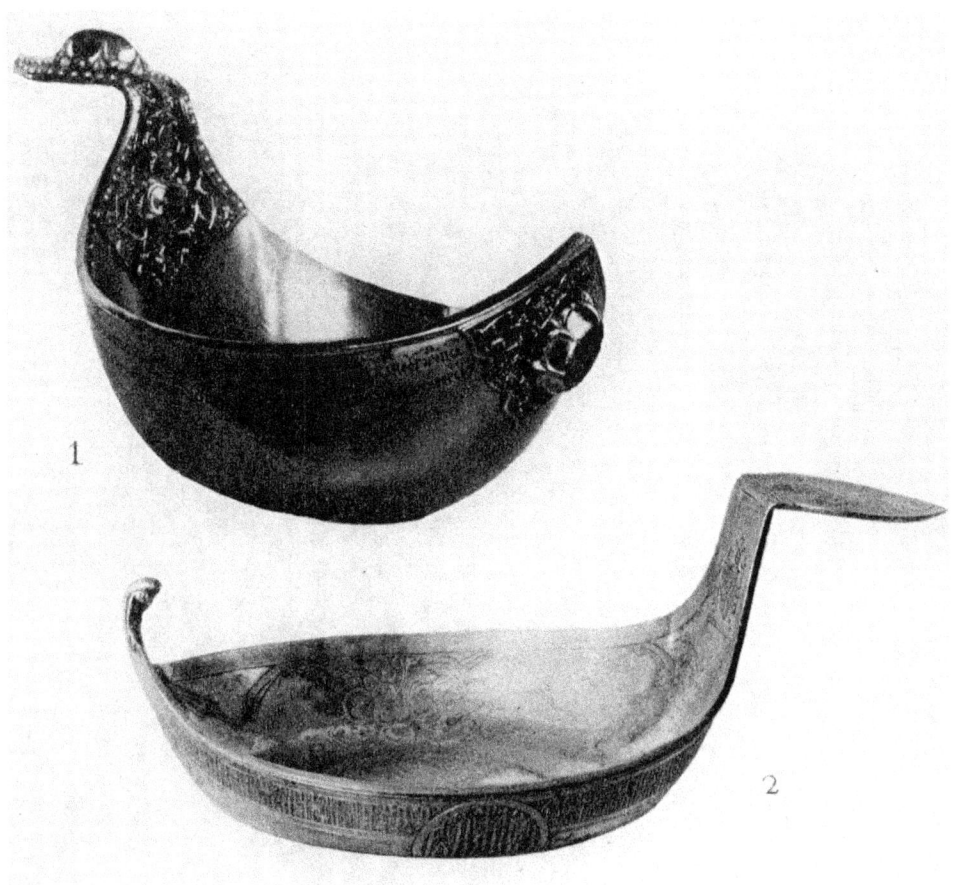

PLATE LXXXIV

PLATE LXXXV

Museum. In the same Treasury is the smaller and rounder kovsh of Joassaff, inscribed : " Kovsh of Joassaff, Archbishop of Pskov and Izborsk," afterwards Patriarch of Moscow (1628–34).

An example of the seventeenth century, embossed with beaded ornaments, is in the Henderson bequest in the British Museum.

The kovsh of the Russian peasant is of wood, like the bratina.

The charka (diminutive of *chara*, a cup or potion) is a small cup, usually fitted with a single handle, for drinking strong liquors or for brandy, as was served before a meal on one of the commercial missions to Russia between 1557 and 1571 of the English merchant, Anthony Jenkinson, mentioned earlier. Like the bratina and kovsh, it is essentially Russian. Among the fifty or more specimens, mostly of the seventeenth century, in the Kremlin, some are inscribed with the names of Tsars from Ivan the Terrible to the Tsarevitch Alexis Petrovitch (1690–1718), son of Peter the Great.

Many are wholly of precious metal, while others are of rock crystal, cornelian, jasper and other semi-precious stones, mounted in gold and jewelled in a truly regal manner. Many and various are the ornamental motives, and, as in the bratina, are occasionally engraved with such admonitions as " Drink if it does not harm you : drink with moderation. It is not wine but drunkenness which is to be blamed." One remarkable specimen of a charka in the Kremlin is cut out of a large piece of opaque amber, mounted in silver-gilt. Another, dated 1609, is of white coral, while yet another rare charka is carved from a piece of ivory. Two of the Tsar Michael are illustrated in colour, No. 8 in *Antiquities of the Russian Empire*. Others may be seen on Plates 181–2 in Filimonov's catalogue, and of these two have two handles and others have three globular feet.

Some important specimens of the seventeenth century, in richly coloured enamels of divers kinds, are in the Henderson collection in the British Museum, two of which are illustrated here, one having three ball feet (Plate LXXXV, Nos. 1 and 2). Others are wholly of silver, or decorated with niello.

Attention should be directed to the great decorative effect of the special Slavonic lettering called *Vyaz*, formed into a continuous kind of monogram, in which the vertical line is dominant, on some of the Russian silver vessels.

The taste for mounting the cocoanut as a cup spread to Russia from the West in the seventeenth century, and at least one specimen of a bratina, formed of a nut and mounted in delicate scrolled filigree of silver-gilt, is known from the electrotype in the Victoria and Albert Museum. Examples of cocoanut cups, both carved and plain, are illustrated in Filimonov's catalogue, together with specimens of the interesting little Russian silver bowls of the seventeenth century, decorated inside and out with flowers in painted enamel, similar to those in the Henderson bequest in the British Museum. The names of the enamellers of these little bowls, as of the makers of Russian goldsmiths' work in general in the sixteenth and seventeenth centuries, remain anonymous. It is claimed that a pupil of the Nouailher family of enamellers at Limoges emigrated to Russia and introduced painting in enamel for bowls and other vessels.

Niello (a variety of black inlaid enamel known to the Romans) was employed as part of the decoration and lettering of Russian gold and silver, both ecclesiastical and secular, in the sixteenth and seventeenth centuries, and was still further developed from the establishment by Peter the Great in 1705 of the celebrated factory at Tula for the manufacture of weapons. Although chiefly engaged in the production of guns and weapons for the army, other interesting work of a domestic character was manufactured there—chairs and tables, caskets and vases, candlesticks and cups, of steel and bronze, frequently damascened in gold and silver and inlaid with niello. Silver plate proper was not wrought at the factory, but cups and other objects are extant from the hands of independent goldsmiths at Tula, as, for example, a small circular bowl of silver-gilt and niello, 1828, in the Victoria and Albert Museum. Niello was practised at St. Petersburg and elsewhere in the eighteenth century. A curious tankard of Scandinavian form, gilt and nielloed and engraved with Scriptural subjects, of about 1700, is in the Victoria and Albert Museum ; and a small beaker of silver-gilt and niello, wrought at Novgorod, once the personal possession of the Empress Anne, is in the Hermitage Museum at Petrograd.

Georg Zeggein, master goldsmith at Munich before his death in 1581, is said to have learned the art of working in silver at Tula.

The Russian snuff-boxes of silver covered with niello, of the nineteenth century, are familiar and common.

If the names of most of the craftsmen who executed the sacred vessels of the Russian Church and of the secular objects already mentioned remain in undeserved obscurity, three names of goldsmiths have survived. One was G. Frobo, the maker of some plates (in the Kremlin) of solid gold for the Tsar Alexis, richly enamelled with the royal eagle in the centre and the arms of eight Russian provinces, originally part of a large service. Research in the archives might lead to the identification of some of his other works.

An earlier goldsmith, one Ivan Formin, was the maker in 1440 of a chalice of marble and gold, in the Troitska monastery (the Trinity Monastery of St. Sergius), after Kiev the richest of monasteries in precious relics, where there is a cross, sent to St. Sergius (fourteenth century) by Philotheos, Patriarch of Constantinople, and mounted in gold and precious stones in the seventeenth century by Andreyko Petrov Ismalov, as inscribed.

Nor must the name be forgotten of Maria Feodorovna, widow of the Emperor Paul I, as a capable medallist and worker in metals and as the maker of a Sacramental service of ivory, gold and enamel, for use in the Russian Church.

Just as the abolition of the national dress by order of Peter the Great and his " westernisation " of Russia created new tastes in dress and ornaments, so, too, did the system of compulsory hallmarking of silver plate, introduced by Peter in 1700, have the effect of making western influence predominant in household plate, largely to the exclusion of the older forms of domestic vessels, the bratina, kovsh and charka. Happily, the Tsar's zeal for western fashions did not go so far as to melt the historic bratini of his predecessors on the throne.

In 1733 a town-mark was a compulsory addition to the marks.

The mark of Moscow was the Imperial double-headed eagle, with the name of the city underneath, until 1741, when it was superseded by the device of St. George and the dragon. The mark of St. Petersburg until 1746 was the same eagle, but crowned, and was replaced by a kedge and anchor in a shield, accompanied by the date on the same punch until 1829.

Although not unknown to Russian goldsmiths before the accession of Peter the Great, tankards of Scandinavian and German forms were now made in greater numbers. Cups, beakers and other drinking vessels became popular and ousted from favour the older national vessels mentioned above. While the forms of these things betray the countries of origin, there is not in every case a slavish imitation of the decoration. Indeed, in many cases a distinctly Russian touch is given to it, as in the tankard made in 1686–7 for the Grand Duchess Sophia Alexeievna, daughter of the Tsar Alexis and half-sister of Peter the Great, a woman of strong will; this is illustrated on page 78 of the catalogue of the Exhibition of Ecclesiastical Art at Moscow in 1913.

Mr. F. J. Varley, in an interesting article in the *Connoisseur* for April, 1918, illustrates some Russian silver of the eighteenth century, showing the influence of Western Europe, from his own collection, now on view in the Victoria and Albert Museum. Four boat-shaped salts, stamped at St. Petersburg in 1795, are typically English in design, and may have been made by, or under the direct influence of, one of the English silversmiths settled there. A plain tankard of Danish type on three pomegranate feet, marked at St. Petersburg in 1705, is in the Victoria and Albert Museum.

That omnivorous collector of works of art, Catherine II, whose purchase of the Walpole collection of pictures from England was her greatest capture, acquired not only Sèvres porcelain and matchless French plate, described in an earlier chapter, but was "justly ambitious," in the words of a writer in the *Morning Advertiser* for April 3, 1786, "to establish and perpetuate refinement and improvement in every science within her dominions, has made every possible exertion to render St. Petersburgh as cultivated, polite and accomplished as London." Craftsmen from other

European countries were tempted by such reports to venture to Russia. From England went at least two London goldsmiths: Robert Hogg, who entered his name on the roll of St. Petersburg goldsmiths on November 14, 1776, and William Donarth on January 18, 1786. Such was the success of Donarth that at his death in 1805 he had five apprentices in his workshop, which was carried on by his widow. An earlier Englishman, one Samuel Gibbs, had been apprenticed to G. Jasper, a German goldsmith in the Russian capital, and became a master goldsmith in 1727. A silversmith of the same name, John A. Gibbs, arrived in St. Petersburg from England in 1804 and became master in 1806. Other English names are recorded.

Of the domestic plate made in the Russian capital in the eighteenth century after the fashions of Western Europe, the following pieces in the Winter Palace are noteworthy: some large centrepieces by Ivan Liebmann, made in 1739–40 in emulation of the works of Claude Ballin, the younger, the French goldsmith whose works are in the same palace. A teapot, decorated in the French style; a plain salver; and a dish cover are by Nicholas Dohm (1720–46). Here are coffee-pots and teapots by J. F. Köpping (1748–80) and J. H. Blohm (1766–86); and part of a dinner service in Louis XVI style by Just Nicolaus Lundt, 1783. All these are illustrated with the priceless old French silver of the eighteenth century in Baron de Foelkersam's catalogue of the collection, together with notes on the Swedish silversmiths working in St. Petersburg in that century.

An important phase of the art of the Russian goldsmith, outside the purview of this book, is the mounting of icons in the precious metals. A discussion of the ancient Russian crowns and regalia in the Kremlin is also inappropriate here, interesting as it is.

Lovers of English plate will remember the wonderful collection of old English plate in the Kremlin, unrivalled in some particulars. This collection has been dealt with by the present author in a separate book.

SCOTLAND

PLATE LXXXVI.

No. 1 Mazer cup, by Alexander Auchinleck, of Edinburgh, c. 1552. H. 16¼ in.
D. 8¼ in. St. Mary's College, St. Andrews.
No. 2 Ewer of crystal and silver-gilt, by George Heriot, the elder, of Edinburgh, c. 1565.
H. 9¼ in. Lord Swaythling Collection.
No. 3 Salt, by Patrick Gairden, of St. Andrews, c. 1670.
St. Mary's College, St. Andrews.
No. 4 Nautilus-shell cup, by Robert Denneistoun, of Edinburgh, 1611-2. H. 8¼ in.
Heriot's Trust, Edinburgh.

PLATE LXXXVII.

No. 1 Gold cup and cover, Edinburgh, 1754-5. H. 10¼ in. Messrs. Crichton Bros.
No. 2 Tankard, by Robert Inglis, of Edinburgh, 1704-5. Captain C. D. Rotch.
No. 3 Quaich, Edinburgh, 1724. Donaldson's Hospital, Edinburgh.
No. 4 Mace of the Corporation of Edinburgh. Maker, George Robertsone, of Edinburgh, 1617. L. 38¼ in.
No. 5 Small mug, by Alexander Forbes, of Edinburgh, 1682-3. H. 3 in.

PLATE LXXXVIII.

Nos. 1-7 Seven silver archery medals, 1618-1628. University of St. Andrews.
No. 8 Gold teapot, by James Ker, of Edinburgh, 1736. Mrs. Leopold de Rothschild.
Nos. 9 and 12 Urn, 1778-9, and coffee pot, 1769-70, both by Patrick Robertson, of Edinburgh. Royal Scottish Museum.
No. 10 Coffee pot, Edinburgh, 1801-2. Mrs. William E. Simms, Kentucky, U.S.A.
No. 11 Caster, Edinburgh, 1746-7. Royal Scottish Museum.

OF all the historic treasures in gold and silver in Scotland which have perished by the hand of the despoiler, or have found their way to the crucible in times of stress or changes in fashion, none would be of greater interest to-day than the gift sent by Mary Queen of Scots to the French poet, Ronsard, from her prison. It is described as a marvellous buffet or sideboard, fashioned in silver to represent a cliff on Mount Helicon, split so deeply by the sacred hoof of Pegasus that the spring of Hippocrene issued from it. Paris, not Edinburgh, was, however, the probable place of workmanship.

The ancient Scottish regalia was doubtless made, at least in part, in Scotland. Indeed, the sceptre which was presented by Pope Alexander VI to James IV in 1494 was largely remade in 1536 by Adam Leys, a goldsmith of Edinburgh.

One symbol of authority survives to-day, in its original condition —the mace of the Corporation of Edinburgh, made in 1617 by George Robertsone while George Craufuird was deacon of the goldsmiths' guild of the Scottish capital (Plate LXXXVII, No. 4).

The mazer cup ($6\frac{1}{4}$ inches high and $8\frac{1}{2}$ inches in diameter) of St. Mary's College, St. Andrews, is not only the oldest piece of Scottish plate with a hall-mark but is the model for other silver cups of the same shape, both for sacred and secular usage in Scotland. It is used as a loving cup at high feasts in the University. Alexander Auchinleck, of Edinburgh, was the maker about 1552 of this historic relic, while Thomas Ewing was the holder of the dignified office of deacon of the guild of goldsmiths in that picturesque capital (Plate LXXXVI, No. 1). The mazers in Edinburgh Castle in 1488, not one of which has survived, were doubtless of the same shape, but without the stem and foot.

The silver cup of the same shape, 8 inches in diameter and $8\frac{1}{8}$ inches high, at St. Salvador's College in the same ancient University, would appear to have lost its original wooden bowl, which has been replaced by one of silver mounted on a high stem. It was made by William Law, of Edinburgh, in 1681, while Edward Cleghorne, a prominent goldsmith, was deacon of the guild. The cup was given by Lady Anne Halkett, a devoted adherent of Charles I and writer on religious subjects, in fulfilment of the wishes of her son, Robert, that if he should return as a student from this College with a good report, she should present a donation to the Church. A sufferer towards the close of her life for her strong and unconcealed political opinions, she ordered the following inscription to be put above the door of her house at Dunfermline :

" Sin word is thrale an thocht is free
Keep weel thy tongue I counsel thee."

It is thought that a " mazer " of this shape prompted the quaint and beautiful passage in Zacharie Boyd's *Last Battell of the Soule*, published at Edinburgh in 1629 : " Take now the cup of salvation, the great Mazer of His mercy, and call upon the name of the Lord."

One other University cup is that which was presented in 1653 to Marischal College, Aberdeen, by Lord Strathnaver, eldest son of the Earl of Sunderland. It is a tall cup on a baluster stem and was made by Walter Melvil, the earliest known goldsmith using the town-mark of Aberdeen, remembered as the maker of the mace of 1650 belonging to King's College, Aberdeen.

Several silver " mazer " cups, inspired by the above St. Mary's mazer, are preserved as Sacramental cups in parishes in the vicinity of Edinburgh, where they were mostly made. Others are in parishes in Fifeshire and elsewhere. Their development may be traced by the aid of the illustrations in the Rev. T. Burns's admirable book on old Scottish Church plate.

Among the secular vessels adapted for sacred use is the beaker, introduced by traders from the Netherlands and by Protestant refugees in the sixteenth century. Aberdeen appears to have been the distributing centre for the Scottish-made beakers, which were seldom made by Edinburgh silversmiths. One such plain beaker was found by the author in 1912 at King's College, Windsor, Nova Scotia. According to the inscription it had belonged in 1663 to the Church of Kearn in Scotland and was made by a goldsmith of Aberdeen. With this beaker was a plain dish, dated 1776, also by an Aberdeen craftsman.

All manner of vessels were used for sacred purposes. For example, John Knox (according to Macdonald's *Days at the Coast*) administered the Sacrament from the turned-up bases of two silver candlesticks, on his visit to the Earl of Glencairn.

The ewer of rock crystal and silver-gilt from Lord Swaythling's collection is a regal and historic piece of about 1565. The maker's mark is that of George Heriot, the elder, the famous Edinburgh goldsmith (who is not to be confused with his son of the same name) and the deacon's mark is that of James Collie or Coln. All the silver-gilt mounts of the crystal body—the cover and handle, the foot and the curious spout, resembling a bird's head—are simple and plain, with no attempt at decoration. Engraved on a disc on the

PLATE LXXXVI

PLATE LXXXVII

SCOTLAND

cover are the arms of Erskine and Murray. The crystal body is carved with a primitive design of flowers. The total height is not more than 9¼ inches. It was a gift from Queen Elizabeth to John, Lord Erskine, 22nd Earl of Mar (Regent of Scotland in 1571) for the baptism of one of his children, though it is not ecclesiastical in shape (Plate LXXXVI, No. 2). The Queen had doubtless commanded George Heriot to send a suitable vessel to the Regent Mar, just as she had sent a German silver cup as a gift to the Protestant Reformer, Heinrich Bullinger, illustrated on Plate LI (No. 2).

In Scottish plate, and indeed in English plate, the nautilus shell cup of Heriot's Trust in Edinburgh stands alone. The shell is richly mounted in silver and rests on a stem of three scrolled monsters on a high foot, and bears the mark of the Edinburgh goldsmith, Robert Denneistoun, with the date-letter for 1611-12 (Plate LXXXVI, No. 4). In this cup George Heriot, the younger, founder of Heriot's Hospital, pledged his friends.

The covered ewer (with its plain basin) in Canongate Church, Edinburgh, is interesting in the history of old silver in that it is one of the earliest extant examples of this shape, whether English or Scottish. Edward Cleghorne, of Edinburgh, was the maker in 1674-5.

Excessively rare, if not unique, in Scottish silver is the salt at St. Mary's College, St. Andrews, which is a copy about 1670 by one Patrick Gairden, a silversmith of that old town, of an English model of the time of Charles I. In ignorance of, or contempt for, their original purpose to support a napkin, the three scrolls have been removed from the top of the salt. An English salt on Plate XXX, illustrates the scrolls in question.

The influence of an English wine cup of the reign of James I (James VI of Scotland) may be traced in the tall and slender baluster stems of certain Sacramental cups peculiar to Scotland. These have large shallow bowls, resembling in shape those of Venetian-glass cups. One of these cups, made in 1638 by John Fraser, of Edinburgh, while Jon Scott was deacon of the guild, has been generously restored by the Earl of Rosebery to the parish of Monifieth in Forfarshire, from which it had strayed; it is illustrated in the *Burlington Magazine* for April 1923.

A silver tankard on Plate LXXXVII (No. 2) is as characteristic of Edinburgh goldsmiths of the late seventeenth and early eighteenth centuries as is a certain type of Scottish pewter flagon or tankard. It differs from the contemporary English tankards in a few details, as is apparent at a glance. This specimen was made by Robert Inglis, of Edinburgh, in 1704-5 and is the property of Captain C. D. Rotch.

In the collection of the late Mr. J. Pierpont Morgan was an example of the date 1695-6, with the marks of the Edinburgh goldsmith, Alexander Forbes, and of the assay-master, John Borthwick, which is illustrated in the catalogue of that important collection. Another tankard, not unlike the Pierpont Morgan piece, was in the collection of the Duke of Cumberland when examined by the author in 1911. The only mark stamped upon it was that of the maker, James or Thomas Ker, of Edinburgh.

These tankards appear to differ from one by John Luke, the younger, of Glasgow, about 1707, a gift of the partners of the "Woollen Manufactorie" in Glasgow to Thomas Thomson, their manager, which was sold at Christie's on December 11, 1923.

No less characteristic of Scottish goldsmiths is a little mug of the seventeenth and early eighteenth centuries, like that shown on Plate LXXXVII (No. 5) by the above Alexander Forbes, dated 1682-3. Some mugs have higher feet than this specimen. They were made at Glasgow as well as Edinburgh, and elsewhere. Sir John H. B. Noble, Bart., is the owner of one with the mark of Aberdeen. Although not of this pattern, a pair of plain mugs by a Glasgow silversmith of about 1730 are mentioned because of the curious name of the maker, Johan Gothelf-Bilsings; these were sold at Christie's on June 23, 1920.

Three Scottish silver "Monteith" bowls are known to the author. The origin of this title for these bowls, from a "fantastical Scot," named "Monteigh," is explained on page 128, and recalls King's poem (c. 1708):

"New things produce new words, and thus Monteth,
 Has by one vessel sav'd his name from death."

One of these bowls, made in 1697-8 by James Cockburne, of

Edinburgh, while James Penman was assay master, is engraved with the arms of Johnston, of Westraw, and when seen by the author was in the collection of the Duke of Cumberland. A very large "Monteith," unusually late in date, embossed with Bacchanalian subjects and fitted with two figure handles, was made in 1782-3 by Patrick Robertson, of Edinburgh, and is in the possession of the Marquess of Londonderry.

Allan Ramsay had in mind a silver or pottery punch bowl when he sang in 1721:

> "Charge me with Nantz and limpid spring,
>   Let sour and sweet be mixt;
> Bend round a health, syne to the king,
>   To Edinburgh's captains next,
> Wha form'd me in sae blyth a shape,
>   And gave me lasting honours,
> Take up my ladle, fill, and lape,
>   And say, Fair fa' the donors."

Caudle cups were made by Scottish silversmiths in the same style as the English. One important covered cup of this kind, decorated with the familiar acanthus leaves, by Alexander Reid, of Edinburgh, 1682-3 (while John Borthwick was assay-master), is in possession of Sir John H. B. Noble, Bart. In the same collection is a pair of rare, plain, octagonal candlesticks, by James Penman, of Edinburgh, 1693-4.

A teapot of a globular shape, with a straight spout, was a popular form among the Edinburgh goldsmiths from the reign of Queen Anne. Some are quite plain and others are slightly chased around the lid with formal scrolls and flowers. Two solid gold teapots of this shape were given as prizes by George II as the "King's Plate" at Edinburgh Races in 1736 and 1737. The first was won by a horse named "Legacy," the winner of the "King's Plate" at Newmarket in the same year. James Ker was the maker of this rare piece, which was in the collection of the late Mr. Leopold de Rothschild (Plate LXXXVIII). A similar gold teapot, in the possession of the Earl of Rosebery, is engraved with the Royal arms and was also made by James Ker in 1737-8, while Archibald Ure was assay-master at Edinburgh. In the collection of Mr. John Girdwood (illustrated in the *Connoisseur* for March 1924) is a silver tea set with a teapot of this same globular shape by William Aytoun, a prominent Edinburgh silversmith in 1733.

The original Scottish quaich or quaigh, a word adopted from the Gaelic for a cup or bowl, was made of a solid block of wood, like the old English mazer, or of small staves of wood, often of different colours, held together by hoops after the fashion of a cask. It was fitted with two handles and occasionally with three. Quaichs of stone, brass, pewter and horn were made by local craftsmen in their leisure moments in the long winter nights in the Highlands and elsewhere, or, in the case of wood, while tending their flocks and herds. One of ebony and white wood, bound with silver hoops, is said to have been made by Archibald, Marquess of Argyll, before his execution; this is in the Museum of the Society of Antiquaries of Scotland in Edinburgh, where there are several quaichs made from different materials.

For the Scottish aristocracy silver quaichs were made in the seventeenth and eighteenth centuries, but the conclusion must not be drawn from this statement that every great family was provided with one. While many quaichs of silver have probably been melted, they are much rarer than the porringers of Colonial America.

Inverness appears to have been a centre for the making of silver quaichs in the north. Sir C. J. Jackson, in the second edition of his work on English Goldsmiths and their Marks, mentions four made by Inverness silversmiths, including one of 1640 in the collection of the late Marquess of Breadalbane, which must be the earliest recorded example in silver. One dated 1770, in the above Edinburgh Museum, was made in that town.

A quaich sold at Christie's on March 24, 1909, for £408 16s. to Messrs. Crichton Bros., had the Glasgow hall-mark for 1665, with the maker's mark of Thomas Moncrur, and is regarded as one of the earliest known pieces of plate with the Glasgow marks. The craftsman has introduced engraved lines on the bowl in imitation of the

SCOTLAND

staves of the wooden quaichs, as may be observed from the illustration in the *History of English Plate*, p. 743. Another early Glasgow silver quaich, by Robert Brock, 1683, is in the collection of Mr. J. A. Holms.

Like other domestic vessels, the quaich was not unknown in use for sacred purposes in churches in Scotland. Two are illustrated in the above-mentioned book on Old Scottish Church plate, by the late Rev. T. Burns. The first, at Alvah, Banff, was made at Edinburgh between 1663 and 1684 by Edward Cleghorne (maker of the fine silver ewer and basin in Canongate Church, Edinburgh), when Patrick Borthwick was deacon of the Goldsmiths' guild, and is, or has been, used as a baptismal basin. Four more in Ayr Parish Church, dated 1722, by Charles Dickson, of Edinburgh, are, or were, in use for Communion cups, baptismal basins and alms bowls.

A silver quaich of the late seventeenth century, described as the work of Matthew Colquhoun, of Ayr, is illustrated in *Scottish National Memorials*, 1890. In the Liverpool Museum is one with the Edinburgh date-letter for 1731-2. One private collection known to the author contains several silver quaichs, dating from about 1665 to 1800, mostly made at Edinburgh, and including one by Thomas Moncrur, of Glasgow, maker of the early quaich already mentioned.

Quaichs are of different sizes, from 4 inches in diameter to larger vessels of over 11 inches in width across the handles.

The silver quaich made at Edinburgh in 1724 is the old loving cup of Donaldson's Hospital in Edinburgh, and previously the personal drinking cup of the founder of that hospital (Plate LXXXVII, No. 3).

In the Earl of Rosebery's collection of old plate is a unique silver quaich copied in 1702-3 by one Anthony Stanley, a goldsmith in Dublin, from an older Scottish quaich.

Gold plate is rare in any country, not least in Scotland. A Scottish gold teapot has been described. Here is a second piece of Scottish origin—a cup and cover decorated in the rococo fashion and fitted with two wooden handles enclosed in gold sockets, which was made at Edinburgh in 1754-5. It is illustrated by the courtesy of

Messrs. Crichton Bros., who have failed to trace the circumstances in which the royal arms of George II and those of the City of Edinburgh were engraved on the cup (Plate LXXXVII, No. 1).

A few pieces of old Edinburgh plate are illustrated on Plate LXXXVIII, comprising a plain caster of English style, dated 1746–7; a coffee-pot, by Patrick Robertson, 1769–70; and a tea-urn by the same goldsmith in 1778–9, which shows no trace in the form of decoration of the influence of the famous Edinburgh-born architect and designer, Robert Adam. These three pieces are in the Royal Scottish Museum at Edinburgh. The fluted coffee-pot, made in Edinburgh in 1801–2, was in possession of Mrs. William E. Simms in Kentucky in 1912 (Plate LXXXVIII, No. 10).

In the *History of English Plate* is an illustration (Fig. 1270) of a fine pierced basket by an Edinburgh silversmith in 1752.

Reference has been made elsewhere in this book to an occasional practice of silversmiths in stamping their own marks on the plate of other craftsmen. A cake or bread basket, decorated in the "Adam" style, in the Victoria and Albert Museum, is not only stamped with the marks of the Edinburgh silversmith, William Davie, for 1775–6, but also the London date-letter for the same year. Mr. Frederick Bradbury has drawn the author's attention to another interesting case where the mark of William Robertson, of Edinburgh, was stamped over the Sheffield mark for 1790 on a pair of candlesticks.

Archery medals of silver are, like the quaich, confined to Scotland. Seventy are preserved at the University of St. Andrews, and others (made as early as 1670–8 by William Scott and Alexander Galloway, of Aberdeen) belong to the old Grammar School of Aberdeen. A fascinating account of these precious relics of the past, illustrated with 173 specimens, was published by the late Mr. A. J. S. Brook in the "Proceedings of the Society of Antiquaries of Scotland" in 1894. The seven medals illustrated on Plate LXXXVIII are the oldest at St. Andrews and are dated between 1618 and 1628. As will be observed, the earlier medals are small and simple shields, engraved with the winners' initials and date—for example, IC, for John Cunningham, of Barns, with the date 1618. In later medals

SCOTLAND

the shield becomes larger and is engraved with the winner's arms. In the eighteenth century they were larger still and were frequently embossed.

The St. Andrews medal was given to the winner of the silver arrow shot for by the students once a year, with becoming enthusiasm, "to keep up that noble ancient exercise of archery, and he that wins it appends to it his coat of arms on a silver plate." Bearers of names illustrious in Scottish history were among the competitors and winners.

Scottish mulls—large or small horns—were frequently mounted in silver for snuffboxes, especially early in the nineteenth century. One of historic interest, for five different kinds of snuff, is in the collection of Sir John H. B. Noble, Bart. It bears an inscription that it was a gift to the Perthshire Regiment of Gentlemen and Yeomanry Cavalry from James Hay, Esq., Captain of the Carse troop, in 1804. The same owner has another interesting relic of a second regiment raised in Scotland to repel the threatened invasion by Napoleon. This is a silver snuffbox, by an Edinburgh goldsmith, and was given by the officers of the Midlothian Regiment of Fencible Cavalry to their Lieut.-Colonel, Sir James Foulis, Bart., in 1800.

No piece of plate has been traced to the workshop of James Gray, the goldsmith who engraved the brass monument of the Earl of Murray, Regent of Scotland, in 1570, in St. Giles's, Edinburgh.

Besides quaichs of divers kinds, the late Marquess of Breadalbane had formed a collection of Scottish silver spoons of the eighteenth and early nineteenth centuries, wrought by goldsmiths outside Edinburgh and Glasgow—at Aberdeen, Arbroath, Banff, Dundee, Elgin, Greenock, Inverness, Leith, Perth and Wick.

Banff ranked next to Aberdeen as a centre of silversmithing in the North of Scotland.

Robert Gairdyne, of Dundee, made some alterations in the cover of the German cup, called "Queen Mary's cup" at Perth, illustrated as a frontispiece to the Rev. T. Burns's book mentioned previously.

In writing of Scottish goldsmiths, the name of James Gilsland, or

Gilliland, of Edinburgh, to whom Raeburn, the portrait painter, was apprenticed, must not be forgotten.

As in London and Dublin, so in Scotland, the seeker after a truly representative collection of the work of native goldsmiths in a public museum, will seek in vain. An interesting group of old Scottish plate is, or was, on loan at the National Museum in Edinburgh from Hon. Lady Binning. It includes a large and fine two-handled bowl and cover, of 1709-10, by James Sympson, and an unusual teapot, of 1758-9, by Robert Gordon, both Edinburgh silversmiths.

PLATE LXXXVIII

PLATE LXXXIX

SPAIN

PLATE LXXXIX.

Ewer (H. 19 in.) and basin (D. 19¾ in.). Late 16th century.
Collection of the late J. Pierpont Morgan, Esq.

PLATE XC.

No. 1   Ewer, of silver-gilt, set with small enamelled plaques, c. 1610.   Lord Dalmeny.
Nos. 2 and 3   Two silver-gilt ewers, c. 1610.   Lord Dalmeny.
No. 4   Inkstand, Madrid. 18th century.   Metropolitan Museum, New York.
No. 5   Silver-gilt ewer, c. 1610.   Royal Palace, Madrid.
No. 6   Cup, silver-gilt. Early 17th century.   Messrs. Crichton Bros.
No. 7   Covered ewer, silver-gilt, c. 1610.   Osma Museum, Madrid.
Nos. 8 and 9   Dish and ewer, silver-gilt, by Fernando Becerril, of Cuenca.
17th century.   Osma Museum, Madrid.

PLATE XCI.

No. 1   Plain caster. Late 17th century.   Collection of Dr. W. L. Hildburgh.
No. 2   Rococo dish, c. 1750, by a goldsmith of Salamanca.
No. 3   Tazza, 17th century, by Aguila and Gonzalez, of Mexico.
No. 4   Covered salt. Early 17th century.   Collection of Dr. W. L. Hildburgh.

SPAIN shares with France and England incredibly serious losses in Royal plate, for nothing now remains of the great collection of the Court of Ferdinand and Isabella, the most brilliant epoch in the history of the country. The conquests in the New World brought vast wealth into Spain, and under Philip II (1556–98) the glory and material prosperity of the country were enhanced. One of the chief monarchs of Christendom, as Philip was, adorned the gigantic Escorial with vast quantities of plate, wrought not only by Spanish goldsmiths but also by foreigners, and never before had the craft of the goldsmith been so extensively patronised. All the great treasure of the Escorial and many other princely houses has since been converted into coin during the civil wars of 1833–1840 and at other times, and the Royal collection to-day contains no Spanish secular plate of the sixteenth century. Nor can a representative collection be seen in any public museum in Spain.

Ecclesiastical silver from medieval times to our own day may, however, be studied with other phases of old Spanish art in the treasuries of the great cathedrals and churches.

Under the sway of the Arphes, a family of goldsmiths of German origin, in the sixteenth century, several of the sacred buildings were enriched with costly custodias (monstrances), great tower-like structures which are peculiar to Spain, and although no examples of their skill in domestic silver have survived, the inference may be safely made that this skilful family were employed in producing domestic silver for the Court and nobles. Enrique de Arphe, working in the Gothic style, is responsible for the great custodia of Cordova in 1513 and one at Toledo in 1524, ten feet high and enriched with 260 silver-gilt statuettes. His son, Antonio, came under the influence of the Renaissance and, to name only one, created the celebrated custodia of Santiago in 1544. The most famous member of the family was Juan de Arphe, grandson of Enrique and author of a work, *Varia Conmensuracion*, which contains the principles of the *cinque cento* style of his work. He it was who made the custodias of Avila in 1571, and of Valladolid, his masterpiece, 6½ feet high, in 1590. His custodia at Seville, begun in 1580 and finished seven years later, is so large and heavy that 24 men are needed to carry it in processions; it was restored in 1668 by Juan Segura, goldsmith.

A superficial study will convince the student that Spanish ecclesiastical silver from the fifteenth to the seventeenth centuries is in general conspicuous for excessive elaboration and reflects the national taste for display, as may be observed in the treasuries of the great churches and in the illustrated catalogue of the *Exposicion Historico-Europea de Madrid*, 1892. Were a truly representative display of domestic silver of these periods available for study the presumption may be made that the same national tendency for exuberant decoration would be generally apparent.

An interesting speculation regarding *provenance* is provided in the golden cup covered with the long lobes or flutes seen on the contemporary plate of other countries, which figures in the fifteenth-century picture of the Adoration of the Magi by the

Spanish master, Lo Fil de Mestre Rodrigo, in the National Gallery in London. In painting this picture the artist may have had this identical domestic cup before him in his studio or had made a drawing of it elsewhere. Nor can anything be identified of the early attempts at goldsmithing of the Spanish painter, Don Juan de Valdes Leal (1622-90), who was apprenticed in 1638 to a goldsmith. But the influence of his early training in the craft is apparent in his fondness for painting gold and silver embroideries, and in the silver in his picture of St. Mark the hermit and St. Eloy, Bishop and silversmith.

No vessels of domestic use and ornament were in greater favour in the sixteenth century in England, France, Italy, Germany, the Netherlands and Spain than the rose-water dish and its accompanying graceful ewer. Judging from the excessively few examples of these Spanish vessels which have escaped the melting-pot, a marked tendency is towards over elaboration as in other Spanish plate, but the important pair acquired by the late Mr. J. Pierpont Morgan are more restrained in the Renaissance style of decoration —masks, straps, vases of flowers, festoons of fruit and terminal figures—than might be expected (Plate LXXXIX). Yet more simple is a silver-gilt ewer, bought from the collection of the Duke of Cumberland by Messrs. Crichton Bros. The fine silver-gilt ewer, 12 inches high, of the early seventeenth century, illustrated on Plate 99 in the catalogue of the exhibition of old plate at St. James's Court in 1902, still retains a touch of the Renaissance.

First introduced at the end of the fifteenth century, and characteristic of Spain and Portugal in the sixteenth century, is a shallow dish or plateau on a short foot, decorated in various styles and subjects, the shape of which was derived from dishes of Valencia pottery of an earlier date. The presence of arms, combined with old traditions and the marks of certain identifiable places, help to distinguish the Spanish from the Portuguese dishes, since the style and decoration and the workmanship are not dissimilar. Two of these Spanish dishes are illustrated on Plates 113 and 114 in the above Madrid catalogue, with two twelve-sided dishes of the sixteenth century, finer than usual, in the Cathedral of Saragossa.

Dishes of this character were common in the Iberian Peninsula. Two have found their way to churches in the British Isles, as gifts at a later date from pious benefactors, and several others have passed into private collections. One is in the church of Llanavan, in Cardiganshire, and is illustrated in the Rev. J. T. Evans's book on the Church plate of that Welsh county. The other, made at Santiago, is at St. Brelade's in Jersey, and is illustrated in Mr. S. Carey Curtis's account of the plate in the churches of that Island. It is decorated in the centre with escallop shells, the distinguishing symbol of St. James the Greater, to whom the Cathedral of Santiago is dedicated. The wide rim is covered with intertwining architectural arches.

A notable example, in the collection of the Baroness James de Rothschild, has a gold coin of Ferdinand and Isabella, issued for Brabant and struck at Kampen, in Holland, at the mint of the Spanish rulers. On the wide rim are figures engaged in fighting various animals and monsters, repoussé and chased. This is illustrated in the catalogue of that notable collection of plate. In St. Mary's Church, Rotherhithe, is a circular dish (without a foot) of the early seventeenth century, embossed with cherubs' heads and grotesque masks and with large plain twisted lobes, like those of Spanish pottery. It was probably a gift from one of the prosperous mariners who lived in this once flourishing parish on the Thames.

Rare among Spanish tazze is the charming piece in the collection of Dr. A. T. Carter, K.C. It is plain, except for a slight chasing of scrolled ornament, in the centre of which is a beautiful enamelled medallion of arabesques. The mark is attributed to Cisneros, of Murcia, about 1550.

The defeat of the Armada in 1588 was a reeling blow to the material prosperity of Spain, with a consequent decline in the art of the goldsmith, which was followed, however, by the most glorious period in the country's literary history and the golden age of Spanish literature.

An early seventeenth century silver-gilt salt with a triangular top for pepper, in Dr. Hildburgh's collection (Plate XCI, No. 4), recalls the salt with a pepper caster at the top, and with scrolled handles, depicted in the picture of a "Repast" attributed to Velasquez, acquired by the National Gallery, Budapest.

The dish and ewer of the seventeenth century in the Osma Museum, Madrid (Plate XC, Nos. 8 and 9), are examples of the work of Fernando Becerril, a member of a notable family of goldsmiths at Cuenca, while the tazza on Plate XCI (No. 3) was wrought by Aguila and Gonzalez, in Mexico, in the same century.

An interesting little Spanish cup of the early seventeenth century —contemporary with the publication of the first edition of *Don Quixote*—decorated with applied shells, the symbol of St. James the Greater, and with typical Spanish ribs, in the manner of a Spanish tazza of the late sixteenth century in the Louvre, has passed through the hands of Messrs. Crichton Bros. (Plate XC, No. 6). Similar ribs, scrolled at the lower ends, form part of the decoration on Mr. Pierpont Morgan's ewer (Plate LXXXIX).

A good deal of Spanish metal work, in silver and metal-gilt, both ecclesiastical and secular, of the early seventeenth century, may be identified from the little plaques of arabesques in cloisonné enamel, as seen on the dish of Mr. J. Pierpont Morgan (illustrated on Plate 25 in the present author's catalogue, 1902), and on the ewer of Lord Dalmeny, described later. Enamels of this kind adorn the crown of the silver-gilt Virgin in the Cathedral of Ciudad Real, illustrated on Plates 141 and 142 of the "Exposicion" catalogue already mentioned. A gilt shield of a morion in the Royal Armoury at Madrid is similarly decorated and suggests collaboration between a silversmith, an enameller and an armourer. Several vessels for sacred purposes, both of silver and inferior metal, in the large collection in the Victoria and Albert Museum, are likewise treated in this manner.

The Pierpont Morgan dish, formerly in the Gutmann collection, is enriched with a shield of enamelled arms of Castile, France and Leon, as well as the rectangular and oval enamels.

At the end of the sixteenth century a characteristic Spanish ewer with a deep cylindrical body, about eight inches high, was evolved mostly by goldsmiths of Toledo, and was extensively made in the early part of the following century. A few of these ewers bear a maker's mark introducing the lamb from the Golden Fleece, like that on the ewer in the Royal Palace at Madrid (Plate XC, No. 5), the meaning of which has not been elucidated. It is, however, conjectured that it was stamped solely on plate intended for the exclusive use of the Court. The same mark is found on a ewer in the Osma Museum. One (with a cover, which is a little unusual) from the Osma Museum in Madrid and three typical specimens, from Lord Dalmeny's collection, inherited from his maternal grandfather. Baron Mayer de Rothschild, are illustrated on Plate XC. Another, wrought at Gerona by Juan de Benavente, has been lent by Sir John Ramsden, Bart., to the Victoria and Albert Museum. Earl Howe is the owner of a ewer of the same shape as Lord Dalmeny's (No. 1). Ewers not unlike the silver ewer of Lord Dalmeny (No. 2) were made of copper early in the seventeenth century.

One distinctive feature of these ewers is the short foot, which is usually plain ; the handles are formed of scrolls of different shapes, including the "harp shape" found on French and English ewers of the second half of the seventeenth century and Irish cups of the following century ; another handle is like that on Lord Dalmeny's ewer (No. 2). The decoration consists of applied straps of various patterns, large scrolls and oval panels, chased on the flat or in slight relief, and arabesques ; some specimens are quite plain, except for a grotesque mask under the large spout, while others are decorated with the small enamelled plaques mentioned above. These little ewers went out of fashion before 1650.

The Spanish plate of the late sixteenth and early seventeenth centuries decorated with escallop shells, the symbol of St. James the Greater, is probably an indication that it was wrought by silversmiths of Santiago di Compostela, the supposed burial place of that Apostle. The little cup mentioned earlier is thus decorated.

Charles I, King of England, would seem to have had a predilection for Spanish silver, for he ordered six candlesticks " of Spanish work " for the funeral of his father, James I, which were placed around the dead King's bed.

Under Philip III the power of Spain began to wane, and with

it a decline is noticeable in the applied arts, a decline which is still more marked in the reign of Philip IV, notwithstanding that one of the supreme artists of all ages, Velasquez, was the Court painter.

That Spanish goldsmiths worked on domestic objects with a plain surface as well as on highly decorated pieces is confirmed by the pair of plain cylindrical casters with a salt, both of the late seventeenth century, in the collection of Dr. W. L. Hildburgh (Plate XCI, No. 1) and by other things seen by the author. In striking contrast are the florid, embossed, circular dishes under baroque influence, of the second half of the seventeenth and of the eighteenth centuries and akin in the heavy embossing to those of Portugal.

Parallel with the decline in the applied arts in Spain in the eighteenth century is the interesting fact that a taste was apparent among the nobles for inkstands, dishes, cruets and other things for the table in imitation of English fashions, though the dominating influence both in silver and furniture was the French, introduced under the Bourbons. An interesting inkstand, made at Madrid by an unknown silversmith, is in the Metropolitan Museum, New York (Plate XC, No. 4). A dish, by a goldsmith of Salamanca about 1750, is a good example of Spanish rococo work (Plate XCI, No. 2).

In Spain, as in Portugal, shaving dishes and ewers were popular in silver and in pottery and porcelain in the eighteenth century. Likewise there were Spanish brass dishes for the same purpose, the most popular of which was like that of "Don Quixote's helmet."

Looting was inseparable from the wars of history, and the great campaigns between the French and the Spanish, English and Portuguese in the Peninsula, are no exception, for both the French and the English carried away pictures, silver and other treasures. A dish and ewer of the eighteenth century (now in the Metropolitan Museum, New York) were taken, according to the inscription, by Major George Halford, of the 2nd battalion of the 59th Regiment, from the Governor's apartments in the castle at the storming of St. Sebastian in 1813. The inscription on a silver dinner or soup plate, in the possession of the Earl of Derby, indicates that it was taken by the Braganza Regiment of Portuguese Cavalry at the battle of Vittoria in the same year. This plate has since been engraved with a portrait of Lord Hill, a distinguished officer in this campaign. To these may be added a pair of silver-gilt rosewater ewers, made in London in 1804 from loot taken from a Spanish galleon, captured by Admiral Lord Anson.

In the important group of Spanish plate in the Victoria and Albert Museum, not the least interesting piece is a large oblong casket, of characteristic workmanship, showing groups of men playing the game of pelota, and divers emblems—by A°. Perez, of Toledo, about 1600.

Just as the fashions of English silversmiths were introduced into the American colonies, so, too, were Spanish tastes in silver and decoration copied in Mexico. A highly important silver ewer in the Rijks Museum, Amsterdam, is stamped with the mark of F. Enriquez, believed to have been a Mexican silversmith of Spanish origin in the late sixteenth and early seventeenth centuries. The tazza, previously mentioned, was made in Mexico. Indeed, the subject of Mexican plate deserves more detailed study.

According to a little book, *La Plata Española*, by Señor E. de Leguina, goldsmiths were working at Toledo, Seville and Burgos in the thirteenth century and in the following century also at Gerona, Barcelona and other places. In the fifteenth century the names of several goldsmiths are recorded in that book at Barcelona, famed for its craftsmen in the precious metals, Burgos, Catalonia, Gerona, Guadalupe, Pamplona, Seville, Toledo, Valencia and Valladolid. The list is extended considerably in the sixteenth century. Of the places recorded, Toledo takes precedence with 80 goldsmiths, the mark being the same as that used on the famous sword-blades made there; Barcelona ranks next with 52, Granada with 30, Madrid with 28, Seville with 22, Burgos with 17, Valladolid with 15, Cordova with 14 and Saragossa with 8. The names of goldsmiths are recorded in about ten other towns, including Salamanca and Valencia.

In the seventeenth century Madrid heads the list with 123 craftsmen, followed at a distance by Toledo with 32, Burgos and Seville each with 20. Barcelona falls from its place of honour to

PLATE XC

PLATE XCI

sixth place in the list. It was in this century that Spanish filigree work was introduced and was made at Cordova and Salamanca, and later at Astorga. A notable filigree tray has been presented recently to the Victoria and Albert Museum by Mr. Lionel A. Crichton.

Such are the changes in the status of these centres of the craft that Cordova ranks first in the eighteenth century with over 220 names, Madrid and Toledo equal with 21, and Burgos and Seville with a dozen each. Silver was wrought at many other places in Spain, including Barcelona, Badajoz, Cadiz, Granada, Santiago, Salamanca, Valencia and Saragossa. At this time the ateliers in Madrid included those of Isaac and Michael Naudin in 1772.

The ateliers of the eighteenth century in Salamanca, Astorga, and Barcelona were thriving. Of the 220 names recorded at Cordova in this century, three of the most successful silversmiths were Christóbal Sánchez y Soto, Damian de Castro and José Francisco de Valderrama. One of the most notable goldsmiths in Madrid in the first half of the century was D. Tomas Buenafuente, who was associated with Bartolome Balmet, of Friburg. In the middle of the century the only jewel makers in the Spanish capital were the two French brothers, Carnay, who are said to have worked mainly, if not entirely, for the Court, and who refused to have any Spaniards in their workshops. The most popular goldsmith's atelier was that of D. Antonio Martinez, who settled in Madrid in 1778 under the patronage of Carlos III, and according to a royal decree issued in that year he was "obliged to teach the construction of fine and ordinary jewels of gold, silver, pinchbeck, and steel, with or without enamels, and repoussé, and the use of the machines and tools by which perfect execution is facilitated." This was one of the most interesting industrial enterprises of the King. Gold and silver plate in the Classical style, as well as jewels, orders and sword hilts, was wrought in the atelier of Martinez. Several of his pupils achieved success early in the nineteenth century, among them being Nicholas Roche and Juan Nivel, Domingo Conde and Ignacio Macazaga, Inocencio Eloria, a worker in bronze, Antonio de Nieva, of Malaga, Jose Marti, Jose Rovira Cayetano Farsult and Francisco Moliner.

In addition to the printed catalogue mentioned above, the following works may be consulted : *Spanish Arts*, by J. F. Riaño ; *Estudio sobre la historia de la orfebreria toledano*, by R. R. de Arellano, 1915 ; and Davillier's book on Spanish plate.

Señor Pedro M. de Artiñano has recently published a book on old Spanish goldsmiths' marks of some fifty different towns, entitled *Catalogo de la Exposicion de Orfebreria Civil Españolo*, in which are a few illustrations of plate, and from which the present author is indebted for information.

SWEDEN

PLATE XCII.

No. 1 Beaker, by Hans Oloffsson, of Stockholm, 1554.   Kulturhistoriska Museum, Lund.
No. 2 Candlestick, by Henning Petri, of Nyköping, c. 1695. H. 13¼ in.   Runtuna Church.
No. 3 Tankard. Late 16th century.   National Museum, Stockholm.
No. 4 Filigree beaker, with cover, by H. V. Torell, of Gothenburg, c. 1690.
No. 5 Candlestick, by J. U. Kickow, of Stockholm, 1689. H. 7¼ in.   Barfva Church.
No. 6 Bridal crown. 17th century.   Edsberg Church.

PLATE XCIII.

No. 1 Box, by Fredrik Peterson Ström, of Stockholm, 1766.
No. 2 Tankard, by Johan Nützel, of Stockholm. Late 17th century.
No. 3 Small bowl, 1660, in a church at Ösmo. H. 5¼ in.
No. 4 Bowl and cover. D. 10¼ in., by Henrik Wittkopf, of Stockholm, 1733.
    Frau Bischof.
No. 5 Tureen and dish, by Jonas Thomasson Ronander, of Stockholm, 1766.
No. 6 Sauce boat, by Pehr Zethelius, of Stockholm, 1776.
    (Nos. 1, 5 and 6 are in the National Museum, Stockholm.)

THE craft of the goldsmith in Sweden achieved prominence under Charles X and Gustavus Adolphus, the second of whom is commemorated by several silver statuettes of German workmanship described on page 219.

Domestic plate was extensively wrought in the seventeenth century, much of it in the German style in design and decoration. The Kremlin in Moscow contains several important and historic examples of Swedish plate of that period, as it does of English, Dutch and German. Most of these were gifts from the Swedish to the Russian Courts and are illustrated in Filimonov's catalogue and in Mr. F. R. Martin's *Schwedische Königliche Geschenke an Russische Zaren*, 1647–1699. Of these mention should be made of a great centrepiece, 14 inches high, composed of four candle-branches and a dish, supported by a five-headed dragon, two casters for sugar and shell-shaped receptacles for sweetmeats or fruit, the work of a Stockholm goldsmith and the gift of Charles XI of Sweden in 1674, with a *giesskanne* in the form of a swan, also made at Stockholm.

The centrepiece is interesting as showing that such objects of the table were made in Sweden, under German influence, several years earlier than in France or England. These two pieces are illustrated on Plate 28 of Mr. Martin's book.

The tankard was the most popular of domestic vessels in Sweden, as it was throughout Scandinavia.

The earlier shape, introduced towards the close of the sixteenth century and continued until about 1650, is tall and cylindrical and in this respect resembles the tankards of Denmark and Norway. One of the most interesting of the early Swedish tankards was made for the Duke Johan of Östergötland and is in the National Museum at Stockholm (Plate XCII, No. 3).

Swedish tankards of the late seventeenth and eighteenth centuries may be distinguished from those of Denmark and Norway in that the bodies are shorter and incline to taper downwards, while the covers tend to be lower and broader and to project outward over the lip. The ball feet and thumbpieces are larger and are decorated. The whole tankard in fact conforms more to some of the German tankards of the seventeenth century and to those made at Riga, like one illustrated on Plate XVII (No. 1). Many are set with coins in the German manner. A comparison may be made between the tankards of Denmark and Norway illustrated on Plates XXV and LXXVIII, and a particularly good Swedish example in the National Museum at Stockholm, on Plate XCIII (No. 2). This is set in the cover with a plaque representing the Queen of Sheba before Solomon, in relief, and was made by the Stockholm silversmith, Johan Nützel, who was working between 1676 and 1715.

Another tankard of the same shape, set with Swedish and other medals, in the Wallace Collection, bears the date-letter for 1695 and the mark of Petter Henning, the elder, of Stockholm, who died in 1714 and whose widow carried on his business as silversmith for 21 years after his death. London can show a second Swedish tankard of about 1720, set with large coins, in the Jones collection in the Victoria and Albert Museum.

Of the same characteristic type is a tankard formerly at Windsor Castle, which has a cover in three stages, the upper two being decorated with scallops and foliated scrolls in relief, while the lower is engraved with scrolls. Inserted in the cover is a medallion of Charles XI of Sweden and Ulrica Eleonora, his Queen, struck by Meybusch in 1683 in commemoration of the birth of their three children, one of whom succeeded as Charles XII. The plain body rests on three large ball feet, decorated with grapes and scrolls. A royal crown and the date 1682 (a year previous to the medallion) are engraved on the tankard, which bears a long inscription in English to the effect that it was given by the Dowager Queen of Sweden (widow of Gustavus Adolphus) to Charles XI and his Queen upon the birth of Charles XII in 1682. Charles XII lost it at the battle of Pultowa (Poltava) in 1709, and when Peter the Great showed the tankard to Count Piper, his prisoner, the Count recognised it as his sovereign's and shed tears upon it. The Tsar gave it to his favourite Scottish physician, Areskine, and after passing through various hands it finally came into the possession of Mr. Robert Vernon, who presented it to William IV in 1831.

The decoration alone proves the fictitiousness of the inscription. Moreover, it is stamped with the date-letter for 1724 and the mark of Gothenburg, with the mark of Abraham Wirgman, the maker of several similar tankards, including one of 1723 in the possession of Prince Eugene of Sweden.

The tankard was given by the King to the Red Cross sale in London in 1918 and has since gone to Sweden. A full account, with illustrations, by Dr. Gustaf Upmark is in *Nordiska Museet Fataburen*, 1919, pp. 148–151. A copy of this tankard, made by John Bridge in London in 1832–3, is in the London Museum. Tankards of the same shape were made in Russia, possibly by silversmiths from Sweden in the eighteenth century.

Tall beakers with wide mouths and narrow bases were popular in Sweden, especially in the eighteenth century. The early specimen on Plate XCII (No. 1), engraved with formal bands of foliage, was wrought by one Hans Oloffsson, of Stockholm, in 1554; it is in the Kulturhistoriska Museum at Lund.

One of the most peculiar of Swedish secular vessels of the second half of the seventeenth century is a covered beaker of delicate filigree work, with or without painted enamelled plaques, standing on ball feet, like one illustrated on Plate XCII (No. 4), the maker of which was H. V. Torell, of Gothenburg. Several of these were examined by the author some years ago in the Old Imperial collections of Russia in the Kremlin and Peter the Great's Gallery in the Hermitage Museum at Petrograd. Three pairs in the last Gallery were gifts from Charles XII of Sweden to Peter the Great in 1699. Two of these pairs are embellished with the enamelled plaques just mentioned, while the third is without enamels. All were made at Stockholm, the last pair probably by Rudolph Wittkopf, who became master goldsmith in 1687, and died in 1722 after a successful career. In the same Gallery is a little écuelle with two flat handles covered with filigree and with three filigree ball feet on the saucer-cover. Stamped upon it are the initials of a Stockholm silversmith, John Stahle (Stahl), who appears to have specialised in filigree work between 1675 and 1700. The same mark is on ten oval dishes of 1698 illustrated (No. 232) in Filimonov's catalogue of the collection in the Kremlin. Four of these filigree beakers and two écuelles are illustrated on Plate 50 of Mr. F. R. Martin's book.

An important example of this characteristic filigree work is the mirror, supposed to have been the gift of Ulrica Eleonora, Queen of Sweden, to the Tsarina Sophie of Russia in 1684, which is illustrated by Mr. F. R. Martin on page 21 of the work mentioned above.

Inappropriate as this filigree work is for such a purpose, Swedish silversmiths were not deterred from making sacred vessels for the service of the Church, as may be observed on a chalice, paten and wafer box of the year 1678 which are illustrated on page 159 of Dr. Upmark's catalogue of the exhibition of old plate at Strängnäs in 1910.

A brief notice has been made in the Danish and Norwegian chapters of the little silver bowls with one or two handles for drinking liquor. Some small bowls in use as font vessels have been found by Dr. Upmark in Swedish churches, though their original intention is manifestly secular, not ecclesiastical. Three different forms are illustrated in his catalogue of the exhibition at Strängnäs.

SWEDEN

An early example of one of these little bowls with two handles, called a *dopskål*, was made by Petter Lenart, of Stockholm, in 1626, the engraved decoration of which is illustrated by Dr. Upmark in *Guld- och Silversmeder i Sverige* 1520–1850 (1925). Two later examples are shown here, on Plate XCIII (Nos. 3 and 4), by an identified goldsmith of 1660 and by Henrik Wittkopf, of Stockholm, 1733.

The Swedish silver candlestick by Johan Ulrik Kickow, of Stockholm, 1689, illustrated on Plate XCII (No. 5), has been copied from a French candlestick, such as the pair in the collection of Mr. Junius S. Morgan, illustrated in the catalogue of the exhibition of old French silver at the Musée des Arts Décoratifs in Paris in 1926. The same shape of candlestick was made also by English goldsmiths as early as 1660. Although secular in origin, the candlestick in question is in the Church of Barfva in Södermanland.

A similar candlestick by a Stockholm silversmith, part of the gift of Swedish plate from Charles XII to the Court of Russia in 1699, is illustrated on Plate 49 in Mr. F. R. Martin's book.

Other secular silver candlesticks in Swedish churches are illustrated by Dr. Upmark in the above-mentioned catalogue, including a German pair with twisted columns, by a Hamburg goldsmith of the end of the seventeenth century, and others of the same shape, by the Swedish silversmiths, Arvid Falck, of Stockholm, 1680–90, and Henning Petri, of Nyköping, about 1695 (Plate XCII, No. 2). Such candlesticks were made at Hamburg in 1655, as is confirmed by those sent by Charles X of Sweden to the Court of Russia in that year, which are shown by Mr. Martin on Plate 19 of his book on the Swedish gifts.

Of this same shape are some by Stockholm silversmiths, in the Kremlin, the gift of Charles XII of Sweden to Peter the Great in 1699, illustrated on Plate 49 of Mr. Martin's book.

Candlesticks of this same pattern with twisted columns were also made in Holland, as is described on page 239.

Two late eighteenth-century pieces of plate by the Stockholm silversmiths, Jonas Thomasson Ronander and Pehr Zethelius, are illustrated on Plate XCIII (Nos. 5 and 6). The sauce boat with two lips and a single handle by the latter craftsman has been derived from the French.

One feature of Swedish goldsmiths' work must not be overlooked in this little survey, namely, the interesting old bridal crowns. Just as the silversmiths of Holland were much engaged in making the silver bands for the picturesque old Dutch head dresses and the craftsmen of Hungary in fashioning the ornaments for the national costume, so, too, were the goldsmiths of Sweden in the seventeenth and eighteenth centuries skilled in making the bridal crowns peculiar to that country. The designs and workmanship resemble the ordinary jewellery of the various districts in Sweden, as do the bridal crowns of Norway. The crowns from Södermanland-Närkingska, for example, are comparatively small and are so designed as to be carried high on the bridal veils; they usually consist of a broad band, set with ornaments of different patterns; upon this band are fixed at intervals five or seven large pierced foliated ornaments, joined at the top to a plain ring, from which may be suspended chased circular discs or be fixed with cherubs' masks at intervals. As in jewellery in Sweden and other countries certain conventional ornaments were reproduced from generation to generation, and consequently it is impossible to determine the precise date of some of these bridal crowns. Dr. Gustaf Upmark in the above-mentioned catalogue contributes a summary of the chief characteristics of the crowns and illustrates two different types of the seventeenth century, from the Churches of Edsberg and Hyltinge. The first of these is illustrated here, on Plate XCII (No. 6).

Gothenburg was an important place in the history of the goldsmith's craft. Here were made the silver tankard and beaker, just mentioned, and here also were wrought, by Herman Hermansson, a silver chalice, paten and wafer box of considerable interest in the history of the Swedish Church and people in America. These sacred vessels were presented in 1718 to Holy Trinity Church at Christina in Pennsylvania by the Mining Company at Falun in Sweden, doubtless at the instigation of the Rev. Erick Björk, at that time minister at Falun, but previously, from 1696 to 1713, in

PLATE XCII

PLATE XCIII

SWEDEN

charge of the congregation at Christina. Anders Ohtz, a goldsmith at Falun, in 1717, was presumably incapable of making such vessels. Illustrations may be seen in the present author's book on the Old Silver in the American Churches.

The fame of Swedish, as of French and English and other foreign silversmiths, was carried to Russia, and a few specimens of their work are described in Baron A. de Foelkersam's catalogue of the plate in the Winter Palace. With the decline in the demand for plate in Sweden in the eighteenth century a goodly number of silversmiths emigrated from that country to St. Petersburg.

In addition to the two important works previously mentioned, Dr. Gustaf Upmark's *Guld- och Silversmeder i Sverige* 1520–1850 (1925), is invaluable for information on old Swedish silver, with its long lists of towns where silver was wrought and of silversmiths' names. Not all these craftsmen were of Swedish origin. A few settled from Germany in the seventeenth century, and among them was a Frenchman, one Abraham Carré, who worked at Stockholm between 1676 and 1715. French decoration prevailed here, as in other countries, in the eighteenth century.

SWITZERLAND

PLATE XCIV.

Ewer (H. 12 in.), dish (D. 15¼ in.), probably Swiss (c. 1595).
Owner, Sir John H. B. Noble, Bart.

PLATE XCV.

No. 1 Lion cup. H. 17¾ in., by Emmanuel Jenner, of Berne, 1690.
Lord Dalmeny's Collection.
No. 2 Tall beaker and cover. H. 12¼ in., by Johann Rudolf Fäsch-Glaser, of Bâle, 1541.
Baron Bruno Schröder's Collection.
No. 3 Owl. H. 14 in., by Nicolaus Matthey, of Neuchâtel, c. 1690.
Lord Dalmeny's Collection.
No. 4 Bishop Parkhurst's beaker. H. 8¼ in., by Felix Keller, of Zurich, 1563.
National Museum, Zurich.
No. 5 Beaker. H. 5⅞ in., by Abraham Gessner (1552-1613), of Zurich.
Victoria and Albert Museum.
No. 6 Bishop Jewel's beaker, 1565. H. 8¼ in. By the same maker and in the same Museum as No. 4.

PLATE XCVI.

No. 1 Triangular salt. 18th century.   National Museum, Zurich.
No. 2 Cup of wood and silver. 16th century. H. 7¾ in.   National Museum, Zurich.
No. 3 Tazza, 1476. H. 8¼ in. D. 8¼ in.   National Museum, Zurich.
No. 4 Globe cup. H. 15 in., by Hans Jacob Stampfer, of Zurich, 1539.
Historical Museum, Bâle.
No. 5 Salt. H. 4¼ in., by Nicolaus Matthey, of Neuchâtel, c. 1690.
Victoria and Albert Museum.

OLD Swiss domestic silver has followed to the melting pot that of other countries in times of personal and national difficulties. Nothing in secular silver could be shown to-day comparable in extent to the important exhibition of pictures and sculpture recently shown at Zurich, which gave an idea of the importance of the art movement in Switzerland between 1430 and 1530. Were such a collection of contemporary silver available, it would perhaps reveal, as do the pictures, the influences of Burgundy, France, Italy and Germany.

Ecclesiastical silver, as has been mentioned before, is outside the scope of this book, though it may not be inappropriate to

SWITZERLAND

mention (as secular vessels of this shape were also made) the plain silver ewer of the fifteenth century from the treasury of Bâle Cathedral, now in the Victoria and Albert Museum.

Dr. Marc Rosenberg illustrates the marks of seventeen towns where silver was wrought in the sixteenth and seventeenth centuries: Baden, Bâle, Berne, Chur, Einsiedeln, Lucerne, Neuchâtel, Neuville, Payern, Rapperswil, Schaffhausen, Sitten, Sursee, Thun, Vevey, Zug and Zurich, and a few others of the eighteenth century. To these may be added Burgdorf and other places not mentioned by Dr. Rosenberg.

An early piece of domestic silver is the cup or tazza from Zug, showing the conventional German lobes, believed to be Swiss work of 1476, in the National Museum, Zurich (Plate XCVI, No. 3).

As the most wealthy and prosperous town, Zurich was an important centre of the goldsmiths as of other arts, and a good collection of old Swiss silver may be seen in the National Museum there. Here was issued in 1549 the very rare pattern book of arabesques for silversmiths, by Rudolph Wyssenbach; and here was made the standing cup, adorned with figures of the Arts and Sciences, by Hans Jacob Stampfer (1505–79), medallist, goldsmith and coin engraver, one of the foremost Swiss craftsmen in the sixteenth century. This cup was presented by the canons of Constance Cathedral to Strassburg in 1545; it is on loan in the Hohenlohe Museum, Strassburg (Schricker, *Kunstchätze in Elsass-Lothringen*, 1896). He was a medallist as well as silversmith and executed portrait medallions of the Reformers, Bullinger, Zwingli and others (Forrer, *Dict of Medallists*). One of his medals of Zwingli is inserted in the sixteenth-century cup of wood and silver of German form in the National Museum, Zurich (Plate XCVI, No. 2).

By the same talented craftsman is the historical cup, shaped like a terrestrial globe, belonging to the University of Bâle, but now deposited in the Bâle Historical Museum. It would seem that it was made in 1539 for Johann Osmolsky, an aristocratic Pole, resident at Bâle, as a suitable gift to his friend, Dr. Theodor Zwinger, by whose influence he had been allowed to buy his house there. Ludovico Demoylin de Rochefort, physician to Margaret of Valois,

Queen of Navarre, and traveller, who settled and died in Bâle, and Dr. Basilius Amerbach, of the Faculty of Law of Bâle University, with the other two friends, Osmolsky and Zwinger, were interested in cartography and forgathered frequently in discussions over this and other congenial subjects, and quaffed wine from this " Poculum Cosmographicum," to their great content (Plate XCVI, No. 4). The whole story is told by Mr. R. F. Burchhardt in *Jahresbericht des Historischen Museum*, 1917, p. 48.

Among the Huguenot refugees in Zurich in 1682 and 1685 were silk weavers, who were probably accompanied by silversmiths, as in England and Holland, though not one is specifically mentioned by Dr. Rosenberg.

Of the double cups of German shape which have escaped the melting pot the specimen in the National Museum at Zurich is of historic and intrinsic interest. It was a gift in 1569 to Colonel Ludwig Pfyffer, of Lucerne, by his captains in commemoration of the campaigns in France against the Huguenots in 1567–1569. The names of these officers are engraved on ribands and their arms on shields. The decorative features are characteristic of the time. One half only of the cup is in the Museum; the other half still remains in the family. The precise *provenance* of the cup cannot be determined in the absence of marks, but it is most probably Swiss.

In the important collection of old plate, English and foreign, of Baron Bruno Schröder, is a large and dignified Swiss beaker of silver-gilt. Engraved on the lip of the cover and the body is some conventional scrolled foliage, which is repeated on the centre of the beaker and on the foot. The finial is a figure of Hercules, holding an enamelled shield of a bear. Inside the cover are the enamelled arms of Von Bärenfels and of the family of Von Hausen of the Upper Rhine. It is inscribed :

WERLI VON BERENFELS 1541.

The maker of this rare piece was Johann Rudolf Fäsch-Glaser, of Bâle, by whom no other piece of plate has been recorded (Plate XCV, No. 2).

The same collection contains a Swiss cocoanut cup of about 1600,

PLATE XCIV

PLATE XCV

set in the cover with a medallion of the arms of the thirteen Swiss cantons and those of the seven confederacies, with the inscription:

SI DUES [DEUS] NOBISCUM QUIS CONTRA NOS.

This inscription appears on the Swiss lion cup mentioned later, and on the English "Bodkin" cup of 1525–6. The two marks have not been identified; one mark may be a variation of that of Zug. It came from the sale of the Earl of Home's silver at Christie's in June, 1919.

Of historic interest are the three beakers in the National Library at Zurich (now deposited in the National Museum), given between 1563 and 1565 to the members of the Cathedral chapter in that city for their convivial gatherings The donors were the three English Puritan Bishops, Robert Horn, of Winchester, John Parkhurst, of Norwich, and John Jewel,* of Salisbury, in appreciation of the hospitality of that society during their exile from England. Bishop Horn, in making his gift, wrote to his friend, the celebrated reformer and chief pastor at Zurich, Heinrich Bullinger (to whom Queen Elizabeth sent the German cup on Plate LI (No. 2), as follows: "And when you daily refresh your remembrance of me in that silver cup, I take it thus, that as nothing can be more gratifying to me than your kindness and esteem, so it is a source of exceeding pleasure to me to be in your frequent recollection, and to be, as it were, constantly before your eyes. But since a cup of so moderate a price must be very small, I have sent you fourteen crowns more, together with my coat-of-arms, as you desire, that you may get a cup made that is larger and more suitable for a large party." Two of the beakers stand on three pomegranate feet, symbols of plenty, and those of Bishops Horn and Parkhurst are enamelled with their arms. Felix Keller (1535–99), of Zurich, the maker of a cocoanut cup in the National Museum at Zurich, was honoured with the commission for making the beakers (Plate XCV, Nos. 4 and 6).

Would that these historic treasures could reveal the thoughts of the consumers of the wine at their festive board, when they daily

---

* The silver image of Peter Martyr, sent from Zurich in 1563 to his friend and guest, Bishop Jewel, has disappeared.

refreshed their remembrance of the episcopal donors who deigned to bestow gifts of loving cups in the jovial bourgeois spirit of Luther.

Bishop Parkhurst's Flemish dish and English ewer are mentioned on pages 58 and 101.

It was a common custom in Switzerland in the thirteenth and fourteenth centuries to establish a convivial meeting-place, called a *Trinkstube*. The custom prevailed during the exile of the three English Bishops, and the ministers of religion, Puritans as they were, and other men of learning had their *Trinkstube*. Each new member was expected to present a silver cup. In 1653 the *Trinkstube* at Zurich just mentioned had as many as 142 silver cups, but in 1656 a third were melted.

The author ventures to suggest that the rose-water dish and ewer shown at the exhibition of Early German Art at the Burlington Fine Arts Club in 1906 may have been executed by a Swiss silversmith. The chief decorative motives of the dish are grotesque figures between birds and strapwork, masks and birds, cornucopiæ and flowers, fruit and a cupid, seated figures of a lady and a warrior. Surrounding the body of the ewer is a broad band, cast in high relief and gilt, with horned caryatid figures between grotesques and elaborate scrolls. On the foot is a design of fish-tailed children sporting with marine monsters (Plate XCIV).

The initials I.I. and A.M., on the enamelled arms, are intended to represent Johannes Jodocus Abbas Muriensis, *i.e.*, those of Johann Jodocus Singeisen, who was Abbot of the monastery of Muri in the Canton of Aargau from 1596 to 1644, and acquired several silver vessels for the adornment and use of that Benedictine foundation. The ewer and dish themselves were probably made shortly before 1596, when the enamelled arms of the monastery, combined with the personal arms of the Abbot, were added to the vessels.

These finely wrought vessels are now in the collection, rich in rare objects of silversmiths' work, of Sir John H. B. Noble, Bart.

At the suppression of this religious house in 1841 some of the fine old stained glass was removed, and is now in the Grossrathsgebäude at Aargau.

A second historical terrestrial globe, over 20 inches high, is

SWITZERLAND

delicately engraved with a map of the world, the other parts of the cup being decorated with ornamental features common to the goldsmiths of the German Renaissance. It is described as of historical interest because it is said to have belonged to Sir Francis Drake, the victor of the Spanish Armada in 1588, and to have been a gift to him from Queen Elizabeth. The maker, Abraham Gessner, a prominent silversmith of Zurich, was 36 years old in 1588, and appears to have specialised in globe-shaped cups. Dr. Rosenberg mentions three others by him and a tazza in the Wallace Collection in London. This cup was sold at Christie's on July 23, 1919, to Mr. S. J. Phillips, of Bond Street. Gessner was also the maker of the beaker in the Victoria and Albert Museum, illustrated on Plate XCV (No. 5).

The tazza just mentioned is inscribed :

> Mit red ich leib und seel verderb
> Not ach und wee wirt sein min Erb
> Fluxs mit dem schwert ich dlant verderb
> Mins givüns kumpt nit ins ander Erb
> Mit list langsam ich dlüt verderb
> Untrüw er erbt von mir min Erb.

In the collection of Dr. Alfred Pringsheim is an important small tazza. This was made at Zurich in the sixteenth century, and is decorated inside with a hunting scene, repoussé and chased.

The characteristically German fashion of cups, in the form of animals and birds, spread with other German conceits into Switzerland. An important lion of historic associations is illustrated on Plate XCV (No. 1). It stands 17¾ inches high, and was made for William III of England in 1690, as a gift, suitably inscribed in Latin, at a festive gathering in celebration of his birthday, to the "Ordo patriciorum atque canditatorum civitatis Bernensis"—a society formed for the young men of Berne in the use of arms and from 1684 for the education of the young patricians in the science of government. At one of the military manœuvres of the society held on May 28, 1690, the English ambassador, Thomas Coxe, conveyed the King's gift.* In the left paw of the lion is a shield of

---

* Ex inform. Dr. Kurz, State Archivist, Berne, and Dr. E. Major, Bâle.

arms of England in translucent enamel and decorating the pedestal are emblems of England, France, Scotland and Ireland. One Emanuel Jenner (1657–1741), of Berne, was the maker. It has descended to Lord Dalmeny from his maternal grandfather, the late Baron Mayer de Rothschild. At least five other pieces of silver by the same silversmith are recorded.

A second lion was made by an unidentified goldsmith of Rapperswil about 1665, and is illustrated on Plate 35 in the present author's catalogue of the late Mr. J. Pierpont Morgan's collection. On the circular base is a view of a city and the following inscription:

> Si Deus Pro Nobis Quis Contra nos
> Sub tuum Presidium confugimus sancta Dei Genitrix.
>
> O Beatissime Ioseph ora pro nobis
> O Beatissime Patrone Dauriane ora pro nobis.

Another rare piece of Swiss silver in Lord Dalmeny's collection is a large owl—the emblem of Pallas Athene—14 inches high, standing on a bird lying on its back. On the top of the large circular pedestal are a snail, frogs and lizard, ungilt, and applied, in the manner of the German goldsmiths of the sixteenth and seventeenth centuries, and repoussé with a serpent, a rat and a tortoise, trees and trunks (Plate XCV, No. 3). Engraved upon it is the following inscription:

> Ob schon all vögel hassen mich,
> Bin ich Kautz und acht es nicht.

The owl is also inscribed:

Juventutis Bernensis Principibus Poculum hoc, ut sui inter pocula memores essent, dono dedit, Philibertus Herwart, Baro Huningæ, Guil: III. M. Brit: Regis ad Helv: Ableg: Extraord:

Philibert Herwart (1645–1721), first Baron de Huningue, commonly called Baron Hervart, was a Protestant refugee who fled to England after 1685 and was Ambassador of William III at Geneva from 1690 to 1702.

Nicolaus Matthey, of Neuchâtel, the maker of this owl, about 1690, also wrought a pair of salts, embossed with flowers and birds

PLATE XCVI

and of the same form as some Dutch and German salts; this pair are in the Victoria and Albert Museum (Plate XCVI, No. 5).

Bâle was an important centre of the goldsmith's craft, and a special mark of the town arms was in vogue from the sixteenth century. An interesting sixteenth-century cup and cover, wrought there, is decorated with sporting scenes and is embellished with the arms of four Swiss cantons and of the city of Zurich, and when last seen by the author was in the collection of Baron Alphonse de Rothschild at Vienna, having come from the Soltykoff collection in 1861.

One of the small Swiss tankards of the same shape as some made in England and Germany between 1550 and 1600 is in the Louvre, and is illustrated on Plate 28 of the catalogue, where it is described as by a goldsmith of Bâle. Belonging to the Coopers Company in London is a cup in the appropriate form of a cooper carrying a tun on his head, the work of an unknown Bâle silversmith of the seventeenth century.

A fish cup of unusually large size, doubtless the cup of a fishermen's guild at Bâle, was made by Johann Brandmüller, of that city, about 1685. It is now in the collection of the Baroness James de Rothschild, of Paris, and is illustrated on Plate 57 of the catalogue.

A prominent family of Bâle silversmiths for over a century, from 1633 to about 1765, was the Fechter family. Dr. Rosenberg, in *Der Goldschmiede Merkzeichen*, enumerates many of their works, including such German-like cups as a cow, a swan, a lion and a horse, and divers cups of other forms. A stag by Sebastian Fechter, the younger, was in the highly important collection of the late Baron Carl von Rothschild.

The small group of old Swiss silver in the Victoria and Albert Museum includes a seventeenth-century tazza, standing on a baluster stem and engraved inside with "Joseph feasting his brethren," by a Zurich silversmith; some cups of the seventeenth century made under German inspiration; and the Matthey salts just mentioned. On loan by Mr. Louis C. G. Clarke in the Museum is a delectable miniature coffee pot, wrought at Geneva, and a globular teapot, bearing the Lausanne mark, both dating from the end of the eighteenth century.

SPURIOUS PLATE

THE subject of the genuineness of old silver as of other old things, whether they be pictures, furniture, glass or porcelain, is seldom absent from the mind of the would-be purchaser. Purchasers there are of unbounded confidence in their own judgments, with a cheerful disregard for advice, who discover their limitations only by costly mistakes not very flattering to their reputations. But the more cautious enter the "antique shops" to be found in all civilised countries with the dominant question, "How am I to tell?" To this question only one answer can be given: intensive study, long experience, and intimacy with examples of proved genuineness, are a sure guide in the long run. When in doubt consult a recognised connoisseur.

The nefarious traffic in forgeries of "antiques" is not, as is too often supposed, the creation of our own time to satisfy the needs of the ever-growing number of collectors of *objets d'art* throughout the world.

In the short review of old French plate, emphasis has been made on the excessive scarcity of domestic plate before the Revolution. It is not surprising, therefore, that faked silver is offered for sale, as are some skilful imitations of French furniture of the eighteenth century. Included among the trifles in spurious French silver are wine tasters.

Competition among collectors for American silver made before the War of Independence (1775–83) is now very keen, especially for things made by Paul Revere, of Boston. His silver is of no more intrinsic interest than many other craftsmen of his time, but, as the eponymous hero of Longfellow's poem, he has earned an exaggerated place in American regard.

Just over a century ago some New York silversmiths sought to improve the value, or at least the "tone," of their wares by stamping imitations of English hall marks upon them. Hugh Wishart (1789–

1816) was one of these men, and among the silver thus stamped is a Sacramental service in the First Presbyterian Church, New York.

Portuguese silversmiths, likewise, imitated the marks of London silver of the late George III period.

Travellers on the Continent have, within the past fifty years, brought back "great treasures" in "old" Dutch, Italian, and German silver, which proved to be of no value other than as bullion. Not a few travellers have returned with the works of Karl Wilhelm Becker, a skilful forger of ancient coins and medals. Some few pieces in the Wallace Collection were probably bought as original specimens, including the silver statuette of a youth in sixteenth century dress and a cup covered with bosses, characteristic of German work of the early sixteenth century, both of which were made in the nineteenth century.

The Marlay bequest to the Fitzwilliam Museum, at Cambridge, contained a goodly number of spurious foreign pieces, which have since been judiciously weeded out.

Many of the large silver ships in private collections have been bought as originals, but are spurious. In some cases, however, the purchasers were not deceived, and did not buy them as old pieces.

The faking of Tudor and other early plate before Charles II is a risky business, involving considerable liability to detection on account of the natural desire of collectors to trace the "pedigree" of such rare pieces. The author has, however, seen in America some amazing specimens of silver, purporting to be of the sixteenth and seventeenth centuries, but so clumsily made as to deceive only the merest tyro.

The Goldsmiths' Company have acquired fifteen hall-marks from genuine English silver between 1570 and 1730, which had been removed from pieces of no great value by "fakers," with the object of inserting them in objects of a more saleable character.

A common and reprehensible practice was to emboss or chase plain old English plate with elaborate agricultural subjects, pastoral and sporting scenes—a practice which was prevalent mostly in the nineteenth century. Be it said in its favour that it was not done with the intention of deceiving the purchaser, who regarded it as an "improvement" on the plain surface of a Charles II tankard. So persistent had the practice become that many owners sent some of their plain plate to goldsmiths, expressly to be decorated in this manner. Tankards of Charles II, Queen Anne, and Georgian periods were thus embellished as prizes for agricultural shows and field sports.

As an illustration of such transformation, a rare tankard of 1671-2 in a well-known collection was embellished in the eighteenth century with scenes from Colonial history, and in order further to embellish it, it was set with Greek coins.

The bodies of Charles II tankards have also been transformed into large casters, and their value thereby increased.

"Faking" of silver and making plate of inferior metal is no new thing, for such practices were not uncommon in Elizabethan times, as is recorded in the *Memorials of the Goldsmiths' Company*. In 1573, one Shakleton, was committed to ward for putting "coarse" feet on a sterling silver salt. In 1578, fifteen members of the Company protested against the evil abuse of some goldsmiths in carrying plate "of much deceptive work" from fair to fair and market to market. George Harves, in 1609, was accused of selling "deceitful" silver hooks and eyes to the Countess of Cumberland. As an excuse he pleaded that "she had treated him hardly in former dealings."

According to the Old Bailey Sessions Papers (printed), transportation was a common punishment in the eighteenth century for crimes against the rules and regulations of the Goldsmiths' Company. For example, Samuel Field and William Hogg were indicted in 1784 for making spoons and buckles of inferior metal covered with "clock-face silver" and stamped with a lion in imitation of the Company's mark and with the alleged maker's mark. Both were transported for fourteen years.

In 1777 a woman goldsmith, one Sarah Cooley, was indicted for stamping shoe buckles of brass and other base metal, coloured to resemble silver, with the lion mark of the Goldsmiths' Company, and was found guilty, as was John Hurst for a like offence.

Many common things, no longer of practical use, have been refashioned and transformed and rendered marketable. For example, plain Georgian snuffer-trays have been converted into inkstands by the simple expedient of adding inkpots to the trays. These are, however, not infrequently converted in this manner at the instigation of the private owners. Imposing looking punch bowls are made by inserting the marks from spoons into the edges of the feet, by the same method adopted by the faker of Irish potato-rings. Simple plain pint mugs are re-hammered into milk jugs, leaving the handles and feet untouched. Plain goblets are transformed into more elegant sugar basins by piercing them and adding a blue glass liner and a handle. An "item" of false silver are many of the cow-shaped milk jugs of the middle of the eighteenth century.

High, some people would prefer to say fantastic, prices were the rule some time ago for Irish silver potato-rings (so called), with the result that the ingenuity of the faker was called into play, to his considerable pecuniary advantage. His *modus operandi* was to work up a ring of the approved pattern, then to cut out the marks from a well stamped old Dublin-made spoon and insert them in the lower rim of the dish-ring, as these objects are properly called. But the faker, trusting in the ignorance of the purchaser, has failed to overcome the difficulty of placing the marks in the correct vertical position, i.e., at right angles to the rim, and is compelled to show them running the wrong way. Another unsuspected trap into which the faker has fallen, is in introducing marks of an earlier date than is usual for these rings, which were only made, except in very isolated instances, during the fifty years between about 1770 and 1820. The faker's ignorance of, or contempt for, periods in fashion, has led him into making sugar basins and cream jugs on three legs, showing marks of Queen Anne and George I, whereas these popular vessels of the tea-table were never made in Ireland before George II, and very rarely in that reign.

Reference has been made in previous chapters to German plate stamped with English marks.

An astonishing piece of deception was practised at Goldsmiths' Hall in London about 1775. It was not uncommon for silver candlesticks, made at Sheffield and stamped with the full marks of the Assay Office of that place, to be bought by London goldsmiths and sent to Goldsmiths' Hall, where the London marks were stamped over those of Sheffield! John Winter, a well-known craftsman, thus suffered at the hands of his competitors in London. His marks on a pair of candlesticks from his workshop are struck over with the mark of John Carter and the London date-letter for 1775-6. Among other London silversmiths who were in the habit of hiding the identity of Sheffield handicraft were Thomas Daniell and John Scofield, and the three partners Richard Carter, Daniel Smith and Robert Sharp. That such an irregularity should be tolerated by the authorities of Goldsmiths' Hall is somewhat remarkable.

One more anomaly of about the same period, by the same body, may be mentioned. Some finely pierced sugar tongs, wrought by Joseph Adams, of Walsall (afterwards one of the original guardians of the Birmingham Assay Office, 1773), were likewise stamped with the London marks. Similarly, some candlesticks, assayed in Sheffield in 1790, have been overmarked at the Edinburgh Assay Office by William Robertson.

This is a subject which has never received any previous notice in books on old plate. For this valuable information the present author is indebted solely to Mr. Frederick Bradbury, the author of the standard work on old Sheffield plate.

INDEX

Aargau, 334
Aarhus, 79, 83
Aberdeen, 304, 306, 310, 311
—— Grammar School, 310
—— King's College, 304
—— Marischal College, 304
Abo, 52, 56
Acton, Lord, 122
Adam, Elias, 222, 223
—— Robert, 136, 139, 146, 148, 151, 152, 157, 310
Adams, Abigail, 6
—— John, 6, 22
—— Joseph, 342
—— Pygan, 11
Adventure, ship, 14
Ægidius (Pieter Gillis), 62, 166
Aguila and Gonzalez, 313
Ailesbury, Marquess of, 91
Aix-en-Provence, 179
Aix-la-Chapelle, 182
Ajtós, 248
Albany, N.Y., First Reformed Church, 15, 230
Aldbury Church, 61
Aldobrandini collection, 212
Aldrich, Thomas Bailey, Mrs., 3, 36
Ales, Alexander, 59
Alexander I., Tsar, 133
—— James, 29, 35
—— VI., Pope, 303
Alexis Petrovitch, Tsarevitch, 297
—— Tsar, 117, 131, 138, 169, 242, 296, 299, 300
Alf, Bishop, 271
Alfassa, Paul, 179
Alkmaar, 244
Allen, John, 3, 14, 26, 28, 39
—— William, chief justice, 159
Allston, William, 129
Altar, 282
Altdorfer, Albrecht, 226
Altenstetter (Attemstetter), David, 214, 216, 217
Althorp, 136
Alvah, Banff, 309

A Magyar Történeti Ötvösmü-Kiállitás Lajstroma, 254
Amber, 187, 297
Amerbach, Basilius, Dr., 332
America, xi, 1-47, 6, 68, 109, 172, 229, 244, 252, 263, 264, 320, 339
—— First Printing Press in, 100
—— Swedish Church in, 328
American Antiquarian Society, 106
—— *Churches, The Old Silver of* (see E. Alfred Jones)
—— Revolution (see Revolution)
—— silversmiths, xi, 1-47, 100, 187, 263, 338
—— Stamp Act, 146
—— War of Independence, 338
Amerigo, 268
Amiens, 179
Amsterdam, 227, 228, 229, 230, 232, 234, 236, 240, 242, 243, 245, 295
—— Rijks Museum, 60, 62, 85, 102, 220, 227, 228, 229, 230, 232, 233, 235, 236, 237, 238, 239, 246, 320
Amyot, Laurent, 65, 67, 277
Ananaspokal, 194
Ancaster, Earl of, 98
Andirons (fire-dogs), 86, 130-1, 222
Andrew II, 247
Andros, Edmund, Sir, 38
Angermair, Christoph, 218
Angers, 179
Anglo-French silversmiths, 39, 44, 133, 139, 147, 149, 152, 153, 154, 155, 156, 173, 261
Anhalt, Prince of, 192
Animals (as cups, etc.), 203-4, 330, 333, 335, 336, 337
Anjou Kings, in Hungary, 248
Annales de l'Académie Royale d'Archéologie de Belgique, 63
Annapolis, 8, 12
—— St. Anne's, 113
Anne Boleyn, Queen, cup, 61, 108
—— Empress of Russia, 296, 299
—— Queen, 8, 27, 113, 130, 137, 139, 140, 146, 147, 149, 153, 307, 340, 341

343

INDEX

Anne, wife of Vladimir of Russia, 292
Annes, Elles, 236
Annesley, Earl, 210, 263
Anonymiana, 112
Anson, Lord, Admiral, 104, 148, 320
Antiques, 11
Antiquities of the Russian Empire, 296, 297
Antwerp, 57, 58, 59, 60, 64, 286
—— Hans of, 57
Apsley House, 159, 290
Arbroath, 311
Arbuthnot, Viscount, 125
Archæologia, 241
Archambo, Peter, 87, 130, 145
Archery medals, 302, 310-1
Ardagh chalice, 255
Areskine, 325
Argyles, 143
Argyll, Duke of, 143, 160
—— Archibald, Marquess of, 308
Armada, The, 316, 335
Armenian silversmiths, 284
Armour, 217-8
Armourers, 217-8
—— Company and Hall, 92, 95, 109, 124
Arnhem, Museum, 235
Arphe family, 314
Arrow, silver, 311
Art in America, 7
Arte Manuelina, 285
Arte Religiosa em Portugal, 286
Ascanio, 269
Ascott, Viscount, 187
Ashburnham sale, 97, 133, 136, 137, 193, 210, 262
Aspremont de Lynden, 59
Astbury ware, 142
Astley, John, Sir, 154
Astorga, 321
Aubry, Claude Augustus, 174
Auchinleck, Alexander, 302, 303
Audenarde, 64
Augsburg, xi, 73, 118, 173, 180, 181, 182, 183, 185, 186, 190, 192, 193, 194, 196, 197, 198, 199, 200, 203, 205, 207, 224, 283, 286
Augusta Sophia, Princess, 155
Auguste, Henri, 170, 176
—— Robert Joseph, 162, 163, 168, 170, 171, 173, 174, 175, 176, 177, 179.
Augustus the Strong, 296

Austin, Josiah, 3, 32
Austria, xi, 48-51
Avery, C. Louise, Miss, 11, 13, 19, 22, 24, 46, 149
Avila, 314
Ayr, 309
—— Parish Church, 309
Ayres, Samuel, 13
Aytoun, William, 308

Baardt, Klaes, 233, 245
Badajoz, 321
Baden, 331
—— Grand Duke of, 183, 204
Bailey, Edward, 12
Bainbridge, Cardinal, 140
Bair, Paulus, 194
Baird, W. A., Mr., 167
Bâle, 166, 330, 331, 335, 337
—— Cathedral, 331
—— Historical Museum, 330, 331
—— University, 331, 332
—— Prince Archbishop of, 266
Ballin, Claude, the elder, 166
—— —— the younger, 151, 152, 166, 173, 224, 301
Balmet, Bartolome, 321
Baltic States and towns, xi, 52-6
Baltimore, 13
Balzac, Edme Pierre, 174
—— Jean François, 178
Bancker, Adrian, 3, 32
Banff, 311
Bánffy, 250
Bang, Hieronymus, 217
Bapst, his book on the French plate of the King of Portugal, 175
—— *Etudes sur l'Orfèvrerie Française du XVIII siècle*, 168, 177
Barber Surgeons Company, 24, 94, 100, 124
Barcelona, 320, 321
Barfva, church, 323, 327
Barnard's Inn, 111
Barry, Standish, 13
Barst, Georg, 201
Bartolo, Giovanni, 266
Basil II, Emperor, 292
Basins, 8, 64, 101-2, 163, 171, 176, 181, 182, 199, 200, 208-11, 227, 230, 233, 235, 246, 268, 285, 305, 309

INDEX

Basins, sugar (and bowls), 28, 33, 34, 37, 44
Baskets, bread and cake, 28, 87, 152, 162, 255, 264, 310
Bateman, Viscount, 169
Bateman-Hanbury heirlooms, 169
Bathory, Clara, 250
Bauch, Meinrad, the elder, 202, 205
Baumgartner, Joh. Jac., 224
—— Ulrich, 214
Baur, Christian, 190
Bavaria, Court and Kings of, 170, 171, 175
Bayonne, 179
Bayr, Melchior, 282
Beakers, 7, 10, 11, 13, 14, 15, 27, 52, 56, 59, 62, 67, 75, 78, 80, 84, 121, 166, 168, 169, 179, 180, 185, 186, 188, 222, 223, 227, 229–230, 236, 242, 247, 250–1, 271, 272–3, 274, 275, 290, 298, 304, 323, 325–6, 328, 330, 332, 333
Beauchamp chapel, 160
—— Richard, 160
Becerril, Fernando, 313, 317
Becker, Andreas, 56
—— Karl Wilhelm, 339
—— Samuel, 205
Becker and Hefner-Alteneck's *Kunstwerke u. Geräthschaften*, 49
Beckford, Captain, 132
Bedford, Duke of, John, 163
Bedstead, 243
Bedwarmers (warming pans), 132, 162, 166, 290
Begeer, Carel, J. A., Mr., author of *Inleiding tot de Geschiedenis der Nederlandsche Edelsmeedkunst*, 229, 232, 233, 236, 237, 238, 239, 240, 244, 245, 246
Behrend, Johann, 52, 55
Behrns, 225
Beja, 290
Bekegle, Charles, 257
Bekerschroef, 236
Belem, monastery, 285, 286
Belgium, 57–64
Bell, 184
Bellekin, 200, 237
Belli, Valerio, 265, 267
Bellows, 86, 132
Belts, 283
Belvoir, 129, 264
Benson, Benjamin, 53
Berg, Magnus, 82, 83, 218

Bergen, N. J., Reformed Church, 1, 15
—— Norway, 79, 271, 272, 273, 275, 276
—— —— Museum, 271, 272, 273
Berger, Florence Paull, Mrs., 46
—— Georg, 217
Berkeley, George, Lord, 142
Berlin, 188, 218, 221, 222, 223, 237
—— Königliche Zeughaus, 217
—— Kunstgewerbe Museum, 48, 181, 197, 199, 204, 206, 213, 214, 226
—— Royal Palace (Schloss), 117, 184, 189, 191, 196, 211
Bernardi, Giovanni, 268
Bernath, M. H., in *Kunstchronik für Kunst u. Kunstgewerbe*, 287
Berne, 330, 331, 335
Bernini, 266
Besançon, 179
Bessel, Magnus, 271, 278
Beutmüller, Georg, 188
—— Hannss, 188
Béziers, 179
Biberon, 208
Biennais, Martin Guillaume, 169, 174, 175
Bigelow, Francis H., Mr., 10, 16, 21, 23, 24, 25, 26, 27, 30, 31, 32, 34, 35, 37, 39, 40, 41, 42, 43, 46, 143, 288
Biller, family, 207, 222, 224
—— Johann Jakob, 223
—— Johann Ludwig, 224
—— Lorenz, 196
Binning, Hon. Lady, 312
Birckenholtz, Paul, 197
Birds, various (as cups, etc.), 199, 201, 204–5, 323, 330, 335, 336, 337
Birmingham, 159
—— Art Gallery, 273
—— Assay Office, 342
Bischof, Frau, 323
Bispham, George Tucker, Esq., 86, 139
Björk, Erick, Rev., 328
Blackwood, Timothy, 258
Blaeu, Wilhelm Jansson, 196
Blake, 158
Blanc, brothers, 283
Blanchard, Asa, 13, 33
"Bleeding bowls," 23–4, 124–5
Blohm, J. H., 301
Blois, 167
Blytt, Micael Hansen, 271, 278

AA

Boat, incense, 92
Bobrinsky, Count, 151
Bodington, John, 152
Boehme, Count, 177
Boelen, Henricus, 1, 15
—— Jacob, 1, 15, 38
Bogaert, Jacques, 233
—— Joannes, 242
Bohdanec, 71
Bohemia, 71, 72, 166
—— Elizabeth, Queen of, 130, 227, 232, 234, 241
—— King of, 135, 188
Bol, Ferdinand, 235
Bolch, Godfred, 80
Bölmann, Hieronymus, 221
Bologna, 267
Bolsward, 233
Bolton, A. T., Mr. (book on Robert Adam), 157
—— Thomas, 261
Bonsach, Baard Gangolphi, 271, 273, 275
Bontecou, Timothy, 11
Book-covers, 245
Bookplates, 10, 11, 30, 45, 160
Bordeaux, 163, 173, 179, 290
Borghese, Pauline, 170
Borland, John Lindall, Major, 264
Borthwick, John, 306, 307
—— Patrick, 309
Boston, England, 43, 117, 119
—— Mass., 5, 11, 14, 15, 17, 19, 22, 25, 26, 28, 29, 30, 32, 41, 45, 117, 143
—— —— Bunch of Grapes tavern, 30
—— —— First Baptist Church, 20
—— —— First Church, 14, 17, 21, 117, 123, 230
—— —— Hollis Street Church, 22
—— —— Museum of Fine Arts, 3, 4, 5, 18, 22, 25, 27, 28, 29, 30, 32, 33, 34, 35, 36, 37, 39, 40, 42, 43, 44, 46, 289
—— —— Old South Church, 14
—— —— Regiment, 30
—— —— St. Botolph Club, 43
Bothwell, 169
Botticelli, 267
Bottles, xii, 86, 117-8, 135, 162, 166
Bottle-stands, or coasters, 43, 44, 158-9, 255, 260, 261
Boucher *fils*, 176
Boudo, L., 12

Bouilhet, H., 179
Boullier, Antoine, 173
Bourbons, The, 319
Bourdon, Sebastian, 210
Bourguet, Simon, 170, 173
Bowie, Bayard, Junr., Mrs., 3, 35
Bowls, 34, 36, 37-8, 44, 56, 75, 78, 84, 91, 125, 167, 178, 181, 196, 232, 237, 260, 271, 288, 298, 312, 323, 326-7
Bowman, Lydia, 41
Boxes, 46, 179
—— condiment and spice, 169, 214
—— snuff, patch, etc., 42, 179, 222, 245, 255, 262-4, 276, 299, 311, 323, 328
—— sweetmeat, 2, 28, 133-4, 262
—— tobacco, 160, 228, 236
Boyd, Zacharie (*Last Battell of the Soule*), 303
Boyle, Captain, 67
Brace, John, 152
Bradbury, Frederick, Mr., 138, 158, 310, 342
Bradford, Daniel, 121
—— Gamaliel, Captain, 37
—— Governor, 121
Braga, 290
—— Cathedral, 285
Braganza, Catherine of, 289
—— Duke of, 288
—— House of, 289
—— Regiment of Cavalry, 319
Bramante, 266
Brandenburg, Elector of, 196
Brandewijkom, 244
Brandmüller, Johann, 337
Brandy bowls, 228, 244, 245, 271, 273, 275
Brasher, Ephraim, 36
Brasses of England, by Macklin, 161
Bratina, xii, 292, 293-5, 297, 298, 299
Bratinka, 294
Bratislava, 74
Braun, E. W., Dr., 74
Braziers, 9, 27-8, 37
Breadalbane, Marquess of, 308, 311
Brechtel, Hans Coenraet, 227, 234
Brekelenkam, 240
Breslau, 199, 200
Brevig, 275
Brevoort, John, 4, 32, 34
Brevnov, 71
Brice, John, 159
Bridal wreaths, 282

INDEX

Bridge, John, 82, 325
Bridger, John, 288
Bridges, Margaret, 22
Brigden, Zachariah, 35, 143
Briot, François, 209
Bristol, 146, 147
—— Bishop of, 125
—— Countess of (Elizabeth Chudleigh), 136, 179
—— Delft ware, 26
British Museum, 26, 49, 76, 84, 89, 90, 95, 96, 105, 106, 107, 110, 124, 140, 163, 164, 169, 180, 184, 185, 187, 192, 213, 226, 269, 294, 297, 298
—————— Waddesdon Collection, 48, 54, 59, 71, 73, 184, 187, 201, 212, 215, 220
Brix, Maurice, Mr. 46
Brock, Robert, 309
Broderers' Company, 197
Brome, Viscount, 160
Brongersma, Hillebrandt, 239
Brook, A. J. S., Mr. 310
Brosamer, Hans, 61, 119, 188, 190, 201, 226
Bruce, 90
Brueghel, Pieter, 62
Bruges, 57, 60, 61, 64, 135, 230
—— Museum, 61
Bruglocher, Johan Jacob, 223
Brunswick, 205, 219
Brussels, 58, 64
—— Museum of Decorative Art, 57, 61, 63
Bryggemanns, S. W., 271
Buccleuch, Duke of, 131, 135, 137, 140, 191, 209, 243
Buck, J. H., 6
—— *Old Plate* by, 43
Buckingham Palace, 132, 233
—— Duke of, 220
Buckland Filleigh, 122
Budapest, 51, 250
—— Museum of Applied Art, 247, 249, 250, 252, 253, 254
—— National Gallery, 317
—— National Museum, 195, 247, 249, 254
Buenafuente, D. Tomas, 321
Bühel, Sebald, 180, 193
Buichle, Louis, 13
Bull, John, Sir, 128
Bullinger, Heinrich, 59, 180, 196, 305, 331, 333

Bunsen, 225
Bunt, Cyril G. E. (Editor of *Goldsmiths of Italy*), 270
Burckhardt, Martin, 74
—— R. F., Mr. 332
Burde, William, 199
Burgdorf, 331
Burghley House collection, 106
—— Lord, 110
Burgis, William, 42
Burgos, 320, 321
Burgundy, 330
—— Dukes of, 61
Burlington Fine Arts Club, 193, 287, 334
Burlington Magazine, 64, 107, 108, 120, 128, 168, 232, 242, 269, 290, 305
Burns, T., Rev., *Old Scottish Communion Plate*, 197, 304, 309, 311
Burt, Benjamin, 3, 5, 32, 36, 42
—— John, 4, 29, 34, 40, 41, 42
—— Samuel, 5, 42
—— William, 5
Bushell, S. W., Dr., 107
Busts, 280
Butler, William, Dr., 58
Butty, Francis, 87, 146
Byzantine artists, 292

Cabaret à chocolat, 175
Cabinets, 184, 214
Cadiz, 321
Caen, 66, 179
Caffieri, 168
Cahier, Charles, 172
Calderwood, Robert, 260, 261, 262
Cam, John, 86
Cambridge Colleges, The Old Plate of the (see E. Alfred Jones)
Cambridge Colleges and University, 88, 91, 103, 106, 109, 110, 113, 122, 124, 125, 141, 148, 151
—— Colleges :
    Christ's, 62, 84, 92, 93, 97, 108, 110, 119, 122
    Clare, 57, 58, 86, 87, 103, 107, 128, 150, 151, 157, 159, 180, 187
    Corpus Christi, 39, 64, 76, 84, 85, 89, 90, 91, 94, 95, 101, 119, 120, 126, 143, 242

Cambridge Colleges (continued):
    Emmanuel, 64, 86, 126
    Gonville and Caius, 84, 94, 126, 230, 242
    King's, 152
    Magdalene, 125
    Pembroke, 84, 90, 92, 148, 157
    Peterhouse, 197
    Queens', 86, 103
    St. John's, 120, 128, 210
    Sidney Sussex, 84, 87, 102, 142
    Trinity, 103, 115, 124
    Trinity Hall, 84, 96, 111
—— Fitzwilliam Museum, 146, 182, 339
—— Mass., 100
—— —— First Parish, 16, 42
Campbell, Jacob, 271, 277
—— James, 277
Can, or cann, 20
Canada, xi, 63, 65-8
Candelabra, 86, 140, 157, 168, 171, 174, 175, 221, 225, 282
Candle-brackets, 40
Candlesticks, 11, 40, 47, 50, 63, 66, 67, 75, 81, 86, 88, 138-140, 157, 160, 161, 162, 166, 168, 169, 174, 175, 177, 221, 228, 233, 239-240, 255, 258-9, 261, 263, 266, 267, 268, 270, 271, 274, 275, 277, 278, 285, 298, 310, 318, 323, 327, 341, 342
—— Hand, 140
—— Taper, 140
Cane, Claude, Colonel, 261
Canisters, 221
Canterbury, St. Augustine's College, 95
Caradosso, 266, 269
Caraglio, Gian Jacopo, 281
Carcy, 66
Carlisle, Abraham, 9
—— Earl of, 169
Carlos III, 321
Carnay, 321
Caroline, Queen, 132
Carpenters' Company, 111, 122
Carré, Abraham, 329
Carroll, Charles, 159
Carse Troop of Perthshire Yeomanry, 311
Carter, A. T., Dr., 316
—— John, 342
—— Richard, 342
Cartier, Messrs., 162, 177

Cartridge-boxes, 279, 284
Cary, John, 53
Casey, Samuel, 13
Casimir the Great, 279, 280
—— Jean, King, 284
Caskets, 169, 181, 214-5, 265, 267, 268, 298, 320
—— Marriage, 245
Cassel, Ernest, Sir, 115, 262
—— Royal Museum, 74, 193, 199, 200, 205, 226
Casson, Randal, Mrs., 134
Castelbolognese, 268
Castello, Gaspare, 281
Casters, 12, 40-1, 62, 155, 156, 162, 166, 178, 225, 228, 239, 271, 274, 275, 277, 278, 302, 310, 313, 319, 323, 340
Castlereagh, Viscount, 51
Catalonia, 320
Catania, 266
Catherine II, 136, 137, 173, 174, 175, 300
Caudle, 126
—— cups, 236, 242, 255, 258
Caxton, 109
Cellini, Benvenuto, 165, 183, 191, 200, 209, 211, 216, 265, 266, 268, 269
Censer, 92
Centrepieces, 151, 157, 180, 184, 224, 265, 301, 323, 324
Chabroles, Mark Henry, 153
Chadwick, Robert, Captain, 56
Chafing-dishes, 27
Chain and pendant, 279, 281
Chairs, 222, 298
Chalices, 50, 66, 72, 73, 75, 82, 88, 92, 242, 272, 279, 280, 284, 285, 290, 299, 328
Chalmers, James, 12
Champlain, 65
Chandeliers, 140, 221
Chandler, Lucretia, 39
Channel Islands, xi, 69-70
Chantilly, 164
Charcoal burner, 242
Chardin, pictures by, 179
Charing Church, 122
Charka, xii, 292, 297, 299
Charlemagne, 182
Charles I, 80, 88, 96, 103, 111, 117, 124, 129, 130, 134, 181, 190, 219, 230, 231, 303, 305, 318

INDEX

Charles II, 23, 35, 38, 40, 41, 80, 98, 99, 100, 102, 103, 107, 111, 112, 124, 126, 129, 130, 131, 132, 133, 134, 135, 138, 139, 140, 141, 156, 169, 178, 202, 231, 232, 243, 256, 258, 262, 289, 339, 340
—— IV, 71
—— V, 59, 60, 105, 163, 267
—— VI, 49, 163
—— IX, 165, 269
—— X of Sweden, 221, 323, 327
—— XI of Sweden, 219, 241, 323, 325
—— XII of Sweden, 55, 219, 325, 326, 327
—— the Bold, 61
Charleston, 12
Charlestown, 32
Charlotte, Queen, 132, 173
Chartier, John, 150
Charvel, Paul, 173
Charvet, Claude Antoine, 178
Chatham, 235
Chatria, Remy, 162, 178
Chatsworth, 242, 264
Chaucer, 109, 110
Chaudet, 171, 172
Cheb, 71, 74
Cheese-dish, 161
Chefdeville, Wilhelm, 283
Chefs-d'œuvre d'Orfèvrerie à l'exposition de Budapest (see Pulsky).
Chelmsford, Mass., First Congregational Society, 1, 2, 17, 23
Chelsea porcelain factory, 155
Cheret, Jean Baptiste, 178
Chester, 141
—— Richard, Captain, 123, 124
Cheveley, Louisa, Mrs., 173
Chichester, 92
"Chinese" decoration, 111, 155, 156-7, 262
—— porcelain, 31, 106-7, 129, 217
Chipchase Castle, 290
Chippendale, 46, 136, 147
Chocolate-pots, 35, 63, 87, 144, 157, 162, 171, 176
Choice of Emblems, 99
Christiaans, Hans, 227, 233
Christian IV, 77, 83, 205, 219
Christiania, 271, 273, 274, 275, 278
Christiansand, 271, 276, 277
Christina, Pa., Holy Trinity Church, 328, 329
Christ's Hospital, 91

Christie's (Christie, Manson and Woods), xii, 27, 93, 95, 97, 98, 100, 102, 109, 111, 116, 119, 123, 125, 129, 130, 133, 136, 137, 140, 141, 145, 146, 149, 154, 169, 186, 193, 195, 208, 210, 214, 216, 258, 261, 262, 263, 270, 288, 306, 308, 333, 335
Christofori, Pietro, 265
Chronique de Nuremberg, 188
Chudleigh, Elizabeth (Countess of Bristol), 136
Chur, 331
Churchill, Charles, General, 118
Ciboria, 63, 71
Cirencester Church, 61
Cisneros, 316
Cisterns, 86, 134-7
Ciudad Real, Cathedral, 317
Civil War, The, 87, 130, 231
Claesz, Leendert, 227, 236
—— Pieter, 229, 239
Clarendon, Earl of, 103, 132
Clarke, James, 13
—— Louis C. G., Mr., 337
Claude, picture by, 167
Clausen, Nicholas, 155
Clearwater, A. T., Judge, 1, 2, 3, 4, 11, 13, 15, 19, 20, 24, 29, 31, 33, 35, 36, 39, 42, 46
Cleghorne, Edward, 303, 305, 309
Clement V, 266
—— VII, 267, 268
Clifford, Lord, 210
—— —— of Chudleigh, 181, 210
—— Thomas, 210
Clifton, John, 259
Clock, 216
Clothworkers Company, 124, 128
Cloyne Cathedral, 257
Cobbet, Thomas, Rev., 17
Coburn, John, 4, 5, 41
Cock, silver, 279, 284
Cockayne, William, 120
Cockburne, James, 306
Cocoanut cups, 67, 84, 94-5, 181, 201, 227, 237, 298, 333
Cocoa-pots, 50
Coddington, John, 13
Coffee-pots, 8, 11, 12, 26, 35-6, 50, 63, 86, 143, 144, 154, 162, 168, 176, 238, 261, 271, 277, 278, 289, 301, 302, 310, 337

INDEX

Coffee services, 10, 156, 157, 178, 225
Coimbra, 290
—— Museum, 286
Coke, Carrie, Miss, 86, 144
Colchester, Holy Trinity Church, 76
Collaert, Hans, 58
Collie, James, 304
Collins, Arnold, 13
—— Samuel, 154
Colman family, 217
—— Desiderius, 217
—— Koloman, 217
—— Lorenz, 217, 218
Coln, James, 304
Cologne, 104, 181, 208
Colonial Dames of America, National Society of, 47
—— furniture, 16, 22
—— silversmiths, 15, 16, 308
Colquhoun, Matthew, 309
Column, silver-gilt, 57, 58
Combermere, Lord, 171
Commonwealth, The, 111, 124
Concord, Mass., First Parish, 22
Conde, Domingo, 321
Coney, John, 2, 3, 5, 14, 16, 22, 23, 25, 26, 27, 28, 29, 31, 35, 39, 40, 42, 45
Connecticut silver, 10, 11, 24
Connoisseur, The, 13, 22, 31, 127, 129, 133, 147, 151, 168, 200, 203, 208, 209, 210, 211, 261, 300, 308
Conrad I, Duke of Mazowsze, 279
Constance Cathedral, 331
Constitution frigate, 36, 44
Cook, Wyndham, collection, 191, 287
Cooke, Richard, 53
Cooley, Sarah, 340
Cooper, Myles, Dr., 20
Coopers Company, 337
Cooqus, John, 243
Copenhagen, 75, 77, 80, 81, 82, 83, 276
—— National Museum, 75, 77, 78, 79, 205, 227, 234, 272
Copley, John Singleton, 5
Coques, Gonzales, 62
Cordova, 314, 320, 321
Cork, 255, 256, 257, 258, 262, 264
Corneli, Willialmi, 256
Cornelius, 256
Cornwallis, Lord, 160

Coronation spoon, 88
Costa, Laurindo, *As Constrastarias em Portugal*, 290
Cotton, John, Rev., 230
—— Michel, 66
Country Life, 95, 109, 110, 115, 117, 125, 238, 262
Courtauld, Augustin, 87, 134, 147, 151, 159
—— Samuel, 134
Courtrai, 63, 64
Cousinet, Ambroise-Nicolas, 175
Cowell, William, 2, 5, 21, 23
Cowper, Earl, 150
Coxe, Thomas, 335
Cracow, 279, 280, 281, 282, 283, 284
—— Cathedral, 280, 281
—— Convent of Clarisses, 280
—— Corpus Christi Church, 284
—— Goldsmiths' Guild, 279
—— Holy Virgin Church, 282
—— National Museum, 279, 283
—— Painters' Guild, 280
—— Sigismund Chapel, 282
Cradle, 171
Craufuird, George, 303
Craven, Earl of, 241
—— Lord, 128
Cream jugs and ewers, 29, 33, 34, 41, 44, 47, 144, 257, 289, 341
Crespin, Paul, 144, 158
Cressener, John, 96
Creutz, G., Count, 177
Crichton Bros., Messrs., xii, 85, 86, 87, 94, 97, 104, 131, 134, 180, 185, 302, 308, 310, 313, 315, 317
—— Lionel A., Mr., 19, 36, 39, 161, 321
Crimea, wine, 293
Cripps, *Old French Plate*, 179
—— William, 146
Crooij, L. and F., Abbés, 64
Crosses, 68, 71, 255, 267, 280, 299
Croughton Church, 115
Crowns, bridal, regal and others, 71, 216, 272, 279, 280, 301, 313, 317, 328
Crozier, 88
Crucifix, 183
Cruets, 154, 156, 157, 319
Cruger, Henry, 146, 147
Cruickshank, Robert, 65, 68

Crystal vessels, 71, 72, 107-8, 165, 176, 181, 182, 184, 187, 188, 191, 207-8, 217, 229, 247, 249-50, 252-3, 265, 267-8, 297, 302, 304
Cuenca, 313, 317
Cumberland, Countess of, 340
—— Duke of, 104, 134, 173, 185, 194, 208, 211, 222, 225, 306, 307, 315
Cummings, Maud A., Miss, 41
Cunningham, John, 310
—— Stanley, Mrs., 37
Cups, 11, 14, 15, 17, 35, 42-3, 48, 52, 53, 54-6, 57, 58, 59, 62, 63, 68, 69, 70, 73, 75, 77, 78, 84, 85, 86, 92, 93-4, 96-7, 108, 109, 115, 117, 119, 120, 122-4, 125, 126, 149-151, 155, 157, 158, 159, 160, 163-4, 165, 166, 168, 172, 180, 181, 182, 184, 185, 188, 189-198, 200, 202, 203, 207, 208, 211, 218, 220, 222, 223, 226, 227, 229, 231, 232, 234, 235-6, 241, 247, 252, 255, 257-258, 259, 261, 262, 263, 265, 267, 292, 293, 294, 295, 298, 300, 302, 303, 304, 305, 309, 311, 313, 314, 315, 317, 318, 330, 331, 332, 335, 337
—— caudle, 11, 15, 22, 23, 38, 69, 86, 125, 126-7, 236, 307
—— ivory, 82, 83
Curtis, George M., Mr., the late, 10, 11, 24, 46
—— S. Carey, Mr., 69, 316
Custodias, 314
Cuthbert, John, 261
Czechoslovakia, xi, 71-4, 280

Dadler, Sebastian, 18
Da Gama, Vasco, 285
Dalmeny, Lord, 84, 85, 87, 115, 148, 191, 219, 313, 317, 318, 330, 336
Dalton, O. M., Mr., 164
Daniell, Thomas, 50, 342
Dankelmair, Thomas, 225
Danske Solvarbejder, by Jörgen Olrik, 79, 81
Dantzig, 204, 208
Darmstadt, Grand Ducal collection and Museum, 206, 221, 226
Dartmoor, 116
Dartmouth College, U.S.A., 30
Dassdorf, Theodor, 225
Dauphiné, 207
David, Gerard, 62

David, Peter, 17, 20
Davie, William, 310
Davies, John, Sir, 107
Davillier, book on Spanish plate, 322
Da Vinci, Leonardo, 267
Dawes, Thomas, 30
De Arellano, R.R., *Estudio sobre la historia de la Orfebreria toledano*, 322
De Arphe, Antonio, 314
—— Enrique, 314
—— Juan, 314
De Artiñano, Pedro M., Señor, *Catalogo de la Exposicion de Orfebreria Civil Español*o, 322
De Benavente, Juan, 318
De Berry, Duc, 163, 164
Deblois, Gilbert, 44
—— Stephen, 28
De Bont, Corneille, 62
De Braij, Salomon, 229
De Castro, Antonio, 287
—— Damian, 321
Decatur, Stephen, Cdre., 13
Declaration of American Independence, 8, 22, 31, 94, 263
Decorative Arts in England, The, 146
Deerfield, First Congregational Church, 18
D'Elzius, François Cornet, 63
Designs, goldsmiths, 223-4, 225-6
D'Este, Ippolito, Cardinal, 268
De Figueiredo, M., 175
De Foelkersam, A., Baron, 53, 80, 173, 174, 175, 223, 224, 270, 301, 329
De Foz, Marquis, 175
De Guerin, T. W. M., Colonel, 69, 70
De Heem, J. D., 235, 237, 239, 244
De Heere, Lucas, 62
De Hesdin, Jacquemart, 164
Dehkant, Georg, 55
De Hooch, Pieter, 131
De Huningue, Baron, 336
De Keyser, Hendrik, 234
De Kjobenhavnske Guldsmedes Mœrker, by Bernhard Olsen, 82, 83
Dekker, drinking song, 90
De Laborde, 179
Delafosse, 179
De Lancey, James, Governor, 39, 143
De Langeron, Anne A., Countess, 284
De Laulne, 110
De Leguina E., Señor, 320

Delft, 233
Del Vaga, Pierino, 268
De Mabuse, Jan., 62
De Marco, G. B. di M., 265
De Mello, 287
Demidoff, 176
De Moriamé, E. J. S., 63
De Nieva, Antonio, 321
Denmark, xi, 75-83, 112, 273, 284, 324
—— Kings of, 82
De Nise (Nys), John, 1, 7, 20
Denneistoun, Robert, 302
D'Oggione, Marco, 267
De Querouaille, Louise Renée (Duchess of Portsmouth), 135
Derby, Earl of, 220, 255, 257, 258, 319
De Rezende, Garcia, 286
Der Goldschmiede Merkzeichen (see Dr. Marc Rosenberg)
De Ring, Pieter, 235
De Rochefort, Ludovico D., 331
De Rooy, Anthony, 228, 240
De Ruyter, Michael, Admiral, 227, 235, 236
Descheverey, Jean Baptiste, 66
De Sequeira, Domingos Antonio, 290
De Seronis, Cesar, 281
Desportes, A. F., 167
Destrée, Joseph, M., 60, 61
De Sutri, A. di D., 266
Dethick, John, Sir, 100
De Vaast, A. V. J., 176
De Valderrama, José F., 321
De Valdes Leal, Don Juan, 315
De Vaudreuil, Marquis of, 43
De Velasco, Don Juan Fernandez, 163, 164
De Voghelaer, Isaac, 212
Devonshire, Duke of, 103, 135, 137, 264
De Wagram, Prince, 171
Dewing, Francis, 45
De Witt, Cornelis, 235
Diana on the Stag, 181, 205-7, 215
Dickson, Charles, 309
Dietmar, Reinhard, 209
Dietrich, Michel, 50, 72
Dietrichson, L., 83
Di Francesco, Frederico, 265
Diggle, John, 141
Dijon, 174, 179
Dinglinger family, 181
—— John Melchior, 181, 225

Dinner plates, 155, 156, 319
—— services, 50, 169, 175, 177, 270, 301
Di Sandro, Antonio, 268
Dishes, 49, 56, 57, 58, 59, 61, 62, 63, 66, 83, 85, 101-4, 116, 154, 162, 167, 169, 177-8, 219-20, 227, 231, 232, 233, 240, 241, 242, 243, 250, 252, 263, 285, 286, 287, 288, 290, 304, 313, 315-6, 317, 319, 334
Dish-rings, Irish, 255, 256, 259-61, 262, 264, 341
Dixwell, John, 5, 25
Dogger Bank, 236
Dohm, Nicholas, 301
Doistau, 176
Dolben, William, Sir, Judge, 125
Domanek, Anton Matthias, 50
Donarth, William, 301
Donker, Gabriel, 53
Donn, Thomas, 53
Don Quixote, 317, 319
Doolittle, Amos, 11
Dopskål, 327
Dorchester, Mass., Second Church, 2, 23
Dordrecht, 227, 228, 230, 238, 239
Dorenfeldt, Peter, 276
Dotte, Franz, 209
Dou, Gerard, 233
Dowthwayte, 113
Drake, Francis, Sir, 335
Dram-cups, 31
Drane, R. B., Mrs., 86, 143
Drentwett, Abraham, 221, 223
—— family, 174, 223
Dresden, 181, 195, 217, 221, 222, 223
—— "Green Vaults," 108, 182, 194, 195, 198, 199, 203, 206, 225, 226, 296
—— Historisches Museum, 249
Dreyer, Salomon, 223
Dublin, 255, 256, 258, 259, 260, 261, 262, 263, 264, 277, 309, 312, 341
—— Assay Office, 263, 342
—— Goldsmiths Company, 263
—— National Museum, 255, 256, 258, 260, 264
—— Trinity College, 264
Dubois, Abraham, 9
—— Isaac, 82
Ducerceau, 110
Duffield, Benjamin, 24
Dulany, Daniel, 159

INDEX

Dulany, Lloyd, 159
Dumee, Nicholas, 87, 146
Dummer, Jeremiah, 1, 2, 5, 14, 15, 16, 22, 23, 25, 40, 42, 47, 138
Dumont, 171, 172
Dundee, 197, 311
Dunfermline, 303
Dunlap, *Hist. of Arts of Design*, 45
Dunmore, Earl of, 46
Dunn, Cary, 34
Duplessis, 179
Durand, Antoine-Sébastian, 177
—— Jonas, 153
Dürer, Albrecht, 185, 218, 248, 282
—— Andrew, 282
Dutch silver, xi
Du Vivier, Hennequin, 164
Dwight, Sally Pickman, Miss, 27, 38, 40
Dyboski, R., 284
Dysart, Earl of, 86, 132

Eagles, 184
East India Company, 142, 287
Eben, Johann Georg, 55
Eckert, Liborius, 73
Ecosse, Jean, 176
Ecuelles, 24, 66, 162, 166, 167, 170, 172-3, 225, 326
Eddis, William, 12
Edenton, N. C., 86, 143, 144
Edinburgh, 302, 303, 304, 305, 306, 307, 308, 309, 310, 311, 312
—— Assay Office, 342
—— Canongate Church, 305, 309
—— Castle, 303
—— Corporation of, 302, 303
—— Donaldson's Hospital, 302, 309
—— Heriot's Hospital, 305
—— Heriot's Trust, 302, 305
—— National Museum, 312
—— Races, 307
—— Royal Scottish Museum, 302, 310
—— St. Giles's, 311
—— Society of Antiquaries, 308
Edsberg, Church, 328
Edward III, 92
—— VI, 98
Edwards, John, 2, 3, 4, 5, 14, 26, 28, 39, 41
—— Joseph, 5

Edwards, Samuel, 5, 32
—— Thomas, 5
Edwardes, John, 288
Efferdinger, Erhard, 49
Efremov, Stepan, 295
Eger, 74
Egersund, 271, 277
Eglesfield, John, 91
Eickhoff, Heinrich, 214
Einsiedeln, 331
Eisenhoidt, Anton, 183
Eissler, Caspar Gottlieb, 224
Eléments d'Orfèvrerie, by Germain, 179
Elertz, Cornelis, 231
Elgin, 311
—— marbles, 158
Elizabeth, Archduchess, 269
—— Empress of Russia, 147
—— Queen, 59, 90, 96, 98, 101, 105, 108, 115, 117, 122, 123, 124, 180, 196, 197, 305, 333
—— —— of Habsburg, 281
Elliott, Mr., 131
Ellis, J., 160
Eloria, Inocencio, 321
Emanuel I, 285, 286
Emden, 181, 191, 209, 212
Enamel, 49, 52, 61, 62, 72, 91, 92, 96, 163, 164, 165, 166, 182, 184, 185, 191, 193, 194, 200, 202, 203, 204, 206, 208, 211, 214, 215, 216, 217, 222-3, 235, 236, 248-9, 254, 265, 267, 268, 269, 280, 281, 282, 284, 292, 294, 297, 298, 299, 317, 318, 321, 326
Enderlein, Caspar, 209
Engelbrecht, Johann, 173, 225
—— Martin, 224
England, xi, 7, 8, 9, 11, 13, 14, 17, 18, 23, 26, 27, 29, 30, 31, 32, 33, 34, 35, 39, 41, 45, 81, 84-161, 118, 168, 169, 173, 178, 183, 186, 193, 194, 201, 208, 210, 212, 217, 220, 223, 225, 230, 232, 235, 236, 240, 243, 252, 256, 270, 282, 289, 300, 301, 313, 315, 324, 332, 335, 336
English Goldsmiths and their Marks (see Sir C. J. Jackson)
English Merchant Adventurers, 191
Enkhuizen, 241
Enriquez, F., 320
Entrée dishes, 157
Enville Hall, 130
Epergnes, 13, 50, 87, 151, 157

Erb, Kornelius, 181, 209
Erfurt, 217
Erhard, Christoph, 207
Erlödy, Francis, Count, 247, 249
Ernst, Georg, 211
—— L., M., 247, 253
Erskine, arms of, 305
—— John, Lord, 305
Escorial, The, 313
Esselbeeck, Michel, 227, 234
Essex, Earl of, 124
Esterhazy, Prince, 50, 222, 247, 250
Eston, C., 85, 98, 106
Estonia, 52
Eton College, 94, 102
Eudel, 176, 179
Eudokia Lopukhina, Tsarina, 115
Eudokia Lukianova, Tsarina, 294
Eudokia Michailovna, Tsarevna, 294
Eugene, Prince, of Sweden, 325
Evans, J. T., Rev., book on Cardiganshire Church Plate 316
Evelyn, 129
Evora, 290
Ewers, 43, 50, 57, 59, 63, 64, 65, 66, 67, 71, 72, 85, 87, 101–4, 108, 135, 162, 165, 166, 167, 169, 171, 176, 177–8, 181, 182, 199, 200, 208–10, 227, 230, 231, 232, 233, 235, 240, 241, 242, 243, 246, 250, 259, 285, 286, 287, 290, 302, 304, 305, 309, 313, 315, 317–318, 319, 320, 330, 331, 334
Ewing, Thomas, 303
Exeter, 85, 98, 105, 106
—— Earl of, 146
—— Marquess of, 86, 135, 169
Exposicion Historico-Europea de Madrid, 314, 315, 317
Eydes, John, 105
Eysler, Johann Leonhard, 223

Falck, Arvid, 327
Falconer's Club, Old, 147
Falun, Mining Company at, 328, 329
Farnham, 120
Farren, Thomas, 160
Farsult, J. R. C., 321
Fäsch-Glaser, Johann R., 330, 332
Fastolfe, John, Sir, 101, 102
Fawdery, John, 144
Fawdery, William, 152
Fechter family, 337
—— Sebastian, 337
Feiff, Jon, 276
Ferdinand III, 72
—— Archduke of Tirol, 165, 269
—— II, Grand Duke of Tuscany, 210
—— and Isabella, 313, 316
Fernando, Don, 288
Field, Samuel, 340
59th Regiment, 319
Figdor collection, 188, 213
Figures, 184, 207, 281
Filigree, 321, 323, 326
Filimonov, Catalogue of the Plate in the Kremlin, 220, 293, 295, 296, 297, 298, 323, 326
Finchenhagen, Martin, 275
Finland, xi, 52, 56
Fire-dogs (see Andirons)
"First Empire" style, 44, 50, 51, 73, 81, 158, 171, 174, 290
Flagons, 8, 17, 69, 83, 85, 109, 111, 114–5, 237, 238, 242, 247, 251–2, 263, 306
Flanders, 60, 61, 62, 64, 135
Flaxman, John, 138, 158, 200
Flemish pictures, 62
Fletcher and Gardiner, 44
—— Richard, Bishop, 95
Flindt, Paul, 188, 195, 200, 203, 208, 226
Florence, 265, 267, 268
—— Pitti Palace, 181, 209, 211, 212, 265, 267
—— Uffizi, 265
Flötner, Peter, 98, 188, 192, 212, 226
Flushing, English Church, 60
Foltyn, Master, 73
Fonthill sale, 200
Forbes, Alexander, 302, 306
Fordoun, 125
Forks, 66, 81, 102, 174, 177, 270, 283
Formin, Ivan, 299
Forrer, *Dict. of Medallists*, 331
Forty, 179
Foulis, James, Sir, 311
Fountains (see Wine fountains)
Foxe, Bishop, 97
Frame, 169
France, xi, 65, 67, 69, 82, 118, 138, 162–179, 209, 212, 233, 241, 245, 269, 313, 315, 324, 330, 336

INDEX

Francis I, 115, 267, 269
Francke, Pieter, 243
Frankfurt-am-Main, 197, 206
—— English Church, 59
—— Municipal Council, 59
—— Museum, 57, 58
Franklin, Benjamin, Dr., 25
Fraser, John, 305
Frederick Augustus I, 182
Frederick, Cardinal, 281
—— I, Elector and Duke of Saxony, 249
—— III, 49, 81, 185
—— IV, 82
French Episcopal Church of the Savoy, 153
French, Hollis, Mr., 39, 46
Freshfield, books on Church plate, 190, 288
Friburg, 321
Friesch Zilver (see Ottema)
Friesland, 228, 245
Friess, Jacob, 206
Frobo, G., 299
Fröhlich, Jacob, 197
Frontenac, Governor, 65
Fruit stand, 220
Fuchs, Nicolaus, 81
Fueter, Daniel Christian, 4, 36, 39
Fulham, All Saints Church, 190
Funete, warship, 236
Furniture, 222, 224, 232, 319

Gaap, Georg Lorenz, 222
Gairden, Patrick, 302, 305
Gairdyne, Robert, 197, 311
Galloway, Alexander, 310
Gamble, Ellis, 153
Garand, Jean François, 162, 163, 176
Gardiner, John, 11
Gardner, J. Starkie, Mr., 97, 109
Garneray, 171, 172
Garnier, Daniel, 86, 133, 173
Garthorne, Francis, 141
—— George, 113, 140
Gauvreau, Pierre, 66
Garvan, Francis P., Mr., collection, 1, 2, 3, 4, 14, 15, 17, 19, 20, 21, 22, 25, 28, 29, 31, 32, 34, 36, 41, 42
Gdańsk, 284
Geertsen, Balthasar, 57
Geneva, 336, 337

355

Genoa, 209
George I, 34, 104, 138, 139, 147, 153, 341
—— II, 34, 208, 307, 310, 341
—— III, 87, 134, 141, 145, 155, 157, 170, 173, 177, 241, 270, 339
—— IV, 131, 141, 157, 159
—— V, 143, 325
Georgia, Russia, wine of, 293
—— U.S.A., 12
Germain, François Thomas, 162, 163, 168, 174, 175, 177
—— Pierre, 176, 179
—— —— II, 162, 178
—— Thomas, 168, 172, 176
Germans, 120
Germany, xi, 82, 166, 180-226, 230, 234, 237, 239, 247, 248, 273, 281, 315, 329, 330
Gerona, 318, 320
Gertzner, Georg, 73
Gessner, Abraham, 330, 335
Ghent, 61, 62, 64
—— Museum, 62
Ghiselin, Cesar, 7
Gibbon, John, 87, 127
Gibbs, John A., 301
—— Samuel, 301
Giessen, University, 197
Gilliland, James, 312
Gillis, Pieter (Ægidius), 62
Gilsland, James, 311
Girdwood, John, Mr., 308
Gjessing, Helge, M., 81, 276
Gladstone, H. N., Esq., 84, 121
Glasgow, 306, 308, 309, 311
—— "Woolen Manufactorie," 306
Glass, 217
—— holders or stands, 236
—— Venetian, 217
Glencairn, Earl of, 304
Glisson, Francis, 126
Globe cups, 181, 185, 195-6, 330, 331, 334-5
Glogier, Hanusz, 280
Gloucester candlestick, 88
—— Duke of, Henry, 135
Glover, Elizabeth, 100
—— Jose, Rev., 100
Goble, Robert, the elder, 257
—— —— the younger, 257
Godfrey, Edmund Bery, Sir, 112
—— Richard, 123

Godin, Edme-François, 175
Godunov, Boris, 292, 296
Goelet, Philip, 4, 7, 31
Golden Fleece, Order of, 318
Golden Roses, 266
Goldschmiedearbeiten in Livland, Estland u. Kurland, by Buchholtz, 56
Goldsmiths Company and Hall, London, 4, 5, 50, 69, 96, 97, 99, 101, 108, 115, 116, 119, 120, 139, 152, 153, 208, 339, 340, 341, 342
—— —— *Memorials of* (see Sir W. Prideaux)
—— —— *Plate of*, by J. B. Carrington and G. R. Hughes, 133, 161
Goltzius, Hendrik, 234, 236, 240
Gonzalez, 313, 317
Goode, John, 86
Gordon, Robert, 312
Goslar, 182
Gotha, 226
—— Royal Collection and Museum, 206, 223
Gothelf-Bilsings, Johan, 306
Gothenburg, 323, 325, 326, 328
Gouel, Gilles, 163
Goulette, 59, 60
Goupel, Marie, 66
Gouthière, 136
Grammont, 64
Granada, 320, 321
Grand Dauphin, 172
Gray, Charles, 12
—— James, 311
Gray's Inn, 29
Graz, Museum Joanneum, 192
Great War, The, 67, 134
Great Yarmouth, New Meeting Chapel, 121
—— —— Old Congregational Church, 121
Greenock, 311
Gregory, Andrew, 256
Greifswald, University, 180, 197
Gren, Michael, 81
Grevenor, H., author (with Thor Kielland) of *Guldsmedhaandverket i Oslo og Kristiania*, 275, 278
Grey, Lady, 130
—— Jane, Lady, 62, 166
Grignon, René, 10
Grochowski, Abraham, 280
Groningen, 237

Grosz family, 216
Groth, Albret, 271, 274, 275, 278
Groton Manor, 106
Guadalupe, 320
Guardiagrele, Nicola di Andrea da, 182
Gueridons, 222
Guérin, J., 179
Guernsey, 69, 70
Guerrière, frigate, 44
Guest, Theodora, Lady, 200
Guildford, 58
—— Corporation, 57, 58, 85, 101
Guilds, 48, 61, 71, 184, 185, 197, 198, 204, 207, 227, 228, 229, 234, 235, 238, 248, 256, 257, 258, 266, 267, 276, 282
Guimarães, 290
Guld-och Silversmeder i Sverige 1520–1850, 327, 329
Gustavus Adolphus of Sweden, 18, 219, 323, 325
—— III, 177
Gutmann collection, 192, 193, 200, 317
Gwynn, Nell, 132, 143

Haarlem, 15, 229, 230, 234
Hadden, Harvey, Mr., 91
Hadley Monken, St. Mary's, 115, 238
Hague, The, 113, 130, 227, 228, 230, 234, 239, 241, 242, 243
—— English Church, 242
Halford, George, Major, 319
Halkett, Anne, Lady, 303
—— Robert, 303
Hals, Dirk, 244
—— Franz, 131, 232
Halsey, R. T. H., Mr., 46
Hamburg, 83, 186, 213, 220, 221, 295, 327
Hamersly, Thomas, 39
Hamilton, James, 12
—— John, 260, 261
—— Palace, sale, 176, 195
Hampton Court Palace, 134, 140
Hancock, John, 43
—— Thomas, 41
Hanmer, Thomas, Sir, 137
Hann, Sebastian, 253
Hanners, George, 35, 36
Hanover, 155, 208, 211, 221, 225
Hanseatic League, 54

INDEX

"Hansel im Keller," "Hansje in den Kelder," 223, 238
Harache, Pierre, 82, 86, 103, 118, 136, 139, 155, 156
Harewood, Earl of, 136
Harland, Thomas, 24
Harness, 282, 283
Harpur, John, Sir, 128
Harrison, William, 116
Hartford, Conn., Christ Church, 149
—— —— First Church, 2, 21
—— —— Wadsworth Athenæum, 25, 33, 289
Hartt, Edmund, 33
Harvard College and University, 16, 22, 29, 40, 42, 45, 100
Harves, 340
Hastier, John, 7, 21
Hauer, Johann, 185
Häufebecher, 192
Haugaard, Niels, 271, 278
Haugh, Samuel, 26
Haussner, Michel, 190
Hauteville, 283
Havard, *Histoire de l'Orfèvrerie Française*, 179
Hawarden Castle, 121
Hay, James, Captain, 311
Hayward, Nathan, Esq., 3, 28
Head-dresses, 245, 328
Hebden, Thomas, 112
Heberstein, 295
Heckenhauer, Joh. Ph., 174
—— Leonhard, 221
Heda, Willem K., 115, 229, 238, 239, 244
Hedeneck, Christoph, 49
Hedon, 113
Helman, 128
Helsingfors, National Museum, 52, 56
Heming, Thomas, 87, 152, 173
Henchman, Daniel, 30
Hendricks, Ahasuerus, 15, 230
Henning, Petter, 324
Henrietta Maria, Queen, 134
Henry III, 88, 283
—— VI, 163
—— VII, 64, 93
—— VIII, 94, 101, 104, 115, 140, 164, 266
—— Matthew, 45
Herbert, Lawrence, 46
Herblin, Jean, 283
Heriot, George, the elder, 302, 304, 305

Heriot, George, the younger, 305
Heriot's Hospital, 305
—— Trust, 305
Hermansson, Herman, 328
Hervart, Baron, 336
Herwart, Philibert, Baron de Huningue, 336
Hesse, Prince of, 192
Heuglin, Johann Erhard, 224
Heywood, Thomas, *Rape of Lucrece*, 295
Hildburgh, W. L., Dr., 313, 316, 319
Hildebrand, Friedrich, 190, 200, 201, 203, 205
Hill, Lord, 320
Hiller, Benjamin, 2, 4, 20, 26, 41
Hist. of English Plate (see Sir C. J. Jackson)
Historic Silver of the American Colonies (see F. H. Bigelow)
Hjorring, 83
Hodder, George, 255, 264
Hogarth, 27, 146, 153, 154
Hogg, Robert, 301
—— William, 340
Hohenfurth, 71
Holbein, Hans, 57, 101, 117
Holford Collection, xii, 214
Holland, 14, 15, 72, 78, 202, 217, 221, 227–246, 232, 235, 236, 237, 240, 241, 242, 243, 327, 328, 332
Holm, Ivar Vigfusson, 76
Holms, J. A., Mr., 98, 309
Holyoke, President, 22
Home, Earl of, collection, 95, 129, 136, 141, 186, 333
Homes, William, 2, 5, 25, 30
Hopkinson collection, 13
Hoppenhaupt, Johann M., 221
Hopton, Ralph, Lord, 230
Horn, Robert, Bishop, 333
Horns, 75-6, 77, 84, 90-1, 183, 227, 228, 229, 271, 272, 282
Horsens, 79, 83
Horsey, Jerome, 283
Hossauer, G., 225
Hostomice, 71
Hough, Atherton, 117
House of Commons, 137
Howard, Thomas, 4
Howe, Earl, 318
—— Lord, Admiral, 261
Howell, James, *Familiar Letters*, 107
Hübner, Paul, 181, 209, 212

Hudson, Seth, Dr., 45
Huertin, 7
Hughes, Henry, 12
Hugo, Victor, 141
Huguenots, 236, 332
Huguenot refugees, 7, 8, 10, 11, 27, 82, 103, 118, 133, 137, 149, 150, 153, 154, 155, 173, 241, 277, 332
Hull, 112
—— Isaac, Commodore, 36, 44
—— John, 2, 5, 14, 23, 24
Humphreys, Richard, 2, 9, 25, 29
Hungary, xii, 72, 74, 207, 247–254, 280, 328
Hunt, Holman, picture, 128
—— Robert, Rev., 96
Hurcomb's, xii
Hurd, Jacob, 1, 2, 3, 4, 17, 21, 22, 27, 32, 34, 35, 36, 37, 39, 42, 43, 44, 66, 146, 277
—— Nathaniel, 30, 43, 45
Hurst, Henry, 1, 17
Hutchinson, Governor, 28
Hyltinge, church, 328

Iberian Peninsula, 286, 287, 316, 319
Iceland, 75, 76
Ice-pails, 137-8, 158, 162, 174, 225, 270
Icons, 292, 301
Ignatius, Abbot, 294
Ilchester, Earl of, 133, 147
Ilg, *Album Kunstindustrieller Gegenstände des Kaiserhauses*, 50, 207, 294
Image, 333
Imlin, Johann Ludwig, 178
Incense, 293, 294
Industry, ship, 37
Inglis, Robert, 302, 306
Inkstands, 8, 31, 87, 134, 140, 263, 313, 319, 341
Insignia, 279
Inverness, 311
Ipswich, Mass., 14, 17
Ireland, xi, 123, 255-264, 336, 341
—— National Museum of (see Dublin)
Ironmongers' Company, 95, 97, 99, 111, 133
Ironsides, 121
Iroquois Indians, 149
Irving, Washington, 230
Islamic glass, 52
Isle of Man, 121, 257
Ismalov, Andreyko Petrov, 299

Italy, xii, 82, 118, 158, 265–270, 281, 315, 330
Ivan IV., "The Terrible," 293, 296, 297
Ivan Ivanovitch, Tsarevitch, 293
Ivanov, Peter, 296
Ivories, 48, 51, 82, 218, 297, 299

Jacobs, Jeronimus, 58
Jackson, C. J., Sir, author of *Hist. of English Plate*, 4, 28, 91, 93, 95, 99, 105, 116, 124, 134, 137, 138, 142, 143, 145, 148, 256, 257, 258, 262, 308, 309, 310
—— James, 12
—— Joseph, 255, 260
Jadwiga, 280
Jagellon, Ladislas, King, 284
Jagiełło, Władysłas, 280
Jäger, Jacob or Johann, 181, 210
Jahrbuch für Genealogie, Heraldik . . . , 53
Jahresbericht des Hist. Museum (Bâle), 332
Jamaica, 176
James I, 95, 102, 106, 117, 122, 163, 195, 197, 305, 318
—— II, 127, 132
—— IV, 266, 303
—— VI, 305
Jamestown Church, Virginia, 38
Jamnitzer family, 184
—— Abraham, 184
—— Albrecht, 184
—— Bartl, 184
—— Christoph, 180, 184, 190, 204, 205, 209
—— Hans, 184
—— Wenzel, 48, 108, 180, 181, 183, 184, 191, 206, 208, 214
Jane Seymour, Queen, 57
Janssens, Hieronymus, 130
Janszen, Simon, 113
Jars, 129
Jasper, G., 301
Jayne, H. F., Mr., 7, 9
Jeffries, William A., Mr., 40, 42, 47
Jenkinson, Anthony, 295, 297
Jenner, Emanuel, 330
Jernegan, Henry, 137
Jersey, 69
—— Earl of, 85, 103, 108
Jessen, P., Dr., books by, 224, 226
Jewel, John, Bishop, 330, 333
Jewellery, 248, 254, 268, 272, 321, 328

INDEX

Joassaff, Patriarch, 119, 297
Johannes, goldsmith, 280
John IV, 288
—— V, 289
—— VI, 290
John Albert, Prince, 281
John, Tsar, 296
John and Ann, snow, 17
John of Gaunt, 91
Johns, Joseph, 255, 259, 263
Johnson, Dr., Dictionary, 109
Johnston, Samuel, Governor, 144
Joiners' Company, 151
Jones, E. Alfred, Catalogue of the Baroness James de Rothschild's Plate and Limoges Enamels, 194, 217, 222, 226, 234, 287, 316, 337
—— —— Catalogue of the J. Pierpont Morgan Plate, 59, 102, 104, 105, 106, 111, 112, 113, 119, 121, 123, 127, 138, 148, 151, 191, 193, 200, 209, 217, 223, 226, 251, 287, 306, 336
—— —— Catalogue of the late Mr. Leopold de Rothschild's Plate, 98, 203, 205, 209, 221, 226, 233
—— —— *The Gold and Silver of Windsor Castle*, 82, 102, 112, 130, 131, 138, 155, 161, 170, 200, 219, 226, 243
—— —— *The Old English Plate of the Emperor of Russia*, 98, 114, 122, 131, 137, 138, 141, 157
—— —— *The Old Plate of the Cambridge Colleges*, 64, 102, 122, 230
—— —— *The Old Royal Plate of the Tower of London*, 186
—— —— *The Old Silver of the American Churches*, 8, 11, 14, 15, 16, 17, 18, 19, 21, 22, 38, 39, 47, 125, 149, 230, 329
—— Elisha, Colonel, 17
—— Inigo, 134
—— Mary, 17
—— William, 156
Jonson, Ben, 109
Joseph, Patriarch (see Joassaff)
Joubert, François, 178
Journal des Luxus u. der Moden, 50
Jppes, Claes, 236
Judit, Ver, 254
Jugs, 144, 268
—— Stoneware (see Stoneware jugs)

Julius II, 266, 269
Junge, Nicholai, 80
Jungfrauenbecher, 141, 181, 202

Kalf, Willem, 237
Kamyn, Erasmus, 283
Kandler, Charles, 137
Karlsruhe, 183
Kassa, 74
Kearn, 304
Kedleston, 136
Keil, Luis, M., 175
Keller, Felix, 330, 333
Kendal, Corporation of, 111
Kent, Earl of, 103
Kentucky, 13
Kenyon, Lord, 125
Ker, James, 302, 306, 307, 308
—— Thomas, 306
Kettenflaschen, 211
Kettles, 10, 27, 31, 37, 87, 145-6, 155, 156, 228, 244, 261
Kickow, Johann Ulrick, 323, 327
Kiel, 215
Kielland, Thor., M. (author of *Sætryk av Norsk Kunsthistorie*; of *Norsk Guldsmedkunst* . . .; and of *Guldsmedhaandverket i Oslo og Kristiania*, 81, 272, 275, 276, 278
Kierstead, Cornelius, 3, 10, 14, 19, 37
Kiev, 292, 299
Kimball, Fiske, Mr., *Domestic Architecture of the American Colonies . . .*, 46
King, poem, 306
—— David, 255, 256, 259
—— L., 45, 160
King's Lynn, Corporation of, 84, 92
Kingston, Evelyn Pierrepont, 5th Earl and 1st Duke of, 136
—— First Church, 15
—— 2nd Duke of, 179
Kipffenberger, Steffan, 199
Kirk German Church, 121
Kirseborn, Jochum, 273
Kirstein, Jean Jacques, 162, 172
Kittery, Maine, First Congregational Church, 13
Kniper, Stanislaus, 284
Knives, 81, 174, 283
Knole, 129, 130, 131, 169

Knopfell, Frederick, 44, 154
Knox, John, 304
Kobenhaupt, Georg, 198
Kolmann, Hermann, 48, 189
Kolsrad, Olaf, 77
Komárno, 74
Komárom, 74
Königsberg, 187
Kornblum, Marx, 48, 50
Kosice, 74
Kovsh, xi, 292, 295-7, 299
Krags, Peder, 81
Krasiński, Casimir, Count, 284
—— Edouard, Count, 279, 284
Krautauer, Ignaz, 48, 51
Kremlin, The (see Moscow)
Küblich, Ferdinand, 80
Kulmbach, Hans, 282
Kunstgewerbe in Livland, Estland u. Kurland, by Neumann, 56
Kunst u. Kunsthandwerk, 50
Kunstschrank, Pomeranian, 215, 216
Kurz, Dr. 335

Labarte, 179
Lacock Church, 84, 93
Lacroix, 179
Ladles, 13, 66, 67
Lafayette, General, 11
Lafrance, Ambroise, 67, 68
Lambe, Jonathan, 87
Lambertsen, Arend, 229
Lambeth Delft ware, 23, 100, 138
Lambrespring, Bartholomew, 160
Lamerie, Paul, 44, 86, 87, 104, 133, 134, 136, 137, 140, 143, 144, 145, 147, 148, 149, 150, 151, 152, 153, 154, 156, 161, 258
Lamp, Sanctuary, 65, 67
Landass, Torje, 271
Landron, François, 66
Lane, W. Coolidge, Mr., 22
Langlois, Jean Etienne, 177
Langton, Thomas, Bishop, 92
Lanier, Benjamin, 283
La Plata Española, 320
La Rochelle, 179
Lasteyrie, 179
Latour, Vincenz, Count, 50
Latvia, 52

Lauch, Balthasar, 195
Launceston, 161
Lausanne, 337
Laval, F. de M., Bishop, 65
Law, William, 303
Lawson, Alexander, 159
Le Blon, 211
Le Blond, Sébastien, 166, 172
Le Brun, 179
Le Coq, André, 82
Lee of Fareham, Viscount, 107, 110, 127, 150, 162, 167, 169, 181, 182, 208, 210
Lee, John, 142
Leeke, Ralph, 125, 136
Leeuwarden, 227, 228, 233, 239, 244, 245, 246
—— Friesch Museum, 60, 227, 228, 233, 239
Lefebvre, Francis, 66
Le Febvre, Marc, 63
Leicester, Earl of, 148
Leinster, Duke of, 133, 262
Leipzig, 195
—— Kunstgewerbe Museum, 195
Leiss, Nikolaus, 197
Leith, 311
Le Jeune, J. M. Moreau, 128
Lelij, Gabynus, 228, 245
—— Johannes, 228, 244, 245
Le Man, G. A., M., book on Jan Looff, 243
Lemberg, 284
Lemon strainers, 9, 31
Lenart, Petter, 327
Lenhendrick, Louis T., 173, 174, 175
Lencker, Christoph, 210
—— Elias, 214
—— Hans, 214
Lenoir, Jean Marie, 82
Lenox and Richmond, Duke of, 135
Lent, John, 25
Le Poinçon de Paris, by M. Henry Nocq, 166
Lepszy, Leonard, M., 284
Le Roux, 7
—— Bartholomew, 82
—— Charles, 32
—— John, 32
Leroy, Marc Antoine, 163
Le Roy, Martin, Mme., 162, 172, 176
Le Sage, Simon, 155
Leslie, Charles, 258
L'Esperance, Pierre, 67
Lessing, Brochure on Eisenhoidt's works, 183

INDEX

Lessing, *Gold u. Silber*, 182, 192, 194, 197, 203, 217
—— and Bruning, Brochure on the Pomeranian *Kunstschrank*, 215
—— on Papal swords, 266
Le Telier, John, 9
Leucker, Nikolas, 197
Levasseur, Michel, 66
Leverett, Knight, 5, 40
Levoca, 74
Levon, A. C., 52, 56
Lewin, Gabriel, 12, 13
Lexington, Ky., 13, 86
—— Mass., First Congregational Society, 45
Leyden, 234, 239, 240
—— Stedelyk Museum, 227, 234, 239, 240
—— University, 234
Leys, Adam, 303
Liebmann, Ivan, 301
Liège, 63, 64
—— Cathedral, 61
Lille, 179
Limerick, 255, 256, 259, 263
Limoges enamel, 118, 165, 212, 298
Limousin, François, 165
Lincoln, Earl of, 103
Lindall, Timothy, 25
Linden, Jürgen, 54, 56
Lindsay, Lionel St. G., Father, 65
Lisbon, 173, 175, 176, 177, 286, 288, 289, 290, 291
—— National Art Museum, 162, 177, 286, 289, 291
Lisburne, Lord, 157
Liverpool Museum, 309
Livingston family, 29
Llanavan Church, 316
Lloyd, John, 255, 261
Locker, John, 255
Lockwood, Luke V., Mr., 46
Löcse, 74
Lo Fil de Mestre Rodrigo, 315
Lofthouse, Seth, 132
Loidt, Ægidius, 75, 77
Loir, Guillaume, 162
Londesborough collection, 216
London, 4, 12, 23, 24, 27, 28, 39, 43, 64, 69, 82, 232, 312, 325, 341, 342
—— guilds, 198

London Museum, 159, 325
—— National Gallery, 62, 115, 131, 166, 167, 232, 238, 240, 244, 315
—— Royal Academy, Diploma Gallery, 267
—— Tower of, 84, 88, 98, 186, 232
—— —— *The Old Royal Plate of* (see E. Alfred Jones)
—— Wallace Collection, 49, 98, 162, 165, 167, 176, 178, 218, 235, 285, 286, 324, 335, 339
Londonderry, Marquess of, 242, 270, 307
Longfellow, 6
—— "Golden Legend," 18
Longworth Church, 117
Looff, Jan, 227, 243
Lord of the Isles, by Sir W. Scott, 90
Lorette, 66
L'Orfèvrerie Française, by H. Bouilhet, 179
L'Orfèvrerie Religieuse en Belgique, 64
Loring, Misses, 42
Losonci, Anthony, 250
Loter, Ieronimus, 73
Louis XIV, 50, 63, 118, 129, 137, 149, 163, 166, 169, 179, 221, 223, 224, 245, 289
—— XV, 50, 170, 177, 289
—— XVI, 50, 51, 56, 81, 170, 171, 172, 174, 175, 177, 245, 270, 289, 301
—— of Hungary, 280
Louisburg, 43, 145
Louvain, 64
Lovelace, Lord, 46
Low Countries, 121, 130, 243
Lowe, Hudson, General, Sir, 172
Lowell, James Russell, 37
Löwenhertz, Mogens Thommesen, 75, 79
Lownes, Joseph, 9
Loyet, Gerard, 61
Lübeck, 54, 185, 272
Luborzyca, 280
Lucan, Lord, 171
Lucas, Guillaume, 166
Lucerne, 331, 332
Ludolf, Conrad, 80, 81
Ludwig, Michel, 186
Luke, John, 306
Lukin, William, 137
Lund, Kulturhistoriska Museum, 323, 325
Lundt, Just Nicolaus, 174, 301
Lüneberg, 48, 182, 183, 189, 203
—— treasure, 188, 197, 203, 226

Lunte, 276
Luselil, 76
Luther, Martin, 180, 197, 334
Luthmer, Catalogue of Baron Carl von Rothschild's collection, 206
Luti, Benedetto, 265
Lutma, Johannes, the elder, 227, 232, 242
—— —— the younger, 227
Luzsenszky, Baron, 253
Lwów, 284
Lynch, Thomas, 94
Lyons, 179

Macazaga, Ignacio, 321
Macdonald, *Days at the Coast*, 304
Maces, 302, 303, 304
MacGregor, clan, xii
Maciej (Matthew), 280–1
Mackensen (Maxson), Andreas, 279, 284
McMullin, John, 9, 21
Macon ou Chalon-sur-Saône, 179
Madras, 287
Madrid, 313, 319
—— Osma Museum, 313, 317, 318, 320, 321
—— Royal Armoury, 60, 217, 317
—— Royal Palace, 60, 313, 318
Madryn Castle, 287, 288
Magdeburg, 196, 222
Mailloux, Joseph, 66
Mainguy, Pierre, 69, 70
Maisonbasse, 66
Maisters, Robert, 53
Majolica ware, 265
Major, E., Dr., 335
Malaga, 321
Malbone, Godfrey, 139
Malesice, 71
Malines, 63, 64
Mallabar, Robert, 53
Manchester Art Gallery, 85, 86, 143, 255, 257, 258, 263
Manning, R. J., Governor, 11
Männlich, Daniel, 211
Mannlich, Heinrich, 219
—— Jakob, 73
Mansfield, John, 4
Mar, Earl of, 305
—— Regent, 305

Marblehead, 14
Marburg, University, 197
Marcinek, Marcian, 281
Marcone, 268
Margaret of Valois, Queen of Navarre, 331
Margaret of York, 61
Margas, Samuel, 155
Maria Feodorovna, Empress, 299
Maria Theresa, Empress, 49, 50
Marie Antoinette, 176
Marie Louise, Empress, 171
Mariano, 268
Markirch, 198
Marlborough, Duke of, first, 104, 118, 136, 137, 167, 242
Marot, Daniel, 241
Marseilles, 174, 179
—— Municipal Council, 172
Marti, Jose, 321
Martin, F. R., Mr., books on the Danish and Swedish gifts to the Court of Russia, 83, 205, 221, 323, 324, 326, 327
Martin, I, 284
Martinez, D. Antonio, 321
Martyr, Peter, 333
Marston, Church, 84, 93
—— John, 30
Mary I, Queen, 59, 108, 124
—— —— II, 113, 143
—— —— of Scots, 169, 302
—— Tudor, 166
Maryland, 12
Mascarene, Jean Paul, General, 31, 35
Maskievitch, Samuel, 292
Massachusetts, 42, 264
—— General Court of, 18
"Master E S," 185
"Master of 1466," 185
"Master of 1551," 208
"Master of the Playing Cards," 185
Matsys, Quentin, 62
Matthey, Nicolaus, 330, 336, 337
Matthias Corvinus, 49, 189, 248
Matthias, Emperor, 206
Maximilian I, 188, 217–8
—— II, 72, 269
—— Elector of Bavaria, 211
Mazarin, Cardinal, 169
Mazers, xii, 76, 84, 88–90, 92, 94, 271, 302, 303, 304

INDEX

Medals and Medallists, 235, 243, 267, 268, 269, 324, 331, 339
Meddelelser om Dansk Guldsmedekunst, by Nyrop, 83
Medford, First Parish, 16
Medina de Pomar, 164
Medway, River, 235, 236
"Meester met den Beker," 240
Meissonier, Juste Aurèle, 148, 155, 179
Melin, Mathias, 62
Melvil, Walter, 304
Memlinc, Hans, 62
Memmingen, 213
Mensma, Nicholas, 228, 239
Ment, Hans, 209
Mentzel, Gottlieb, 174, 220, 221
Mercers Company, 92, 100, 126, 199
Merchant Taylors Company, 256
Methuen, Lord, 84, 93, 149
—— Treaty, 289
Metsu, 244
Mettayer, Lewis, 136, 137
Metz, 179
Mexico, xi, 313, 320
Meybusch, 325
Michael Angelo, 269
Michael, Tsar, 293, 294, 296, 297
Michel, Andreas, 194
Michelin, François Martin, 162
Middelburg, 227, 243
Midlothian Regiment of Fencible Cavalry, 311
Mignot, Daniel, 208
Mildmay, Lady, 106
Milk-pots, 8, 341
Miller, Hannss, 209
—— Jacob, the elder, 206
—— Thomas, 1, 17
Millner, Thomas, 1, 17
Milton, 92
Minott, Samuel, 21
Mirrors, 169, 222
Miskolcz, 247, 252
Miskolczi, 252
Mitre, 71
Modena, Palazzo Coccapani, 287
Moffatt, H. C., Mr. (see *Oxford Plate*).
Molenbeker, 238, 239
Moliner, Francisco, 321
Molinier (see Pulszky)
Möller, Fridrich Romanussen, 271, 274

Möller, Jacob Andersen, 271, 275, 278
—— Lauritz Nilsen, 276
—— Romanus F., 271, 274
Monatsbecher, 192
Moncrur, Thomas, 308, 309
Monifieth, 305
Mons, 63, 64
"Monsieur Monteigh," 128, 306
Monstrances, 49, 64, 182, 280, 281, 282, 286, 314
Montagu, Samuel, Sir, 138
Montgermont, 176
Monteith bowls, 29, 38, 87, 128, 242-3, 259, 264, 306-7
Montpellier, 179
Montreal, 65, 68
Moore, Jo:, 257
—— Robert, 12
More, Thomas, Sir, 117
Moreau, 171, 172
Morgan, J. Pierpont, collection, 59, 84, 85, 86, 87, 97, 98, 102, 106, 111, 113, 119, 121, 123, 127, 138, 141, 148, 151, 157, 180, 181, 185, 187, 191, 192, 193, 195, 199, 200, 202, 209, 212, 213, 215, 217, 223, 230, 251, 287, 306, 313, 315, 317, 336
—— —— —— Catalogue of Plate (see E. Alfred Jones)
—— —— Catalogue of Jewels, 230
—— ——, Esq., Junr., 109
—— Junius S., Esq., 168, 172
Moringer, Ulrich, 186
Morions, 165, 317
Morning Advertiser, 300
Morris, Samuel, 9
Morse, 269
—— Nathaniel, 26, 45
Moscow, 296, 300
—— Ascension Convent, 294
—— Cathedral of the Annunciation, 293
—— —— Assumption, 140
—— Exhibition of Ecclesiastical Art, 300
—— Kremlin, The, 85, 97, 120, 122, 124, 131, 181, 184, 185, 190, 192, 199, 202, 204, 205, 206, 219, 220, 221, 222, 226, 239, 240, 242, 243, 293, 295, 296, 297, 299, 301, 323, 326, 327
——, Patriarch's Treasury, 109, 114, 115, 119, 214, 296, 297
Mostyn Lord, 64, 128, 168

Motta e Silva, Cardinal, 172
Motzfeldt, Magdalene, 79
Moulinar, 7
—— John, 33, 41
Mozart, Anton, 215
Mugs, 17, 20, 21, 22, 26, 69, 70, 86, 141–2, 302, 306, 341
Mulliner, Colonel, 87, 146
Mulls, 311
Munich, 171, 175, 191, 198, 211, 214, 217, 223, 231
—— National Museum, 202
—— Reiche Kapelle, 193
—— Schatzkammer and Silberkammer, 168, 170, 173, 178, 199, 211, 214, 224, 226
Munster, Peace of, 229
Murat, Prince, 171
Murcia, 316
Muri, Monastery, 334
Murray, 305
—— Earl of, 311
—— John, 45
Mustard-pots, 41
Myers, 39
—— John, 10

Nagyszeben, 252, 253
Namur, 64
Nantes, Edict of, 7, 69
Nantwein, St., 191
Naples, 173
—— Museum, 268
Napoleon, 140, 159, 170, 171, 172, 173, 175, 269, 311
Narva, 55
National Art-Collections Fund, 99
Natural History Museum, 237
Naudin, Isaac, 321
—— Michael, 321
Nautilus-shell cups, 48, 49, 59, 96, 181, 184, 199–201, 204, 205, 227, 237, 284, 302, 305
Neal, Daniel, 6
Neapolitan ambassador, 170
Needleworkers, English, 88
Nefs, 63, 164, 265
Negyes, 252
Neisser, Lucas, 210
Nelme, Anthony, 133, 145
Nelson, Lord, 138, 235

Nelson, M. D., Mrs., 87, 145
Neponset, Church of Unity, 2, 23
Netherlands, The, 96, 237, 257, 304, 315
Nettlecombe chalice, 92
Neuchâtel, 330, 331, 336
Neuville, 331
New Bern, N. C., 14
Newcastle, 113
New England, 11, 13, 17, 19, 21, 22, 23, 24, 26, 117
—— —— Guards, 43
Newfoundland Fisheries, 154
New Haven, 11, 19, 37
Newkirke, Joseph, 2, 24
New London, 14
Newman, Samuel, Rev., 117
Newmarket, America, 31, 129
—— England, 307
Newport, R. I., 13, 19
Newton, John, 145
Newton of Lyme, Lord, 101
New York, 9, 10, 11, 12, 13, 15, 18, 19, 20, 21, 24, 25, 27, 28, 32, 33, 34, 37, 38, 39, 40, 41, 45, 46, 82, 87, 230, 338
—— —— Cathedral of St. John the Divine, 125
—— —— First Presbyterian Church, 18, 339
—— —— Historical Society, 2, 19, 38, 85, 86, 149
—— —— King's College, 20
—— —— Metropolitan Museum, 2, 3, 4, 11, 24, 26, 29, 31, 32, 34, 37, 38, 42, 46, 146, 176, 180, 187, 192, 198, 206, 215, 220, 285, 289, 313, 319
Nicholas V, 266
Nichols, James, 12
Nicholson, John, 255, 264
Niello, 185, 190, 191, 192, 228, 265, 279, 284, 293, 294, 298
Nielsen, Hans, 75, 80
Nijmegen, 228, 240, 242
Nikon Ragozin, 294
Nîmes, 179
Nivel, Juan, 321
Nivelles, 64
Noble, John H. B., Sir, Bart., 70, 98, 124, 134, 156, 173, 231, 258, 260, 262, 290, 306, 307, 311, 330, 334
Nocq, Henry, M., 174, 178, 179
Nordiska Museet Fataburen, 325

INDEX

Norfolk, Duke of, 97
Norman Conquest, 87
Norreys, Lord, 125
Northbourne, Lord, 86, 133
North Mimms Church, 187
Northwode, John, 89
Norton, Mary, 17
Norway, xi, 78, 81, 82, 271-8, 324, 328
—— King of, 75
Norwich, 58, 95, 98
—— Bishop of (see John Parkhurst).
—— Corporation of, 102
Nouailher family of enamellers, 298
Novgorod, 298
Noyes, John, 5
Nuremberg, xi, 118, 120, 180, 181, 183, 184, 185, 186, 187, 188, 189, 190, 192, 193, 194, 195, 197, 198, 199, 200, 202, 203, 204, 205, 207, 208, 209, 210, 212, 214, 215, 217, 219, 220, 222, 223, 224, 280, 282, 286
Nutmeg-graters, 31
Nuttall, 12
Nützel, Johan, 323, 324
Nyhoff, 231
Nyköping, 323
Nyrop (see *Meddelelser . . .*)
Nys, Johan (see De Nise)

Oberdieck, Gerhardt, 222
Ochterveldt, Jacob, 232
Odense, 75, 80, 83
Odiot, Jean Baptiste Claude, 170, 171, 174, 179
Oertel, 179
Oettinger, Andreas, 193
Ohtz, Anders, 329
Oil and Vinegar frames, 52, 156, 162, 177, 178, 245
Old Silver of the American Churches (see E. Alfred Jones)
Old Silver Work, 97, 109
Oldenburg horn, 183
—— Prince of, 177
Olearius, 292
Olmütz, 73, 280
Oloffson, Hans, 323, 325
Olomouc, 73, 280
Olrik, Jörgen, Mr., 75, 79, 81
Olsen, Bernhard, Mr., 82, 83
Onclebagh, Gerret, 19, 41

Opava, 73
Oporto, 285, 288, 289, 290, 291
Orange, Prince of, 241
—— Princess of, 242
—— —— Mary, 130
Orfèvrerie Civile Française, by Nocq, Alfassa and Guérin, 179
Orfèvreries de style Empire exécutées par Claude Odiot, by H. Bouilhet, 179
Orfèvreries Tournaisiennes . . ., 63
Orford, Earl of, 147
Orléans, 179
Orth, Jeronimus, 199
Oslo, 278
Ösmo, 323
Osmolsky, Johann, 331, 332
Osnabrück, 182
Östergötland, Johan, Duke of, 324
Osterley, 136
Osterode, 194
Ostrich-egg cups, 71, 73, 74, 84, 95-6, 119, 181, 201-2, 204
Otis, Jonathan, 13
Ottema, N., Mr., book, *Friesch Zilver*, 246
Oudry, Jean-Baptiste, 167
Outrebon, Jean-Louis, 163
Owen, Jeremiah, 18, 19
Oxford, 88, 91, 94, 103, 106, 109, 113, 125, 141, 148, 151, 190
—— Colleges:
    All Souls, 90, 213
    Christ Church, 87, 134, 180, 187
    Corpus Christi, 88, 97, 101, 126
    Exeter, 94, 95
    Jesus, 128
    Magdalen, 128
    Merton 126
    New, 88, 92, 94, 97, 106
    Oriel, 89, 94, 164, 169
    Queen's, 91, 94, 141, 167
    St. John's, 45, 160
    Worcester, 187
—— All Saints' Church, 115, 238
—— Ashmolean Museum, 57, 110
Oxford Plate, by H. C. Moffatt, 45, 94, 106, 194
Oxner, Johann Georg, 211, 223

Paca, William, Governor, 22, 142

INDEX

Pagé, Jacques, 66
Pagolo, 269
Palissy pottery, 184, 209
Palmer, Augusta, Lady, 87, 145
Palmerston, Viscount, 151
Palumba, Vicenzo, 281
Pamplona, 320
Pamunkeys, Queen of, 127
Pantin, Simon, 142, 147
Pap-bowls, 144
Paraguay, 51
Paris, 66, 67, 82, 103, 162, 163, 164, 165, 166, 167, 168, 169, 170, 171, 172, 173, 174, 175, 176, 177, 178, 179, 217-223, 235, 269, 281, 302
—— Cluny Museum, 266
—— Louvre Museum, 57, 59, 165, 172, 176, 180, 190, 192, 212, 226, 233, 235, 240, 317
—— Musée des Arts Décoratifs, 166, 168, 172, 177, 327
Parish, Henry, Mrs., 3, 29
Parker, Matthew, Archbishop, 64, 101, 110
—— Viscount, 128
Parkhurst, John, Bishop, 58, 85, 101, 196, 330, 333, 334
Parr, John, 197
Parst, Georg, 201
Pascal, 87
Patens, 279
Pau, 179
Paul I, Emperor, 299
—— III, Pope, 265
Paull, Florence, Miss, 46 (see Berger)
Pavia, Mrs., 287
Payern, 331
Payne, Humphrey, 160
Peacham, Robert, 90
Peacock, James, 121
Peffenhauser, Anton, 217
Pegge, Dr., 112
Pelham, Betty, 25
—— Charles, 25
—— Henry, 25
Pelican cups, 84, 121, 181
Pelletreau, 7
Pembroke (America), 150
Penfold, John, 143
Penicaud, Jean, II, 165
Penman, James, 307
Penn, William, 7, 24

Pennsylvania, 159
—— *Gazette*, 45
—— Historical Society, 8
—— Museum, 1, 2, 4, 10, 20, 25, 28, 29, 34, 40, 42, 46, 47
—— Provincial Assembly, 8
Pepperell cups, 13
—— William, Sir, 42, 87, 145
Pepys, 89, 94, 124, 125, 126, 127, 132, 139
Perchard, James, 69
—— John, 69
Perez, A°., 320
Perfume-burner, 162, 167
Pergolesi, 157
Permoser, Balthasar, 199
Perpignan, 173, 179
Perry, Marian Lincoln, Mrs., 3, 30
Perth, 311
—— St. John's Church, 197
Perthshire Regiment of Yeomanry, 311
Perugia, 265
Peter the Great, 115, 296, 297, 298, 299, 300, 325, 326, 327
—— Joanna, Miss, 86
Peterson, Peter, 98
Petit, Charles, 103, 166
Petit-Boulogne, J. B., 162
Petri, Henning, 323
Petrograd, 177
—— Hermitage Museum, 52, 53, 205, 224, 243, 294, 299, 326
—— Winter Palace, 80, 86, 87, 120, 144, 151, 155, 163, 168, 175, 195, 223, 224, 228, 243, 270, 301, 329
Petzolt, Hans, 189, 194
Pewterers' Company, 153
—— —— *Hist. of* (Welch's), 153
Pfeiff, Jon, 276
Pfyffer, Ludwig, Colonel, 332
Philadelphia, 7, 8, 9, 10, 18, 20, 21, 24, 25, 27, 29, 32, 33, 40, 42, 44, 45, 263
—— Christ Church, 7, 8, 263
—— Independence Hall, 3
—— Second Presbyterian Church, 17
Philip II, 57, 58, 60, 313
—— III, 163, 318
—— IV, 51, 319
Philip the Good, 61
Phillips, Edmund A., Mr., 99
—— S. J., Messrs., 149, 169, 335

INDEX

Philotheos, Patriarch, 299
Piastowski, Samuel, 284
Pichon, Jerome, Baron, 164, 176, 179
Pickman, Benjamin, Colonel, 42, 43
—— Benjamin Toppan, 43
—— Dudley L., Esq., 1, 17
Pierrepont, Evelyn, 136
Pineau, 179
Piper, Count, 325
Pit, A., Dr., 246
Pitt, William, 148
Pitti Palace (see Florence)
Pius II, 265
—— IV, 286
—— VI, 269
Plaques, 222, 324
Plateaus, 285, 287, 315
Platel, Pierre, 103, 118, 150, 155
Plates, 174, 222, 299
Platt, Berendt, 271, 274
Plessis, Joseph O., Bishop, 66, 67
Płock, 279
—— Cathedral, 279
Plomer-Ward heirlooms, 109
Plummer, John, 112
Plymouth, 99
Podkamień, 282
Poggini, Domenico, 268
—— Gianpagolo, 268
Poitiers, 163, 179
Poland, xii, 279–284
—— Kings of, 279, 284, 294
Pollard, William, 21, 41
Polozk, 296
Poltava, 325
Pondt, Jan, 228, 245
Pontran, Abraham, 18
Pootholt, Bernardus, 237
Popta treasure, 239
Porringers, 23, 24–6, 34, 125, 127, 172
Portland, Duke of, 135, 145, 181, 220, 242, 264
Portsmouth, Corporation of, 97, 119
—— Duchess of, 135
—— N. H., 13
—— —— South Parish, 1, 15
Portugal, xii, 50, 175, 177, 285–291, 315, 319
—— Royal Collection of, 162, 168, 173, 175, 289
Posen, 283
Posset cups, 26, 125

Potato-rings (see Dish-rings)
Potwine, John, 11, 27
Powell, William, Mrs., 33
Poznań, 283
Pozsony, 74
Prague, 51, 71, 72, 73, 231
—— Cathedral, 71
—— Church of St. Loretto, 49
—— Museum, 73
Premysl Otakar II, 71
Prevost, Jean Jacques, 170
Prideaux, W., Sir, *Author of Memorials of the Goldsmiths' Company*, 116, 120, 153, 154, 340
Priester, Johann Jakob, 222
Prince, Charles, Mrs., 3, 32
—— Job, 10
Prince of Orange, snow, 43
Pringsheim, Alfred, Dr., 180, 185, 190, 213, 335
Prior, Matthew, 142
Privy Council Office, 134
Pro Patria, ship, 236
Providence, R. I., 13
Provins, 162
Prud'hon, 171, 172
Prussia, East, 187
"Przeworsk," 283
Przezdziecki and Rastawiecki's book on plate in Poland, 279, 281
Przybyło, Gregorz, 281
Puiforcat, M., collection of, 162, 163, 166, 168, 176, 178
Pulszky, Radisicz and Molinier, *Chefs-d'œuvre d'Orfèvrerie à l'exposition de Budapest* (1884), 49, 251, 253, 254
Punch bowls, 29–30, 31, 35, 36, 125, 127–9, 153, 260, 307
—— ladles, 31, 129
Puritans, 121
Pusey horn, 91
Pyne, Benjamin, 86, 131, 133, 135, 155

Quaichs, 172, 259, 275, 302, 308–9, 311
Quaritch, 167
Quary, Robert, Colonel, 8
Quebec, 43, 65, 66, 67, 173, 277
—— Archbishop's Palace, 66, 178
—— Basilica, 66
—— General Hospital, 65, 67, 68

Quebec, Ursuline Convent, 43, 66
Queen, H.M. The, 265, 270
Queenborough, 235
Queen Charlotte, warship, 261
"Queen Mary's cup," 197, 311
Quethiock, 161
Quilon, King of, 286
Quincy, Mass., 22
Quintard, Peter, 11
Quippe, Bernhard, 199

Rabe, Admiral, 76
Race prizes, 86, 128-9, 150-1, 307
Radisicz (see Pulszky)
Radnor, Earl of, 62
Radziwill, Nicholas, 283
Raeburn, 312
Rákoczi, 250, 253
—— Francis, Prince, 253
Ramsay, Allan, 307
Ramsden, John, Sir, Bart., 223, 231, 318
Randers, 83
Rantoul, Lois B., Mrs., 3, 35
Ranvoyzé, Etienne, 66
—— François, 65, 66, 67, 277
—— Pierre, 66
Raphael, 269
Rapperswil, 331, 336
Raven, Andrew, 143, 260
Read, Hercules, Sir, 241
Reckheim, 59
Reformation, The, 59, 87, 89, 183, 229, 276
Refugees, 153, 155
—— Huguenot (see Huguenot Refugees)
—— Protestant, 121
Regalia, Russian, 301
—— Scottish, 266, 302
Rehlein, Martin, 180, 195
Rehoboth Church, R.I., 117
Reid, Alexander, 307
Reims, 179
Reliquaries, 61, 228, 266, 279, 280, 281, 282
Rembrandt, 131, 232, 233
Remerdes, Mathias, 271, 275
Remington, Thomas, 53
Remsen, Margaret S., Miss, 38
Remy, Pierre, 283
Renart, Louis, 169
Rennes, 179

Renvoize (see Ranvoyzé)
Reval, 52, 53
—— English merchants cup, 53
—— Schwarzhäupterhaus, 52, 53
Revere, Paul, 1, 2, 3, 4, 5, 16, 21, 22, 30, 32, 33, 34, 36, 37, 39, 41, 42, 45, 144, 161, 338
—— —— Mrs., 5
Revolution, American, 5, 7, 11, 20, 24, 35, 40, 44, 68, 146
—— French, 67, 168, 338
Rey, Nicholas, 284
Reynolds, Joshua, Sir, 134, 153
—— William, 262
Rhinelander, T. J. Oakley, Esq., 87, 147
Rhode Island Tracts (No. 13), 26
Riaño (see *Spanish Arts*)
Ribe, 83
Riboulau, Isaac, 149
Richardson, Alexander, 262
—— Francis, 1, 7, 20, 42
—— George F., Mrs., 27
—— Joseph, 1, 3, 4, 8, 9, 20, 29, 32, 42
—— Nathaniel, 8
Richmond and Derby, Countess of, 93
—— Duchess of (Frances Stewart), 167
—— Races, 157
Riedinger, 222
Riesenpokal, 191, 219
Riga, 52, 53, 54, 55, 324
—— English factory, 56
—— Goldsmiths' Guild, 54
—— Kompagnie der Schwarzen Häupter, 52, 54, 55, 56
Ring, gold, 279, 281
Ringkobing, 83
Rio de Janeiro, 175
Ritter, Jeremias, 185
—— Wolff Christoff, 204
Ritter (le), Christoff, 214
Roberdet, goldsmith, 169
Robert, Christopher, 3, 35
Robertson, Patrick, 302, 307, 310
—— William, 310, 342
Robertsone, George, 302
Rochdale, Lord, 110, 125
Roche, Nicholas, 321
Rochester, 235
—— Cathedral, 118
—— 4th Earl of, 103
Rodney, Lord, Admiral, 262

INDEX

Roestraeten, Pieter, 135, 232, 242
Roettiers, Jacques, 162, 174
Rogers, Daniel, 13
Roguier, 171, 172
Rolle, Lord, 159
Rolles, Philip, 85, 86, 104, 136, 149
Rollinson, William, 45
Rollufsen, Borchart, 75, 79
Rome, 222, 266, 268, 286
—— King of, 171
Romney, 123
Ronander, Jonas T., 323, 327
Ronsard, 302
Roosevelt, Nicholas, 1
Rosalind, brig, 67
Rosebery, Earl of, 111, 135, 136, 141, 171, 242, 275, 305, 307, 309
Rosenberg, Marc, Dr., 50, 51, 53, 60, 61, 62, 72, 73, 183, 184, 188, 192, 193, 195, 197, 198, 199, 200, 209, 212, 213, 224, 226, 246, 253, 295, 331, 332, 335, 337
Rosenborg Castle, 58, 80, 82, 183, 219, 222
Rotch, C. D., Captain, xii, 2, 27, 118, 302, 306
—— Francis, 27
Rotherhithe, St. Mary's Church, 316
Rothschild, de, Alfred, Mr., 96, 98, 206
—— Alphonse, Baron, 337
—— James, Baroness, 119, 162, 176, 180, 181, 184, 189, 190, 194, 202, 207, 215, 216, 217, 222, 227, 231, 234, 245, 287, 316, 337
—— —— Catalogue of collection (see E. Alfred Jones)
—— Lady, 200, 204, 205, 207, 211
—— Leopold, Mr., the late, 98, 181, 189, 191, 193, 194, 203, 205, 207, 209, 221, 233, 307
—— —— Mrs., 267, 302
—— Mayer, Baron, 219, 318, 336
—— Salomon, Baroness, 223, 235
—— von, Carl, Baron, 196, 206, 337
Röttenbock, Hans, 195
Rotterdam, 236, 238, 245
Rouen, 179
Rouse, William, 10
Rowe, 99
Roxburghe, Duke of, 157
Royal Charles, warship, 236
Royal United Service Institution, 172
Rubens, 219
Rüblev, 292

Rudolph II, 72, 201, 212, 216, 231
—— IV, 48
—— King, 71
Ruel, Jörg, 200, 205
Ruggles, Timothy, General, 25, 27
Rundell, Bridge and Rundell, 158, 161
Runtuna, Church, 323
Rupert, Charles G., Esq., 255, 258
Russia, xii, 119, 136, 137, 173, 292–301, 325, 329
—— Collections of, 109, 117, 173
—— Court of, 83, 141, 205, 219, 221, 323, 327
—— Tsars and Emperors of, 98, 114, 140, 205, 220
—— *The Old English Plate of the Emperor of Russia* (see E. Alfred Jones)
Russian Church, 292, 299
—— —— Patriarchs of, 292, 297
Rutland, Duke of, 102, 135, 138, 264
Ryssenberch, Hans, 52

St. Agnes, 163, 164
St. Andrews, 305
—— St. Mary's College, 302, 303, 304, 305
—— St. Salvador's College, 303
—— University, 302, 303, 310, 311
St. Benet Fink, Church, 110, 288
St. Brelade's, Jersey, 316
St. Eligius, 71
St. Elizabeth, 247
St. Eloy, 315
St. Esprit, Order of, 165
St. George and the Dragon, 206
St. Giles's, Cripplegate 118, 121
St. Helena, 171
St. Ives, 123
St. James's Court, Exhibition at, 95, 138, 150, 167, 315
St. James the Greater, 316, 317, 318
St. Mark the Hermit, 315
St. Mary Abbotts, Kensington, 288
St. Michael's Parish, Maryland, 26
St. Olaf, 271
St. Omer, 179
St. Petersburg, 136, 174, 175, 298, 300, 301, 329
St. Sebastian, 319
St. Sergius, 299
—— monastery, 292, 299

St. Sigismund, 279, 281
St. Stanislas, 281
St. Wenzel, 71
Saddlers' Company, 28, 84, 85, 95, 100
Saffron Walden, almshouses, 89
Salamanca, 313, 319, 320, 321
—— Bishop of, 268
Salem, Mass., 21, 25, 42
—— —— Essex Institute, 3, 42, 43
Salisbury, Bishop of, 196
—— St. Martin's, 132
Salting collection, 193
Saltonstall, Richard, Colonel, 288
Salts, xii, 28-9, 40, 41, 81, 84-5, 97-101, 116, 124, 153, 155, 162, 165, 170, 175, 212-4, 225, 232, 239, 265, 267, 268-9, 300, 302, 305, 313, 316, 319, 330, 336, 337, 340
Salvers, 31, 38, 39-40, 87, 132, 147, 155, 233, 261, 264, 301
Salzburg, 193
Samovar, 162
Sánchez y Soto, Christóbal, 321
Sandeman, Ernest A., Mr., 288
Sanderson, Robert, xi, 1, 2, 4, 5, 14, 15, 22, 23, 24
Sandomierz, 280
Sandys, Lancelot, 264
Santiago di Compostela, 314, 316, 318, 321
Saragossa, 315, 320, 321
Sasseville, François, 67
Sauce-boats, 29, 41-2, 148-9, 155, 162, 225, 255, 264, 323, 328
Saur, Corwinian, 185
Savannah, 12, 44
Saxony, Court and Kings of, 221, 225, 295
Scallop shells, 156, 176
Scandinavia, 75, 186, 272, 273, 275, 278, 324
Scarlett, William, 148
Scarsdale, Lord, 136
Sceptre, 303
Schaats, Bartholomew, 2, 25
Schaeffler, Daniel, 182, 211
Schaffhausen, 331
Schaller, Hans, 192
Schelderup, Johann, 79
Schmidt, Christoph, 196
—— Johannes, 196
—— Nicolaus, 200, 210
Schneeweis, Urban, 181, 195
Schofield, John, 342

Schongaur, M. 189
Schricker, *Kunstschätze in Elsass-Lothringen*, 331
Schröder, Bruno, Baron and Baroness, collection, xii, 85, 107, 108, 181, 184, 186, 201, 208, 213, 216, 217, 225, 230, 236, 259, 330, 332
Schurman and Luthmer's book on the Grand Duke of Hesse's plate, 187
Schuyler, Peter, Colonel, 149
Schweinberger, Anthoni, 201
Sconces, 130, 131, 169, 221-2
Scot, Jon, 305
Scotland, xi, 121, 172, 229, 275, 302-312
Scott, Walter, Sir, 90, 199
—— William, 310
Scottish National Memorials, 309
Scottish Regalia, 302
Scrope, Archbishop, 89
Sebastian, King of Portugal, 217
Sedlec, 71
Segura, Juan, 314
Selle, John Ludwig, 225
Services, 171, 174
Setubal, 290
Setzbecher, 192
Seville, 314, 320, 321
Sèvres porcelain, 128
Seychelles nut, 201
Sforza, Bona, Queen, 281, 282
Shakespeare, 102, 131
Shakleton, 340
Sharp, Robert, 136, 342
Sharpe, John, 257
Shaving dishes and ewers, 141, 285, 289
Sheerness, 235
Sheffield, 139, 140, 157, 277, 310, 341, 342
—— Plate, 33, 43, 138, 140, 157-8
Shelburne, Earl of, 262
Shelby, Isaac, Governor, 33
Shelley, Giles, 19
Sheppey, Isle of, 235
Sheraton, 46
Shields, 165
—— Thomas, 29
Ships, 63, 181, 199, 215-6, 265, 339
Shrine, 230
Shropshire, Robert, 12
Shurtleff, William, Rev., 15
Siberia, 294

INDEX

Sibmacher, Hans, 119, 191, 203, 208, 226
Sigismund I, 281, 282
—— III, 283
Signay, Joseph, Archbishop, 66, 67
Sikmann, Jörg, 217
Silber, Jonas, 212
Sill, William, 53
Simms, William E., Mrs., 302, 310
Simpkins, William, 5, 41
Singeisen, Johann Jodocus, Abbot, 334
Sitten, 331
60 *Planches d'Orfèvrerie*, by Eudel, 179
Skien, 275
Skinners' Company, 120, 121, 127
Skottowe, Timothy, 26
Sleath, Gabriel, 136
Sleeper, Henry Davis, Mr., 39
"Sleepy Hollow," 230
Sligo, Marquess of, 95, 231, 260, 261
Slytter, Johan, 79, 271, 273
Smith, Anders Hansen, 276, 277
—— Daniel, 136, 342
—— John, Captain, 4
Smollde, Thomas, 53
Sneyd heirlooms, 102, 140
Snuffers and trays, 40, 140, 175, 341
Soane Museum, 27
Soap-box, 176
Södermanland–Närkingska, 328
Solis, Virgil, 190, 192, 208, 226
Soltykoff collection, 337
"Sons of Liberty," 30
Sophia Alexeievna, Grand Duchess, 300
—— Princess, 241
Sophie, Tsarina, 326
Sorö, 75, 76
Sotheby's, 133, 138, 287
Soumaine, Simeon, 2, 21, 32, 38
Soupière, 176, 178
South Carolina, 11, 12
Soutter, Robert, Mrs., 3, 35
Spain, xii, 51, 118, 163, 164, 177, 285, 286, 313–322
Spalding, Philip L., Mr., 28
Spanish Arts, by J. F. Riaño, 322
Sparrow, horse, 150
Speier, 196
Spencer, Earl, 62, 86, 103, 104, 118, 120, 135, 137, 156, 159, 161, 162, 167, 169, 173, 177, 189, 228, 240, 242

Spencer, John, 136
Spice-boxes, 155, 178
Spinola, General, 62
Spittoons, 290
Spitzer collection, 191, 192
Spoons, xii, 11, 43, 66, 68, 79, 88, 174, 177, 244, 245, 270, 277, 278, 283, 284, 290, 311, 341
Spout cups, 26–7, 111
Sprimann, Charles, 174
Sprimont, Nicholas, 148, 155, 156
Sproat, John, 17
Spurious Plate, 338–342
Staffordshire ware, 145
—— Regiment, 264
Stags, 48, 49, 253
Stahl, Stahle, John, 326
Stamford, Conn., Congregational Church, 11
Stamford and Warrington, Earl of, 130
Stampfer, Hans Jacob, 196, 330, 331
Standishes, 31, 134
Stanley, Anthony, 259, 309
—— William, 242
Starr, Isaac, Dr., 1, 20
Statues and Statuettes, 80, 170, 175, 181, 207, 218–9, 279, 339
Stavanger, 81, 271, 273, 276, 277
—— Exhibition of silver at, 81, 276
Stavoren, 228
Steen, Jan., 239, 240
Stegner, Matthias, 49
Stenglin, Philipp, 223
Sterne, Laurence, 127
—— Richard, Archbishop, 127
Stewart, Frances (Duchess of Richmond), 167
—— Lord, 51, 171
Sthin (Stin), Thomas, 251
Stirling, Lord, 35
Stobnica, 279
Stockbauer (see Munich, Reiche Kapelle)
Stockholm, 323, 325, 326, 327, 329
—— Historical Museum, 185, 206, 323, 324
Stoneware and pottery jugs, 26, 104–6, 109
Storr, Paul, 138, 148, 161, 170, 264
Stoss, Wit, 280
Strängnäs, Exhibition of silver at, 326
Strassburg, 162, 172, 178, 179, 181, 190, 196, 198, 209, 216, 331

Strathnaver, Lord, 304
Straub, Hannss, 214
—— Heinrich, 193
Straubing, 213
Strauss, Bernard, 218
Ström, Frederik P., 323
Stromayr, Georg, 50
Strong, John, 12
Strzempiński, Thomas, Bishop, 280
"Studley bowl," 84, 91
Stwosz, 280, 281
Sugar basins, 261, 263, 289, 341
—— tongs, 11, 342
Sunderland, Earl of, 304
Sursee, 331
Surtouts-de-table, 51, 173, 174
Sussex, Duke of, 242
Swan, William, 3, 42
Swaythling, Lord, collection, 84, 85, 86, 87, 93, 95, 96, 98, 99, 100, 102, 109, 110, 120, 122, 132, 138, 144, 149, 152, 167, 213, 302, 304
Sweden, xii, 56, 78, 138, 221, 239, 273, 275, 323-9
—— King of, 177
Sweetmeat boxes (see Boxes)
—— baskets and dishes, 129, 152, 228, 245, 323
Swift, Jonathan, Dean, 262, 263
—— John, 43, 86, 144
Switzerland, xii, 330-7
Swords, 249, 266, 281, 282, 321
Sykes, Richard, 53
Syllabub cup, 26
Sylvius, Balthasar, 229
Sympson, James, 312
Syng, Philip, the elder, 8, 263
—— —— the younger, 3, 4, 8, 9, 20, 28, 31, 263
—— —— III, 9
—— Richard, 152
Syoncope, 88
Szepesi, Joannes, 252
Szillassi, Johann, 74

Tabard Inn, 110
Tables, 222, 298
Taft, Lydia B., Mrs., 2, 4, 22, 41
Tait, D., Archdeacon, 123

Tankards, 7, 12, 13, 15, 16, 17, 18, 19, 20, 26, 32, 49, 52, 53, 73, 75, 77, 78-9, 81, 85, 107, 109-114, 141, 172, 176, 180, 186-8, 198, 209, 218, 237, 238, 247, 252, 253, 255, 256, 258, 262, 264, 271, 273-5, 276, 277, 284, 298, 300, 302, 306, 323, 324-5, 328, 337, 340
—— Ivory, 48, 51
Taming of the Shrew, 102
Tanner, John, 13
Tanqueray, Ann, 87, 144
Tara brooch, 255
Tarnów, Cathedral, 280
Tarrytown, 230
Taudin, James, 153
Taylor, Thomas, Mr. (Chipchase Castle), 290
—— William, 147, 148
Tazze, 38-9, 59, 60, 86, 118-9, 131-2, 147, 167, 180, 192, 209, 212, 227, 231, 239, 243-4, 253, 261, 279, 288, 316, 317, 320, 330, 331, 335, 337
Tea-caddies, 9, 87, 145, 245, 271
Teapots, 10, 12, 26, 31-4, 35, 36, 37, 44, 50, 65, 68, 87, 142-3, 144, 171, 181, 222, 225, 255, 262, 263, 264, 289, 301, 302, 307-8, 312, 337
Tea services, 10, 33, 156, 157, 178, 225
Tea-urns, 37, 146-7, 157, 302
Tearle, Thomas, 87
Teleki, Dominic, Count, 254
—— Michael, 254
Temple, Inner, 120, 122
—— Middle, 122
Ten Eyck, T., 32
Terborch, Gerard, 233, 240
Termonde, 64
Terry, Carden, 255, 264
—— Fred, 124
Thackara and Vallance, 45
Thames, River, 235, 316
Thayer, Nathaniel B., Mrs., 5
Thelot, Johann Andreas, 222
Thirty Years War, 218, 219, 283
38th Foot, 264
Thomason, Edward, Sir, 159
Thomire, 171
Thompson, John, 141
—— William, 263
Thomson, Thomas, 306
Thrones, 80, 155

INDEX

Thun, 331
Thünckel, Johannes, 220
Thuringia, Margrave of, Louis, 247
Thurston, Herbert, Rev., 269
Tiara, papal, 269
Tichborne, 261
Tipping, Fearon, Colonel, 105, 144, 167
Tirol, Ferdinand of, Archduke, 72
Toilet services, 50, 132-3, 154, 155, 167, 171, 173, 175, 177, 224, 262, 278
Toledo, 314, 317, 320, 321
Tong cup, 108, 109
Tongres, 64
Toppan, Robert N., Mrs., 32
Torel, William, 88
Torell, H. V., 323, 326
Tornekrans, Henrik C., 76
Toulon, 179
Toulouse, 179
Tournai, 63, 64, 97
Tours, 179
Townshend, Charles, 150, 160, 255, 260
—— William, 255
—— —— S., Mr., 39
Toynbee, Paget, Mrs., 145
Transylvania, 247, 252, 253, 254
Travelling service, 269
Trays, 13, 33, 147, 157, 261, 270
Treasury, The, 134
Treby, George, 154
Treffler, Johann Christoph, 211
Tresse, Margaret, 7
Trinity House, Corporation of, 123
Triptychs, 215
Tristram Shandy, 127
Troitska monastery, 292, 299
Trondhjem, 272
Troppau, 73, 74
Trouvain, Antoine, 40, 132
Troyes, 179
Tryall, horse, 31, 128
Tryon, William, Governor, 46, 146
Trzemeszno, 279
Tula, 298, 299
Tumbler cups, 4, 31, 141
Tunis, 59
Turaberin, Timothy, Don Cossack, 296
Tureens, 50, 87, 147-8, 157, 162, 170, 171, 174, 176, 177, 179, 270, 323
Turell, Ebenezer, Rev., 16

Turin, 270
Turnberry Castle, 90
Tutbury horn, 91
Tyler, Andrew, 2, 5, 25
Tyng, Edward, 43
Tyniec, Abbey of, 280
Tyrol, 207

Ude, Johannes, 146
Ulm, 181, 193, 205, 213
Ulrica Eleonora, Queen, 325, 326
Ulrich, Boas, 181, 215
United Service Institution, 138
Unna, Hans, 53
Upmark, Gustaf, Dr., 325, 326, 327, 328, 329
Upnor Castle, 235
Urbino, 213
Ure, Archibald, 308
Ustí nad Labem, 71
Utrecht, 227, 230, 237, 244

Valadini, L., 265, 270
Valencia, 320
—— pottery, 315
Valentin, 73
Valladolid, 314, 320
Van Abeele, Peter, 235
Van Aelst, Willem, 237
Van Bassen, Bartelmees, 134
Van Beyeren, Abraham, 237, 244
Van Cortlandt, Anne S., Miss, 3, 37
Van de Rijn, J. D., Captain, 236
Van der Beken, Nicaise, 58
Van der Helst, B., 228, 229
Van der Passe, Crispin, 234
Van der Spee, Jacques, 57, 61
Van der Spiegle, Jacobus, 1
Van der Strate, Ian, 233
Van der Weyden, Roger, 62
Van Doorslaer, G., Dr., 63
Van Dyck, 219
—— —— Peter, 1, 21, 32
Van Dyke, Richard, 44

Van Giffen family, 238
Van Haensbergen, Joh., 239
Van Jaesvelt, Reynere, 58
Van Kerkwijk, A. O., M., 227, 236, 237, 243
Van Kessel, Th., 231
Van Limburg, Herman, 164
—— —— Jehannequin, 164
—— —— Pol, 164
Van Meunincxhove, Jan., 135
Van Nievkercke, Loys, 61
Van Streek, J., 240
Van Vianen, style, 186, 231, 234
—— —— Adam I., 186, 220, 227, 230, 233, 242
—— —— —— II, 231
—— —— Christian, 231, 232
—— —— Ernst Janszoon, 234
—— —— Paul, 72, 227, 231, 243
—— —— Willem Eernstensz, 230
Van Weemaer, Jacomiinje, 233
Varia Conmensuracion, 314
Varley, F. J., Mr., 296, 300
Vases, 158, 222, 242, 298
Vassall, Spencer Thomas, Lt.-Col., 264
Vassili III, Tsar, 296
Vatican, The, 267
Vauquer, Jean, 167
Vejle, 83
Velasquez, 317, 319
Venetian glasses, 92, 116
—— goldsmiths, 249
Venice, 188, 212, 269, 282
Verduyn, Pieter, 239
Vermay, Jean, 60
Vermeer, 131
Vermeyen, Jean, 60
Vernon, John, 33, 36
—— Lady, 171
—— Robert, 325
—— Samuel, 2, 13, 19
—— Thomas, 25
Verocchio, 267
Veszprém, 248
Vevey, 331
"Vexier pokal," 223
Viborg, 77, 83
Vicente, Gil, 286
Vicenza, 267

Victor, J., 243
Victoria and Albert Museum, xii, 19, 26, 36, 39, 56, 62, 63, 67, 75, 84, 87, 88, 91, 92, 95, 98, 99, 100, 105, 106, 107, 109, 110, 118, 120, 121, 123, 126, 130, 132, 134, 136, 142, 144, 148, 151, 157, 158, 161, 169, 173, 180, 191, 193, 195, 199, 213, 217, 218, 226, 231, 234, 237, 239, 243, 244, 245, 246, 257, 258, 262, 263, 264, 267, 269, 270, 284, 285, 287, 291, 294, 295, 296, 298, 300, 310, 317, 318, 320, 321, 324, 330, 331, 335, 337
Vienna, 48, 49, 51, 72, 73, 96, 166, 171, 177, 183, 213, 217, 337
—— Congress of, 51
—— Geistliche Schatzkammer, 215
—— Imperial Museum, 48, 49, 51, 71, 72, 162, 178, 180, 181, 185, 188, 200, 201, 202, 203, 205, 207, 209, 216, 218, 226, 227, 231, 265, 267, 268, 294
—— Industrial Art Museum, 225
Vilant, William, 1, 9, 20
Villiers, Clementina, Lady, 108
Vilna, 280, 283, 284
Vintagers, 207
Vintners' Company, 95, 98, 141, 202
Virginia, 11, 13, 96, 127, 142
—— Company, 4
—— Historical Society, 127
Virton, 64
Vittoria, 320
Vladimir of Russia, 292
Voet, E., Mr., Junr., 246
Von Bärenfels, 332
Von Bore, Kethe, 197
Von der Renne (n), Salomon, 204
Von Drach, *Silberarbeiten Cassel*, 199
Von Drolshagen, 52, 53
—— —— Bruno, 53
—— —— Jürgen, 53
Von Falkenstein, Zavis, 71
Von Guericke, Otto, 196
Von Hausen, 332
Von Hohenreid, J. B. K., 49
Von Köln, Heinrich, 56
Von Oppenheim, Albert, Baron, 287
Von Raitenau, W. D., Prince-Archbishop of Salzburg, 211
Vos, Johannes, 245
Vrede, warship, 236

INDEX

Wadsworth, Alexander, F., Mrs., 1, 15
—— Athenæum, Hartford, 25, 33
Waggon and tun, 199
Wainwright, Francis, Col., 14
Wakelin, John, 147, 148
Walker, Joseph, 255, 258
Wall, John, 50
Wallace Collection (see London)
Wallbaum, Mathaeus, 181, 206, 214, 215
Wallenstein, 219
Walpole, Horace, 145
—— Collection, 300
—— Society, New York, 46
Walsall, 342
Walsh, 92
—— Stephen, 263
Walter, John H., Mr., 24
Walton, William, 7
Warburg, 183
Ward, Joseph, 152
—— Richard, 43
Warham, Archbishop, 106
Warming-pans (see Bed-warmers)
Warner, Andrew E., 13
—— John, 255, 264
—— Joseph, 13
Warren, J. C., Mrs., 86, 151
—— Peter, Sir, Admiral, 145
Wars of the Roses, 87
Warsaw, National Museum, 279, 284
—— Shooting guild, 284
Warwick Castle, 191
—— Earl of, 160
—— St. Mary's, 160
Washington, 44
—— George, General, 11 f.n.
Watch-cases, 167
Waterloo, 170
Watts, W. W., Mr. (author of *Old English Silver*), 161, 232
Webb, Caleb, 255, 258
Webster, C. A., Rev., 257
Wechter, Georg, 119, 186, 190, 191, 208, 226
Wedgwood ware, 158
Weenix, J. B., 240
Weghorst, Philip L., 75, 81
Weimar, 223
Weishaupt, 175, 214
Welbeck, 129, 264
Welch (see Pewterers' Company)
Wellington, Duke of, 108, 159, 171, 240, 290
Wellis, Simon, 288
Wentworth, John, Governor, 30
Wessel, Joachim, 187
Wessely, *Das Ornament*, 189, 224, 226
Westminster Abbey, 88
Weston, Mass., 17
Westraw, Johnston of, 307
Weye, Bernhard H., 224
Wharton, William F., Hon., 16
Whawell sale, 287
Wheatley, George, 262
Wheelock, Eleazer, Rev., 30
Wheelwright, Esther, 43
Whieldon ware, 142, 148
White, Fuller, 156
—— Miles, Junr., Mrs., 13
Whitechapel Church, Virginia, 113
Whitehall Palace, 134
Whiting, Ebenezer, 12
Whitney, Geoffrey, *Choice of Emblems*, 99
Whittemore, William, 13
Wick, 311
Wickes, George, 42, 86, 150, 261
Wickhart, Andreas, 218
Wied, Prince of, 231
Wieliczka, 280, 282
Wiener Neustadt, 48
Wilhelm, Henry, 190
Wilkes, John, 30
Willaume, David, 27, 82, 103, 133, 137, 145, 150
William III, 113, 130, 133, 135, 137, 140, 141, 143, 153, 154, 241, 242, 335, 336
—— IV, 325
—— the Silent, 227, 241
Williamson, G. C., Dr., 230
—— Samuel, 18
—— William, 255, 259
Wilno, 280, 284
Wilson, Rev., Dr., 151
Wiltberger, Christian, 9
Winchester, Bishop of, 196
—— College, 93, 94, 101, 109, 119, 125
—— Marquess of, 125
Winckler, David, 198
Windmill cups, 80, 223, 227, 238

www.ingramcontent.com/pod-product-compliance
Lightning Source LLC
Chambersburg PA
CBHW080933300426
44115CB00017B/2799